Mass Media
and
American Politics

Mass Media
and
American Politics

Seventh Edition

Doris A. Graber
University of Illinois at Chicago

CQ PRESS

A Division of Congressional Quarterly Inc.
Washington, D.C.

CQ Press
1255 22nd Street, NW, Suite 400
Washington, DC 20037

Phone: 202 729-1900; toll-free, 1-866-427-7737 (1-866-4CQ-PRESS)

Web: www.cqpress.com

Cover design: ION Graphic Design Works

⊗ The paper used in this publication exceeds the requirements of the
American National Standard for Information Sciences—Permanence of
Paper for Printed Library Materials, ANSI Z39.48-1992.

Printed and bound in the United States of America

09   08   07   06   2   3   4   5

Library of Congress Cataloging-in-Publication Data

Graber, Doris A. (Doris Appel),
  Mass media and American politics / Doris A. Graber.—7th ed.
    p. cm.
  Includes bibliographical references and index.
  ISBN 1-56802-917-9 (alk. paper)
  1. Mass media—Social aspects—United States.   2. Mass media—
Political aspects—United States.   I. Title.

HN90.M3G7 2005
302.23′0973–dc22

                                                    2005018309

To
Jack, Jim, Lee, Susan, Tom—
my very special students

Contents

c h a p t e r o n e

c h a p t e r t w o

c h a p t e r   t h r e e

c h a p t e r   f o u r

c h a p t e r   f i v e

c h a p t e r   s i x

c h a p t e r   s e v e n

c h a p t e r   e i g h t

c h a p t e r   n i n e

c h a p t e r   t e n

c h a p t e r   e l e v e n

c h a p t e r   t w e l v e

Tables, Figures, and Boxes

Tables

Figures

Boxes

Preface

W HEN THE PREVIOUS EDITION OF THIS BOOK went to press, the nation had just experienced the horrors of the September 11, 2001, terrorist attacks on U.S. soil. Many commentators predicted that nothing would ever be the same again in the U.S. public sphere. The predictions of major changes have been accurate and include the news media. One word, *fragmentation,* sums the main changes. In the past a few major newspapers, a handful of wire services, and three large television networks were the main news providers. Now a bevy of round-the-clock cable television stations and news Web sites covers much of the breaking news and sets the agenda for competitors with slower news cycles.

Audiences have become fragmented, switching from traditional media to the newer venues. The major established networks still attract the largest audiences, but viewership has declined sharply. The same holds true for newspaper and news journal readers. Competition for audiences and advertisers has become fiercer. It pressures news media to publish breaking news at a pace that often precludes careful checking of sources. It also prompts them to become ever more entertaining, because audiences sample multiple print and broadcast venues in pursuit of news that interests and pleases them. In the wake of changing demographics, personal and business lifestyles, and, above all, advancing technologies, what new vistas does the mass media scene present four years after that fateful September day in 2001? And what are the main political implications?

To answer these questions we must identify the general characteristics of the U.S. mass media system as well as the political, economic, and technological forces that generate change. The seventh edition of *Mass Media and American Politics* does just that. It features up-to-date information about the structural and organizational characteristics of the current media system and the developments that continually modify its contours. The media are in transition. Narrowly targeted news offerings exist side by side with mass-appeal programs, and the boundaries between print and broadcast media are blurring. What mix of information sources will ultimately prevail, and how that mix will change the political as well as the media scene, remains an intriguing mystery.

The data featured in this new edition come from the rich array of current political communication studies, including my own research on television's impact on citizens' understanding of politics. The book's approach continues to be interdisciplinary and objective, offering a variety of viewpoints on controversial issues. From this evidence and the ample up-to-date citations of information sources, readers should be able to form their own opinions and evaluations. The book's approach is direct and clear to suit the needs of novices in this area of knowledge without sacrificing the scholarly depth, documentation, and precision that more advanced readers require.

The book focuses on news disseminated by television and newspapers because these media are still the chief sources of current information for people in public and private life. Each chapter also features analysis of the impact of the Internet and cable television on the information stream and on politics. I emphasize the many public policy issues raised by the "new" media because average citizens must understand their implications so that they can voice their concerns when policies are in the making.

Although the scope continues to broaden, a major portion of political communication research still concentrates on the relationship between media and politics during elections. This new edition of *Mass Media and American Politics*, like prior editions, takes a much broader approach. It covers the impact of media on all spheres and phases of political life at all levels of government in normal times and times of crisis.

Chapters 1 and 2 set the stage with descriptions of the mass media as institutions in the U.S. political system. The chapters explain how governmental structures and functions affect journalists and media institutions and how the media, in turn, influence politicians and the work of all branches of government. The discussion highlights the consequences of proliferation of media outlets and the continuing debates about appropriate regulatory policies. Chapter 3 completes the analysis of the legal, political, and economic framework in which U.S. media operate. I analyze the legal rights of citizens, public officials, and journalists to gather and publish information and to seek protection from damaging publicity.

Chapter 4 deals with the many factors that play a part in creating stories about particular events and people under ordinary circumstances. It highlights media structures, personnel, and operational concerns. The chapter incorporates new research demonstrating that entertainment programs have become an important forum for politicians and a source of political information that attracts audiences because these programs use appealing dramatic or humorous formats. In Chapter 5 I describe news patterns during crises, such as major natural disasters and wars. The chapter clarifies how news media play major supporting roles that facilitate the difficult tasks facing governments when normal functions are disrupted. Chapter 6 deals with the ethical problems and political consequences of political activism by journalists. I define the boundaries journalists face when they investigate misbehaviors by public officials, by business tycoons, or by religious leaders. In Chapter 7 I explore the wealth of information political communication scholars have accumulated about political learning and opinion formation, along with theories about media-induced asocial and prosocial behavior. Much of the material about learning from news stories is based on my own ongoing research.

The powerful influence of the media in a variety of political situations is the subject of Chapters 8–11. These situations include media coverage of elections (Chapter 8) and the interplay between the media and such major political institutions as the presidency and Congress (Chapter 9). In these chapters I pay particular attention to the changes that Internet news offerings have brought about. The media's role in the judicial system and at state and local levels is set forth in Chapter 10. The discussion covers news about courts at the national and state levels and about the criminal justice system. It also dwells on the shortcomings of news about state and local political issues. Chapter 11 details the growing impact of news media on the conduct of foreign policy; I explore several recent theories about selecting events abroad for coverage. Based on my research of censorship in wartime, I analyze the difficult trade-offs when First Amendment freedoms must be balanced against national security concerns. The book concludes with a discussion of policy trends and the new technologies and political forces shaping them (Chapter 12). The boxed vignette about Web logs (blogs) and bloggers in Chapter 12, like vignettes in other chapters, casts a spotlight on an especially intriguing media issue.

The changes in this new edition reflect the political and technological events that have transpired since 2000, the rich crop of new mass media studies, and much-appreciated suggestions from colleagues and students who have used the book. I am indebted to my research assistants, especially James Smith, who created new, up-to-date tables and tracked down other data. The editorial team at CQ Press and its freelance staff provided their usual strong support that greatly eased the many chores that are part of authoring books. Special thanks must go to Colleen Ganey, Molly Lohman, and Kerry Kern, who managed to squeeze an incredible amount of editorial and production work into a far too tiny time slot. My husband, as always, has cheered me on even when time spent on the book interfered with other plans. As always, Tom's loving support has been legendary. He is a major partner in all I do.

Doris A. Graber

Mass Media
and
American Politics

Media Power and Government Control

T HE FEDERAL OCCUPATIONAL SAFETY and Health Administration (OSHA) was created in 1970 to protect U.S. workers from preventable injuries and deaths in the workplace. When inadequate regulations, lax inspections, or minor penalties for major violations inhibit OSHA's mission, workers and their families suffer, and the economy loses valuable human resources. This is why reporters from the *New York Times* decided in 2003 to investigate reports of hundreds of severe injuries in the McWane Company's cast iron pipe factories. The reporters wanted to see if adequate safety rules were in place and if OSHA was monitoring these dangerous workplaces.[1] During the investigation, these reporters and others from the Public Broadcasting Station's *Frontline* program and the Canadian Broadcasting Corporation discovered that 2,197 U.S. workers had been killed over a ten year period ending in 2002 because employers ignored safety regulations. "Workers decapitated on assembly lines, shredded in machinery, burned beyond recognition, electrocuted, buried alive—all of them killed, investigators concluded, because their employers willfully violated workplace safety laws." OSHA had investigated these cases but sought prosecution for only 7 percent despite repeated promises to press for criminal charges.[2]

Spurred by the prospect of massive adverse publicity in major news media, OSHA announced a strengthened enforcement program and special investigations of McWane plants in 2003. OSHA administrator John Henshaw acknowledged that the news stories had prompted the action. The stories had been able to overcome OSHA's customary reluctance for forceful law enforcement and its reluctance to risk the rage of powerful companies and their supporters. The McWane companies and other high

1

risk operations also took notice of the news stories. They pledged greater attention to safety rules even at the expense of worker productivity. Most important, follow-up investigations in 2004 showed that conditions had improved substantially and workers felt much safer.[3]

Political Importance of Mass Media

[4]As the OSHA story shows, the impact of news stories on political leaders and on citizens' views about public policies and public officials demonstrates how mass media, in combination with other political factors, can influence U.S. politics. News stories take millions of Americans, in all walks of life, to the battlefields of the world. They give them ringside seats for space shuttle launches or basketball championships. They allow the nation to share political experiences, such as watching presidential inaugurations or congressional investigations. These experiences then undergird public opinions and political actions.[5]

Print, audio, and audiovisual media often serve as attitude and behavior models. The images that media create suggest which views and behaviors are acceptable and even praiseworthy and which are outside the mainstream. Audiences can learn how to conduct themselves at home and at work, how to cope with crises, and how to evaluate social institutions like the medical profession or grocery chains. The mass media also are powerful guardians of proper political behavior, because Americans believe that the press should inform them about government wrongdoings. Media stories also indicate what different groups deem important or unimportant, what conforms to prevailing standards of justice and morality, and how events are related to each other. In the process the media set forth cultural values that their audiences are likely to accept in whole or in part as typical of U.S. society. The media thus help to integrate and homogenize our society.

Media images are especially potent when they involve aspects of life that people experience only through the media. The personal and professional conduct of politicians, political events in distant lands, frenzied trading at stock exchanges, medical breakthroughs, or corrupt corporate dealings are not generally experienced firsthand. Rather, popular perceptions of these aspects of life take shape largely in response to news and fictional stories in media. Like caricatures, media stories often create skewed impressions because they cannot report stories in detail or full context. For example, thanks to a heavy focus on crime news and fiction stories, television exaggerates the likelihood of an individual becoming a victim of crime. Viewers therefore fear crime excessively, especially if they watch a lot of television.[6]

Attention to the mass media is all-pervasive among twenty-first-century Americans. The average high school graduate today has spent more time in front of a television set than in school, particularly during his or her preschool and elementary school days. Even in school, media are the basis for much learning about current events. An average adult in the United States spends nearly half of her or his leisure time watching television, listening to the radio, reading newspapers and magazines, or surfing the Web. Averaged over an entire week, this amounts to more than seven hours of exposure per day to some form of mass media news or entertainment. Television, relayed over the air, via cable, through the Internet, or through a videotape recorder, occupies three-fourths of this time. Despite considerable dissatisfaction with the quality of television programs in all of these modalities, television remains the primary source of news and entertainment for the average American. It is also the most trusted source of information.[7]

Sixty percent of people responding to a national survey in late spring 2004 said that they had watched television news the day before. Additionally, 42 percent claimed to have read a daily newspaper the day before, and 40 percent said that they had paid attention to radio news.[8] The ability to attract such vast audiences of ordinary people, as well as political elites, is a major ingredient in the power of the mass media and makes them extraordinarily important for the individuals and groups whose stories and causes are publicized (Table 1-1).

Politically relevant information is often conveyed through stories not concerned explicitly with politics. In fact, because most people are exposed far more to nonpolitical information, make-believe media, such as movies and entertainment television, have become major suppliers of political images. During the 2004 presidential election campaign, for example, the 15 percent of TV viewers who watched Comedy Central's the *Daily Show* received far more coverage of the Republican and Democratic Conventions than network television audiences. Young viewers in particular regularly cite *Late Show* with David Letterman and the *Tonight Show* with Jay Leno as their main sources of political information.[9]

Such entertainment shows portray social institutions, such as the police or the schools, in ways that either convey esteem or heap scorn. These shows also express social judgments about various types of people. For instance, television in the past often depicted African Americans and women as socially inferior and with limited abilities. This type of coverage conveys messages that audiences, including the misrepresented groups, may accept at face value, even when the portrayals distort real-world conditions. Audience members may also think that social conditions and judgments shown on television are widely accepted and therefore socially sanctioned.[10]

TABLE 1-1   News Consumption Patterns, 2000 and 2004 (in percentages)

Medium	2000	2004	Change
Local TV news	56	59	13
Newspapers "read yesterday"	46	42	−4
Radio	43	40	−3
Nightly network news	30	34	+4
Online news "three or more days"	23	29	+6
Fox News	17	25	+8
CNN	21	22	+1
Network morning shows	20	22	+2
TV news magazines	31	22	−9
Sports news on ESPN	23	20	−3
National Public Radio	15	16	+1
News magazines	12	13	+1
NewsHour with Jim Lehrer	5	5	0
C-SPAN	4	5	+1
Business magazines	5	4	−1

SOURCE: Adapted from the Pew Research Center for the People and the Press, "Internet Sapping Broadcast News Audience," June 13, 2000, and "News Audiences Increasingly Politicized," June 8, 2004, http://people-press.org.

NOTE: Both surveys are based on national telephone samples of adults reporting "regular" use of a news medium. The 2000 survey sampled 3,142 adults; the 2004 survey, 3,000.

Not only are the media the chief source of most Americans' views of the world, but they also provide the fastest way to disperse information throughout society. Major political news broadcasts by twenty-four-hour services like CNN or Fox News spread breaking stories throughout the country in minutes. People hear the stories either directly from radio or television or secondhand from other people.

All of the mass media are politically important because of their potential to reach large audiences. However, the influence of each medium varies depending on its characteristics, the nature and quantity of the political messages it carries, and the size of the audience reached. Print media, including media featuring printed text on the Internet, generally supply the largest quantities of factual political information and analysis. They need readers who are literate at appropriate levels. Electronic media, especially television broadcasts, provide a greater sense of reality, which explains why audiences find electronic media more credible than print media. Moreover, large segments of the U.S. population have limited reading skills and find it far easier to capture meanings from pictures and spoken language. Electronic media also convey physical images, including body language and facial expressions, much more effectively than print media. They are especially well suited to attract viewers' attention and arouse their emotions. Many people find it easier to gather insights on events and issues through audiovisual media.[11]

Functions of Mass Media

What major societal functions do the mass media perform? Political scientist Harold Lasswell, a pioneer in media studies, mentions three things: surveillance of the world to report ongoing events, interpretation of the meaning of events, and socialization of individuals into their cultural settings.[12] To these three, a fourth function must be added: deliberate manipulation of politics. The manner in which these four functions are performed affects the political fate of individuals, groups, and social organizations, as well as the course of domestic and international politics.

Surveillance

Surveillance involves two major tasks. It throws the spotlight of publicity on selected individuals, organizations, and events, which may then make them matters of concern to politicians and the public. Surveillance may determine which political demands surface and which remain hidden. It may force politicians to respond to situations on which their views would not have been aired otherwise. In contrast with such public surveillance, private surveillance serves the private needs of individual citizens, informing them about events of interest. Private surveillance may lead to political activities, but its primary functions are gratifying personal needs and quieting anxieties. The media, as Marshall McLuhan, another pioneering media scholar, observed, are "sense extensions" for individuals who cannot directly witness most of the events of interest to them and their communities.[13]

Public Surveillance. Newspeople determine what is news—that is, which political happenings will be reported and which will be ignored. Their choices are politically significant because they affect who and what will have a good chance to become the focus for political discussion and action.[14] Without media attention the people and events covered by the news might have less influence on decision makers—or none at all. Conditions that might be tolerated in obscurity can become intolerable in the glare of publicity. Take the workplace injuries in unsafe pipe-making factories. Without the public airing of the situation, reforms would have been unlikely. Politicians are keenly aware of the media's agenda-setting power. This is why they try mightily to time and structure events to yield as much favorable publicity as possible and to forestall damaging coverage.

Not all media surveillance spurs beneficial reactions, of course. Misperceptions and scares created by media stories have undermined confidence in good policies and practices, good people, and good products on many occasions. The human and economic costs have been vast. For example, dubious stories that impugned the safety of bioengineered foods caused millions of dollars of losses in the affected industries.

If media stories overemphasize crime and corruption in the inner city, scared residents may move to the suburbs, leaving the inner city deserted and even less safe and deprived of tax revenues. Speculation that international conflicts or economic downturns are in the offing may scare investors and produce fluctuations in domestic and international stock markets and commodity exchanges. Serious economic (and hence political) consequences may ensue.

Fear of publicity can be as powerful a force in shaping action as actual exposure. Politicians and business leaders know what damage an unfavorable story can do and act accordingly, either to avoid or conceal censurable behaviors or to atone for them by public confessions. President Bill Clinton, whose eight-year term was pockmarked with scandals, tried valiantly to hide some of them by forceful denials of allegations. But whenever proof made the charges undeniable, he escaped much public wrath by publicly apologizing for his misbehavior.[15]

The media can doom people and events to obscurity by inattention as well. When the media have more information than they can transmit, many important stories remain untold. Time and space constraints are most stringent for the news venue with the largest audiences—network television newscasts. Newspeople also ignore important events that do not seem "newsworthy" by accepted journalistic criteria or that fail to catch their attention. Conscious attempts to suppress information for ideological or political reasons are another, less frequent reason for lack of coverage.

For many years left-wing social critics have faulted mainstream U.S. journalists for using their news selection power to strengthen white middle-class values and suppress socialist viewpoints. These critics claim that the media deliberately perpetuate capitalist exploitation of the masses, in line with the ideological preferences of media owners. Critics also claim that the media have intentionally suppressed the facts about dangerous products, such as alcohol and tobacco, and about the socially harmful activities of large corporations, which may be responsible for water and air pollution or unsafe consumer goods.[16] By the same token, right-wing critics complain that the media give undue attention to enemies of the established social and political order in hopes of undermining it. Each camp cites a long list of stories to support its contentions.[17]

YOUR TAX DOLLARS AT WORK: CONGRESS STARTS THE DAY WITH THE PLEDGE.

Reprinted by permission: Tribune Media Services.

Journalists reject these charges. They deny political motives in news selection and defend their choices on the basis of the general criteria of newsworthiness (treated more fully in Chapter 4). They, too, can muster evidence from news stories to support their claims. At the heart of controversies over the ideological bias of the media lie two basic questions that cannot be answered conclusively. The first concerns people's motivations. How can one prove what motivates journalists to act in certain ways? Lacking proof, is it fair to ascribe motivations to them in the face of their denials? The second question relates to story effects. To what degree can media stories produce the goals that owners of print and electronic media and news professionals are allegedly seeking? If the desired effects are unattainable, the critics' concerns are moot.

Besides calling attention to matters of potential public concern, the media also provide cues about the importance of an issue. Important stories are covered prominently—on the front page with big headlines and pictures or as a major television or radio feature. Less important matters get buried in the back pages or have brief exposure on television or radio. However, nearly all coverage, even when it is brief and comparatively inconspicuous, lends an aura of significance to publicized topics. Through the sheer fact of coverage the media can confer status on individuals and organizations. The media "function essentially as agencies of social legitimation—as forces, that is, which reaffirm those ultimate value standards and beliefs, which in turn uphold the social and political status quo." [18]

Television made African American civil rights leaders and their causes household names. Martin Luther King Jr. and Jesse Jackson became national figures in part because television showed them giving speeches and leading marches and protests. In King's case, television captured the riots following his assassination. An individual who wins a hearing on radio or television often becomes an instant celebrity, whether he or she is a political candidate, like 2004 presidential contender John Kerry, whose efforts to win an election were widely publicized; a social crusader, like Ralph Nader, whose goals became front-page news; or a convicted murderer or terrorist, like Osama bin Laden. Their unpublicized counterparts remain obscure and bereft of political influence.

Because publicity is crucial for political success, actors on the political scene deliberately create situations likely to receive media coverage. Daniel Boorstin has labeled events arranged primarily to stimulate media coverage "pseudo-events." [19] Such events range from news conferences called by public figures even when there is no news to announce to physical assaults on people and property by members of protest groups who want to dramatize grievances. Newspeople who must cover such events may feel manipulated and resentful, but they are loath to allow competing media to scoop them.

When events are exceptionally significant or have become widely known already, or when the story is reported by competing media, the journalism community loses control over the news flow. For example, journalistic standards demand the reporting of news about prominent persons and major domestic or international events.[20] Aside from such unavoidable events, coverage is discretionary for a wide range of people and events.

The power of the media to set the agenda for politics is not controlled by a system of formal checks and balances as is the power of the U.S. government. Media power is not subject to periodic review through the electoral process. If media emphases or claims are incorrect, remedies are few. Truth in advertising laws protect citizens from false advertising of consumer goods but not from false political claims or improper news selection by media personnel. The courts have interpreted restrictions on the news media as impairing the constitutional rights to free speech and a free press. Media critic Jay Blumler expresses the dilemma well:

> Media power is not supposed to be shared: That's an infringement of editorial autonomy. It is not supposed to be controlled: That's censorship. It's not even supposed to be influenced: That's news management! But why should

media personnel be exempt from Lord Acton's dictum that all power corrupts and absolute power corrupts absolutely? And if they are not exempt, who exactly is best fitted to guard the press guardians, as it were?[21]

Private Surveillance.   Average citizens may not think much about the broader political impact of the news they read, hear, and watch. They use the media primarily to keep in touch with what they deem personally important. The media are their eyes and ears to the world, their means of surveillance. The media tell us about weather, sports, jobs, fashions, economic conditions, social and cultural events, health and science, and the public and private lives of famous people.

The ability to stay informed makes people feel secure, whether or not they remember what they read or hear or see. Even though the news may be bad, at least people feel that there will be no startling surprises. News reassures us that the political system continues to operate despite constant crises and frequent mistakes. Reassurance is important for peace of mind. But it also tends to encourage political quiescence, because there is no need to act if political leaders seem to be doing their jobs. For good or ill, the public's quiescence helps maintain the political and economic status quo.[22]

Other significant private functions that the mass media fulfill for many people are entertainment, companionship, tension relief, and a way to pass the time with minimal physical or mental exertion. The mass media can satisfy these important personal needs conveniently and cheaply. People who otherwise might be frustrated and dissatisfied can participate through the media vicariously in current political happenings, in sports and musical events, in the lives of famous people, and in the lives of families and communities featured in the news.[23]

Interpretation

Media not only survey the events of the day and bring them to public and private attention, they also interpret the events' meanings, put them into context, and speculate about their consequences. Most incidents lend themselves to a variety of interpretations, depending on the values and experiences of the interpreter. The kind of interpretation affects the political consequences of media reports. For example, since 1962 the way in which the media interpret the legal and social significance of abortions has changed considerably. Abortion almost universally used to be considered murder. The abortionist was the villain and the pregnant woman was an accomplice in a heinous crime. Now abortion is often cast into the frame of women's rights to control their bodies and to protect their physical and mental health.

What spawned the switch in media interpretation and eased the change in public attitudes toward abortion? The experience of a beloved television personality. Sherri Finkbine, hostess of *Romper Room,* a popular children's show in the 1960s, had taken thalidomide during her pregnancy before the drug's tragic effects on the unborn were known. Once she learned of the potential harm, she feared giving birth to a severely malformed baby and had an abortion in 1962. Instead of reporting the action as murder, as had been the custom, news media throughout the country defended Finkbine's decision to terminate her pregnancy. To steer clear of the negative connotations of the word *abortion,* journalists used a new vocabulary. They talked of "surgery to prevent a malformed baby," of "avoiding the possibility of mothering a drug-deformed child," and of the necessity of inducing a miscarriage to spare a child from loathing "its own image and crying out against those who might have spared it this suffering."[24]

Numerous circumstances influenced the type of interpretation that the Finkbine story received. In the end, it hinged on journalists' decisions, made independently or in response to pressures, to frame the story in a specific way and to choose informants accordingly. Journalists' inclinations help decide how the news will be framed, which in turn determines its likely impact.

By suggesting the causes and relationships of events, the media may shape opinions without explicitly telling audiences which views to adopt. For example, linking civil strife during the cold war to left-wing agitators ensured that the U.S. public would view violent protests with considerable alarm. Linking the protests to internal corruption and social oppression would have put the problems into a far less threatening light.

News presentations can predetermine people's conclusions in countless ways.

> We [journalists] can attribute any social problem to official policies, the machinations of those who benefit from it, or the pathology of those who suffer from it. We can trace it back to class or racial inequalities, to ideologies such as nationalism or patriotism, or to resistance to the regime. We can root the problem in God, in its historic genesis, in the accidental or systematic conjuncture of events, in rationality, in irrationality, or in a combination of these or other origins. In choosing any such ultimate cause we are also depicting a setting, an appropriate course of action, and sets of virtuous and evil characters, and doing so in a way that will appeal to some part of the public that sees its own sentiments or interests reflected in that choice of a social scene.[25]

The items that media personnel select to illustrate a point or to characterize a political actor need not be intrinsically important to be influential in shaping opinions and evaluations. They do not even need exposure in respected media outlets. This is why House Speaker–designate Bob

Livingston resigned from Congress in 1998, when he learned that the publisher of the pornographic *Hustler* magazine was about to publicize charges of adultery about him. Livingston had confessed extramarital liaisons to his colleagues in Congress but feared that an explosion of adverse media publicity would devastate his party and his career.

Socialization

The third function of major mass media that Lasswell mentions is political socialization (Chapter 7). It involves learning basic values and orientations that prepare individuals to fit into their cultural milieu. Before the 1970s, studies largely ignored the mass media because parents and the schools were deemed the primary agents of socialization. Research in the 1970s finally established that the media play a crucial role in political socialization.[26] Most information that young people acquire about their political world comes directly or indirectly from the mass media. The media present specific facts as well as general values, teaching young people which elements produce power and success; they also provide the young with behavior models. Because young people lack established attitudes and behaviors, they use such information to develop their opinions.

Most of the new orientations and opinions that adults acquire during their lifetime also are based on information from the mass media. People do not necessarily adopt the precise attitudes and opinions that media suggest; rather, mass media information provides the ingredients that people use to adjust their existing attitudes and opinions to keep pace with a changing world. The mass media deserve credit, therefore, for a sizable share of adult political socialization and resocialization. Examples of resocialization—the restructuring of established basic attitudes—are the shifts in sexual morality and racial attitudes that the public has undergone since the middle of the last century and the changing views on relations with mainland China and with Russia.[27]

Manipulation

Journalists at prominent news venues periodically become major players in the game of politics; they do not just play their traditional role as chroniclers of information provided by others. The most common way for a journalist to break out of the role of political bystander is through an investigation. Many major print and electronic media enterprises operate their own investigative units, because investigative stories are very popular.

The purpose of many investigations is to *muckrake*. Journalists who investigate corruption and wrongdoing to stimulate government to clean up the "dirt" they have exposed are called muckrakers. The term comes from a rake designed to collect manure. President Theodore Roosevelt was the first to apply the term to journalism. Muckraking today may have several different goals.[28] The journalist's primary purpose may be to write stories that expose misconduct in government and produce reforms. Or the chief purpose may be to present sensational information that attracts large media audiences and enhances profits. Other manipulative stories may be designed to affect politics in line with the journalist's political preferences (Chapter 6).

Effects of Mass Media

The public believes that the media influence politics and public thinking. Politicians act on the basis of the same assumption. But many studies fail to show substantial impact. Why is there such a discrepancy between many social science appraisals of mass media effects and the general impression, reflected in public policies, that the mass media are extremely influential?

There are three major reasons. First, many studies, particularly those conducted during the 1950s and 1960s, took a narrow approach to media effects, looking for only a few specified effects rather than all possible effects. Second, theories about learning and how to test it have enhanced the belief that media have minimal effects because people often fail to recall specific facts mentioned in news stories. Third, social scientists have great difficulty measuring media effects because these effects are part of a complex combination of social stimuli.

Early Studies

U.S. social scientists began to study the effects of the mass media primarily in one narrow area: vote change as a result of media coverage of presidential elections. Among these early studies, several are considered classics. *The People's Choice* by Paul Lazarsfeld, Bernard Berelson, and Hazel Gaudet, all of Columbia University, reported in 1944 how people made their voting choices in Erie County, Pennsylvania, in the 1940 presidential election. Sequels to the study followed in short order. The best known are *Voting: A Study of Opinion Formation in a Presidential Campaign, The Voter Decides,* and *The American Voter.*[29]

Focus on Vote Choices. The early studies were based on the assumption that a well-publicized campaign changes votes. If it did not, this would indicate that the media lacked influence. Subsequent studies have shown that this reasoning is faulty. There may be measurable media influence even when vote choice remains stable. Besides, media effects vary depending on the office at stake and the historical period. At the time of the early voting studies, change of vote choice was quite uncommon because most voters adhered to party lines, regardless of media coverage. Subsequently, party allegiance weakened among many voters, so that the opportunities for media influence on vote choice are now far greater.

Had the investigators concentrated on other settings, such as judicial or nonpartisan elections (for which few voting cues outside the media are available), they might also have discovered greater media-induced change in attitude. Substantial media influence might have been found even in presidential elections if changes in people's trust and affection or knowledge about the candidates and the election had been explored. Such changes constitute important media influences that are crucial components of a variety of political behaviors aside from voting.

The early voting studies focused almost exclusively on effects on individuals; they failed to trace effects on the social groups to which individuals belong and through which they influence political events. Gay men might not change their votes after hearing a candidate attack their lifestyle. But they might urge their association to testify against legislation favored by the candidate. They might even participate in violence in the wake of news stories reporting hate crimes against the gay community. In turn, these activities may have major political repercussions. Yet the early studies of media effects ignore such sequential impacts on the political system and its component parts.

The findings that media effects were minimal were so pervasive that social science research into mass media effects fell to a low ebb after an initial flurry in the 1940s and 1950s. Social scientists did not want to waste time studying inconsequential effects. Despite the seemingly solid evidence of media importance, they did not care to swim against the stream of established knowledge. As a consequence, study after study dealing with political socialization and learning ignored the mass media.

Learning Theories. The early findings were all the more believable because they tied in well with theories of persuasion. Mass media messages presumably miss their mark because they are impersonal. They are not tailored to the interests of specific individuals, as are the messages of parents, teachers, and friends. They do not permit immediate feedback, preventing the instant revision of messages that makes them more suitable for the receiver. Furthermore, compulsion to listen to mass media messages is rare and there is no need to answer. Hence it is easy to ignore them.

Although there is a lot of truth to these claims, they fail to consider that television can be a very personal medium. Audiences frequently interact with the television image as if what appears on screen were actually present in front of them. They may look on television commentators and actors as personal friends. Viewers often imitate people and situations on television, and they may identify with specific characters.

Further support for the minimal-effects findings come from various cognitive consistency theories. They postulate that average individuals dislike being presented with information that is incompatible with cherished beliefs. To avoid a painful experience that might require changing established beliefs, people expose themselves to the media selectively. Social scientists have evidence that people are indeed selective in their use of the media and search for information that reinforces what they already believe and know. But, as will be discussed more fully in Chapter 7, the phenomenon is limited.

Recent Research

When researchers resumed their investigations of mass media effects in the wake of persistent evidence of strong media impact, they cast their net more broadly. They began to look beyond media effects on voting to other effects during elections and in other types of political situations. In this vein, researchers have confirmed media impact on factual learning, on opinion formation, and on citizens' political activities. They also have looked beyond the individual to effects on political systems and subsystems in the United States and elsewhere and found strong media effects.[30]

Even if it were true that media are nothing but passive conduits of information, people throughout politics consider the media to be powerful and behave accordingly. In light of this evidence, it is obvious that media coverage often has a strong impact on ongoing political developments, in shaping the views and behaviors of political elites and other selected groups, and in influencing the general public's perception of political life. As Theodore White put it, albeit with some exaggeration:

> The power of the press in America is a primordial one. It sets the agenda of public discussion; and this sweeping political power is unrestrained by any law. It determines what people will talk and think about—an authority that in other nations is reserved for tyrants, priests, parties, and mandarins.[31]

No major act of the U.S. Congress, no foreign adventure, no act of diplomacy, no great social reform can succeed in the United States unless the press prepares the public mind.[32]

Although research of media effects has made great strides thanks to improvements in research designs and techniques, research into mass media effects remains hampered by serious measurement problems.

Measuring Complex Effects. Mass media effects are difficult to measure, both at the individual and societal levels, because the effects are highly complex and elusive. The most common measuring device at the individual level—self-assessment of impact elicited during interviews—is notoriously unreliable. Researchers lack tools to measure human thinking objectively. Even when people engage in overt behavior, one cannot judge accurately what messages may have prompted the behavior. Actions spring from a variety of motivations, so it is difficult to isolate the media's part.[33]

Assessing the impact of particular news stories is especially difficult because mass media audiences already have knowledge and attitudes that they bring to bear on new information. Because researchers rarely know precisely what these attitudes and knowledge consist of, or the rules by which they are combined with new information, the researchers cannot pinpoint the exact contribution that particular mass media stories have made to an individual's cognitions, feelings, and actions. To complicate matters further, the impact of the mass media varies depending on the subject matter. For instance, media impact is greater on people's perceptions of unfamiliar issues than on their perceptions of familiar issues, especially when the people have faced them personally.

Establishing effects at the societal level is even more difficult. A good example is the "CNN effect," which was widely credited as propelling President George Bush to dispatch U.S. troops to Somalia in 1992. The term refers to the belief that news media, like the Cable News Network (CNN), directly inflame public opinion by showing gripping pictures of ongoing crises. The public's clamor for action then forces government to take hasty action. Media coverage becomes the dog that wags the public policy tail.

In the Somalia case, CNN and other television networks had aired reports and pictures of widespread starvation and devastation in the summer months of 1992. These pictures presumably inflamed the public and aroused pressure groups that forced members of the Bush administration, against their better judgment, to airlift relief supplies and later to dispatch U.S. troops to Somalia. The rescue effort ultimately failed, and U.S. lives were lost.[34]

Political scientists Steven Livingston and Todd Eachus reached a different conclusion about the respective roles of the news media and the Bush administration in determining U.S. policy in Somalia. After examining a variety of sources, including *New York Times* and *Washington Post* stories about U.S. humanitarian relief policies and after interviewing key government decision makers and long-term relief personnel in Somalia, Livingston and Eachus concluded that plans for relief efforts had been underway for more than a year prior to CNN coverage of the tragedy. Government officials, including concerned members of Congress who had traveled to Somalia, rather than television news stories, had been the spur to action.

Despite persuasive evidence that extensive media coverage of the tragedy followed, rather than preceded, President Bush's announcement of the military airlift and other relief measures on August 14, 1992, many observers still argue that media mobilization of public opinion was an essential prerequisite for the Somalia intervention. They claim that the administration would have avoided the airlift in the absence of media coverage of the tragedy. Absolute proof, one way or the other, does not exist. Inability to prove the scope of mass media impact beyond a doubt has made social scientists shy away from assessing media influence on many important political events. Some social scientists even go to the other extreme and deny that effects exist simply because the effects defy precise measurement. This is unfortunate, because many other elusive effects can be observed in the field and studied in the laboratory.

Measurement of media effects also has suffered because many effects are unanticipated. For example, the stock market is highly sensitive to news reports that might have economic consequences. A brief story about one patient's "miracle cure" from an unusual disease may send drug company stocks soaring even when the story is barely a blip on the audience's attention screen.

Statistical versus Political Significance.   Social scientists often underestimate media impact because they falsely equate statistical significance with political significance. Media impact on a statistically insignificant number of individuals can still have great political consequences. For example, during an election, only 1 or 2 percent of the voters may change their votes because of media stories. That is a statistically negligible effect. From a political standpoint, however, the impact may be major, because many important elections, including several presidential elections, have been decided by a tiny margin of votes. The 2000 presidential race was decided by a fraction of less than 1 percent of the vote in Florida. Overall, more than 105 million votes were cast for president. An "insignificant" 1 percent of that total still represented more than 1 million people.

On a smaller scale, if a broadcast of details of a race riot attracts a few listeners to the riot site and stimulates some to participate, the situation may escalate beyond control. In the same way, the impact of a single news story may change the course of history if it induces one assassin to kill a world leader or convinces one world leader to go to war.

Influencing Elites.   Another major problem with social science research on mass media effects is that it has concentrated on measuring the effects on ordinary individuals rather than on political elites. The average individual, despite contrary democratic fictions, is fairly unimportant in the political process. Mass media impact on a handful of political decision makers usually is vastly more significant because it influences how they conduct political affairs. This is why governments everywhere, in authoritarian as well as democratic societies, try to control the flow of information produced by the media lest it thwart their political objectives.[35]

Who Should Control News Making?

Attempts by governments to control and manipulate the media are universal because public officials everywhere believe that media are important political forces. This belief is based on the assumption that institutions that control the public's information supply can shape public knowledge and behavior and thereby determine support for government or opposition to it. Although media control occurs in all societies, its extent, nature, and purposes vary for several reasons. Political ideology is a major one. In countries in which free expression of opinion is highly valued and in which dissent is respected, the media tend to be comparatively unrestrained. The right of the press to criticize governments also flourishes when the prevailing ideology grants that governments are fallible and often corrupt and that average citizens are capable of forming valuable opinions about the conduct of government. Finally, freedom of the press, even when it becomes a thorn in the side of the government, is more easily tolerated when governments are well established and politically and economically secure. In nations where governments are unstable and resources insufficient to meet the country's needs, it may be difficult to tolerate press behavior that is apt to topple the government or retard its plans for economic development.

Nowhere are the media totally free from formal and informal government and social controls, even in times of peace. On the whole, authoritarian governments control more extensively and more rigidly than nonauthoritarian ones, but all control systems represent points on a continuum. There are also gradations of control within nations, depending on the current regime and political setting, regional and local variations, and the nature of news. The specifics of control systems vary from country to country, but the overall patterns are similar.[36]

Types of Control Systems

Authoritarian control systems are based either on a totalitarian ideology and are designed to control and use the media to support ideological goals or they are nonideological and simply represent a desire by the ruling elites to control media output tightly so that it does not interfere with their conduct of government. Examples of nonideological authoritarian control can be found in states ruled by military governments or in which constitutional guarantees have been suspended. Examples of control based on communist ideology are found in Cuba and China.

There are also two types of nonauthoritarian approaches to control—libertarian and social responsibility. They differ in philosophy about the role the media ought to play in countries in which media enjoy a great deal of freedom. When journalists in democratic societies subscribe to the libertarian philosophy, they feel free to report whatever they deem interesting for their audiences. By contrast, when social responsibility philosophies prevail, newspeople expect to contribute to the betterment of society, spurring media audiences to behave in socially responsible ways. Journalists in the United States and Western Europe furnish examples of both these philosophies. Often libertarian and social responsibility journalism occur simultaneously, or they may alternate during successive historical periods.[37]

In today's world, fully or partially authoritarian systems of media control prevail in most countries, although many governments profess to want democratization and are struggling in that direction. Nonetheless, government attempts to control internal and external news flows persist because governments fear that unrestrained media will lead to political instability, often attributable to deliberate misinformation.

Authoritarian systems operate on the assumption that government must control the media because they are essential for engendering support for the government's mission (Table 1-2). The media may point out minor deficiencies or corruption of low-level officials and suggest adjustments in line with prevailing policies, but criticism of the basic system or its rulers is considered destructive.

TABLE 1-2   The Media Take Different Roles under Different Regimes

Authoritarian regime assumptions	Nonauthoritarian regime assumptions
Governments know and serve people's best interests.	Governments are fallible and corrupt.
Media should support the government and its major policies.	Media should attack the government when officials and policies seem flawed.
News should engender support for major policies.	News should stimulate critical thinking about major policies.
News and entertainment programs should be selected for their social values.	News and entertainment programs should be selected for audience appeal.

SOURCE: Composed by the author.

Beyond that, the media are free to choose the stories they wish to publish, so long as government officials agree that these stories do not interfere with public policies. In totalitarian societies the likely political and social effects of a story—rather than its general significance, novelty, or audience appeal—determine what will be published and what will be buried in silence. For instance, news about accidents, disasters, and crimes is often suppressed because it does not contain socially useful information that is apt to strengthen people's allegiance to the political system. Even entertainment programs, such as music and drama performances and even cartoon shorts in movie theaters, must carry appropriate social messages or have historical significance. The government supports such entertainment financially because it serves the important public purpose of shaping people's minds in support of the political system.

Role of Media in Democracies

In democracies, the public sees journalists as its eyes and ears. Journalists must scrutinize government performance and report their findings. If media scrutiny causes governments to fall and public officials to be ousted, democracy is well served.

Although this is the theory behind the role of media in democratic societies, the practice is less clear-cut. In the United States, for example, neither newspeople nor government officials are completely at ease with the media's watchdog role (Box 1-1). The media limit their criticism to what they perceive as perversions of fundamental social and political values or noteworthy examples of corruption and waste. They rarely question the fundamentals of the political system.

Because journalists depend heavily on the established elites as their sources of news, their links to the existing power structures are strong. They may even share information with government agencies, including law enforcement bodies such as the Federal Bureau of Investigation and the Central Intelligence Agency. When disclosure might cause harm, reporters in a democratic society occasionally withhold important news at the request of the government. This has happened repeatedly during terrorism incidents when the lives of hostages were at stake and in the preparation stages of military interventions. Government officials, in an effort to keep their images untarnished by media attacks, may try to control the media through regulatory legislation or rewards and punishments (Chapter 9).

The chief obligation of the news media in democratic societies is to provide the general public with information and entertainment. According to the U.S. version of the *libertarian* philosophy, anything that happens

BOX 1-1
Enticing the Media Watchdog to Bark

Throughout the political life of the United States, the mass media have been considered a watchdog. This watchdog "barks" by telling stories that alert the public to wrongdoing by government officials. Many public-spirited citizens have used their resources to support journalists who act as watchdogs. For example, Berda Marks Goldsmith endowed the annual $25,000 Goldsmith Prize for Investigative Reporting to reward journalists "whose investigative reporting in a story or series of related stories best promotes more effective and ethical conduct of government, the making of public policy, or the practice of politics." [1]

The Pulitzer Prizes for journalism, valued at $7,500, were endowed by newspaper publisher Joseph Pulitzer in 1904. They have been awarded annually since 1917 and are the most prestigious recognition of journalistic excellence—1,516 entries competed for the prize in 2000, a typical year. Pulitzer himself was a courageous and successful fighter for the causes of good government. His efforts to curb corruption in government and business contributed mightily to the passage of antitrust legislation and regulation of the insurance industry.

Pulitzer articulated his vision of the role that can be played by good journalism in a 1904 article in the *North American Review:*

> Our Republic and its press will rise or fall together. An able, disinterested, public-spirited press, with trained intelligence to know the right and courage to do it, can preserve that public virtue without which popular government is a sham and a mockery. A cynical, mercenary, demagogic press will produce in time a people as base as itself. The power to mould the future of the Republic will be in the hands of the journalists of future generations. [2]

That is quite a challenge! How well is the U.S. press meeting it?

---

1. Kennedy School of Government, Harvard University, "Shorenstein Center Goldsmith Awards Program," www.ksg.harvard.edu/presspol/goldsmith/goldprize.htm.
2. The Pulitzer Prizes, "History of the Prizes," www.pulitzer.org.

that seems interesting or important for media audiences may become news. It should be reported quickly, accurately, and without any attempt to convey a particular point of view. Subjects with the widest audience appeal should be pervasive, which explains the ample doses of sex and violence. Audience appeal is then expected to translate into good profits for media owners either through fees paid by audience members or through advertising revenues. Although audiences may learn important things from the media, libertarians believe that teaching is not the media's chief task. Nor is it their task to question the truth, accuracy, or merits of the information supplied to them by their sources. Rather, it is left to the news audience to decide what to believe and what to question.

By contrast, adherents to the tenets of social responsibility believe that news and entertainment presented by the mass media should reflect social concerns. Media personnel should be participants in the political process, not merely reporters of the passing scene. As guardians of the public welfare, they should foster political action when necessary by publicizing social evils, like rampant industrial pollution of air and water. In a similar vein, undesirable viewpoints and questionable accusations should be denied exposure, however sensational they may be. If reporters believe that the government is hiding information that the public needs to know, they should try to discover the facts and publicize them.

Social responsibility journalism and totalitarian journalism have some philosophical resemblances. Both approaches advocate using the media to support the basic ideals of their societies and to shape people into more perfect beings. Proponents of both schools of journalism are convinced that their goals are good and would not be achieved in a media system dominated by the whims of media owners or audiences. But the similarities should not be exaggerated. Social advocacy in democratic systems lacks the fervor, clout, and single-mindedness it has in systems in which the government monopolizes the media.

Social responsibility journalism rarely speaks with a single uncontested voice throughout society. Nevertheless, it frightens and antagonizes many news professionals and news audiences. If one agrees that the media should be used to influence social thought and behavior for "good" purposes, it becomes difficult to determine which purposes deserve to be included in that category. Critics of social responsibility journalism point out that journalists do not have a public mandate to act as arbiters of social values and policies in a society that has many disparate visions of truth and goodness. Newspeople lack the legitimacy that in a democracy comes only from being elected by the public or appointed by duly elected officials.

Whatever the merits or faults of these arguments, today social responsibility journalism is popular with a sizable proportion of the news profession.[38] Pulitzer prizes and other honors go to journalists who have success-fully exposed questionable practices in the interest of social improvement. The most prominent "villains" targeted for exposure are usually big government and big business.[39]

Models of News Making

Beyond the basic concerns reflected in the philosophies of libertarians and social responsibility advocates, there are many other guiding principles for reporting events. For example, news making can be described in terms of five distinct models: the mirror model, the professional model, the organizational model, the political model, and the civic journalism model. Each represents judgments about the major forces behind news making that shape the nature of news and its political impact.

Underlying Theories

Proponents of the mirror model contend that news is and should be a reflection of reality. Journalists observe the world around them and report what they notice as accurately and objectively as possible. "We don't make the news, we just report it," is their slogan. The implication is that newspeople impartially report all significant happenings that come to their attention. Critics of the mirror model point out that this conception of news making is unrealistic. Millions of significant events take place daily, forcing journalists to choose which items they wish to report. Events that are publicized inevitably loom disproportionately large compared with unpublicized events. The way the story is told in words and pictures further distorts reality.

In the professional model, news making is viewed as an endeavor of highly skilled professionals who put together a balanced and interesting collage of events selected for importance and attractiveness to media audiences. There is no pretense that the end product mirrors the world. Because audience appeal is a crucial consideration for economic reasons, anticipated audience reaction is especially influential in determining which stories pass scrutiny and which are ignored.

The organizational model, sometimes called the bargaining model, is based on organizational theory. Its proponents contend that the pressures inherent in organizational processes and goals determine which items will be published. Pressures spring from interpersonal relations among journalists and between them and their information sources, from professional norms within the news organization and from constraints arising from technical news production processes, cost-benefit considerations, and legal regulations.

The political model rests on the assumption that news everywhere reflects the ideological biases of individual newspeople as well as the pressures of the political environment in which the news organization operates. The media cover high-status people and approved institutions; people and events outside the dominant system or remote from the centers of power are generally ignored. Supporters of the prevailing system are pictured as good guys, opponents as bad guys.

In the 1990s public journalism, or civic journalism, became popular, spurred by widespread concern that average citizens shun participation in public affairs and distrust government and the news media. Proponents of the civic journalism model believe that the press can ascertain citizens' concerns and then write stories that help audiences play an active and successful role in public life.[40] Journalists must articulate and explain public policy choices in understandable language. They must facilitate a public dialogue that encourages and respects diverse views. After consensus has been reached among the clients of a particular news channel, the channel and its clients then must vigorously champion appropriate public policies.

None of these models fully explains news making; rather, the process reflects all of them in varying degrees. Because the influences that shape news making fluctuate, one needs to examine individual news making situations carefully to account for the factors at work. Organizational pressures, for instance, depend on the interactions of people within the organization. Audience tastes change or are interpreted differently. Perceptions of "facts" differ, depending on reporters' dispositions. Moreover, the precise mix of factors that explains news making in any particular instance depends largely on chance and on the needs of a particular news medium.

Control Methods

Societies use four types of controls on the press: legal, normative, structural, and economic. All governments have laws to prevent press misbehavior, such as forbidding publishing deliberate falsehoods. All societies also have social norms that the press generally heeds. For example, in a conservative country, ridiculing sacred concepts or widely accepted beliefs, behaviors, institutions, and individuals would lead to social condemnation. The way media organizations are structured, operated, and financed also shapes their product, as is clear when one compares the policy discretion enjoyed by publicly and privately owned media. Russia's government-controlled and financed media, for example, dare not criticize the government's war against rebels in Chechnya. Privately owned media in

Russia have no such hesitation. Similarly, in those European democracies where governments regularly intervene in social welfare matters, regulation of political communication is far more heavy handed than in liberal, individualistically oriented countries like the United States and England.[41]

The combination of methods by which governments control the media varies, and so do the major objectives of control. To ensure that news stories remain supportive of most government policies, authoritarian societies use legal, structural, and economic means to restrict access to mass communications to voices friendly to the regime. By contrast, nonauthoritarian regimes rarely make formal attempts to deny foes of the regime access to the media. However, they often use legal and normative pressures to avert potentially disastrous political news or news that violates widely cherished social norms.

Governments can control media content by limiting entry into the media business. For example, the government may require licenses for entry and grant them only to people it deems desirable. Control through franchise is quite common, especially for electronic media, because the capacity of the broadcast spectrum is limited. Franchises often bestow monopoly control. In most democracies, newspapers rarely need licenses, and access to the Internet has remained equally unrestricted. In the United States, for instance, anyone with sufficient money can start a newspaper or newsletter or create a Web site.

Media also may be controlled through the manipulation of access to news. Information may be put beyond the reach of media by declaring it to be "confidential" and by barring reporters from government archives. For instance, the government may release information only to favored publications, in effect putting less favored ones out of business. In 1993 President Clinton took the unusual step of limiting reporters' easy access to the White House communication office by closing off a connecting hallway to the press room.[42]

Authoritarian governments often limit what information may be published. In some countries nothing can be printed or broadcast until the government censor has approved it. At times governments will direct papers or magazines to make deletions after their product has been prepared for printing or is already printed. This leaves tantalizing white spaces or missing pages. Government officials often write or edit television and radio scripts, and media outlets must broadcast these without editorial changes. In the past, totalitarian countries could frequently block all unapproved communications from abroad. Practices included jamming foreign broadcasts and prohibiting the import of foreign printed materials. In the Internet age, tight controls have become well-nigh impossible.

All governments use treason and sedition laws to control media output. Treason and sedition can be defined broadly or narrowly. Anything that is critical of the government can be called treasonable or seditious, especially in times of war. In democratic societies, media and the government are in perennial disagreement about the exact location of this point. Governments lean toward protection; the media lean toward disclosure. People judged guilty of treason or sedition may be sentenced to prison or even executed. Given the severity of the penalty, disobedience is rare. Most journalists avoid difficulties with official censors and with treason and sedition laws by refraining from using material that is likely to be objectionable. Government censorship then becomes replaced largely by self censorship.

The First Amendment to the U.S. Constitution, which provides that "Congress shall make no law . . . abridging the freedom of speech, or of the press," has given the media an exceptionally strong basis for resisting government controls in the United States. The courts have ruled, however, that the protection is not absolute. On occasion, it must give way to social rights that the courts consider to be superior. For example, media are forbidden from publicizing the names of CIA secret agents because that would endanger them and destroy their usefulness.

A limited number of controls, such as regulatory laws, court decisions, and informal social pressures, guard against excesses by the media. In the United States the courts have been loath to impose restraints prior to publication, such as granting injunctions that would stop publication of information on the grounds that it would cause irreparable harm. But informal social and political pressures and the fear of indictments after publication have restrained presentation of potentially disturbing stories. In addition, information about sexual abuse of children by priests or stories of abuse of prison inmates have often been suppressed because they might produce a backlash from audiences or powerful politicians.

Besides guarding state survival through treason and sedition laws, government controls commonly shield sensitive governmental proceedings, protect individual reputations and privacy, and safeguard the prevailing moral standards of the community. Curbs on publication of government secrets—so-called classified information—often engender controversy because governments tend to be overzealous in controlling material that they deem potentially harmful to themselves. Finally, most governments also have laws protecting the reputations of individuals or groups and laws against obscenity (Chapter 3).

Defining the limits of government control over information dissemination raises difficult questions for democratic societies. Does official censorship, however minimal, open the way for excessive curbs on free expression? What guidelines are available to determine how far censorship should go? What types of material, if any, can harm children? Or adults?

Should ethnic and racial slurs be prohibited on the ground that they damage minorities' self-image? The answers are controversial and problematic.

In addition to formal control of potentially damaging news, many informal restraints control the actual production and flow of news. All government units, and often many of their subdivisions, have their own information control systems by which they determine which news to conceal or release and how to present it (Chapter 9).

The limitations on the freedom of publication in democratic societies raise questions about the actual differences in press freedom in nonauthoritarian and authoritarian societies. Is there really a difference, for example, in the independence of government-operated television networks in France and in North Korea? The answer is a resounding "yes." The degree of restraint varies so sharply that the systems are fundamentally different. In authoritarian societies the main objective of controls is to support the regime in power. In democratic societies the media are usually free to oppose the regime, to weaken it, and even to topple it. Although the media rarely carry their power to the latter extreme, the potential is there. It is this potential that makes the media in nonauthoritarian societies a genuine restraint on governmental abuses of power and a potent shaper of government action.

Summary

The mass media are an important influence on politics because they regularly and rapidly present politically crucial information to huge audiences. These audiences include political elites and decision makers, as well as large numbers of average citizens whose political activities, however sporadic, are shaped by information from the mass media.

Decisions made by media personnel about what and whom to cover determine what information becomes available to media audiences and what remains unavailable. By putting stories into perspective and interpreting them, reporters assign meaning to the information and indicate the standards by which it ought to be judged. At times, reporters even generate political action directly through their own investigations or indirectly through their capacity to stimulate pseudo-events.

Although social scientists still find it difficult to pinpoint the scope of media impact on particular political events, politicians and their governments everywhere are keenly aware of the political importance of the media. Therefore, these governments have policies to shape the media's political role in their societies. These policies have been buttressed by constitutional and legal rules as well as by a host of informal arrangements. In this chapter we have described briefly how the basic policies, constitutional arrangements, and legal provisions differ in authoritarian and democratic regimes.

Notes

1. David Barstow and Lowell Bergman, "At a Texas Foundry, an Indifference to Life," *New York Times,* January 8, 2003.
2. David Barstow, "U.S. Rarely Seeks Charges for Deaths in Workplace," *New York Times,* December 22, 2003.
3. PBS Frontline, "A Dangerous Business?" www.pbs.org/wgbh/pages/frontline/shows/workplace/.
4. For a brief overview of current knowledge about mass media effects, see W. Lance Bennett, *News: The Politics of Illusion,* 5th ed. (White Plains, N.Y.: Longman, 2003); and Leo W. Jeffres, *Mass Media Effects,* 2d ed. (Prospect Heights, Ill.: Waveland Press, 1997).
5. George Gerbner, Larry Gross, Michael Morgan, and Nancy Signorielli, "Charting the Mainstream: Television's Contributions to Political Orientation," *Journal of Communication* 32 (1982): 106–107. See also Richard Campbell, *Media and Culture* (New York: St. Martin's Press, 1998), part I.
6. Pew Research Center for the People and the Press, "Internet Sapping Broadcast News Audience," June 13, 2000, www.people-press.org.
7. Pew Research Center for the People and the Press, "News Audiences Increasingly Politicized," June 8, 2004, www.people-press.org.
8. Ibid., www.people-press.org/media00sec1.htm.
9. Julia Keller, "Unconventional Wisdom," *Chicago Tribune,* August 2, 2004. See also Michael X. Delli Carpini and Bruce A. Williams, "Let Us Infotain You: Politics in the New Media Environment," in *Mediated Politics: Communication in the Future of Democracy,* ed. W. Lance Bennett and Robert M. Entman (Cambridge: Cambridge University Press, 2001), 160–181; Jeffrey P. Jones, *Entertaining Politics: New Political Television and Civic Culture* (Lanham, Md.: Rowman and Littlefield, 2004); Liesbet van Zoonen, *Entertaining the Citizen: When Politics and Popular Culture Converge* (Lanham, Md.: Rowman and Littlefield, 2004).
10. Robert M. Entman and Andrew Rojecki, *The Black Image in the White Mind: Media and Race in America* (Chicago: University of Chicago Press, 2000).
11. For a discussion of many aspects of visual presentations, see Gregory Stanczak, "Visual Research: Method and Representation," *American Behavioral Scientist* 47, no. 12 (2004): 1471–1642.
12. Harold D. Lasswell, "The Structure and Function of Communication in Society," in *Mass Communications,* ed. Wilbur Schramm (Urbana: University of Illinois Press, 1969), 103.
13. Marshall McLuhan, *Understanding Media: The Extensions of Man* (New York: McGraw-Hill, 1964).
14. Chapter 4 gives a more detailed definition of news. Evidence that the media set the agenda for national issues is presented in David L. Protess and Maxwell McCombs, eds., *Agenda Setting: Readings on Media, Public Opinion, and Policy-making* (Hillsdale, N.J.: Erlbaum, 1991). For a more recent discussion of

agenda setting for news consumers, see Wayne Wanta, *The Public and the National Agenda* (Mahwah, N.J.: Erlbaum, 1997).

15. Larry J. Sabato, Mark Stencel, and S. Robert Lichter, *Peep Show: Media and Politics in an Age of Scandal* (Lanham, Md.: Rowman and Littlefield, 2000). The authors discuss the appropriate ways to deal with scandal stories.

16. Examples of such criticism can be found in Bennett, *News: The Politics of Illusion;* Robert W. McChesney, *Rich Media, Poor Democracy* (New York: New Press, 1999); and Michael Parenti, *Inventing Reality: The Politics of the News Media,* 3d ed. (New York: St. Martin's Press, 1993).

17. An example of a conservative Washington, D.C.–based media analysis group is Accuracy in Media, which publishes periodic reports of its media investigations. For claims that journalists in the elite media are ultraliberal, see S. Robert Lichter, Stanley Rothman, and Linda S. Lichter, *The Media Elite* (New York: Adler and Adler, 1986).

18. Jay G. Blumler, "Purposes of Mass Communications Research: A Transatlantic Perspective," *Journalism Quarterly* 55 (summer 1978): 226.

19. Daniel Boorstin, *The Image: A Guide to Pseudo-Events* (New York: Atheneum, 1971).

20. Criteria of what constitutes *news* are discussed fully in a historical context in Kevin G. Barnhurst and John Nerone, *The Form of News* (New York: Guilford Press, 2001). Also see Samuel P. Winch, *Mapping the Cultural Space of Journalism* (Westport, Conn.: Praeger, 1997).

21. Blumler, "Purposes of Mass Communications Research," 228.

22. The results of reassuring publicity are discussed by Murray Edelman, *The Symbolic Uses of Politics* (1964; reprint, Urbana: University of Illinois Press, 1985), 38–43.

23. Robert Kubey and Mihaly Csikszentmihalyi, *Television and the Quality of Life: How Viewing Shapes Everyday Experience* (Hillsdale, N.J.: Erlbaum, 1990), chap. 5, 7.

24. Marvin N. Olasky and Susan Northway Olasky, "The Crossover in Newspaper Coverage of Abortion from Murder to Liberation," *Journalism Quarterly* 63 (1986): 31–37.

25. W. Lance Bennett and Murray Edelman, "Toward a New Political Narrative," *Journal of Communication* 35 (1985): 156–171.

26. The early writings include David Easton and Jack Dennis, *Children in the Political System: Origins of Political Legitimacy* (New York: McGraw-Hill, 1969); Fred I. Greenstein, *Children and Politics* (New Haven: Yale University Press, 1965); Richard Dawson and Kenneth Prewitt, *Political Socialization* (Boston: Little, Brown, 1969); and Robert D. Hess and Judith Torney, *The Development of Political Attitudes in Children* (Chicago: Aldine, 1967). Examples of the studies in the 1970s are Sidney Kraus and Dennis Davis, *The Effects of Mass Communication on Political Behavior* (University Park: Pennsylvania State University Press, 1976); Steven H. Chaffee, "Mass Communication in Political Socialization," in *Handbook of Political Socialization,* ed. Stanley Renshon (New York: Free Press, 1977). Also see Wendy M. Rahn and Rebecca M. Hirshorn, "Political Advertising and Public Mood: A Study of Children's Political Orientations," *Political Communication,* 16 (1999): 387–407; and Robert D. Putnam, *Bowling Alone: The Collapse and Revival of American Political Community* (New York: Simon and Schuster, 2000).

27. Benjamin I. Page and Robert Y. Shapiro, *The Rational Public: Fifty Years of Trends in Americans' Policy Preferences* (Chicago: University of Chicago Press, 1992);

Benjamin I. Page, *Who Deliberates?* (Chicago: University of Chicago Press, 1996); Shanto Iyengar and Donald Kinder, *News That Matters: Television and American Opinion* (Chicago: University of Chicago Press, 1987); and Doris A. Graber, *Processing the News: How People Tame the Information Tide*, 3d ed. (Lanham, Md.: University Press of America, 1993); James Mann, "Covering China," *Media Studies Journal*, 13, no. 1 (1999): 102–107; John Zaller, "Monica Lewinsky and the Mainspring of American Politics," in *Mediated Politics: Communication in the Future of Democracy*, ed. W. Lance Bennett and Robert M. Entman (Cambridge: Cambridge University Press, 2001), 252–278.

28. David L. Protess, Jack C. Doppelt, James S. Ettema, Margaret T. Gordon, and Fay Lomax Cook, *The Journalism of Outrage: Investigative Reporting and Agenda Building in America* (New York: Guilford Press, 1991), 8–12. Also see Sabato, Stencel, and Lichter, *Peep Show.*

29. Paul Lazarsfeld, Bernard Berelson, and Hazel Gaudet, *The People's Choice* (New York: Columbia University Press, 1944); Bernard Berelson, Paul Lazarsfeld, and William McPhee, *Voting: A Study of Opinion Formation in a Presidential Campaign* (Chicago: University of Chicago Press, 1954); Angus Campbell, Gerald Gurin, and Warren E. Miller, *The Voter Decides* (Evanston, Ill.: Row, Peterson, 1954); and Angus Campbell, Philip E. Converse, Warren E. Miller, and Donald Stokes, *The American Voter* (New York: Wiley, 1960).

30. For examples, see the case studies presented in Frank Esser and Barbara Pfetsch, eds., *Comparing Political Communication: Theories, Cases, and Challenges* (Cambridge: Cambridge University Press, 2004).

31. Theodore White, *The Making of the President, 1972* (New York: Bantam, 1973), 327.

32. Ibid.

33. For a discussion of the problem and examples, see Jan E. Leighley, *Mass Media and Politics: A Social Science Perspective* (Boston: Houghton Mifflin, 2004).

34. This account is based on Steven Livingston and Todd Eachus, "Humanitarian Crisis and U.S. Foreign Policy: Somalia and the CNN Effect Reconsidered," *Political Communication* 12 (1995): 413–429.

35. Jeffres, *Mass Media Effects*, presents an excellent overview of the media effects literature.

36. The discussion is modeled on Fred Siebert, Theodore Peterson, and Wilbur Schramm, *Four Theories of the Press* (Urbana: University of Illinois Press, 1963). For a critique of the model, see Daniel C. Hallin and Paolo Mancini, *Comparing Media Systems: Three Models of Media and Politics* (Cambridge: Cambridge University Press, 2004).

37. For a brief account of media history in the United States, see Timothy E. Cook, *Governing with the News: The News Media as a Political Institution* (Chicago: University of Chicago Press, 1998), 17–60. Also see Kevin G. Barnhurst and John Nerone, *The Form of News* (New York: Guilford Press, 2001), which traces changes in form and substance of news delivered by U.S. media.

38. David H. Weaver and G. Cleveland Wilhoit, *The American Journalist in the 21st Century* (Mahwah, N.J.: Erlbaum, 2005). Public journalism embodies most of the principles of social responsibility journalism. See Edmund D. Lambeth, Philip E. Meyers, and Esther Thorson, eds., *Assessing Public Journalism* (Columbia: University of Missouri Press, 1998); Michael Schudson, "The Public Journalism Movement and Its Problems," in *The Politics of News, The News of Politics*, ed. Doris Graber, Denis McQuail, and Pippa Norris (Washington, D.C.: CQ

Press, 1998); and Theodore L. Glasser, ed., *The Idea of Public Journalism* (New York: Guilford Press, 1999).

39. See, for example, Dean Alger, *Megamedia: How Giant Corporations Dominate Mass Media, Distort Competition, and Endanger Democracy* (Lanham, Md.: Rowman and Littlefield, 1998).

40. Lambeth, Meyers, and Thorson, *Assessing Public Journalism*; Schudson, "The Public Journalism Movement."

41. Hallin and Mancini, *Comparing Media Systems.*

42. John Anthony Maltese, *Spin Control: The White House Office of Communication and the Management of Presidential News,* 2d ed. (Chapel Hill: University of North Carolina Press, 1994), 232–233.

Readings

Aufderheide, Patricia. *Communications Policy and the Public Interest: The Telecommunications Act of 1996.* New York: Guilford Press, 1999.

Bennett, W. Lance. *News: The Politics of Illusion.* 5th ed. White Plains, N.Y.: Longman, 2003.

Campbell, Richard, Christopher R. Martin, and Bettina Fabos. *Media and Culture: An Introduction to Mass Communication,* 4th ed. Boston: Bedford/ St. Martin's, 2005.

Cook, Timothy E. *Governing with the News: The News Media as a Political Institution.* Chicago: University of Chicago Press, 1998.

Graber, Doris A., ed. *Media Power in Politics.* 4th ed. Washington, D.C.: CQ Press, 2000.

Hamilton, James T. *All the News That's Fit to Sell: How the Market Transforms Information into News.* Princeton: Princeton University Press, 2004.

Hess, Stephen. *News and Newsmaking.* Washington, D.C.: Brookings, 1996.

Jamieson, Kathleen Hall, and Paul Waldman. *The Press Effect: Politicians, Journalists, and the Stories That Shape the Political World.* New York: Oxford University Press, 2003.

Kaid, Lynda Lee. *Handbook of Political Communication Research.* Mahwah, N.J.: Erlbaum, 2004.

Norris, Pippa. *A Virtuous Circle: Political Communications in Postindustrial Societies.* Cambridge: Cambridge University Press, 2000.

Schudson, Michael. *The Sociology of News.* New York: Norton, 2003.

Ownership, Regulation, and Guidance of Media

WHEN SOVIET LEADER MIKHAIL GORBACHEV announced in 1989 that his government would relinquish control over the nation's news media and allow opposition voices to be heard, democratic leaders everywhere hailed it as the birth of freedom in a hitherto totalitarian society. But openness, it seems, was short lived. Vladimir Putin, the former KGB secret police agent who became president in 2000, reasserted control over the media. Using subterfuge his government took control of all major privately owned media deemed hostile to the Putin regime. The message to media was clear—support the government or face shutdown or even imprisonment. The country's last remaining independent television station—TVS—succumbed in June 2004 and was replaced by a state-run sports channel. During elections in 2004 debate was stifled by laws, later voided by the courts, that threatened media with closure if they criticized the political candidates' positions. Other laws restrained questioning the wisdom of public policies.[1]

Putin's strenuous efforts to regain control over all independent media enterprises is a typical, contemporary version of battles fought by governments for control over the nation's information supply to ensure that it supports the reigning government and damages the opposition. Concern about who will wield media power has been a central issue in U.S. politics since colonial days. In this chapter we will weigh the pros and cons of various forms of government and private sector control of the mass media, as well as the implications of changing patterns. We will also assess the impact of environmental pressures on the mass media industry, such as economic constraints and citizen lobbies. The policy issues involved in media control are so complex, so intertwined with political preferences, that no ownership and control system stands out clearly as "best." All have advantages

31

and drawbacks. It therefore is no wonder that attempts in the United States to legislate about media ownership and control have produced little agreement on what the laws should be.

Control and Ownership: Public and Semipublic

The different forms of control and ownership of the media affect not only media economics but also the substance of media output, in line with the old adage, "He who pays the piper calls the tune." People concerned about self-serving politicians are likely to oppose government ownership and operation of the media. They also are apt to be leery about extensive government regulation of privately owned and operated media. By contrast, people who distrust the business ethics of private individuals and corporations, especially huge ones, do not want unfettered media control in private hands.

The Crux of the Debate

When governments own and operate major television channels, or regulate them heavily, as is quite common throughout the world, programming tends to uncritically support government policies, even in democratic countries. However, the British government's experience with operating radio and television through the nonpartisan British Broadcasting Corporation does show that governments can avoid direct political interference.[2]

Private control of television, if divided among many owners, is likely to bring more conflicting interests into play than government control. Even when large corporations monopolize control, their business interests are apt to be diverse and often incompatible so that they support different policies. Nonetheless, when business enterprises control broadcasting, the prevailing political values reflected in the choice of programs are likely to be mainstream and middle class. Moreover, the pressures springing from profit considerations lead to the types of offerings that yield high financial returns. Mass appeal, rather than fostering particular social or cultural concerns, becomes the primary goal when advertising revenues finance media enterprises. Advertisers who pay for the privilege of reaching audiences want to attract large numbers of potential customers, particularly eighteen- to forty-nine-year-olds who are the most active shoppers. Governments are free from commercial pressures because they can use tax money to finance whatever programs they believe to be in the public interest. They must consider intragovernment power struggles, but they do not need to consider the economic consequences of the size of their audience.

At present, when most Americans distrust government more than business, private ownership and control of the mass media is their preferred option. Consequently, the bulk of television fare is geared to simple, emotion-laden programming that attracts large, diverse audiences. Controversial or troublesome issues that may antagonize or deplete media audiences and diminish advertising revenues are largely shunned.

Popular, "lightweight" programming draws the wrath of many people, particularly intellectual elites. They can be accused of intellectual snobbery for claiming that the mass public's tastes are inferior to their own. Some critics argue erroneously that people would choose high-brow, intellectual programs over fluffy entertainment if they had the chance. Proof is plentiful that the public does indeed prefer light entertainment to more serious programs.[3] In 1998, for example, President Clinton's State of the Union message attracted 53 million viewers. Some months later, a broadcast in which he promised to discuss an inappropriate sexual relationship with a White House intern attracted 68 million. Later that year, the finale of the popular *Seinfeld* show on NBC drew 76 million viewers, topping the audience for the president's yearly report by more than 40 percent. In print news, magazines featuring sex or violence far outsell journals that treat political and social issues seriously. In fact, scholarly political journals frequently require subsidies to remain in print. Huge crowds are willing to pay heavily in time and money to see movies featuring heinous crimes and explicit sex. The most popular pay television channels show what is euphemistically called "adult entertainment," whereas channels devoted to highbrow culture languish and often perish.

Related to concerns about news media domination by powerful public or private interests is the fear of undue influence if only a small number of organizations share media control. Diversity of media ownership presumably encourages the expression of diverse views, which, to many Americans, is the essence of democracy. The marketplace where ideas and opinions are debated must be wide open. But there is no agreement on exactly how many owners are required for sufficient diversity.[4] Americans appear to be more concerned about the concentration of media ownership in comparatively few hands than about control of the media by business. Social reformers, however, are more concerned about business control, claiming that it fosters tabloid journalism and suppresses discussion of pressing social problems.

How the Public and Semipublic System Works

In the United States outright government ownership and control over media has been limited. However, it is growing as more local governments own cable television systems or operate channels on privately owned systems. Government ownership raises serious unresolved questions about the limitations, if any, to be placed on the government's rights to use these outlets to further partisan political purposes.[5]

The federal government is most heavily involved in broadcasting, with local governments in second place. The federal government controls broadcasts to U.S. military posts throughout the world through the American Forces Radio and Television Service in the Department of Defense. It also owns foreign propaganda outlets. The Voice of America Broadcast system (VOA), for example, broadcasts more than 900 hours of news programs weekly to a foreign audience of 91 million through radio, television, and the Internet. VOA has 1,200 affiliate stations and communicates in fifty-three languages.[6]

Broadcasting by semipublic institutions is another control option. The public broadcasting system, for example, represents a mixture of public and private financing and programming and public and private operation of radio and television stations. Created through the Public Broadcasting Act of 1967, the public broadcasting system supports educational and public service television stations whose programs generally do not attract large audiences. These stations need subsidies because they usually cannot find enough commercial sponsors to pay for their shows.

In 2004 members of the public broadcasting system included 349 noncommercial television stations, primarily operated by community organizations and colleges and universities, and 760 noncommercial radio stations linked together as the independently financed National Public Radio (NPR).[7] The administrative arrangements for the public broadcasting system have been complex. The Corporation for Public Broadcasting (CPB), staffed by political appointees, has handled the general administration, but it has been kept separate from the programming side of the operation to insulate public broadcasting from political pressures. A separate Public Broadcasting Service (PBS) has produced television programs, often in collaboration with state-supported foreign broadcast systems, such as Britain's BBC or France's Antenne Deux or Japan's NHK. The Independent Television Service, created by Congress in 1991, has awarded grants to independent producers for "programming that involves creative risks and addresses the needs of underserved audiences." [8]

The attempt to keep the CPB from influencing programming has failed. The corporation does not tell public television stations what programs they should feature. Instead, it has guided programming by paying for some types of programs and refusing to pay for others. This has constituted purse-string control of programming by government. The results have earned praise along with scorn. In radio, NPR was created both to produce and distribute programs. Because cost considerations made it impossible to include all noncommercial radio stations, only the largest, best-organized ones were included and are eligible for CPB funding grants and participation in NPR programs.

Private foundations, big business enterprises, and large corporations have subsidized 22 percent of the public broadcasting system income (Table 2-1). The Reagan administration authorized PBS to engage in some commercial broadcasting of economic news and to accept a limited amount of advertising. All of these changes have enhanced corporate influence over programming. The general public also has influenced public broadcasting through donations that constitute 26 percent of the income of public broadcasting systems and through community advisory boards. Nevertheless, securing adequate financing is an enduring problem. Dependence on federal funds, even when these funds constitute less than 20 percent of total funding, entails some subservience to federal control, despite barriers to direct government influence.

An emphasis on experimental programs—cultural offerings such as plays, classical music, and ballet—and a stress on high-quality news and public affairs programs distinguishes public television broadcasts from commercial television.[9] The nature and quality of programming varies widely because public television represents a decentralized bevy of local stations. The audience for public television, except for its children's programs, has been small, rarely comprising more than 2 percent of television viewers. Even minority groups, to whom a number of public broadcast programs are targeted, prefer commercial entertainment. Still, PBS serves nearly 100 million people weekly, and more than 22 million listen off-and-on to NPR programs. Because of the limited appeal of public broadcasting and the need to reduce public expenditures, there has been some pressure to disband the system completely and reallocate its frequencies to commercial channels. Some of its programs then might be shown on commercial cable stations, possibly with federal subsidies.[10]

Supporters of the system contend that it provides special services that commercial television neglects because they lack mass appeal. Innovations pioneered by public broadcasting have spread to commercial broadcasting, these supporters say. For example, public broadcasting played a leading role in developing captions for individuals with hearing impairments. At the turn of the century, it led in pioneering digital television, including interactive news and feature programs. Public radio and public television also were among the first to move to satellite distribution that made it possible to deliver multiple national programs to communities. Nonetheless, the future of public broadcasting seems precarious.

TABLE 2-1   Income Sources of the Public Broadcasting System, 2001 (includes nonbroadcast income)

Income source	Millions of dollars	Percentage of budget
State/local government and colleges/universities	593	26
Subscribers and auction/telethons	588	26
Federal government	385	17
Business and industry	361	16
Other	174	8
Foundations	141	6
Private colleges/universities	36	1
Total income	2,278	100

SOURCE: Public Broadcasting Policy Base, "Public Broadcasting System Revenues, 1982–2001," www.current.org/pbpb/statistics/totalrevs.html.

NOTE: Public broadcasting system includes 694 Corporation for Public Broadcasting–qualified public radio stations and 352 public television stations.

Patterns of Private Ownership

The overarching feature of media ownership in the United States is that it is predominantly in private hands. Arrangements vary from individual ownership, where one person owns a newspaper or radio or television station, to ownership by huge corporate conglomerates. Owners include small and large business enterprises, labor groups, religious and ethnic organizations, and many other types of interests represented in society. Explaining private media control patterns is relatively simple, agreeing on their consequences is not.

Business Configurations

"Independents"—individuals or corporations that run a single media venture and nothing else—are a vanishing breed in the media business. Multiple owners have become the norm. These are individuals or corporations who own several media of the same type—mostly radio or television stations or cable channels or newspapers. Because there are fewer than 1,500 daily newspapers in the entire United States and fewer than 2,000 commercial television stations, one might question whether society is well served when most of these media are held by group owners. Nevertheless, this has been the trend. In 2002, for example, the ten largest newspaper groups controlled 51 percent of the country's newspaper circulation.[11]

By 1997 national and regional chains controlled more than 80 percent of daily papers in the United States.[12] The twelve largest groups controlled more than 400 dailies with a circulation of nearly 35 million. Gannett was the leader in circulation in the United States with ninety-two daily papers followed by Knight Ridder (thirty-five), Advance/Newhouse (twenty-five), and Dow Jones (twenty).[13] Most of these newspaper groups also own papers published less frequently, as well as radio and television stations. Although ownership figures change constantly as papers are bought and sold, the relative rankings remain fairly stable. The proportion of circulation that chain-owned papers control has been growing over the decades, but not by leaps and bounds (Table 2-2). Although individual papers within chains generally enjoy editorial-page autonomy, they tend to be more uniform in political endorsements than are independently owned papers.[14]

Crossmedia ownership has been less common than multiple ownership. This occurs when an individual or corporation owns several types of media, such as newspapers *and* television stations or newspapers *and* radio stations. Crossmedia ownership is worrisome when one owner controls all media in the same region. Congress prohibited such monopolies in 1975, except where they already existed. Lobbying by large media enterprises led to an easing of crossownership restrictions in 2004 in markets with at least four independent television stations.[15] Implementation of the new rules has been stayed pending resolution of legal challenges.[16] Newspapers can enter an unlimited number of markets but intramarket newspaper competition has become rare. Ninety-eight percent of all U.S. cities have only one daily newspaper.[17] Suburban dailies, which flourish in a few major cities, do not alter the situation substantially because their coverage of major news stories usually is limited. However, even in one-newspaper towns, the news supply is not monopolized thanks to intermedia competition encompassing print, television, and radio outlets.

A market is the area in which a medium attracts a substantial audience. For instance, each television station has a signal that can be received clearly by people living within a certain radius of the station. All of the people within that radius who can receive the signal are considered within the market. This means that they can be expected to respond to advertising for products and services provided by program sponsors. Crossmedia ownership dispersed over various markets, rather than within a single market, is thriving. Gannett Company, for example, owned 101 daily newspapers, 22 television stations, and more than 130 Web sites in 2004.

A fourth pattern encompasses conglomerates—individuals or corporations that own media enterprises along with other types of businesses. The General Electric Company (GE) is an example (Figure 2-1).

TABLE 2-2   U.S. Newspaper Circulation, October 2003–March 2004

Daily		Sunday	
Newspaper	Circulation	Newspaper	Circulation
USA Today[a]	2,192,098	New York Times	1,677,003
Wall Street Journal	2,101,017	Los Angeles Times	1,392,672
New York Times	1,133,763	Washington Post	1,025,579
Los Angeles Times	983,727	Chicago Tribune	1,000,570
Washington Post	772,553	New York Daily News	802,103
New York Daily News	747,053	Philadelphia Inquirer	769,257
Chicago Tribune[b]	693,978	Dallas Morning News	755,912
Newsday	580,346	Houston Chronicle	740,002
Detroit News/Free Press	579,755	Detroit News/Free Press	705,148
Houston Chronicle	549,300	Boston Globe	686,575

SOURCE: Audit Bureau of Circulation.

[a] Numbers are based on best days only: Monday–Thursday.
[b] Numbers are based on best days only: Wednesday–Friday.

Conglomerates raise fears that their nonmedia business interests may color their news policies. If, for instance, there is a need to reduce the size of the military or to oppose construction of a missile system, the management of a conglomerate such as GE, which holds many defense contracts, may not examine these questions open mindedly. In major urban centers most media fall into the multiple-owner, crossmedia, and conglomerate classifications. For instance, the Tribune Company owns the *Chicago Tribune* as well as television and radio stations in Chicago, along with the Chicago Cubs baseball team. In 2003 Tribune media holdings included thirteen daily newspapers throughout the country, twenty-six television stations in twenty-two markets, one radio station, and one national cable outlet. Its subsidiary Tribune Media Services served as a major syndication outlet of news, features, and entertainment content sold to news outlets throughout the world.[18] All major television and radio stations in Chicago are owned by the national television networks and conglomerates or members of conglomerates.

Radio and television stations that remain under single ownership for the most part are small with comparatively weak signals. The number of media outlets controlled by various entrepreneurs ranges widely and fluctuates considerably, especially in an era of widespread consolidation. Since the turn of the century, many news media companies have added multiple Web sites to their holdings, as well as online versions of their newspapers and television programs, along with newspapers serving special groups like

FIGURE 2-1 The Diverse Holdings of the General Electric Company

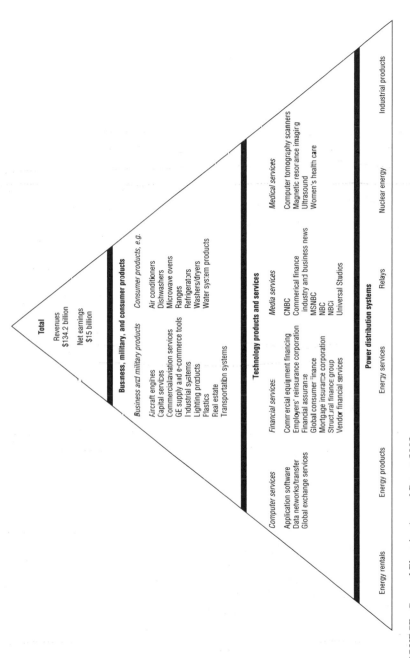

SOURCE: General Electric, *Annual Report*, 2003.

Hispanics or young readers. But one cannot judge the sweep of control exercised by any group merely by looking at the number of its outlets. Three additional factors need to be considered: prestige of each media institution, market size, and competition within the market.

Media Influence Variables: Prestige, Market Size, and Competition

The prestige a media enterprise enjoys is an important component of its political influence. Journalism has widely accepted standards of professionalism, just as do law or medicine or engineering. As part of this system of norms, certain members and products are accepted widely as models for the profession. Other news professionals watch what information these high prestige news organizations present, how they present it, and what interpretations they give to it; they then adjust their own presentations accordingly. Critics derisively call this the "jackal syndrome" or "pack journalism." For political news, the *New York Times* is the lion whom the jackals follow. In television, major network anchors are models for the profession. The upshot is that the many voices in the media marketplace sing in unison much of the time. Newcomers quickly join the chorus and hum the tunes orchestrated by the prestige leadership.

Media enterprises also gain influence based on the size of their market rather than the total number of markets accessible. The hundreds of newspaper and broadcast markets in the United States vary widely in audience size. In such major metropolitan areas as New York, Chicago, or Los Angeles, a market with a fifty-mile radius may have a population of several million people. The same radius for a station in Wyoming might cover more cows than people.

Competition within most media markets used to be quite limited. A single newspaper and a handful of radio and television stations were the rule. That picture has changed dramatically in the wake of technology advances. Nonetheless, most Americans still get the bulk of their political news from one daily newspaper and over-the-air television. In 2004, for example, when asked about attention to news on the previous day, 60 percent of respondents had used television and 42 percent had read a newspaper. When asked in another survey to name their most important sources of news, 83 percent cited television, 42 percent cited newspapers, while 19 percent cited radio and 15 percent cited the Internet (Box 2-1).[19]

Nonetheless, the mushrooming of additional, readily available news sources amounts to a communications revolution. As the Project for Excellence in Journalism's 2004 report on the state of the news media notes: "Journalism is in the midst of an epochal transformation, as momentous

BOX 2-1
Radio Is Alive and Well

Radio continues to be an immensely important source of public information. Although 60 percent of the public watched television news in 2004, and 42 percent sought news from daily papers, a hefty 40 percent tuned in to radio news. Even larger numbers used the radio to listen to music. Most listeners tune in on car radios, primarily during the morning and evening work commute. Listening time averages three hours on week days and six hours on weekends.

Concentration

In the wake of the 1996 Telecommunications Act, which eliminated most restrictions on buying and selling stations, radio station ownership has become highly concentrated. The largest chain, Clear Channel Communications, owns more than 1,200 stations and distributes many of the leading syndicated programs. Clear Channel and its closest competitor, Viacom's Infiniti Broadcasting, control close to 40 percent of the revenue of the entire radio industry.

Consolidation has encouraged national programming so that major talk radio stars like Rush Limbaugh, Howard Stern, Don Imus, and Dr. Laura Schlessinger are heard throughout the country. But most programming remains locally produced and tailored to the tastes of local listeners. Most large markets feature more than fifty stations. Chicago, for example, has more than one hundred stations, both AM and FM. Offerings include talk radio and news, either singly or in combination, sports reports, ethnic programs, and various religious programs. The rest offer a large variety of musical formats. Although fans of classical music may complain that only a single station features their "high quality" music, diversity certainly prevails.

Rules for Survival

Radio is a perfect example of the chameleon-like ability of U.S. mass media to adapt to new technologies and new types of competitors. Predictions that television and its spin-off technologies would kill radio and movies have been utterly wrong. Radio has boomed, thanks to technologies like the transistor and FM and XM radio, and thanks to the targeting of its programs. More than twenty radio formats now cater to distinct demographic groups. News-talk formats, both political and personal, have been growth leaders. Age, income, gender, race, and ethnicity are major programming cleavage lines that appeal to advertisers who like to target their products to likely customers. Ten percent of the billions of dollars spent on advertising across the nation goes to radio stations.

SOURCE: Much of the information about radio comes from Richard Campbell, *Media and Culture*, 4th ed. (Boston: Bedford, 2005), chap. 4.

probably as the invention of the telegraph or television. Journalism . . . is becoming more complex. We are witnessing conflicting trends of fragmentation and convergence simultaneously, and they sometimes lead in opposite directions." [20] Americans are receiving their news from an ever-growing number of outlets, but the most widely used outlets are increasingly owned by fewer giant conglomerate corporations that draw their programs primarily from a shrinking number of suppliers. More excellent news is available than ever before, but so is more trashy, sensationalized, and often false information.

The three original networks—ABC, CBS, and NBC—which once supplied news to three-quarters of the nightly audience, have been joined by the highly successful Fox network, as well as less powerful networks like WB, UPN, Spanish-language networks, satellite TV, and hundreds of cable channels. The networks' share of nightly viewers has shrunk to 40 percent.[21] When the Federal Communications Commission (FCC) compared the number of broadcast news outlets available to Americans living in communities of various sizes at the dawn of the twenty-first century, it found that, on average, the number of outlets had more than tripled since 1960. Congress had ordered the research to ascertain whether it was time to scrap rules restricting companies from owning multiple news enterprises in the same market. The rules were designed to ensure that the limited number of broadcast frequencies would represent a wide spectrum of interests. The conclusion of majorities in Congress, hotly disputed by the minority, was that a substantial loosening of restrictions was in order because advancing technology has multiplied available channels. Besides, companies eager to increase their holdings claimed that economies of scale would allow them to improve their offerings. They would also be better able to compete with unregulated cable and satellite television and the Internet.

Opponents of deregulation have pointed out that large conglomerates, like the Tribune Company, Viacom, and News Corp., already control the most popular stations and often share programs, contrary to the government's communication diversity goals. They also claim that loosening the existing restrictions encourages replacing local programming with bland generic coverage suitable for large, diverse markets. The competition between giant corporations and smaller enterprises, like the fight between supermarkets and Ma and Pa grocery shops, will end with the giants garnering most of the rights to exclusive stories and most of the advertising revenues while the dwarfs' economic base crumbles.

To lend weight to counter arguments, opponents of deregulation point out that deregulation of radio in 1996 led to a frenzy of mergers that ended with a handful of giant corporations, led by Clear Channel Communications and Infiniti Broadcasting Corporation, dominating the industry. Clear Channel grew from 43 to more than 1200 stations nationwide. Altogether, twenty-one companies had each acquired more than forty stations.[22] Some observers hailed this development as beneficial to consumers because larger companies have more resources to produce sophisticated programming. Others condemned it as a major disaster that shrank the diversity of offerings and reduced experimentation and creativity. Other factors to consider in gauging the political influence of various media enterprises is the decline in audience, especially among the young. But decline figures may be deceptive because the fragmentation of news channels and the multiplication of news content on entertainment programs make it hard to judge people's political news sources. On the encouraging side, evidence shows that people do watch the news when something exciting occurs.

The most concentrated control over the information supply rests in the hands of the wire service companies. A huge share of the news stories appearing in nearly every market in the country originates from the wires of the Associated Press (AP). The roots of this organization go back to 1848, when six New York newspapers formed a cooperative association to share the cost of collecting foreign news. Out of this initial effort grew a handful of large organizations that employ reporters scattered throughout the world to collect and report news. News stories and bulletins are transmitted electronically to subscriber newspapers and radio and television stations. A handful of other wire services, such as those operated by the *New York Times, Los Angeles Times,* and *Chicago Tribune,* serve their own papers along with a large array of subscribers.

Media outlets either rewrite wire news stories and bulletins or use them verbatim. The proportion of wire service stories used directly or in rewritten form may vary from less than 10 percent to 80 percent or more of all stories, depending on each media outlet's resources for carrying its own news. For many newspapers, a look at the mix of wire stories on any particular day will foretell accurately the mix of wire stories carried by the paper. Wire service stories tend to predominate for foreign news and even for national news for smaller papers and stations that cannot afford their own correspondents. This means that a small number of wire service companies dominate a large share of news production in the United States.

The Limits of FCC Rules

Despite the strong pressures for deregulation in the United States at the dawn of the twenty-first century, the federal government continues to regulate private electronic media to ensure that they "serve the public interest, convenience, and necessity" as mandated by the Communications Act of 1934 and its 1996 counterpart. The FCC, a bipartisan body appointed by the president and confirmed by the Senate, handles most regulation.[23] The FCC was a seven-member body until the summer of 1984 when, for financial reasons, Congress downsized it to five commissioners. In 1986 the appointment term was shortened from seven to five years, ensuring faster turnover of commission personnel and greater control by the government. In theory, the commission is an independent regulatory body. In practice, congressional purse strings, public and industry pressures, and presidential control over appointment of new members, including the responsibilities of naming the chair, have greatly curtailed the FCC's freedom of operation. The commission's independence is weakened also because its rulings can be appealed to the courts, which frequently overturn them. Conflicting political pressures from outside the agency as well as internal political pressures further limit FCC policy making so that it tends to be "a reactive rather than an innovative system sluggish to respond to change in its environment, particularly to technological change. . . . Clearly there are problems with this kind of policy-making system." [24] On balance, the FCC's record of setting goals and enforcing its rules has earned it the reputation at best of being an ineffective watchdog over the public interest and at worst an industry-kept, pressure-group-dominated lapdog.

The FCC controls only over-the-air television. Cable television and the Internet have been excluded because they are considered "common carriers"—channels carrying information rather than sources of information. U.S. print media are also beyond the FCC's reach. However, like cable and the Internet, they are subject to general laws like those limiting monopolies and trusts. These regulations become operative when the eight largest firms in a particular type of business control more than half of the market and the twenty largest firms control three-quarters or more. Concentration in the news media business has remained substantially below these levels. The Justice Department does permit economically weak newspapers to combine their business and production facilities, free from antitrust and monopoly restraints, as long as their news and editorial operations are kept separate.

FCC control takes four forms: rules limiting the number of stations owned or controlled by a single organization, examinations of the goals and performance of stations as part of periodic licensing, rules mandating public service and local interest programs, and rules to protect individuals from damage caused by unfair media coverage. Although none of these rules prescribe specific content, all of them were designed to increase the chances that content would be diverse and of civic importance.

Rules Limiting Station Ownership

As explained earlier, to prevent high concentrations of media ownership and to ensure diversity of information sources, the FCC limits the number of stations that television and radio owners may control. It also limits the size of the audience that may be within the range of any one group of owners, allowing over-the-air television no more than 39 percent of the market share.[25] Nonetheless, such networks as ABC, CBS, NBC, and Fox, through their many network-owned and independent affiliates, are within reach of more than 90 percent of the nation's audiences.

The networks have full control over stations they own. But they also dominate programming on their affiliates, thereby reaching nearly all of the nation's television households. In the past the networks produced only a limited number of television and radio entertainment programs for their own use. The bulk of entertainment programming came from other sources. That changed drastically in the 1990s with the removal of FCC prohibitions, which previously barred the merger of program production enterprises with program distribution enterprises.

Television station ownership has been enormously profitable. Local television news stations made close to 40 percent profits in 2003, compared to half that rate for newspapers.[26] But the mushrooming of outlets since the 1990s is increasing competition and reducing profitability. Costs for news collection are rising. Consequently, many stations have slashed their news budgets and downsized units, often at the expense of quality of coverage. Advertising revenues have also declined because the pool of large advertisers shrank in the wake of business mergers.

Thus far, no initial investment has been required to get a license from the government, although pressures to change this are mounting. The FCC estimates that auctioning licenses to the highest bidder could yield the federal government billions of dollars, considering that licenses of profitable stations—with their profit margins of up to 50 percent—currently trade for millions of dollars because the demand exceeds the supply.

Licensing as Performance Control

By its power to grant and renew a radio or television license, the FCC determines who may own valuable communication properties. What performance standards does it use for license decisions? Communication law mandates that television and radio must "serve the public interest, convenience, and necessity." [27] But beyond requiring broadcasters to ascertain community needs and interests by talking with community leaders, there are no guides for interpreting these rules. Even the requirement to keep in touch with community leaders was dropped in 1984. In the absence of specific performance requirements, the power to grant and renew licenses has not turned into a tool to foster high quality. When processing licenses the FCC usually looks at the mix of programs, the proportion of public service offerings, and the inclusion of programs geared to selected groups. It does not scrutinize the subject matter of broadcasts in detail. This hands-off attitude has applied to both program inclusions and exclusions. However, the FCC has set limits on the amounts of advertising permitted in children's shows. Ads may not exceed twelve minutes per hour on weekdays and ten and a half minutes on weekends.

The FCC has used its power to grant new licenses to ensure service geared to the information needs of socioeconomic groups different from those already served by existing stations. To decide among several qualified applicants for new broadcasting stations, the FCC may use a lottery that is tilted to favor women, minorities, labor unions, and community organizations that are underrepresented in the ownership of telecommunications facilities. Once a license has been granted, owners hold it for good unless they discriminate or commit fraud or receive many complaints about poor programming. Owners may sell their licenses at will, earning huge profits on the sale.

Since the 1970s numerous civic groups have entered renewal hearings to protest the type of programming offered or omitted by a particular station. As a result of such pressures, the FCC reluctantly has withdrawn licenses from a few stations over the years. For example, a Chicago station lost its license in 1990 for neglecting informational programs and showing obscene movies.[28] However, the 1996 Telecommunications Act makes license withdrawal more difficult. It specifically forbids the FCC from continuing its practice of comparing the merits of new applicants with those of existing license holders in license renewal applications.

Compared with regulatory agencies in other countries, even in Western Europe, Canada, and Australia, the FCC controls the electronic media with a very light hand. The members of the FCC could, if they wished, rigorously define what constitutes "programming in the public interest." They could enforce FCC rulings more strictly and verify station performance records at license renewal time. The threat of license withdrawal for rule violations could be used as a much more powerful deterrent to misbehavior and a much stronger guide to programming. That does not happen because political cross-pressures are strong and the FCC staff is much too small to cope with all their assigned duties. In fact, the FCC is chronically behind schedule, even for such routine matters as the publication of its annual reports.

Public Service and Local Programming

In the past the FCC stipulated the minimum time that ought to be devoted to public service programs on television. Under the 5-5-10 rule, which is no longer enforced, 5 percent of programming had to be devoted to local affairs, 5 percent to general news and public affairs, and 10 percent to nonentertainment programs. Beyond checking a television station's log to ascertain that it recorded the minimum amount of public service programming, the FCC did not examine the nature and quality of programs labeled "public service." In 1991 the FCC directed stations to maintain a record of educational and informational programs for children. But it set no quality standards, even though the record is a requirement for license renewal.[29] A year later Congress passed the Cable Television Consumer Protection and Competition Act, requiring cable television systems to dedicate some of their channels to local broadcast television stations. The Supreme Court has upheld these "must carry" rules as content-neutral measures to assure that over-the-air broadcasters have access to publics that they might otherwise be unable to reach.[30]

Fair Treatment Rules

The FCC also has made rules about access to the airwaves for candidates for political office and for people who have been subjected to media attacks, usually through stories that allege that they have acted illegally or unethically (Chapter 3).

The Dangers of Big Business Control

The steady trend toward consolidation in the media industry increasingly has left control of information in the hands of a few very large organizations. Economic factors are largely responsible for mergers. Producing television programs and gathering worldwide news are expensive. Only large, well-financed organizations able to spread their costs over many customers can provide the lavish media fare that attracts ample audiences. Is it sound public policy to allow further consolidations? Will centralized control bring undesirable uniformity and neglect local needs? Does the absence of newspaper competition in U.S. cities prevent diverse viewpoints from reaching the public?

Although there have been some troubling cases, the fears underlying these questions have proven largely groundless. There has been little change in the uniformity of news in the wake of media mergers; the multiplication of cable, satellite, and Internet television has diversified the media market-place everywhere.[31] Nor is there solid evidence that media giants squelch antibusiness news. In fact, there has been an upswing of antibusiness news that has tarnished business giants like Microsoft, Nike, Nestle, Wal-Mart, and Firestone.[32] The choices that media make to cope with an oversupply of news do not conform predominantly to conservative political orientations.[33]

The charge that media owners pressure journalists into supporting the existing political system also is not borne out. U.S. journalists in large organizations, like their colleagues in small, independently owned enterprises, want to appeal to their audiences. This is why their stories usually reflect the values of mainstream U.S. society, regardless of the journalists' personal political orientations.[34] However, there is a real danger that serious news increasingly will be overwhelmed by "infotainment" programs in the wake of the mergers of news enterprises with entertainment giants, especially when the public prefers such shows to hard-news offerings. "News you can use"—news relating to everyday life needs like food, medical care, and transportation—is on an upswing. Still, an ample supply of hard news remains available on cable stations, on news radio, and on the Internet.

Compared to offerings by small, individually owned enterprises, large enterprises have been able to offer qualitatively superior programs. They can absorb the losses that are often incurred in producing expensive documentaries and public service programs. Large enterprises also can spend more money on talented people, research, investigations, and costly entertainment shows. They can afford to send their reporters to all parts of the world to cover breaking stories firsthand. When FCC rules have compelled small stations to offer nonnetwork programs, cost considerations have forced them to fill their nonnetwork hours with cheap canned movies or syndicated quiz or talent shows. Obviously, current policies designed to reduce media concentration and encourage local programming have failed to meet their objectives. These policies must be reconsidered, keeping in mind the media's mandate to serve the public interest of a democratic society. Antimerger, prolocal programming reforms are difficult to accomplish because large business enterprises maintain close ties with high-level politicians, giving the businesses considerable clout when policies are drafted and enforced.

Pressures by Media Associations and Advertisers

Media lobbies are another means of controlling mass media policies. Radio and television interests, especially the networks and their affiliated stations, are active lobbyists. Most belong to the National Association of

Broadcasters (NAB), a powerful Washington, D.C., lobby despite the diversity and often clashing interests of its members. A number of trade associations and publications, such as *Broadcasting* magazine, also lobby, often at cross-purposes. For newspapers the American Newspaper Publishers Association (ANPA), now merged with several other press associations, has been one of the most prominent groups. These organizations try to influence appointments to the FCC and to guide public policies affecting new technologies that may threaten established systems or practices. For instance, the network lobbies for many years tried to stifle cable television and to acquire control over domestic satellites. The National Cable Television Association and the National Association of Broadcasters have used members' stations to urge support for their policy recommendations. On other occasions, such as the passage of the Telecommunications Act of 1996, they have tried to downplay coverage that might arouse unwanted opposition.

To forestall regulation by outside bodies, the media industry has developed mechanisms for self-control. The NAB has had a radio code since 1929 and a television code since 1952 that set rules on program content and form. The NAB modernizes both codes periodically. Individual codes in major broadcast enterprises and codes adopted by the Council of Better Business Bureaus have supplemented or superseded industrywide codes. Print press self-policing has developed along similar lines. Scholars, too, have set forth codes of journalism ethics. Most codes are quite vague, mandating honesty, fairness, independence, and concern for the public interests. Media outlets then decide what these principles mean in practice. Overall, the impact of industrywide codes has been limited. Typically, they apply only to an organization's members who explicitly subscribe to them. Penalties for code violations have been minimal. The codes have been useful in blunting demands by pressure groups for government intervention to set and enforce standards. For instance, congressional leaders lifted a threat to pass laws limiting excessively violent and sexually explicit shows on programs available to children in return for industry promises to develop a rating system to guide parents.

In the 1970s advertisers began to influence program content by withdrawing their commercials from programs they considered to be obscene or excessively violent. Sears Roebuck was one of the earliest and largest advertisers to do so. McDonald's, American Express, and AT&T refused to place commercials on such shows. Other large advertisers, such as Procter and Gamble, retained consultants to seek out acceptable programs for their advertisements and avoid unacceptable ones. With advertisements on such top-rated shows as the Super Bowl yielding more than $2 million for a thirty-second spot, threats of withdrawal have had some impact on programming.[35]

While reductions in programs featuring sex and violence have been welcome, other changes have been problematic. There is deep concern that advertisers, spurred by pressure groups, may become unofficial censors. For instance, General Motors canceled its sponsorship of an Easter-time program on the life of Jesus because evangelical groups objected to the content. A CBS documentary on gun control, opposed by the gun control lobby, suffered crippling withdrawals of advertising. Fearing similar punishments from fundamentalist religious groups, the networks have refused advertising designed to instruct viewers about the use of condoms for protection against unwanted pregnancies and acquired immune deficiency syndrome (AIDS). Such unofficial censorship at the behest of advertisers is worrisome.

Citizen Lobby Control

Citizens' efforts to affect the quality of broadcasting began in earnest in 1966, when the Office of Communication of the United Church of Christ, a public interest lobby, challenged the renewal of a TV license for WLBT-TV in Jackson, Mississippi, accusing the station of discriminating against African American viewers.[36] African Americans then constituted 45 percent of Jackson's population. The challenge failed, but it was the beginning of efforts by many other citizens groups to use pressure tactics to challenge license renewals.

Citizen groups won a major victory in 1975 when the FCC refused to renew licenses of eight educational television stations in Alabama and denied a construction permit for a ninth because citizen groups had charged racial discrimination in employment at these stations. There also had been complaints that programs dealing with affairs of the African American community had been unduly excluded.[37] Since then numerous stations have yielded to pressure for increased minority employment and programming rather than face legal action.

During these decades many citizens' groups formed to lobby for better programming, more accurate news, and tighter government controls. Typical ones were Accuracy in Media (AIM), a well-financed conservative media-monitoring organization, and its liberal counterpart, Fairness and Accuracy in Reporting (FAIR); the Coalition for Better Television, representing fundamentalist religious groups; Action for Children's Television, which disbanded in 1992; the National Black Media Coalition; and the National Latino Media Coalition.

Despite the substantial impact of such groups on FCC rule making and licensing procedures, citizens' national lobbying efforts declined in the 1980s and have never regained their original vigor.[38] One reason has been the difficulty of sustaining citizen interest over time, another was lack of financial support and loss of leadership. The broadcast lobby defeated efforts to obtain public funding for citizens' lobby groups, and foundation support has dried up. Many groups also were discouraged when the appeals courts reversed substantial victories won in the lower courts and when the U.S. Supreme Court voided the 1996 Computer Decency Act.[39] Some citizens' groups have redirected their energy into local lobbying to ensure that cable systems in their locality serve the interests of various publics at reasonable prices to consumers.

In addition to the more than sixty organizations concerned exclusively with media reform, other organizations, such as the Parent Teacher Association (PTA), the National Organization for Women, and the American Medical Association, have lobbied on a variety of media issues. They have shown concern about stereotyping, access to media coverage and to media employment and ownership, advertising on children's programs, and enforcement of FCC program regulations. The groups' tactics include monitoring media content, publicizing their findings, and pressuring broadcasters, advertisers, media audiences, and government control agencies. PTA members have pressured advertisers, who, in turn, have succeeded in reducing the number of violent programs shown in the early evening. Legal maneuvers have ranged from challenges of license renewals to damage suits for the harmful effects of media content.

Assessing the precise influence of these organizations is difficult because many of their goals overlap with other forces that affect media policy. Some of the causes for which they have worked, such as for measures fostering good programming for children, have prospered over the years, however, and part of the credit undoubtedly belongs to them. Yet these groups have a long road to travel before they can match the influence enjoyed by the broadcast lobby in protecting its interests even when they run counter to the concerns of many citizens.

Summary

In this chapter we have examined the most common types of ownership and control of the media. The national government owns and operates vast overseas radio and television enterprises. At home it partially controls a far-flung system of public television and radio broadcasting that provides an alternative to commercial programming.

For the average American, these government-controlled systems are peripheral compared with privately owned print and electronic media enterprises. The major political problem in the private sector is concentration of ownership of media and concentrated control over news and entertainment programs. The control of large business conglomerates over much of media output has caused concern that the public is ill served. These conglomerates' aim to attract large audiences leads to lightweight programming at the expense of serious fare, and challenges to mainstream politics are rare.

We have looked into the structure of the media business and government regulations designed to assure a diverse supply of information. We also have tried to evaluate the impact of the existing system on the supply of political news that citizens need. Many prevailing views about the interrelation between media structures and functions have little merit. Business ownership has enhanced the focus on soft news and entertainment but it has not led to programming dominated by business perspectives. Ownership of news enterprises has not shielded big business from harsh criticism often in the form of investigative reports. Coverage of local news has not withered in the wake of media mergers, and large, rather than small, enterprises have excelled in providing news and entertainment. Obviously, further research could provide a sounder basis for media policy making that will ensure that U.S. media truly serve the public interest.

Media owners, as well as industry lobby groups and citizens' lobbies, shape media operations and products. The diversity of influences brought into play when news and entertainment are produced make it impossible to assess the precise impact of these influences on media content in general or even on a particular story. In the next chapter we will focus on legal aspects of news production for additional clues to the mystery of what shapes the news.

Notes

1. Freedom House, "Freedom in the World 2004," www.freedomhouse.org/research/freeworld/2004.
2. Daniel C. Hallin and Paolo Mancini, *Comparing Media Systems: Three Models of Media and Politics* (Cambridge: Cambridge University Press, 2004). This book describes different government control styles in selected western democracies.
3. Examples of the types of shows that attracted the largest audiences in November 2004 are *CSI: Crime Scene Investigation* (31.5 million viewers); *Desperate Housewives* (24.2 million viewers), *CSI: Miami* (22.5 million viewers), *Survivor: Vanuatu* (20.4 million viewers), and *ER* (18.9 million viewers). In addition, there are the ever-popular sports events, such as the Super Bowl, entertainment industry awards presentations, and such competitions as *Who Wants to Be a Millionaire?* and news magazine shows like *Sixty Minutes*.
4. Ben H. Bagdikian, *The New Media Monopoly* (Boston: Beacon Press, 2004); Robert Picard, "Media Concentration, Economics, and Regulation," in *The Politics of News, the News of Politics,* ed. Doris Graber, Denis McQuail, and Pippa Norris (Washington, D.C.: CQ Press, 1998). For a negative view of the "marketplace of ideas" concept, see Benjamin Ginsberg, *The Captive Public: How Mass Opinion Promotes State Power* (New York: Basic Books, 1986), 98–148.

5. "Despite the expressed insulation of public broadcasters from federal editorial domination, case law specifically allows broadcast program decisions to be dictated by political officials when the state is licensee. Therefore, potential conflict exists between First Amendment and political interests." William Hanks and Lemuel Schofield, "Limitations on the State as Editor in State-Owned Broadcast Stations," *Journalism Quarterly* 63 (winter 1986): 798.

6. The Virtual Reference Desk, "Government Agencies," www.virtualref.com/govagency/.

7. Public Broadcasting Station, www.pbs.org; National Public Radio, www.npr.org.

8. Ibid.

9. A content analysis of political discourse on PBS led to the conclusion that stories focused primarily on the strategic aspects of domestic politics and the economy and featured the views of political elites, especially insiders drawn from government and the business world. William Hoynes, "Political Discourse and the 'New PBS,' " *Press/Politics* 7, no. 4 (2002): 34–56.

10. For an impassionate analysis of the trials and tribulations of U.S. public television, see James Ledbetter, *Made Possible By . . . The Death of Public Broadcasting in the United States* (London: Verso, 1997).

11. Project for Excellence in Journalism, *The State of the News Media 2004*, www.stateofthenewsmedia.org.

12. Dean Alger, *Megamedia: How Giant Corporations Dominate Mass Media, Distort Competition, and Endanger Democracy* (Lanham, Md.: Rowman and Littlefield, 1998), 31.

13. Ibid., 92.

14. Media critic Dean Alger claims that quality deteriorates when papers are acquired by a chain. Ibid., 180–182.

15. Federal Communications Commission, www.fcc.gov. See also Jeff Chester, "Strict Scrutiny: Why Journalists Should Be Concerned about New Federal and Industry Deregulation Proposals," *Press/Politics* 7, no. 2 (2002): 105–115.

16. Major media companies hope to bring the issue to the U.S. Supreme Court with the support of the proderegulation George W. Bush administration. Leon Lazaroff, "Media Giants Ponder FCC Appeal," *Chicago Tribune*, November 25, 2004.

17. Alger, *Megamedia*, 31, 130–134.

18. Tribune Company's "2003 Annual Report" and its Web site, www.tribune.com.

19. Pew Research Center for the People and the Press, "Biennial Media Consumption Survey," 2004, http://people-press.org/.

20. Project for Excellence in Journalism, "The State of the News Media 2004," www.stateofthenewsmedia.org.

21. Ibid.

22. Ibid.

23. In decisions about media mergers, the Federal Trade Commission also plays a major role.

24. Erwin G. Krasnow, Lawrence D. Longley, and Herbert A. Terry, *The Politics of Broadcast Regulation*, 3d ed. (New York: St. Martin's Press, 1982), 284.

25. The FCC rules state the limit as 45 percent. But in response to complaints by members of Congress, 39 percent has been accepted as a compromise.

26. Project for Excellence in Journalism, "The State of the News Media 2004."

27. 47 U.S.C.A. §307(a), 1934.

28. Steven Morris, "FCC Denies WSNS-TV New Broadcast License," *Chicago Tribune,* September 20, 1990.
29. Congress members have introduced many contradictory bills to address news and public service programming requirements. Most of the bills die early in the game. *CQ Weekly* is an excellent source for tracking these legislative developments.
30. *Turner Broadcasting Systems v. FCC,* 520 U.S. 180 (1997).
31. David Pearce Demers, *The Menace of the Corporate Newspaper: Fact or Fiction?* (Ames: Iowa State University Press, 1996); W. Lance Bennett and Timothy E. Cook, "Journalism Norms and News Construction: Rules for Representing Politics," *Political Communication,* special issue (winter 1996). For contrary views, see Alger, *Megamedia,* 153–194; and Robert W. McChesney, *Rich Media, Poor Democracy* (New York: New Press, 1999).
32. Jarol B. Manheim, *The Death of a Thousand Cuts: Corporate Campaigns and the Attack on the Corporation* (Mahwah, N.J.: Erlbaum, 2001).
33. Bennett and Cook, "Journalism Norms and News Construction."
34. For a discussion of journalists' political orientations and professional values, see Chapter 4.
35. Bloomberg News, "Fox Asks $2.4 Million Per Ad for Super Bowl," *Chicago Tribune,* December 30, 2004.
36. *Office of Communication of the United Church of Christ v. FCC,* 359 F.2d 994 (D.C. Cir. 1966).
37. Krasnow, Longley, and Terry, *The Politics of Broadcast Regulation,* 54–62.
38. Ibid., 56–57.
39. *Reno v. American Civil Liberties Union,* 521 U.S. 844 (1997).

Readings

Aufderheide, Patricia. *Communications Policy and the Public Interest: The Telecommunications Act of 1996.* New York: Guilford Press, 1999.
Bagdikian, Ben H. *The New Media Monopoly.* Boston: Beacon Press, 2004.
Campbell, Richard, Christopher R. Martin, and Bettina Fabos. *Media and Culture: An Introduction to Mass Communication.* 4th ed. Boston: Bedford/St. Martin's, 2005.
Compaine, Benjamin, and Douglas Gomery. *Who Owns the Media: Competition and Concentration in the Media Industry.* 3d ed. Mahwah, N.J.: Erlbaum, 2000.
Croteau, David, and William Hoynes. *Media/Society: Industries, Images, and Audiences.* 3d ed. Thousand Oaks, Calif.: Pine Forge Press, 2003.
Einstein, Mara. *Media Diversity: Economics, Ownership, and the FCC.* Mahwah, N.J.: Erlbaum, 2004.
Graber, Doris, Denis McQuail, and Pippa Norris, eds. *The Politics of News, the News of Politics.* Washington, D.C.: CQ Press, 1998.
Krasnow, Erwin G., Lawrence D. Longley, and Herbert A. Terry. *The Politics of Broadcast Regulation.* 3d ed. New York: St. Martin's Press, 1982.
Price, Monroe E., and Marc Raboy, eds. *Public Service Broadcasting in Transition: A Documentary Reader.* New York: Kluwer Law International, 2003.
Zarkin, Kimberly. *Anti-Indecency Groups and the Federal Communications Commission: A Study in the Politics of Broadcast Regulation.* Lewiston, N.Y.: E. Mellon Press, 2003.

c h a p t e r   t h r e e

Press Freedom and the Law

H OW PREVALENT IS PRESS FREEDOM? The disappointing answer is "not very," and the situation is deteriorating in a world gripped by fears of terrorism. Forty-three percent of the world's people, living in seventy-one countries, do not enjoy a free press at all, and another 40 percent, living in forty-nine countries, enjoy only partial press freedom. That leaves just 17 percent of the world's people in seventy-three countries benefiting from full press freedom.[1] These ratings are based on four sets of criteria: laws and regulations that influence media content, political pressures and controls over media content, economic influences over media content, and such repressive actions as censorship and physical violence, including the killing of journalists (Box 3-1).

The United States, along with most western democracies, ranks among the countries where, according to Freedom House's 2004 survey, print and broadcast media and the Internet are essentially free, though most fall considerably short of a perfect score. Why and how has the United States maintained its high press-freedom rankings for more than sixty years? What does press freedom, guaranteed by the U.S. Constitution, mean in practice? How can the freedom of privately controlled institutions to choose, frame, and report all news be reconciled with protection of society from irresponsible news stories that damage public interests? How can an unfettered media establishment be kept responsive to the many voices that should be heard? In this chapter we will begin to shed light on these puzzles by probing problems that arise when a free press claims the exclusive right to decide what to publish and, in the process, clashes with demands by citizen groups for different types of stories. We will then turn to barriers to information that the government claims is too sensitive to publish. Finally, we will examine restraints on publication that legislators and courts have imposed to safeguard private and public interests.

The First Amendment to the U.S. Constitution is the basis for press freedom. The amendment guarantees that "Congress shall make no law . . . abridging the freedom of speech or of the press." This makes the press the only private enterprise in the United States to which the Constitution grants a privileged status. The interpretations of the scope of this privilege, however, have fluctuated since the First Amendment was ratified in 1791, and federal and state courts have interpreted it in diverse ways.[2]

The nation's founders granted this special status to the press because they considered the right to express opinions and to collect and disseminate information free from government interference as the bedrock of a free society.[3] If restraints are needed to protect society from pernicious publicity, they must not come through "prior restraint." Government can forestall publication only if it "will surely result in direct, immediate, and irreparable damage to our nation or its people." [4] The belief in the political importance of a free press has stood the test of time and remains a cornerstone of U.S. democracy. Therefore, any factor that affects the interpretation or the scope of this basic right is a matter of major political significance.

Access to the Media

The notion of government "by the people" implies that the people have a right to make their voices heard. Practically speaking, this means that they must be able to use the mass media to state their views. The civil rights movement of the 1960s and the many environmental protection crusades that have swept the country, for example, never could have gathered widespread support without mass media publicity. Did the reformers have a *right* to mass media publicity for their views and for their organizing activities? The answer is "no." In fact, it is difficult for most people, other than journalists or major public figures, to gain access to the media.[5] Media personnel decide what stories to publicize and whose views to present, leaving many views without a public forum. There is simply not enough time and space available to accommodate all who want to be heard. Internet Web sites remain only a partial solution to the problem.

Uncontrolled Media

U.S. courts usually have held that the freedom of the print media to determine what they will or will not print, and whose views they will present, is nearly absolute. Cable television and the Internet thus far enjoy the same freedom, because, like the telephone, they are considered "common carriers" in the business of transporting other people's messages. However, this issue remains contested because many legislators and large numbers of the public favor restraints on press freedom, especially to protect children from unsavory information. As it stands now, as long as uncontrolled media stay clear of deliberate libel and slander and do not publish top-secret information, legal restraints do not hamper their publishing decisions.

The U.S. Supreme Court defined print press rights in the case of *Miami Herald Publishing Company v. Tornillo* (1974).[6] At issue was the constitutionality of a Florida statute that gave a right to immediate reply to candidates for public office who had been personally attacked by a newspaper. The rebuttal had to match the format of the original attack, and it had to be placed in an equally prominent spot in the newspaper. The law had been passed to deal with the problem of personal attacks published very late in a campaign, giving candidates little time to respond. The consequence might be loss of the election.

The case arose in 1972 when Patrick Tornillo Jr., leader of the Dade County Teachers Union, was running for the Florida state legislature. Just before the primary the *Miami Herald* published two editorials objecting to Tornillo's election because he had led a recent teachers' strike. Tornillo demanded that the paper print his replies to claims made in the editorials. The paper refused. After Tornillo lost the primary decisively, he sued the paper.

When the case reached the U.S. Supreme Court in 1974, the Court ruled unanimously that newspapers can print or refuse to print anything they like. No one, including a candidate whose reputation has been damaged, has the *right* to obtain space in a newspaper. Therefore, the Florida right to reply statute was unconstitutional. The decision reaffirmed what had been the thrust of the law all along. Private citizens may request that a story or response to a personal attack be printed and that request may be granted, but they have no right to demand publication.[7]

Controlled Media

The rules are different for the broadcast media, because limited channel space makes them semi-monopolies. Besides, entry into the broadcast media business requires a license from the government. In return for the privilege of broadcasting over the public airwaves, license holders must adhere to government regulations. These include rules ensuring that the license holders respect the limited rights of access to the airways that Congress has mandated.

BOX 3-1
What Makes the Press Free?

Every year Freedom House, a nonprofit, nonpartisan organization, reports on press freedom throughout the world. Each country's public information system is rated either as free, partially free, or not free. The criteria that Freedom House use to measure press freedom summarize the many ways in which governments around the world can and do interfere with the freedom of their news media.

Freedom House divides its rating system into three broad categories: the legal environment worth thirty points, the political environment worth forty points, and the economic environment worth thirty points. Scores in all three categories are based on surveys of local conditions. Overall scores then determine annual ratings.

Appraisal of the legal environment entails judgments of the laws and regulations that could restrain media content and the government's inclination to use them. Freedom House also examines the positive impact of constitutional and other legal guarantees of freedom of expression and the existence of readily usable freedom of information laws. On the negative side, the impact of security legislation is considered, along with the impact of criminal statutes and penalties for libel and defamation. Institutional factors are important as well. They include the independence of the judiciary and of official media regulatory bodies, registration requirements for media outlets and journalists, and the freedom of journalists to organize to promote their concerns.

Under the category of political environment, Freedom House evaluates how free the media are in choosing their content. That requires checking the editorial independence of state-owned media and privately-owned media as well as assessing ease of access to information and ease of access to people who are sources of information. Official censorship and self-censorship are other areas of concern, as is the freedom of local and foreign reporters to cover the news without harassment. Reporters need to be spared intimidation by the state or other actors, including protection from arbitrary imprisonment, violent assaults, and other threats.

The economic environment category includes factors that might impair the operation of a free press due to unfavorable economic conditions; burdensome conditions for ownership; excessive ownership concentration; high costs of establishing media, producing news, and distributing it; and pressures brought by withholding of subsidies or advertising. Corruption and bribery may also affect media content adversely, as may the lack of transparency.

Judged by these criteria, the press freedom record for 2004 is a sorry one. It shows that 43 percent of the world's population live in countries where freedom of expression is severely constrained. Another 40 percent live in countries where there is only some freedom for open discussion of controversial issues. A mere 17 percent of the world's people live in countries where the press is labeled "free," though never totally so. The leaders in press freedom are small European democracies: Denmark, Sweden, Norway, Finland, Iceland, Belgium, and Switzerland. At the unfree end of the scale are North Korea, Cuba, Burma, Turkmenistan, and Libya. The United States ranks seventeenth out of 192 countries and is rated as a free-press country.

SOURCE: Freedom House, "Press Freedom Survey 2004," www.freedom house.org.

Considering that broadcast channels have mushroomed, many members of Congress and many broadcasters and communication scholars have urged ending differential treatment of broadcast media based on the assumption of broadcast channel scarcity. Moreover, the distinctions among print and broadcast media are becoming increasingly blurred because print media now use many broadcast technologies to disseminate their messages. The argument therefore goes that all media should be free from government interference in making publishing decisions.

What kinds of messages has Congress deemed urgent enough to mandate their airing? Section 315 of the Communications Act of 1934 and its many subsequent amendments and interpretations mentions the public's access rights to broadcast media. The right falls into three categories: the equal time provision, the fairness doctrine, and the right of rebuttal. All of these rights arise only after a station has broadcast the information in question.

The Right to Equal Time. If a station gives or sells time during an election campaign to one candidate for a specific office, it must make the same opportunity available to all candidates for that office, including those with few backers. However, if the station refuses time to all candidates for the same office, none of them has a right to demand access under Section 315. The rules exclude coverage provided through regular news programs and specifically exempt talk shows.

Stations constrained by the all-or-none equal time rule often opt for "none," particularly for state and local offices and when many candidates are competing for the same office. This keeps many viable candidates off the air and has led to widespread dissatisfaction with the equal time rule and demands to abandon it. To make it possible to stage lengthy debates among mainline candidates for major offices without running afoul of the equal time provisions, the FCC exempted them from equal time rules in 1983, allowing radio and television broadcasters to stage political debates at all political levels among a limited array of candidates chosen in a nondiscriminatory way. Candidates who feel that they have been unfairly shut out may appeal to the FCC. The ruling applies even to public television stations.[8]

The Right to Fair Treatment.   The fairness doctrine has had a broader reach than the equal time provision because it is not limited to candidates for political office. It mandates free air time for the presentation of issues of public concern and the expression of opposing views whenever a highly controversial public issue has been discussed on television.

Like the equal time provision, the fairness doctrine (suspended in 2000) has had unintended consequences. It has impoverished public debate by suppressing controversy, because the media frequently shied away from programs dealing with controversial public issues to avoid demands to air opposing views in place of regular revenue-producing programs. It was difficult to decide who, among many claimants for airtime, had the right to reply to controversial programs.[9] Although the rule will likely never be reinstated, the pressures and litigation produced by the fairness rule have made the media more receptive to featuring opposing views. For example, it has become traditional to allow spokespersons for the opposition to offer rebuttals after presidential, gubernatorial, and mayoral speeches covering major policy issues. The temper of the times has thus curbed editorial freedom, even without legal constraints.

Is there a right of reply to contentious statements made in business commercials? The oil industry, environmentalists, and the drug industry, among other groups, have used commercials to advocate controversial public policies. Commercial firms and public interest groups have petitioned for time to respond because press freedom rules do not apply automatically to commercial messages. In fact, free expression in commercial messages has been constrained severely through truth-in-advertising laws administered by the Federal Trade Commission. If courts order the media to make time available to respond to commercial messages, must the time be free of charge? The answer is unclear because the courts have spoken with forked tongues. Media willingness to allow replies has been quite mixed.

The Right of Rebuttal. The 1969 landmark case *Red Lion Broadcasting Co. v. Federal Communications Commission* established a broad scope for the right of reply when individuals are assailed on radio or television in a way that damages their reputations.[10] The case arose because a book about a conservative senator was attacked on a program conducted and paid for by the ultraconservative Christian Crusade. Fred Cook, the book's author, asked for rebuttal time, free of charge. The station was willing to sell him reply time but refused free time, disclaiming responsibility for the content of programs prepared by clients who had bought air time.

The U.S. Supreme Court sided with Cook, who received the right of rebuttal, at station expense, on the grounds that maligned individuals deserve a right to reply and that the public has a right to hear opposing views. The decision proved to be a hollow victory for supporters of free access to the airways, however, because stations sharply curtailed air time available for controversial broadcasts, fearing rebuttal claims.

The *Red Lion* case is also noteworthy as an example of political manipulation of the regulatory process. The Democratic National Committee had paid for and orchestrated Cook's protest as part of an effort to generate an avalanche of demands for rebuttals that would force stations to cancel conservative radio and television programs to avoid the costs of free rebuttal time.[11] This did, indeed, happen. By 1975, 300 of 350 stations that carried the Christian Crusade had dropped it.

Problems of the Status Quo

Apart from the right to reply to a personal attack and the right of rival candidates to have equal broadcast time, individuals have no access rights. There is no way to bring messages to public attention through the mass media if the media are unwilling, aside from using advertisements, e-mail, or a Web site or chat room on the Internet. Public television enjoys complete editorial freedom as well. When public television in Alabama canceled the film *Death of a Princess* in response to protests by Saudi Arabia's royal family and threats of economic boycott, a group of citizens charged unfair denial of their right of access to information. The federal district court disagreed.[12] The station, not the public, had the right to decide what to feature and what to reject.

Single networks or stations often secure exclusive broadcast rights to popular events, such as major baseball and basketball games. This practice is another restraint on information dissemination. Networks have negotiated exclusive contracts even for such public spectacles as the rededication of the Statue of Liberty during its centennial and the Olympic Games in Athens, Greece, in 2004. The television networks also have been very restrictive in airing programs by freelance reporters who are unaffiliated with the network. Similarly, professional organizations frequently restrain the flow of news to the general public. For instance, when scientists discovered a treatment that could cut AIDS patients' pneumonia deaths by half, they withheld the news for five months to ensure that the glory of being the first to announce the good news would go to a bona fide medical journal, the renowned *New England Journal of Medicine.* If the scientists had violated journal rules by releasing data to the public prior to publication in a medical journal, their research reports could have been rejected for publication thereafter.[13]

People in public office who want access to the mass media to explain their views face problems similar to those of private individuals. Although the media are likely to be more sympathetic to their requests, on many occasions coverage is denied or granted only outside primetime. Several speeches by Presidents Nixon, Ford, Reagan, Bush, and Clinton were not broadcast at all because the media considered them partisan political statements or claimed that they contained nothing new. Others were carried by only a few stations, forcing the president to compete against regular broadcasts and reducing his audience sharply. Presidents prevent access problems by tailoring their requests for media time to the needs of the media. In particular, they avoid schedule conflicts with major sports events.

The question of access rights to the airwaves also has been raised in connection with interest groups. Several groups have asked for more children's programs, even though they would be of little interest to the majority of adult listeners and viewers. The FCC has concurred that children constitute an important special audience whose needs for distinctive programming must be met. The FCC has pressured stations to increase programming, often with a veiled threat that failure to oblige would lead to mandatory rules. Stations have been reluctant to add children's programs because their revenues are comparatively low, particularly after the FCC shortened the time allowed for advertising to spare immature viewers from temptations.

Other audiences whose right of access to special programs has been recognized sporadically include African Americans, Hispanics, and lovers of classical music, to name a few. Occasional rulings have forced the electronic media to set aside time for broadcasts geared to such groups, whose needs might be ignored if the forces of the economic marketplace were allowed full rein. The FCC has further protected the interests of these groups by giving preference in license applications to stations whose output is likely to serve neglected clienteles. In light of the growing number of cable, television, and radio outlets, making access easier for everyone, government protection of special interest groups is declining. In 1981 the Supreme Court freed the FCC from any obligation to weigh the effects of alternative program formats on different population groups when making licensing decisions. The Court's ruling arose from a series of cases in which radio stations had changed their format, for instance, from all news to all music.[14]

Other Approaches to Media Access

Attempts to gain access to the mass media through independently produced programs, individual requests for airtime, and FCC rulings that support the interest of minority audiences have been only moderately successful. Other routes to access are even less satisfactory. Letters to the editor and op-ed essays are examples. Because of lack of space, most papers publish only a tiny portion of the letters and opinion pieces they receive. The *New York Times,* for example, receives more than 60,000 letters annually and publishes 4–5 percent of them, limiting length strictly. Even with these stringent controls, space devoted to letters equals the space allotted for editorials in the *Times.* Editors select the letters and op-ed essays to be published, using a variety of criteria that disadvantage average people. Unusual messages or those sent by someone well known are most likely to be printed.

Another avenue to access is through paid advertisements. Labor unions, business enterprises, lobby groups, and even foreign governments have placed advertisements on the air or in major newspapers to present their side of disputes and public policy issues. Usually only large companies can afford the steep purchase price, which may run into thousands of dollars for full-page advertisements and national broadcast exposure. Print and electronic media occasionally have refused to publish advertisements or sell airtime when messages seemed to them too controversial—on topics such as the energy crisis and the Arab–Israeli dispute, for example. Public concern about the denial of advertising space has lessened in the wake of creation of the Internet, where Web sites disseminate messages to computer users around the world. However, access to that message system is a less effective way to reach the general public than the daily papers and major over-the-air broadcasts, although this could change.

When people who are eager to publicize their views cannot afford paid messages, they may try to gain attention by creating a sensational event and inviting the media to witness it. A young Chinese dissident used the tactic in 1992, when he invited the media to watch his display of posters commemorating the brutal suppression of China's prodemocracy movement in Beijing's Tiananmen Square. The ensuing free publicity reached millions of people worldwide. Few publicity seekers meet with such success, and many fail miserably, as happened to a man who invited the media to a self-immolation to protest unemployment in 1983. Camera crews filmed the action while the protester suffered life-threatening burns. The story received nationwide coverage, but the emphasis was on the callousness of the film crew that did not stop the burning. The unemployment issue was well-nigh ignored.[15]

The rise of lobby groups eager to ensure broad access rights to people with minority viewpoints, and the FCC's sympathy for their pleas, have made broadcasters more sensitive to pressures for access by political activists. But even if radio or television station management is willing to grant access to such people, especially when they have engaged in newsworthy activities, there still is the problem of insufficient time to air every claimant's views. Despite the multiplication of television and radio channels in the wake of technological advancements, there will never be enough channels or even newspaper pages to publicize all important views to large audiences. Even the Internet does not guarantee everyone wide public exposure. Concerned citizens have neither the time nor the capacity to listen to all significant views and put them into proper perspective. In fact, the capacity to broadcast and publicize already far exceeds the audience's capacity to listen and assimilate. Studies of cable television users have shown that regardless of the number of channels available and the important stories they feature, the average viewer rarely taps into more than six channels.

Access to Information

Access to information involves two major issues: who shall have access and what information must be open for public inspection.

Special Access for the Media?

The right to publish without restraint means little if journalists are refused access to sources of information. Supreme Court decisions have denied that the media enjoy special rights in this regard. Neither ordinary citizens nor media personnel have a constitutional right to gather information.[16] In fact, "the First Amendment does not guarantee the press a constitutional right of special access to information not available to the public generally."[17] This even includes such mundane matters as the addresses of

people who have been arrested.[18] The Court rejected the argument that
the First Amendment entitles the press to special rights of access because
of its duty to scrutinize the political scene on behalf of the public.

Without special access rights, journalists can be barred from many
politically crucial events, thus depriving the public of important information. Closed White House and State Department meetings are examples.
The media often are excluded from pretrial hearings and grand jury proceedings that determine whether evidence of wrongdoing justifies indictments. The press also has no right to attend conferences of the Supreme
Court at which the justices reveal why they decided to hear certain cases
and declined to hear others. Media people may be barred from attending
sessions of legislative bodies closed to the general public. Such sessions
ordinarily deal with confidential information that may require protection
or with matters that might prove embarrassing to legislators. Because such
proceedings and sessions frequently involve high political stakes, participants often leak news about them to journalists.

Journalists have no right to be admitted to sites of crimes and disasters when the general public is excluded. Nor do they have the right to
visit prisons or to interview and film inmates, even for the purpose of
investigating prison conditions and confirming rumors of brutality. The
Supreme Court has stressed in several cases that reporters could get the
information they needed without special access privileges.[19] This suggests
that the Court is willing to grant access in situations in which information
about prison conditions is totally lacking. Many of the Supreme Court's
decisions regarding access to information were highly controversial, as
shown by five-to-four divisions among the nine justices. This clash of views
has made media access rights an area of ongoing legal development.

In wartime, military officials often bar news personnel from combat
zones by denying transportation to these areas or by keeping invasion
plans secret. That was the case during the buildup to the Persian Gulf War
in 1990–1991 and during the war itself. Despite press protests and a suit
filed by news outlets against incumbent President George Bush and the
Department of Defense, the government effectively throttled free access to
news. Following the Gulf War the Department of Defense issued new regulations to ease media access in similar future situations. But such regulations rarely make a difference in practice because of the military's culture
of secrecy.

By custom, although not by law, newspeople often receive preferred
treatment in gaining entry to public events. Press passes ensure media
access to the best observation points for presidential inaugurations, space
shuttle landings, and political conventions. The media often are admitted
to the scene of events, such as accidents and crimes, while the general

public is kept out. Access, however, is purely at the discretion of the authorities in charge.[20]

Access to Government Documents

Government documents are other important sources of political information that are often off-limits to the public and media. The Freedom of Information Act, signed by President Lyndon B. Johnson on July 4, 1966, and amended in 1974 to make the act more enforceable, ostensibly opened many government files to the news media and the general public.[21] Burdensome application requirements and the costs of duplicating information have limited its usefulness for news personnel. In recent years, the intricacies of scanning computerized records that were encoded in outdated ways have raised additional access hurdles. Nonetheless, the act has enabled important disclosures, such as CIA involvement in political upheavals in foreign countries, illegal financial dealings by members of Congress, and the government's failure to protect the public from chemical and biological hazards and ineffective drugs. Most reporters, however, prefer covering readily available current news to using the Freedom of Information Act to dig into government files to unearth past misdeeds.

Some serious abuses have marred the act's reputation as a bulwark of freedom. Organized crime and narcotics traffickers have used it to spot threats to their activities, and business firms have used it to spy on competitors. To cope with these and other abuses, Congress has amended the act repeatedly. Fees charged to businesses for information have been raised to cover the full costs of inquiries. Fees have been lowered for media enterprises to encourage their search for information. Although most of the changes have garnered widespread approval because they attempted to resolve acute problems, most have also faced criticism as either an undue expansion of First Amendment rights or as an unsavory contraction.

General Rules.   Many types of public documents remain unavailable to reporters despite the pervasiveness of freedom of information laws at all levels of government. Most laws provide for access to public records, but various political jurisdictions define *public records* differently. Laws obviously constitute a public record, but are citizens entitled to inspect the minutes of the meetings that preceded passage of a law, or tapes of the proceedings, or exhibits that a legislative committee considered before passing the law? In many states the term *public record* does not include any information about the genesis of laws and regulations.

The computerization of government records is raising many new access issues. The courts have acknowledged that information stored in government computers constitutes a public record, but they have yet to decide definitively what access rights exist. For example, it is unclear whether journalists have the right to ask for specific data within a database, or whether that entails the creation of a new "record" that public agencies are not required to supply. Must government agencies facilitate computer access by installing user-friendly programs? The *Congressional Record,* for example, could not be searched effectively until full text-searching facilities were developed. What about data stored in now obsolete files that current personnel cannot retrieve? It will take many years to find satisfactory answers to such questions and to develop reasonable policies.

Applicants for information often must demonstrate a special need for it. They must specify precisely what information they want, which is difficult to do without knowing what is available. Administrators determine how specific the request must be and whether and how applicants must demonstrate that they truly need the information. A widely used rule of thumb about access to information is that disclosure must be in the public interest and must not do excessive harm. Access should be denied if the harm caused by opening records is greater than the possible benefit. Accordingly, a reporter's request for the records of welfare clients for a story on welfare cheating probably would be denied because it is embarrassing to many people to have others know that they need public assistance. Because there are no precise guidelines for determining what is in the public interest and what degree of harm is excessive, the judgments of public officials who control documents are supreme.

Many state legislatures are unwilling to leave access policies to the discretion of administrative officials. Therefore they construct detailed lists of the kinds of records that may or may not be disclosed. That approach is unsatisfactory, too, because legislators cannot possibly foresee all types of requests. Release of records may then be forestalled simply because the legislation does not specifically mention their contents.

Governments routinely bar certain types of documents from disclosure. For example, examination questions and answers for tests given by government agencies usually are placed beyond public scrutiny. If they did become public, the value of these examinations might be totally destroyed. However, if the fairness and appropriateness of examination questions for public jobs are in doubt, public scrutiny of questions and answers might be beneficial. Favoritism in grading exams of the protégés of the powerful is a common abuse that also is difficult to expose without access to graded exams.

Other data that governments frequently keep from media personnel are business records that could advantage competitors, such as bids for government contracts. Because corruption is common in awarding government contracts, reporters often are very interested in what companies have bid or what promises they made in return for contract awards. Without access to the records, investigative reporting of suspected fraud or corruption is impossible. However, secrecy is warranted because publicizing the details of a bid could give an unfair advantage to another firm to underbid the lowest bidder by a few dollars and clinch the contract.

Clearly, some restraints on access are essential to protect individuals and business enterprises, especially now when access to computerized government information can make every citizen's life an open book. Yet restraints make betrayals of the public trust easier. The cloak of secrecy may conceal vast areas of corruption. Finding the right balance between protection of individuals and their business ventures and protection of the public interest through media access is extremely difficult and controversial.

Historical and National Security Documents.   Access to the official and private records of major public officials is also limited. These records are usually unavailable to the media and the general public until twenty-five years after the public official's death. The lengthy limit was selected to spare possible embarrassment to people in the official's public and private network.[22] When exceptions are made to the twenty-five-year rule, they are frequently contested in court, as happened when former president Richard Nixon unsuccessfully sued to recover control of many of his records about the Watergate affair that had been released to the media. The closure of the private records of public officials is part of the privacy protection afforded to all individuals, but it serves a public purpose as well. For uninhibited discussion in policy making, assurance of confidentiality is essential. Without it, officials will posture for an audience rather than freely address themselves to the issues under consideration. The danger of inhibiting free discussion also explains why deliberations prior to legislative or judicial decisions are generally closed to public scrutiny.

The media ordinarily cannot publish documents concerning matters of national security. Examples are CIA intelligence data and information about prospective negotiations or sensitive past negotiations. Media may also be restricted in publishing news about weapons the United States has adopted or stories indicating that security devices are not operating properly. In some cases, however, such information is available in open files, in traditional media, or on the Internet so that it can be pieced together into a coherent story.

Overall the government annually labels more than 1 million documents as classified, which means that access to them requires special permission. It places many more beyond easy access because they contain information taken from previously classified documents. In addition, state and local officials withhold massive numbers of documents. The Clinton administration eased the jams in information flow at the federal level by putting the burden of proof on the government that secrecy was essential, rather than requiring applicants to prove otherwise. Still the problems of access to classified documents remain staggering.[23]

The most difficult aspect of security censorship is to determine which information is truly sensitive and must be protected and which information should remain open to media personnel and the public. A graphic illustration of this perennial battle is the *Pentagon Papers* case. Daniel Ellsberg, a former aide to President Lyndon Johnson's National Security Council, claimed that foreign policy information in a Department of Defense study of the U.S. entrapment in the Vietnam War had been classified improperly as top secret. He copied the information surreptitiously and gave it to prominent newspapers for publication. He hoped that its release would turn people against the war. The executive branch considered his actions a criminal breach of wartime security and sued Ellsberg and the media that printed the information.

In *New York Times Co. v. United States* (1971), the Supreme Court absolved the media, ruling that the government had been overly cautious in classifying the information as top secret.[24] In the Court's view publication did not harm the country. Although the case cleared Ellsberg and the media of the charges, it left the government's contention unchallenged that officials may be prosecuted when they jeopardize national security by disclosing classified information to the press. That happened to Samuel Loring Morison, a naval intelligence analyst who was convicted in 1985 on espionage charges for providing a British military magazine with intelligence satellite photographs.[25]

The Supreme Court decision in the *Pentagon Papers* case and subsequent lower court rulings did not end the public controversy. Analysts still disagree about whether the disclosures from the *Pentagon Papers* damaged the national security of the United States. Those who concur with the Court point out that much of the information released had been available already. Dissenters counter that the information had never been compiled in a single document and published in such prominent sources as the *New York Times* and the *Washington Post*. They also refer to the dismay expressed by many European leaders about publicizing events that they had deemed confidential.

Before the Nixon years, if a government agency decided that certain information needed to be kept from the media, the prevailing presumption, shared by the courts, was that the agencies charged with guarding national security are best qualified to assess such matters. That has changed. Disputes about the safety of disclosing national security information are particularly difficult to settle because both the clamor of the

New York Times reporter Judith Miller, author of controversial stories about Iraq's weapons of mass destruction; attorney Floyd Abrams, famous for defending First Amendment rights, and *Time Magazine* reporter Matthew Cooper are shown discussing shield laws in December 2004. Cooper faces a jail term for refusing to testify about his contacts with confidential sources.

media to obtain access and the government's contention that the information requires protection are often self-serving. What is dubbed "the public interest" may be simply the reporters' interest in furthering their careers, or the publishers' interest in making money, or the government's interest in shielding itself from embarrassment.

At times, security issues, such as information about hostage situations, are resolved through informal cooperation between the government and the media or through self-censorship. For instance, news organizations worldwide voluntarily withhold news about hostage incidents or kidnappings when news stories could jeopardize delicate negotiations to rescue the victims. Information about these instances is hard to obtain because neither the media nor the government want to publicize their collaborative efforts to suppress news. If the information leaks out, all collaborators often deny it. Given that pattern, it was surprising when it became public knowledge in 2001 that the chief executives of the nation's major television networks had pledged to honor National Security Adviser

Condoleezza Rice's request to abstain from broadcasting messages from Osama bin Laden, the alleged mastermind behind the 2001 terrorist assault on the United States. Rice had contacted the executives shortly after the event. She justified her request on the grounds that taped broadcasts by bin Laden might contain encoded messages encouraging further terrorism.[26]

Executive Privilege. The doctrine of executive privilege is deeply intertwined with the question of limits on secrecy. Chief executives have the right to conceal information that they consider sensitive. This privilege extends to all of their communications with their staffs. Prior to the Nixon years the courts usually upheld executive privilege, but decisions since then suggest that the scope of the privilege is shrinking. Efforts to make leaking of information a crime have also mostly failed. However, it is a crime to leak the names of CIA agents.[27]

Silence by various government departments and agencies also sharply restricts political news available to the media. Undisclosed information frequently concerns failures, incidents of malfeasance, malfunctions, or government waste. Agencies guard this type of news zealously because disclosure might harm the agency or its key personnel. Chief executives at all levels of government often issue directives restraining top officials from talking freely to journalists. President Reagan even ordered lie detector tests for officials to check compliance with disclosure rules, but he later rescinded the directive. Although not usually enforceable, directives that muzzle public officials tend to reduce the flow of information to the press and the public.

Except for the ever-present opportunity to get information through leaks, reporters find it difficult to penetrate the walls of silence surrounding publicity-shy agencies. Instead, the media rely on an agency's press handouts or publicity releases or on secondary reports from agency personnel. These usually reflect the sources' sense of what is news, rather than the reporters'.[28] Occasionally, reporters on the trail of stories that would be highly embarrassing to government officials find themselves under strong pressure to stop their inquiries or suppress publication of the damaging news.[29]

Private Industry Documents

Although the problem of government secrecy as a restraint on information collection is formidable, it is small compared with the problem of access to news stories covering the private sector. Numerous enterprises whose operations affect the lives of millions of Americans as much or more than many government agencies shroud their operations in secrecy.

If asbestos companies or major tobacco companies want to exclude reporters from access to information about their business practices, they can do so with impunity. So can drug companies, repair shops, or housing contractors as long as the information has not surfaced in an official proceeding like a court case or government report. Fear that a company might sue a media organization for millions of dollars is also a powerful deterrent to airing questionable business practices. Even *60 Minutes,* renowned for its fearless investigative reports, has occasionally caved in to such pressure. That happened in 1995 when the program temporarily shelved an interview with a tobacco industry whistle blower because exceptionally high legal expenses loomed.[30]

The Freedom of Information Act does not cover unpublished records of private businesses, except for the reports made to the government about sales or inventory figures or customer lists. As noted earlier, many of these reports are withheld from the public on the ground that business cannot thrive if its operational data are made available to its competitors. Moreover, the chances that withheld information will be disclosed through leaks are infinitely less in business than in government. Employees can be pledged to secrecy as a condition of employment and fired if they break their vow.

Individual Rights versus the Public's Right to Know

Thus far we have focused on barriers to the free flow of information imposed by the mass media to protect editorial freedom or by government or industry to shield sensitive information. But there are equally important barriers to circulation of information imposed by individuals or on behalf of individuals for the purpose of protecting the right to privacy, the right to an unprejudiced trial, the right to gather information freely, and the right to a good reputation.

Privacy Protection

How much may the media publish about the private affairs of people in public and private life without infringing on the constitutionally protected right of privacy? How much do privacy rights exclude from public scrutiny? The answers depend on the status of the people involved. Private individuals enjoy broad, though shrinking, protections from publicity; public officials and people who have become public figures because their lives are of interest to the public do not enjoy such protections.

In general, state and federal courts have been fairly lenient in permitting the media to cover details about the personal affairs of people when they are revealed in public records. A 1975 Georgia case involving a young woman who had been raped and murdered epitomizes this trend. The family wanted to keep the victim's name out of stories discussing the crime. Nonetheless, the news media published the victim's name and gruesome details of the crime. The family sued for invasion of privacy, claiming that there was no need to disclose the name and that Georgia law prohibited releasing the names of rape victims. The U.S. Supreme Court disagreed and overturned the Georgia law. It held that crime was a matter of public record, making the facts surrounding it publishable despite protests by victims and their families.[31]

Circumstances may turn private individuals into public figures. This happened to Oliver Sipple, who attended a public rally featuring President Ford. Sipple prevented an assassination attempt on the president by grabbing the would-be assassin's gun. When newspeople checked his background they discovered that he was homosexual and included this information in subsequent stories. Sipple brought suit for invasion of privacy, but the courts denied his claim, saying that he had forfeited his right to privacy by seizing the gun. That action had made him an "involuntary public figure." Individuals also may lose their right to privacy when they grant interviews to reporters. Reporters are free to round the story out with "newsworthy" observations that were not part of the interview. Reporters are also free to publish facts that were told to them in confidence, though they usually honor their pledge of keeping an interviewee's name confidential.[32] If reporters, without malice, misrepresent some of the facts, this, too, is tolerated. The rationale is that the public is entitled to a full story, if it gets any story at all, and that fears of privacy invasion suits should not unduly inhibit reporting.

Many privacy invasion cases involve unauthorized photographs of people currently or previously in public life. When Jacqueline Kennedy Onassis, the widow of President John F. Kennedy, sued one particularly obnoxious photographer, the court ruled that even though she was no longer the first lady, she remained a public figure. Therefore, pictures could be taken and printed without her consent. The court, however, ordered the photographer to stop harassing her.[33] The courts have also permitted reporters to keep the homes of relatives of murder suspects under photographic surveillance and to film police officers during compromising sting operations. In fact, reporters are free to publish pictures taken in public settings without asking their subjects' permission.

To strengthen privacy protection, the courts in recent years have permitted subjects of unsolicited investigative reports to use trespass laws to stop the media. An example is the trespassing judgment won by the owners of a fashionable New York restaurant against CBS after reporters had entered the premises and filmed violations of the city's health code.[34] The courts also have been increasingly willing to protect people against willful inflictions of emotional pain by news media. However, the Supreme Court ruled unanimously in 1988 that the work of satirists and cartoonists enjoys full First Amendment protection.[35] It denied a plea for privacy protection and for compensation from Rev. Jerry Falwell for emotional injury inflicted by a salacious attack by *Hustler* magazine.

Because relatively few cases of privacy invasion generate law suits, privacy protection rests primarily on the sensitivity of the news media. And the media are not very sensitive. Even mainstream newspapers feature columns devoted to celebrity gossip, and tabloid papers and television shows of the same genre revel in this type of journalism. When Rev. Jesse Jackson learned in 2001 about an impending story about a daughter that he had fathered out of wedlock, he knew that efforts to protect his privacy would be futile. Therefore, like many other prospective victims of embarrassing publicity, he chose to announce the story himself. In the current news climate it has become impossible to protect newsworthy individuals from the "feeding frenzy" of print and electronic tabloid journalists. Once the proverbial cat is out of the bag, all join the chase, including serious news professionals who do not want to ignore stories that draw large audiences.[36] Efforts by several states to prohibit privacy invasion when the news lacks "social value" are unlikely to succeed over objections that they violate the First Amendment.[37]

Fair Trial and the Gag Rule

The courts favor a broad scope of disclosure for most people in public life, but they insist on a limited scope of disclosure in their own bailiwick. The courts used to guard zealously the right of accused persons to be protected against publicity that might influence judge and jury and harm their cases. This has been true even though scientific evidence showing that media publicity influences parties to a trial is scant and inconclusive.[38]

The stern posture of the courts in censoring pretrial publicity is weakening, however. In 1983 two Supreme Court justices refused to block a nationwide television broadcast about a sensational murder case scheduled for trial three weeks later. The trial involved seven white New Orleans police officers accused of the revenge slaying of four African American men suspected of participating in the murder of a white police officer. In the same vein, a federal court refused to prevent television stations from showing tapes of a cocaine transaction incriminating John DeLorean, a well-known automobile maker and jet-set celebrity. DeLorean's attorneys had argued that the pretrial publicity would make it impossible to find an impartial jury. In another case the courts ruled that incriminating tapes used in a corruption trial of several members of Congress could be shown publicly, even though some of the defendants had not been tried as yet and the convicted defendants were appealing the case.[39] When prominent national political figures have asked to have their trials moved out of Washington, D.C., because of prejudicial pretrial publicity, the courts have almost invariably refused their requests.[40] That did not happen in the case of Timothy McVeigh. His lawyers were able to have his 1997 trial moved away from Oklahoma City, the scene of his politically motivated bombing that killed 168 people and wounded 500 more.

Two murder cases, *Shepherd v. Florida* (1951) and *Sheppard v. Maxwell* (1966), brought the question of media coverage of court cases to wide public attention.[41] In these cases the U.S. Supreme Court held that the defendants, convicted of murder, had not had a fair trial because of widespread media publicity. As Justices Robert H. Jackson and Felix Frankfurter stated in *Shepherd v. Florida*, "The trial was but a legal gesture to register a verdict already dictated by the press and the public opinion [it] generated." [42] The Court overturned the convictions.

Judges have the right to prohibit the mass media from covering some or all of a court case before and during a trial, even when the public is allowed to attend courtroom sessions. Gag orders interfere with the media's ability to report on the fairness of judicial proceedings. They also run counter to the general reluctance of U.S. courts to condone prior censorship. Nonetheless, the courts have upheld gag laws as a necessary protection for accused persons. Judges may make rules restraining filmed coverage or may bar it completely without presenting evidence that the information covered by the gag order would impede a fair trial. Gag orders may extend even to judges' rulings that tell the media to refrain from covering a case. Thus the fact of judicial suppression of information may itself be hidden.

Numerous reporters have gone to jail and paid fines rather than obey gag rules because they felt that the courts were overly protective of the rights of criminal suspects and insufficiently concerned with the public's right to know. A 1976 decision, *Nebraska Press Association v. Stuart,* partly supports the reporters' views.[43] In that case the Supreme Court reversed a gag order in a murder trial. The Court declared that judicial maneuvers short of gag laws should forestall careless reporting that interferes with the rights of defendants. For example, trials can take place in different jurisdictions if there has been excessive local publicity. People can also bring suits against media enterprises or individual reporters who act irresponsibly by publicizing testimony from closed sessions of the courts, taking unauthorized pictures, or bribing court personnel to leak trial testimony.

The policy on gag laws is still unclear, however. Some lower courts have failed to comply with Supreme Court directives or have evaded the spirit of decisions. For example, instead of gagging the press, judges have placed gags on all the principals in a case, including the plaintiffs and defendants, their lawyers, and the jury, to prohibit them from talking about the case, particularly to members of the press. In an increasing number of cases, judges have barred access to information by closing courtrooms to all observers during pretrial proceedings as well as trials. However, this has not stopped legal personnel, including prosecutors, from leaking information to the press when that seems advantageous.

During the 1980s the Supreme Court struck down several of these restrictions or limited their use by specifying the circumstances under which media access may be denied. In *Richmond Newspapers v. Virginia* (1980), the Court ruled that the public and the press had an almost absolute right to attend criminal trials.[44] In the same vein, the justices declared in 1984 that neither newspeople nor the public may be barred from observing jury selection, except in unusual circumstances.[45] The Supreme Court appears to be moving closer to the notion that the public's access to judicial proceedings is part of the First Amendment rights guaranteed by the Constitution. A change in direction seemed possible following adverse public reaction to televising the 1995 murder trial of O.J. Simpson as if it were a daily soap opera serial. However, people have complained little about this type of coverage in subsequent high-profile trials, such as Michael Jackson's trial for child molestation or Scott Peterson's trial for the murder of his pregnant wife. In fact, television programs like *America's Most Wanted,* which focuses on dramatic crimes, attract large audiences.

Shield Laws

Digging into the affairs of public officials and other prominent citizens or exposing the activities of criminals or dissidents often requires winning the confidence of informants with promises to conceal their identity. Newspeople contend that compulsion to reveal the identity of their sources or surrender unpublished bits of information could hamper their investigations. If reporters disclose such information, they break their word to informants. Feeling betrayed, the sources are likely to dry up. This is why reporters want laws to shield them from subpoenas forcing them to testify.

However, failure to disclose information may allow criminals to go unpunished and innocent victims to be denied justice. Law enforcement agencies may find it difficult to penetrate dissident and terrorist groups that journalists have been able to use as sources. This is why media organizations at times agree to comply with subpoenas fully or partially. For instance, CBS agreed to surrender portions of unused filmed scenes from the hijacking of a TWA airliner to facilitate the prosecution of the hijackers.[46] A 1999 survey of 400 news organizations by the Reporters Committee for Freedom of the Press showed that 36 percent of the print media and 77 percent of the broadcast media had received one or more subpoenas for disclosure of information they had gathered on the job.[47]

The Supreme Court has ruled that newspeople generally do not have a common law right to protect their sources in the face of a subpoena. Nor may they shield records or editorial deliberations from judicial scrutiny if these records are needed to prove libel, except when the needed information is available from unshielded sources.[48] However, more than half of the states have shield laws to protect reporters from forced testimony. Shield laws give journalists most of the rights enjoyed by lawyers, doctors, and clergy to keep relations with their clients confidential. Shield laws also may bar searches of news offices to discover leads to crimes.

Shield laws do not ensure absolute protection. For example, when the right of reporters to withhold the names of their sources clashes with the right of other individuals to conduct a lawsuit involving criminal offenses, state shield laws and common law protections must yield. In 2004 a federal judge ordered two reporters jailed for up to eighteen months for refusing to tell a grand jury the names of government officials suspected of leaking confidential government information.[49] Likewise, a television reporter was convicted in 2004 of criminal contempt for refusing to say who gave him an FBI videotape showing a politician taking a bribe.

Some journalists advocate a federal shield law to protect all newspeople throughout the country and to reduce the costs of litigation when they resist forced disclosure. Others, fearing that such a law would provide conditional shielding only, prefer to do without shield laws of any kind; they contend that the First Amendment constitutes an absolute shield. These differences of opinion have taken steam out of the pressure for a federal shield law. Members of the judiciary also deny that shield laws are needed, but for different reasons. In the words of Justice Byron R. White, "From the beginning of our country, the press has operated without constitutional protection for press informants, and the press has flourished." Hence the absence of shield laws has "not been a serious obstacle to either the development or retention of confidential news sources by the press." [50]

Libel Laws

Legislators designed libel laws to provide redress when published information has unjustly tarnished a person's reputation. To win a libel suit, a plaintiff must prove that the defendant's negligence or recklessness led to the publishing of information that exposed the plaintiff to hatred, ridicule, or contempt. For years, libel suits, even when lost in court, dampened investigative reporting. That changed substantially in 1964 for cases involving public officials. The police chief of Montgomery, Alabama, brought an action for libel because an advertisement in the *New York Times* had charged him with mishandling civil rights demonstrations. The Supreme Court absolved the newspaper, ruling in *New York Times v. Sullivan* that a public official who claims libel must be able to show that the libelous information was published "with knowledge that it was false or with reckless disregard of whether it was false or not."[51] The *Sullivan* rule has made it very difficult for public officials to bring suit for libelous statements made about them. Malicious intent and extraordinary carelessness are hard to prove, especially because the courts give the media the benefit of the doubt. By the same token, the Sullivan rule has made it much easier for media to publish adverse information about public officials without extensive checking of the accuracy of the information prior to publication.

Since the 1974 decision in *Gertz v. Robert Welch,* the Supreme Court has narrowed the "public figure" category.[52] In that case the Court held that a person who had not deliberately sought publicity would be deemed a public figure only in exceptional—as yet unspecified—circumstances. Therefore, a prominent lawyer, whose name had been widely reported in the news, was not a public figure and could sue for libel.[53] However, the best protection for public figures from unscrupulous exposure by the media comes from the informal and formal codes of ethics by which most journalists abide. The increasing number of suits by public figures against media people also have become a damper on careless reporting because these suits are costly in time and money, even when the media are exonerated, which happens nearly half the time. The average initial awards in the ten to twenty cases that go to trial each year run to millions of dollars. These awards usually are sharply reduced if the case is appealed. Nonetheless, financially weak institutions cannot afford to risk multimillion-dollar judgments that might force them out of business.[54]

The battle between freedom of the press and the right of individuals to be protected from harmful publicity is full of confusing developments. The courts have pulled back from the position that, except for the right to a fair trial, individual rights are largely subordinate to press freedom. The courts have done so by distinguishing the rights of private individuals from those of public figures and by construing the category of public figures more narrowly. This leaves private individuals with substantial rights to bar the media from publishing potentially libelous or embarrassing facts. It remains unclear whether libel suits may be brought to challenge expressions of demonstrably false opinions.[55] The emergence of the Internet has raised several new issues in libel law that remain to be settled. Most important, who bears responsibility for publishing libels? Early decisions suggest that browsers, such as Netscape or Google, are not responsible for screening content for libels and other illegal content such as foul language or obscenity.

Other Restrictions on Publication

As we discussed in Chapter 1, all governments prohibit the publication of information that, in their view, would harm the public interest. The United States is no exception. Censorship is most prevalent in matters of national security involving external dangers, national security involving internal dangers, and obscenity. In each category there is general agreement that certain types of information should not be publicized. There is very little agreement, however, about where the line ought to be drawn between permitted and prohibited types of material. We have already discussed the controversy surrounding the release of the *Pentagon Papers*. Additional examples involving external security will be presented in Chapter 11.

Internal security news primarily entails investigations of allegedly subversive groups and reports on civil disturbances. The Patriot Act of 2001, passed in the wake of the terrorist attack on the United States in September of that year, vastly expanded the scope of government surveillance over messages potentially related to internal security. Because many of its provisions are under challenge as violations of First Amendment rights, the ultimate chilling impact of the law on free expression is uncertain. Moreover, some of its most restrictive provisions will expire in 2005 unless reauthorized (Chapter 5).[56]

Constraints on internal news also involve media portrayal of asocial behavior that might lead to imitation. Attempts to limit the portrayals of crime and violence, either in general or on programs to which children have access, are examples (Chapter 7). Closely related to restraints on the depiction of crime and violence are restraints on publication of indecent and obscene materials and broadcasts that include offensive language or that portray sexual matters or human excretion. Censorship advocates fear that such broadcasts may corrupt members of the audience, particularly children, and lead to imitation of undesirable behavior. They contend that publication of indecent and obscene materials, particularly in visual form, violates community standards and therefore should be prohibited by law. This argument rests on the notion that the public should have the right to prohibit the dissemination of material that offends its sense of propriety.

Despite the huge popularity of pornography, as shown by the millions of people who buy pornographic magazines, pay for pornographic movies and stage shows, rent pornographic videos, and visit pornography sites on the Internet, laws in many places bar free access to such information. FCC rules require scheduling indecent programming only between midnight and 6:00 a.m., when children are unlikely to be watching television. Obscene programming is barred at all times. Indecent material has been defined by the FCC as "material that depicts or describes, in terms patently offensive by contemporary community standards for the broadcast medium, sexual or excretory activities or organs." Obscenity has been defined by the Supreme Court as "something that, taken as a whole, appeals to the prurient interest; that depicts or describes in a patently offensive way sexual conduct; and that lacks serious artistic, political, and scientific value." [57] Congress has repeatedly tried to pass laws that would make it difficult for children and adolescents to view pornography. The 1996 Communications Decency Act and the 2000 Child Online Protection Act are examples. Ultimately, the Supreme Court declares most such measures unconstitutional. [58]

Nonetheless, regulation of racy materials has become more heavy-handed largely because lobby groups have escalated indecency complaints from 111 in 2000 to more than a million in 2004. [59] FCC fines for indecent programming have risen from $48,000 in 2000 to nearly $8 million in 2004 for offenses ranging from entertainer Janet Jackson's bared breast during the 2004 Super Bowl to the use of profanity by U2 lead singer Bono and the appearance of scantily dressed actors during the 2004 Olympic Game opening ceremonies. Obviously, puritanical sentiments are becoming more prevalent, better organized, and receive more support from a government dominated by conservatives.

Another example of protective censorship is the ban since 1971 on cigarette advertising on radio and television. It is designed to protect susceptible individuals from being lured into smoking by seductive advertisements. Pressures for additional areas of protective censorship have been considerable and range from pleas to stop liquor, sugared cereal, and casino gambling advertisements to requests to bar information dealing with abortion or drug addiction. Legislatures and courts have rejected most of them except when advertising on children's programs was involved. [60]

So-called hate broadcasters also remain a gray area in broadcast law, which has achieved new prominence because hate messages abound on the Internet. Indeed, the Internet had more than 2,000 racial hate Web sites at the end of 2000. [61] Contrary to the expressed public policy of the nation, many small over-the-air and cable stations or individual programs routinely attack racial, ethnic, and religious groups. As with broadcasts using obscene language, these attacks violate many citizens' sense of propriety. Nevertheless, the FCC has been reluctant to withhold licenses from the offending parties because genuine freedom of expression includes "freedom for the thought we hate," as Supreme Court Justice Oliver Wendell Holmes said long ago. Although formal restraints remain few, informal restraints have mushroomed. Television and radio stations have disciplined or dismissed reporters and commentators who made comments offensive to such groups as African Americans, women, and homosexuals.

Summary

In a democratic society, citizens have the right and civic duty to inform themselves and to express their views publicly. The press, as the eyes and ears of the public, must be protected against restraints that could interfere with its ability to gather information and disseminate it freely. In this chapter we have seen that despite such legislation as the Freedom of Information Act of 1966, lots of information about government activities remains unpublished. Either it has been classified as secret for security reasons or it has not been released to the public because it could embarrass individuals, including government officials, or it has escaped media scrutiny simply because of the flood of available information. If the participants so desire, they may exclude the public and press from many executive sessions of legislatures, grand jury sessions, pretrial proceedings in the courts, and other official meetings.

People have challenged nearly all types of exclusions in the courts as unconstitutional restrictions on the right of access to information. The courts have ruled that most of the exclusions are compatible with constitutional guarantees of free speech and press. They also have ruled, for the most part, that news professionals enjoy neither greater rights of access to information than does the general public nor, in the absence of shield laws, greater freedom to protect their access to information by refusal to disclose their sources.

The right to publish information in mass media venues is also limited. Here the public is most seriously restricted because newspeople claim the exclusive right to determine what to publicize and what to omit. The power of print media to exclude stories is nearly absolute, except for social pressures to report issues that are vital to the public. Under current rules and regulations television must grant equal access to political candidates for the same office. The fairness rules requiring exposure of opposition views and the right of rebuttal are in limbo.

Even when access to a media forum is ensured, the right to publish is not absolute. News has been suppressed because of public policy considerations, such as the need to safeguard external and internal security and the need to protect the moral standards of the community. The scope of permissible censorship has been the subject of countless inconclusive debates and conflicting court decisions in a perennial contest between legislators eager to censor objectionable messages and judges equally eager to wave the banner of First Amendment rights.

The right to publish also conflicts on many occasions with the rights of individuals to enjoy their privacy, to be protected from disclosure of damaging information, and to be safe from publicity that might interfere with a fair trial. The courts have been the main forum for weighing these conflicting claims, and the scales have tipped erratically from case to case. Two trends stand out from the haze of legal battles: The right to a fair trial generally wins over the freedom to publish, and private individuals enjoy far greater protection from publicity than do people in public life. Shifting definitions of what turns a private person into a public person have blurred this distinction, however.

When one looks at the massive restraints on the rights of access to information, the rights of access to publication channels, and the right to publish information freely, one may feel deep concern about freedom of information. Is there cause for worry? Taking a bright view, as Justice White did in a 1972 case, "the press has flourished. The existing constitutional rules have not been a serious obstacle" stopping the press from investigating wrongdoing.[62] The press as watchdog may be chilled by legal restraints, but it is not frozen into inaction. From the perspective of champions of First Amendment rights, this may be small comfort. Many current political trends, including pressures by private organizations to enforce the norms of "political correctness," point toward greater restraints and greater public tolerance for restraints, especially when social and national security are involved. Self-censorship is on the rise as well. For example, on Veterans Day 2004 many stations skipped their traditional showing of the World War II classic movie—*Saving Private Ryan*. They feared that the violence and harsh language in the film would subject them to FCC fines. Constant vigilance to deter such impairments of First Amendment rights is the price of preserving the heritage of freedom of thought and expression.

Notes

1. Freedom House, "Press Freedom Survey 2004," www.freedomhouse.org.
2. Robert F. Copple, "The Dynamics of Expression under the State Constitution," *Journalism Quarterly* 64 (spring 1987): 106–113.
3. For an analysis of how well these rights have been used, see Doris A. Graber, "Press Freedom and the General Welfare," *Political Science Quarterly* 101 (summer 1986): 257–275.
4. Justice Potter Stewart in *New York Times v. United States*, 403 U.S. 713 (1971).

5. Jerome Barron, *Freedom of the Press for Whom? The Right of Access to the Mass Media* (Bloomington: Indiana University Press, 1973).
6. *Miami Herald Publishing Company v. Tornillo*, 418 U.S. 241 (1974).
7. For a full discussion of the case, see Fred W. Friendly, *The Good Guys, the Bad Guys, and the First Amendment: Free Speech vs. Fairness in Broadcasting* (New York: Random House, 1977), 192–198.
8. *Arkansas Educational Television Commission v. Forbes*, 523 U.S. 666 (1998).
9. Stephen Labaton, "Court Rejects F.C.C. Mandate to Broadcast Political Replies," *New York Times*, October 12, 2000.
10. *Red Lion Broadcasting Co. v. Federal Communications Commission*, 395 U.S. 367 (1969).
11. Friendly, *The Good Guys*, 32–42.
12. *Muir v. Alabama Educational Television Commission*, 688 F.2d 1033 (5th Cir. 1982). First Amendment problems encountered when governments own media are discussed by William Hanks and Lemuel Schofield, "Limitations on the State as Editor in State-Owned Broadcast Stations," *Journalism Quarterly* 63 (winter 1986): 797–801. The right of public broadcasters to editorialize was upheld in *League of Women Voters v. FCC*, 731 F.2d 995 (D.C. Cir. 1984).
13. "AIDS Panel Delayed News of Treatment," *New York Times*, November 14, 1990.
14. *FCC v. WNCN Listeners Guild*, 450 U.S. 582 (1981).
15. W. Lance Bennett, Lynne A. Gressett, and William Haltom, "Repairing the News: A Case Study of the News Paradigm," *Journal of Communication* 35 (spring 1985): 50–68.
16. *Zemel v. Rusk*, 381 U.S. 1 (1965).
17. *Branzburg v. Hayes*, 408 U.S. 665 (1972).
18. *Los Angeles Police Department v. United Reporting Publishing Corporation*, 528 U.S. 32 (1999).
19. See, for instance, *Pell v. Procunier*, 417 U.S. 817 (1974); *Saxbe v. Washington Post Co.*, 417 U.S. 843 (1974); and *Houchins v. KQED*, 438 U.S. 1 (1978).
20. *Wilson v. Layne*, 526 U.S. 603 (1999).
21. The act was an amendment to the 1946 Administrative Procedure Act—5 U.S.C.A. 1002 (1946)—which provided that official records should be open to people who could demonstrate a "need to know" except for "information held confidential for good cause found" (Sec. 22). The 1966 amendment stated that disclosure should be the rule, not the exception, with the burden on government to justify the withholding of a document (5 U.S.C.A. Sec. 552 and Supp. 1, February 1975).
22. Douglas Jehl, "Clinton Revamps Policy on Secrecy of U.S. Documents," *New York Times*, April 18, 1995.
23. Neil A. Lewis, "New Policy on Declassifying Secrets Is Debated," *New York Times*, January 4, 1994.
24. *New York Times Co. v. United States*, 403 U.S. 713 (1971).
25. *United States v. Morison*, 844 F.2d 1057 (4th Cir.), *cert. denied*, 488 U.S. 908 (1988).
26. Doris A. Graber, "Terrorism, Censorship, and the 1st Amendment: In Search of Policy Guidelines," in *Framing Terrorism: The News Media, the Government, and the Public*, ed. Pippa Norris, Montague Kern, and Marion Just (New York: Routledge, 2003), 27–42.
27. John J. Lumpkin, "Lawmaker Revives Proposal for Plugging Leaks to Media," *Chicago Tribune*, August 24, 2001.

28. Doris A. Graber, *Public Sector Communication: How Organizations Manage Information* (Washington, D.C.: CQ Press, 1992), 49–61.
29. Kristina Borjesson, ed., *Into the Buzzsaw: Leading Journalists Expose the Myth of a Free Press* (Amherst, N.Y.: Prometheus, 2002).
30. William Glaberson, " 'Sixty Minutes' Case Illustrates a Trend Born of Corporate Pressure, Some Analysts Say," *New York Times,* November 17, 1995.
31. *Cox Broadcasting Corp. v. Cohn,* 420 U.S. 469 (1975).
32. *Cohen v. Cowles Media Co.,* 501 U.S. 663 (1991).
33. *Gallella v. Onassis,* 487 F.2d 986 (2d Cir. 1973).
34. *Le Mistral Inc. v. Columbia Broadcasting System,* 402 N.Y.S.2d 815 (1978).
35. *Hustler v. Falwell,* 485 U.S. 46 (1988). See also Robert E. Drechsel, "Mass Media Liability for Intentionally Inflicted Emotional Distress," *Journalism Quarterly* 62 (spring 1985): 95–99.
36. Larry J. Sabato, *Feeding Frenzy: Attack Journalism and American Politics* (New York: Free Press, 2000).
37. Linda Greenhouse, "National Enquirer Forces Trial on Invasion-of-Privacy Issue," *New York Times,* December 5, 1995.
38. Although judges often command jurors to strike improper information presented in court from their memory, they disclaim the ability to wipe out media information that jury members might have received outside the courtroom.
39. For examples of the court's reasoning, see *U.S. v. Alexandro,* 459 U.S. 835 (1982); *U.S. v. Jannotti,* 457 U.S. 1106 (1982).
40. An example is Michael K. Deaver, a Reagan White House aide indicted for perjury. In his request for a change of venue, he presented the court with 471 hostile news clips from Washington, D.C., papers.
41. *Shepherd v. Florida,* 341 U.S. 50 (1951); *Sheppard v. Maxwell,* 384 U.S. 333 (1966).
42. *Shepherd v. Florida,* at 69.
43. *Nebraska Press Association v. Stuart,* 427 U.S. 539 (1976).
44. *Richmond Newspapers v. Virginia,* 448 U.S. 555 (1980).
45. *Press-Enterprise v. Riverside County Superior Court,* 464 U.S. 501 (1984). The controversy arose because the Riverside County, California, superior court closed jury selection in a rape and murder case. The Press–Enterprise Company of Riverside sued to gain access to the court proceeding and to the relevant transcripts.
46. Alex S. Jones, "CBS Compromises on Subpoena for Videotapes of Hostage Crisis," *New York Times,* July 27, 1985.
47. Reporters Committee for Freedom of the Press, "Agents of Discovery," 2001, www.rcfp.org/agents/.
48. *Anthony Herbert v. Barry Lando and the Columbia Broadcasting System Inc.,* 441 U.S. 153 (1979).
49. Adam Liptak, "Judges Skeptical of First Amendment Protection for Reporters in C.I.A. Leak Inquiry," *New York Times,* December 9, 2004; Loren Manly and Adam Liptak, "At Leak Inquiry's Center, a Circumspect Columnist," *New York Times,* December 31, 2004.
50. *Branzburg v. Hayes,* at 699.
51. *New York Times v. Sullivan,* 376 U.S. 254 (1964), at 279–280.
52. *Gertz v. Robert Welch,* 418 U.S. 323 (1974).
53. *Time Inc. v. Firestone,* 424 U.S. 448 (1976); *Hutchinson v. Proxmire,* 443 U.S. 111 (1979); *Wolston v. Reader's Digest,* 443 U.S. 157 (1979).
54. Libel Defense Resource Center, "Press Release, February 26, 2001," www.ldrc.com/damages01.html.

55. Linda Greenhouse, "Ruling in Libel Case, High Court Says Some Opinion Isn't Protected," *New York Times,* June 22, 1990.
56. Electronic Privacy Information Center, "The USA Patriot Act," www.epic.org/ privacy/terrorism/usapatriot.
57. *Miller v. California,* 413 U.S. 5 (1973), at 15. Definition quoted in Tim Jones, "Broadcasters Get Long-Awaited Indecency Guidelines," *Chicago Tribune,* April 7, 2001.
58. See, for example, *Reno v. American Civil Liberties Union,* 521 U.S. 844 (1997). For an editorial opinion about such censorship laws see "Congress Quietly Censors the Web," *Chicago Tribune,* December 23, 2000. The fate of the Child Online Protection Act remains in limbo. See Linda Greenhouse, "Court, 5-4, Blocks a Law Regulating Internet Access," *New York Times,* June 30, 2004.
59. Stephen Labaton, "Indecency on the Air, Evolution at F.C.C.," *New York Times,* December 23, 2004.
60. *Greater New Orleans Broadcasting Association v. U.S.,* 527 U.S. 173 (1999); *44 Liquormart, Inc. v. Rhode Island,* 517 U.S. 484 (1996).
61. Lisa Guernsey, "Mainstream Sites Serve as Portals to Hate," *New York Times,* November 30, 2000.
62. *Branzburg v. Hayes,* at 699.

Readings

Carter, T. Barton, Marc A. Franklin, and Jay B. Wright. *The First Amendment and the Fifth Estate: Regulation of Electronic Mass Media.* 6th ed. New York: Foundation Press, 2003.

Carter, T. Barton, Marc A. Franklin, and Jay B. Wright. *The First Amendment and the Fourth Estate: The Law of Mass Media.* 9th ed. New York: Foundation Press, 2004.

Godwin, Mike. *Cyber Rights: Defending Free Speech in the Digital Age.* Cambridge: MIT Press, 2003.

Gunther, Richard, and Anthony Mughan. *Democracy and the Media: A Comparative Perspective.* Cambridge: Cambridge University Press, 2000.

Heins, Marjorie. *Not in Front of the Children: Indecency, Censorship, and the Innocence of Youth.* New York: Hill and Wang, 2001.

Liebman, Lance M., Paul Schwartz, and John Thorne. *Telecommunications Law.* New York: Foundation Press, 2004.

McGlone, Catherine. *New York Times v. Sullivan and the Freedom of the Press Debate: Debating Supreme Court Decisions.* Berkeley Heights, N.J.: Enslow Publishers, 2005.

Sadler, Roger L. *Electronic Media Law.* Thousand Oaks, Calif.: Sage, 2005.

Teeter, Dwight L., and Bill Loving. *Law of Mass Communications: Freedom and Control of Print and Broadcast Media.* 11th ed. New York: Foundation Press, 2004.

Tillinghast, Charles H. *American Broadcast Regulation and the First Amendment.* Ames: Iowa State University Press, 2000.

News Making and
News Reporting Routines

AMERICAN JOURNALISTS ARE WORRIED about the direction in which their profession is moving. In a 2004 nationwide survey, 61 percent of national broadcast journalists thought that the direction was wrong. So did 42 percent of print journalists. Why? The answer is that journalists believe the quality of their work is declining. They complain that the news has become shallower and is often irrelevant to the public's major concerns. All too often errors lace the news and excessive sensationalism demeans it. Many journalists even complain that pervasive pressures from advertisers and business owners, who want their values and views to prevail, are compromising the integrity of news reporting.

How justified are these worries? Are the pessimists right that mass-mediated news is deteriorating, or is the situation far more optimistic, as many journalists believe, especially when they work locally in communities throughout the country? In this chapter we provide insights on these issues by focusing on reporters and their work under normal circumstances. In the next chapter we will address news making during crisis.

Profile Sketch of U.S. Journalists

How do journalists decide which information to report as "news" and how to shape it into news stories? These questions can be answered from three theoretical perspectives. Personality theory explains professional behavior in terms of personality and social background factors. Organization theory focuses on the impact of organizational goals and pressures on the behavior of members of news production organizations. Role theory maintains that stories will vary depending on the professional role conceptions that media personnel adopt. For instance, journalists who see themselves as impartial reporters of the news will behave differently from those who see themselves as partisan reformers.

Personality and Social Background Factors

What are some of the personality and background factors that influence the substance and shape of news? Data collected by the Pew Research Center for the People and the Press for its study of "How Journalists see Journalism in 2004" help answer this question. The findings are based on telephone and online interviews conducted in 2004 with 547 randomly selected print and broadcast journalists in the United States working for daily and weekly newspapers, radio and television stations, and news services and magazines.[1]

The social profile of newspeople resembles the profile of other professionals in the United States. Eighty-three percent of the respondents in the Pew study were white, 67 percent were male, and 94 percent had graduated from college, though many did not major in journalism. Education appears to be the single most important background characteristic that shapes newspeople's general philosophy of reporting. Like most people with a social science or humanities degree, journalists tend to be socially more liberal than the general population and to have a keener sense of social responsibility.

Journalists are less likely than the general population to describe themselves as conservative. In 2004, 7 percent of national journalists (12 percent at the local level) professed to conservative leanings compared to 33 percent of the general public. Roughly one third claimed to be liberal and more than half called themselves moderate.[2] The overall tone of stories selected is in tune with the political orientations of media personnel, albeit leaning a bit more toward the middle of the political spectrum. Economic and social liberalism prevails, especially in the most prominent media organizations. So does a preference for an internationalist foreign policy, caution about military intervention, and some suspicion about the ethics of established large institutions, particularly big business and big government. However, despite perennial complaints about partisan bias in election campaign coverage, most studies show that media personnel treat the major parties fairly.[3] Anticipation of scrutiny and criticism encourage such evenhandedness. The extent to which biased reporting based on party preferences is a problem in U.S. media is not fully known, because scholars have rarely investigated media bias outside the election context.[4]

Minority journalists and women present a slightly different demographic profile. For example, African American, Hispanic, and Asian journalists are more likely to be women. Overall, the proportion of nonwhite journalists has risen, but the proportion of women has remained steady at roughly one-third of the total. It is lowest in the wire services and television and highest in weekly newspapers and news magazines. By contrast, nonwhite males have their highest representation in radio and television and their lowest representation in weekly newspapers. Women and minority males are much more likely to call themselves Democrats than are male white journalists, and they are less likely to claim to be independents. Overall, nonwhites constitute a far smaller proportion of the journalism workforce than one might expect, given their growing numbers in the U.S. population.

Bloggers are a new addition to the journalism workforce, and their demographics, training, and biases remain somewhat of a mystery. Bloggers are people who have publicly accessible Web sites where they report their thoughts—more or less continuously—on topics that interest them. In fact, "blog" messages (a contraction for Web-log) are posted on the Web every seven-and-a-half seconds. Whether bloggers deserve to be called part of the journalism workforce has become an issue, because journalists are increasingly incorporating information from blogs into regular news stories. In 2004, for example, journalists publicized blogs covering the presidential campaign and election, the Florida hurricanes, and the Asian tsunami. Bloggers broke the story about Senate Majority Leader Trent Lott's racist remarks that later forced his resignation. A blogger first published photographs of a planeload of coffins returning U.S. war dead that strengthened opposition to the war in Iraq at a time when official policy called for suppressing such graphic footage. Even when the mainstream press does not pick up blogs, they may circulate widely. A law professor at the University of California at Los Angeles, for example, claims that his blogs attract more than 10,000 readers every day.[5] And the Pew Internet and American Life Project estimates that by the end of 2004 the audience for blogs had grown to a respectable 32 million viewers.[6]

Is it really important to know who the bloggers are? What effect do demographic characteristics have on the news product? The evidence is inconclusive, making it debatable whether adequate coverage of the nation's problems requires media organizations that are a microcosm of the larger society.[7] If demographically distinct groups are uniquely qualified to assess their own needs, then racial, ethnic, and gender underrepresentation in the media is harmful. Proponents of facsimile representation point out that most general media emphasize established white middle-class groups and values while neglecting the concerns of minorities and poor people. The media also stress urban rather than rural affairs and focus heavily on male-dominated sports. These patterns suggest that news output does reflect reporters' backgrounds and interests. But it may also suggest that news patterns are designed to cater to the tastes of the kinds of audiences that advertisers find most attractive.[8] Reporters' unique life experiences are also important in shaping their stories. In fact, idiosyncratic factors explain why newspeople who have similar backgrounds will nonetheless focus on different stories or will give a different emphasis to the same news story or entertainment plot. For instance, Washington, D.C.–based reporters routinely use friendships with well-connected government officials to get important scoops. As a result of close personal ties with these officials, the reporters are apt to become captives of their Beltway sources' perspectives on the world. In the end, personality factors and role demands intertwine with organizational factors to set the broad boundaries of what is acceptable news.

Organizational Factors

Colleagues and settings strongly influence newspeople. Every news organization has its own internal power structure that develops from the interaction of owners, journalists, news sources, audiences, advertisers, and government authorities. In most news organizations today, the ideology of working journalists is slightly to the left of middle America, quite similar to that of liberal Democrats. Still, most journalists support the basic tenets of the current political and social system.

By and large, print and broadcast journalists believe that many of the structural changes in the news business in the twenty-first century have harmed the quality of journalism. This includes the incorporation of media enterprises within large corporate entities (discussed in Chapter 2), which has increased the emphasis on high profits and led to cutbacks in staff and other resources for gathering news. Accordingly, collection of serious news has suffered. The pressure to produce news around the clock with diminished resources accounts for bouts of sloppy, error-prone reporting. Not all organizational changes have been harmful, however. For example, most journalists say that the Internet has made journalism better because it is an excellent source of information easily available to anybody with a computer. Besides, knowing that the accuracy of news reports can be checked readily on the Web by news consumers has forced reporters to be more circumspect in their reports.

According to journalists, poor quality of news content and poor writing are the most serious threats to the profession, along with loss of audiences and decreasing profits (Table 4-1). Technological changes and the general business environment also pose threats, as do loss of credibility

TABLE 4-1   The State of Journalism: Most Important Problems Facing Reporters
(in percentages)

	National		Local		
Problem	Print	Broadcast	Print	Broadcast	Internet
Quality of coverage	32	51	30	37	32
Business pressures	31	28	36	33	32
Credibility	39	15	33	12	19
Media environment	15	14	6	9	27
Ethics	6	4	6	5	4

SOURCE: Adapted from Pew Research Center for the People and the Press, http://people-press.org/reports/display.php3?ReportID=214.

NOTE: Based on a survey of 547 national and local print, broadcast, and Internet journalists. Respondents were drawn from national and local media samples representing a cross-section of news organizations and their personnel. They were interviewed between March 10 and April 20, 2004. Percentages add up to more than 100 percent because respondents were able to answer "yes" to more than one question.

and concerns about ethical lapses. Print and broadcast journalists differ in their appraisal of the health of the profession, as do reporters working in national media and local media. Variations in conditions within each sector rather than variations in judgments are the explanation.

Organizational pressures begin to operate even before the job starts. Most journalists join news organizations and remain with them only if they share the organization's basic philosophy. To win advancement, professional recognition, and approval from their colleagues, reporters learn quickly which types of stories are acceptable to their editors and colleagues. Relationships with colleagues are particularly important within large, prominent news enterprises in which newspeople receive their main social and professional support from coworkers rather than from the community at large.[9] The opposite holds true in small towns, where newspeople often interact freely with community leaders and receive their support.

Despite the substantial evidence of media influence on U.S. politics, most newspeople deny that they should be concerned about the real-life impact of their stories. Journalists insist routinely and appropriately that government and business must take responsibility for the intended and unintended consequences of their actions. Yet journalists reject responsibility for the consequences of their own work even while claiming to subscribe to social responsibility journalism. Journalists commonly argue that journalism is a craft and not a profession. Eschewing candor to protect their flanks, they allege that they simply report the news found in the marketplace—nothing more.

Role Models

Although editors and reporters throughout the country take cues and follow interpretations about stories from the eastern media elite—the *New York Times, Wall Street Journal,* and *Washington Post*—these journalists shape their basic news policies according to their own views about the role that media should play in society. The effects of the social responsibility role compared with other stances were discussed in Chapter 1. News stories also vary depending on whether newspeople see themselves largely as objective observers who must present facts and diverse views voiced by others or as interpreters who must supply meanings and evaluations.

Reporters differ widely on that score in western democracies. Divisions are especially sharp among proponents of traditional journalism and advocates for civic or public journalism.[10] Civic journalism fans believe that reporters must tailor the news so that it not only informs citizens about important happenings but also helps them to take collective action to resolve problems.[11] Beyond turning reporters into interpreters of what the news means or should mean, this approach also turns them consciously into participants in the political process. Although this may be laudable in many instances, civic journalism sacrifices journalists' role as neutral observers. When journalists are asked about the core values of their calling, most acknowledge neutrality as a core value that serves their audience's interests. Other highly rated values are acting as the public's watchdog over government, supplying news needed for citizenship duties, and analyzing complex problems to help the public understand them.[12] Over the past decade journalists have become less concerned about getting the news out quickly, serving all segments of the public, and entertaining the audience. Journalists in traditional media feel that many of the mushrooming new media serve these goals.

What do journalists identify as "news"?[13] Old-time journalists would say that it is news when a man bites a dog, but not when a dog bites a man. Why not? U.S. journalists see it as their role to cover exceptional events rather than ordinary ones. What seems exceptional depends on the conditions within a particular society at a particular point in time. It also depends on journalists' perception of which of the many extraordinary events that surround them is likely to interest their audiences and deserves and needs coverage. That is what makes news stories a human creation rather than a natural event that journalists merely describe. The fact that the decision of what is news hinges on multiple subjective judgments explains why there is much disagreement about what ought to be news on a given day. But it also explains the great deal of uniformity of story types in U.S. print and electronic media.

Gatekeeping

A small number of journalists have final control over story choices. They are often called *gatekeepers* and include wire service reporters, Web editors and other reporters who initially choose stories, the editors who assign the reporters and accept or reject what they submit, disc jockeys at radio stations who present five-minute news breaks, and television program executives. In general, fewer than twenty-five people within a large newspaper or television organization are involved in the final decision of what news to use.

These few, particularly those who make news choices for nationwide audiences, wield a tremendous amount of political power because their choices determine what will be widely available as "news." This is why in public opinion polls that rank the political influence of U.S. institutions, the news media routinely rank among the top ten. When pollsters asked a national sample of Americans which telephone call the president should answer first if a topnotch editor, business leader, church figure, and educational leader called simultaneously, most chose the newspaper editor.[14] As discussed in Chapter 1, news stories influence the issues about which ordinary people as well as political elites think.[15] Of course, media gatekeepers are not entirely free in their story choices. Coverage of major events, such as wars, assassinations, and airline hijackings, is almost mandatory. Other events can be included or omitted at will, within the limits set by news conventions. On an average evening, somewhat more than half of the stories on each major television network represent unique choices. The figures are slightly lower for print media.

Gatekeepers also select the sources through whose eyes the public views the world. Government officials are the main source of most political stories reported by the wire services and national and local media (Table 4-2). This gives public officials an excellent chance to influence the slant of the news. However, when highly controversial issues are at stake, gatekeepers usually turn to unofficial sources as well.[16] Basing the news on a narrow spectrum of sources can lead to biased reporting. Reporters may give the widest publicity to the views of "celebrity" authorities in tangentially related fields and ignore important specialists.

A study of sources used for stories about welfare reform, consumer issues, the environment, and nuclear energy concluded that journalists favor sources that reflect their own inclinations.

> On welfare reform, liberal sources predominate over conservative ones. On consumer issues they look to Ralph Nader, the public interest movement, and liberal activist groups. On pollution and the environment, they select activist

TABLE 4-2   Sources of Front-Page News Stories (in percentages)

Source	*Times/ Post* staff stories	*Tribune* staff stories	*Chronicle* staff stories	Wire services staff stories	Total stories
Government officials	51	49	48	60	52
U.S.	(32)	(23)	(13)	(34)	(29)
State	(6)	(5)	(16)	(2)	(6)
Local	(5)	(12)	(17)	(1)	(7)
Foreign	(9)	(10)	(2)	(23)	(10)
Group-linked person[a]	29	27	30	15	27
Private person	14	20	17	7	14
Foreign person	4	4	3	17	5
Other	2	1	2	1	1

SOURCE: Author's research.

NOTE: Based on content analysis of 1,151 news stories attributed to staff or wire services writers and published in the *New York Times, Washington Post, Chicago Tribune,* and *San Francisco Chronicle.* Data drawn from constructed week analysis from June 1, 2003, to June 1, 2004. Totals may not add up to 100 percent due to rounding.

[a] "Group-linked" persons are members of a group but are not necessarily official spokespersons for the group. This includes experts, medical staff, nonprofit organizations, and sources speaking on behalf of a private company.

environmental groups and, once again, liberal leaders. On nuclear energy, antinuclear sources are the most popular.   Journalists by no means depend exclusively on liberal viewpoints. They cite a mixture of public and private, partisan and nonpartisan, liberal and conservative sources. But the liberal side consistently outweighs the conservative.[17]

Sources who have gained recognition as "experts" through media publicity tend to be used over and over again while other, less publicized, sources are neglected.

When multiple media cover the same story, as happens routinely, they often use sources representing different elites. When that happens, the thrust of the story may vary widely even though the underlying facts are the same. For example, when researchers looked at 167 stories about a major stock market crash in 1987, they found that the causes and effects of the crash were assessed in quite diverse fashion by the *CBS Evening News, Newsweek,* the *New York Times,* and the *Wall Street Journal.* The three print media had relied most heavily on experts from the financial sector as primary sources, drawing 38, 52, and 65 percent of their sources, respectively, from this sector. Government sources and academics took second and third place but appeared far less frequently. For CBS, government sources came first, followed by sources from the business sector and the financial sector. CBS was also unique in drawing heavily (44 percent) on unnamed sources.[18]

The use of different sources led to disparate appraisals of the causes of the crash and hence different impressions about needed remedies. In *Newsweek* the national debt and presidential policies were the chief causes; in the *New York Times* it was the debt and computerized trading. *Wall Street Journal* sources emphasized computerized trading and the foreign trade deficit. On the *CBS Evening News,* the national debt was the chief villain, with twice the emphasis it had received in other sources. Presidential policies and partisan politics were other important causes. When it came to estimating the effects of the crash, all but the *Wall Street Journal* mentioned improved cooperation between president and Congress as a likely outcome. Beyond that, speculations about probable effects diverged widely, presenting media audiences with clashing images about the country's economic problems.

Highly respected national newscasters also are extraordinarily influential in putting their versions of news events on the political agenda. By singling out news events for positive or negative commentary, these media figures may sway public and official opinions. At the turn of the century, if anchors Peter Jennings, Tom Brokaw, or Dan Rather declared that health care legislation would lower the quality of medical care or that a U.S. military presence along the coast of China would risk war, popular support for these policies was likely to plunge.[19] A sixty-second verbal barrage on the evening news or a few embarrassing questions can destroy programs, politicians, and the reputations of major organizations. But in the age of Internet and cable television, the power of these newscasters is waning (Box 4-1).

Because Americans like to view their media as effective guardians of the public interest, society usually focuses on the positive consequences of news story choices. Negative or questionable consequences should not be overlooked, however. For example, Peter Braestrup, chief of the Saigon bureau of the *Washington Post* during the Vietnam War, argued in his book *Big Story* that unwise story choices and interpretations about the conduct of the war misled the public and government officials.[20] Similarly, when it became clear in 2004 that reports about Iraq's possession of weapons of mass destruction had been false, the *New York Times* and *Washington Post* assumed some of the blame for the consequences. Better reporting, they argued, could have aborted the costly war against Iraq.[21]

General Factors in News Selection

As mentioned earlier, what becomes news depends in part on the demographics, training, personality, and professional socialization of news

BOX 4-1
When Giants Fall

History is full of tales about giants in the world of politics, the arts, the sciences. Alexander the Great comes to mind, as do Michelangelo and Einstein. But with depressing regularity, eras of giants always come to an ignominious end. Lilliputians tie down sleeping Gullivers so they can move no longer. So it seems to be with the era of the giant news anchors in U.S. network television. When the clock rang in the twenty-first century, just three aging giants were left—Tom Brokaw, Dan Rather, and Peter Jennings. No progeny of potentially equal stature stood in the wings. The declining significance of network news, as its audiences dwindled and its resources were slashed, and the wounds from network scandals, make it unlikely that we will ever again see an age of giant anchors in broadcast journalism.

Tom Brokaw retired at the end of 2004 after twenty-one years in the anchor chair. Dan Rather stepped down in the spring of 2005, twenty-four years after succeeding legendary anchor Walter Cronkite. Pundits were predicting that Peter Jennings's reign as anchor was coming to an end in an era when television was looking for young faces to attract young viewers, rather than aging, and often ailing, plainspoken super-reporters.

Dan Rather's retirement seemed particularly jarring because it happened in the wake of a scandal that scarred his image. In the middle of a hotly fought presidential election, *CBS Evening News* and *60 Minutes* had broadcast a story that impugned the character of incumbent president George Bush, who was running for reelection. The story, based on documents that could never be authenticated, alleged that Bush had used political connections to get a lieutenant's commission in the National Guard and had subsequently failed to carry out his duties but, thanks to his mentors, had escaped the usual penalties for such behavior.

A panel charged with investigating how the network produced, edited, and broadcast this flimsy story concluded that Rather and his team had violated multiple journalism norms. Their failures had included sloppy fact-checking, uncritical reliance on obviously biased sources, and slanted presentation of interview contents. The panel did

(Box continues, next page)

absolve Rather of the charge that his personal dislike of President Bush had fueled the report, but there are many doubters on that score.

The broader implications of the case aroused much commentary. Some believed that the already low credibility of journalists had suffered a death blow that would kill network television news before long. Others saw the accusation of overt political bias in the news as just another example of the political polarization that is sapping civility in political discourse throughout the nation. Even more ominous, some viewed the incident as further evidence of a society riddled with corruption and self-seeking among its leaders in politics, the press, and even religion.

Be that as it may. One thing is clear, another set of giants has fallen and with it the power of network television to unify and lead public opinion. Round-the-clock cable television may partly fill the void, or perhaps the growing horde of bloggers or some new venue, as yet unrecognized, will fill it. The crystal ball is cloudy, and clearing seems far away. We do know what we have lost, but we cannot yet assess the magnitude of the consequences or the merits of what is to come.

personnel. In the United States this means, by and large, upwardly mobile, well-educated white males whose political views are liberal and who subscribe in ever larger numbers to the tenets of social responsibility journalism (discussed in Chapter 2). News selection also hinges on norms within a news organization and how newspeople conceptualize their professional roles, plus pressure from internal and external competition.

Within each news organization, reporters and editors compete for time, space, and prominence of position for their stories. News organizations also compete with each other for audience attention, for advertisers, and, in the case of the networks, for affiliates. If one station or network has a popular program, others often will copy the format and try to place an equally attractive program into a parallel time slot to capture their competitor's audiences and advertisers. Likewise, papers may feel compelled to carry stories simply because another medium in the same market has carried them.

News personnel operate within the broad political context of their societies in general and their circulation communities in particular. Most have internalized these contexts so that they become the frame of reference for the personnel. As media scholar George Gerbner observed long ago, there is "no fundamentally nonideological, apolitical, nonpartisan news gathering and reporting system." [22] For example, if a reporter's political context demands favorable images of religious leaders, news and entertainment will reflect this outlook. That used to be the case in the United States until the twenty-first century, when multiple stories unveiled sexual misconduct by priests.[23]

Political pressures also leave their mark. Media personnel depend on political leaders for information and are therefore vulnerable to manipulation by them. Powerful elites flood the media with self-serving stories that are often hard to resist. Intensive, frequent contacts between journalists and leaders and the desire to keep associations cordial may lead to cozy relationships that hamper critical detachment. Wooing reporters to elicit favorable media coverage is the mark of the astute politician. Reporters often succumb to the blandishments of politicians for fear of alienating powerful and important news sources.

Economic pressures are even more potent than political pressures in molding news and entertainment. Newspapers and magazines need to earn profits. Except for publications that are subsidized by individual or group sponsors, media enterprises must raise most of their income from subscriptions and advertisers. Therefore, media offerings must appeal to large numbers of subscribers or potential customers for the products that advertisers sell. This means that news organizations must direct their programs and stories either to general audiences in the prime consumption years of life (roughly ages twenty-five to forty-five) or to selected special audiences that are key targets for particular advertiser appeals. For example, toothpaste, laundry detergent, and breakfast cereals are best marketed to the huge nationwide audiences who watch the regular nighttime situation comedies or detective stories; expensive cameras, fancy foreign sports cars, and raft trips down the Amazon are most likely to find customers among a select few. Advertisers for such products are attracted to journals with well-to-do subscribers such as *National Geographic* or the *Wall Street Journal,* as well as to specialized cable channels and television documentaries.

Producers of broadcasts directed to nationwide audiences try to maintain a smooth flow of appealing programs throughout the prime evening hours to keep audiences from switching channels. As long as a program is unobjectionable, most audiences will remain with the station. Such considerations deter producers from mixing serious, audience-losing programs with light entertainment in prime time. The fear of losing the audience for an entire evening has also been a major reason for opposing the expansion of the nightly network news to a full hour.

The desire to keep audiences watching a particular station even affects the format of news and public service programs. Stations select newscasters for their physical attractiveness. The stations encourage informal banter, and nearly every newscast contains some fascinating bits of trivia or a touching yet inconsequential human-interest story. The news becomes "infotainment"—a marriage of information and entertainment values. Networks avoid complicated stories for fear of confusing audiences, just as they slight "dull" economic news irrespective of importance. However, journalists often underestimate the public's tastes for serious presentations, as shown by the popularity of the televised congressional debates about U.S. involvement in the Persian Gulf War in 1991 and by the massive audiences for presidential addresses.

Criteria for Choosing Specific Stories

In addition to deciding what is publishable news, gatekeepers must choose particular news items to include in their mix of offerings. The motto of the *New York Times,* "All the News That's Fit to Print," is an impossible myth; there is far more publishable news available than any daily news medium can possibly use. Gatekeepers also must decide how they want to frame each item so that it carries a particular message. For instance, when journalists cast stories about controversial policies like health care reform as games of strategy, as they are wont to do, the policy issues blur and lose importance.[24] In 1993 and 1994, for example, 67 percent of the health news coverage was framed as political gaming, with stories focusing on who was winning and losing supporters for their favorite policy. Only 25 percent of the stories addressed substantive issues in health care reform. When political scientist Regina Lawrence studied use of the game frame in the 1996 debate about welfare reform, she discovered that use of the frame hinged on the context. When the story was linked to elections or political battles in Washington, D.C., the game frame was prevalent. That was not the case when the story was linked to state policies or issues concerning implementation of reforms.[25]

The criteria newspeople use in story selection relate primarily to audience appeal rather than to the political significance of stories, their educational value, their broad social purposes, or the reporter's own political views. This holds particularly true for television, where viewer numbers, demographic characteristics, and viewer attitudes are constantly monitored by rating services, such as A.C. Nielsen and the American Research Bureau (ARB). For both radio and television, advertising rates are based on audience size. An increase in audience size of just 1 percent can mean millions of dollars in additional advertising income. Newspaper advertising rates are also based on paid circulation, which is monitored by an independent agency, the Audit Bureau of Circulation. News outlets rarely ask audiences if they would prefer different programs to the existing fare. The fact that people watch or listen to or purchase papers in large numbers is assumed to prove that they like what they get.

The emphasis on audience appeal and the economic pressures that mandate it need to be kept in mind when evaluating the totality of media output. These factors explain why the amounts and kinds of coverage of important issues often are not commensurate with their significance in the real world at the time of publication. For instance, television news coverage of crime reached record highs in 1995 because journalists believed that the public wanted extensive coverage of the O.J. Simpson murder trial and several other sensational cases. The combined story totals for health issues, the economy, and federal budget talks fell substantially below crime story totals, leaving the impression that these stories mattered less than the crime sagas.[26] Stories like the Clinton sex scandals, the death of Britain's Princess Diana, or the custody fight over Cuban child refugee Elian Gonzalez received inordinate amounts of coverage at the expense of more significant events. News also projects distorted images when peaks in coverage of events like urban riots or terrorist attacks do not match peaks in actual happenings. Peaks in news about street crime typically do not coincide with peaks in street crime as recorded by police.[27]

Discrepancies between the frequency of newsworthy events and their coverage are especially well illustrated by crime news reporting (Table 4-3). In 2002, 49 percent of the local crime stories reported by the *Chicago Tribune* dealt with murder and 17 percent with sexual assaults. These crimes constituted less than 2 percent of all crimes recorded in police statistics. Another 34 percent of the *Tribune* stories covered less serious crimes like assault, robbery, burglary, theft, and arson. These crimes constituted 98 percent in the official record.[28] Even considering that murder and sexual assaults are more serious than these other crimes, the huge discrepancy in coverage seems unwarranted.

Newspeople use five criteria for choosing news stories. First, stories must picture conditions that could have a strong impact on readers or listeners. Stories about health hazards, consumer fraud, or pensions for the elderly influence people more than do unfamiliar happenings with which they cannot identify. To make stories attractive, newspeople commonly present them as events that happened to ordinary people. Inflation news becomes the story of the housewife at the supermarket; foreign competition becomes the story of laid-off workers in a local textile plant. In the process of personalization, the broader political significance of the story is often lost, and the news is trivialized.[29]

Violence, conflict, disaster, or scandal is the second criterion of newsworthiness. Wars, murders, strikes, earthquakes, accidents, or sex scandals involving prominent people are the kinds of things that excite audiences.

TABLE 4-3   Police versus Newspaper Crime Reports in Chicago, 2002

Crime	Police reports of Chicago crime		Tribune reports of Chicago crime		Tribune reports of all crime		Tribune reports of crime outside Chicago	
Murder[a]	651	(0.3%)	74	(48.6%)	93	(43.6%)	167	(45.7%)
Sexual assault	2,024	(1.0%)	26	(17.1%)	60	(16.4%)	34	(15.9%)
Assault[b]	22,905	(11.8%)	32	(21.1%)	73	(20.0%)	41	(19.2%)
Theft/robbery/burglary/arson[c]	167,725	(86.8%)	20	(13.2%)	65	(17.9%)	45	(21.3%)
Total	193,305	(100.0%)	152	(100.0%)	365	(100.0%)	213	(100.0%)

SOURCE: Compiled from police crime reports and *Chicago Tribune* index 2002.

[a]Murder includes manslaughter, assassination, mass murders, and serial murders.
[b]Assault includes aggravated assault and aggravated battery.
[c]Theft includes motor vehicle theft.

In fact, inexpensive mass newspapers became viable business ventures in the United States only when the publishers of the *New York Sun* discovered in 1833 that papers filled with breezy crime and sex stories far outsold their more staid competitors. Mass sales permitted sharp price reductions and led to the birth of the "penny press." People remember dramatic behavior better than they recall the more standard fare. A 1987 story of a toddler rescued from a well has become one of the best-remembered events of recent decades. Other widely memorable events include the O.J. Simpson murder trial that started in 1994, the Elian Gonzalez custody case in 2000, and the 2004 Abu Ghraib prisoner abuse cases.

A third element of newsworthiness is familiarity. News is attractive if it pertains to well-known people or involves familiar situations of concern to many. This is why newspeople try to cast unfamiliar situations, such as mass famines in Africa, into more familiar stories of individual babies dying from malnutrition. The amazing amount of detail that people can retain about the powerful and famous demonstrates that the public is keenly interested in celebrities. More than four decades after the assassination of President Kennedy in 1963, many Americans still remember details of the funeral ceremony, as well as where they were when they heard the news of the killing. The sense of personal grief and loss has lingered, bridging the gap between the average person's private and public worlds. People value the feeling of personal intimacy that comes from knowing details of a famous person's life. People harbor somewhat similar feelings even toward the cast members of soap operas and reality dramas. People often adopt television stars as part of their families. They avidly follow the trials and tribulations of these people and may even try to model themselves after them.

Proximity is the fourth element of newsworthiness. Strong preference for local news signifies that people are most interested in what happens near them. Next to news about crime and health, people pay most attention to local news, far ahead of news about national and international affairs.[30] Local media flourish because they concentrate on events close to home; these outlets use roughly 75 percent of their space for local stories. Nonetheless, the public receives so much news from Washington, D.C., and a few major metropolitan areas that these cities and their newsmakers have become familiar to the nation. This, in a sense, makes such occurrences "local" in what media analyst Marshall McLuhan has called the "global village" created by television.

The fifth element is that news should be timely and novel. It must be something that has just occurred and is out of the ordinary, either in the sense that it does not happen all the time—such as the regular departure of airplanes or the daily opening of grocery stores—or in the sense that it is not part of people's everyday lives.

Among these five basic criteria, conflict, proximity, and timeliness are most important, judging from analyses of actual news choices. A story's long-range significance is a lesser concern. It does play a part, however, when major events occur, like national elections, the death of a well-known leader, or a calamitous natural disaster. Nevertheless, news makers select and frame most stories primarily to satisfy the five criteria.

Gathering the News

News organizations establish regular listening posts, or "beats," in places where events of interest to the public are most likely to occur. In the United States, beats at the centers of government cover political executives, legislative bodies, court systems, and international organizations. Places in which deviant behaviors are most apt to be reported, such as police stations and hospitals, are monitored. Fluctuations in economic trends are recorded at stock and commodity markets and at institutions designed to check the pulse of the nation's business. Some beats, such as health or education, are functionally defined. Reporters assigned to them generally cover a wider array of institutions on a less regular schedule than is true of the more usual beats.

Stories emanating from the traditional beats at the national level, such as the White House, Capitol, or Pentagon, have an excellent chance of publication, either because of their intrinsic significance, the prominence of their sources, or simply because they have been produced by beat reporters on the regular payroll. In the *New York Times* or *Washington Post,* for example, stories from regularly covered beats outnumber other stories two to one and capture the bulk of front-page headlines.[31]

All major media monitor similar beats. Consequently, overall news patterns—the types of stories that are covered—are relatively uniform throughout the country and change in tandem. For instance, there has been a shift away from hard news, if one defines hard news as "breaking events involving top leaders, major issues, or significant disruptions in the routines of daily life, such as an earthquake or airline disasters."[32] The trend has been toward softer news and features. Table 4-4 documents the variations in prominence of news topics by news venue. Notable differences include the dearth of foreign affairs coverage in nonelite newspapers and local news and the lack of news about government operations in the morning network news shows and local news. The heavy emphasis on crime news in the morning news and local news is also notable, as is the universal neglect of news about science and technology.

Thanks to more available space, newspapers carry more nonpolitical news. In fact, it is remarkable that they devote nearly half of the newshole—

TABLE 4-4 Frequency of News Topic Mentions, January 8–October 6, 2003

Topic	Print[a] general	Print elite front	Network a.m. TV[b]	Network p.m. TV	PBS *News Hour*	Cable news[c]	Local news[d]
Government	21	26	8	26	24	29	10
Foreign affairs/military	8	21	21	21	39	24	5
Domestic affairs	19	22	10	22	11	6	14
Crime	7	7	18	7	2	11	24
Business	4	6	2	6	11	3	7
Celebrities/entertainment	8	1	11	1	1	7	7
Lifestyle	23	8	14	8	3	9	10
Science	2	3	2	3	3	1	4
Accidents/disasters	3	4	11	4	4	10	12
Other	4	2	3	2	2	3	6

SOURCE: Adapted from Project of Excellence in Journalism, "The State of the News Media, 2004," www.stateofthenewsmedia.org.

[a] Print data in the "general" category are based on content analysis of 5,867 articles in sixteen randomly chosen newspapers of various circulation sizes. Twenty-eight sampling dates were randomly chosen from January 8 to October 6, 2003. Samples were taken from the front page, the metro page, and the lifestyle pages. In the "print elite front" category, data are based on the front pages of the largest circulation papers only.

[b] Network television news data are based on content analysis of 2,000 stories on weekday morning and evening newscasts on all three networks plus the *NewsHour* on PBS. One hundred and ten hours of news programming were analyzed, spread over twenty days.

[c] Cable television data are based on 5,570 story segments aired on five sample days on CNN, Fox News, and MSNBC. For each sample day, sixteen hours of news programming were examined for each venue.

[d] Local news data are based on program analyses of 154 stations from 1998 to 2002. Coding categories do not precisely match those used for the other venues but are reasonably comparable. The domestic affairs category combines "social" issues and "health/consumer" issues.

the space available for news stories, rather than advertising and announce-ments—to nonpolitical stories. Overall, readers of elite newspapers and viewers of evening television news on the networks, cable, or public television receive an ample supply of diverse political news. Readers of nonelite newspapers and viewers of the morning news do less well, and viewers of local news trail with less than a third of offerings covering hard news topics. Unfortunately, these venues attract the largest and youngest audiences.

News organizations, including the giants in the business, cannot afford to have full teams of reporters and camera crews dispersed across the country. In fact, economic declines have forced them to contract their bases. Even in good times, national networks generally station teams in only half a dozen cities where the equipment, support staff, and news personnel are good. Locations are not selected with an eye to covering all parts of the nation equally well or to providing diverse settings. Chance thus determines which locations receive coverage for routine stories and which do not.

Walter Lippmann once said that the press is like "the beam of a searchlight that moves restlessly about, bringing one episode and then another out of the darkness into vision. Men cannot do the work of the world by this light alone. They cannot govern society by episodes, incidents, and eruptions." [33] The extremely uneven, often sparse, coverage of news about the states is an example. Table 4-5 shows the percentage of network news stories devoted to individual U.S. states in broadcasts monitored from September 2003 to August 2004. The table also reports each state's population as a rough measure of its political significance. Fourteen states were covered by fewer than twenty-five stories annually and another thirteen by no more than fifty. Such sparse coverage by network television denies these states a national audience. At the other end of the spectrum, events in nine states and the District of Columbia were detailed in 101–556 stories. In presidential election years the most populous states and states with special political significance receive the lion's share of coverage.

The distribution of picture coverage is equally uneven. Most pictures are taken in East Coast cities, such as Washington, D.C., and New York, with a sprinkling of pictures from Chicago and Los Angeles. Of course, reporters will cover special events anywhere in the country. Every network reports presidential election debates, wherever they are held, and routinely follows presidential travels, whether the destination is tiny Hope, Arkansas, President Clinton's hometown, or the Great Wall of China. States receive exceptional coverage when major news happens there. Newsworthy events in remote sites are most likely to be covered if they involve prominent people and are scheduled in advance so that news venues can plan to have media crews available.

TABLE 4-5   Network Coverage of State News, September 2003–August 2004

Annual number of stories	States		Percentage of mentions	Percentage of population
24	Alaska	Montana	5.0	7.5
	Arkansas	Nebraska		
	Delaware	North Dakota		
	Hawaii	Rhode Island		
	Idaho	Vermont		
	Indiana	West Virginia		
	Maine	Wyoming		
25–50	Alabama	Nevada	11.7	15.4
	Connecticut	New Mexico		
	Kansas	Oklahoma		
	Kentucky	Oregon		
	Louisiana	South Dakota		
	Minnesota	Utah		
	Missouri			
51–100	Arizona	New Jersey	26.6	31.6
	Georgia	North Carolina		
	Illinois	South Carolina		
	Maryland	Tennessee		
	Massachusetts	Washington		
	Michigan	Wisconsin		
	Mississippi			
	New Hampshire			
101–150	Colorado	Virginia	12.2	9.4
	Iowa			
	Pennsylvania			
151–556	California	Texas	44.5	36.1
	Florida	Washington, D.C		
	New York			
	Ohio			

SOURCE: Data compiled from the Vanderbilt Television News Archive. Population totals based on electoral vote allocation for the 2004 presidential election.

NOTE: N = 4,117 mentions in stories.

Prior planning is even important for more accessible events. News organizations need time to allocate reporters and camera crews and edit pictures and stories. The need to plan ahead leads to an emphasis on more predictable events, such as formal visits by dignitaries, legislative hearings, or executive press conferences. The development of portable camera equipment to produce videotapes that can be broadcast with little further processing has greatly eased—though not eliminated—this problem. "Spot news" can now be filmed and broadcast rapidly, often via satellite transmission. This is only one of hundreds of examples of the profound impact of technology on the content of news.

News Production Constraints

Many news selection criteria reflect the pressure to edit and publish news rapidly. That is why pseudo-events—events created to generate press coverage—constitute more than half of all television news stories. Reporters attend events like bridge dedications or county fairs because it is an easy and quick way to get fresh story material. Politicians love such photo opportunities. When access to a newsworthy event is difficult, reporters resort to interviews with on-scene observers or ever-available "experts" anywhere in the country eager to discuss the situation. Since interviews are a comparatively cheap way to collect story material, they have become increasingly common in an era of strained resources.

Once stories reach media news offices, editors must make selections quickly. Ben Bagdikian, a former *Washington Post* editor, in a classic study of gatekeeping at eight newspapers, found that editors usually sift and choose stories on the spot.[34] They do not assemble and carefully balance them with an eye to the overall effects of a particular issue of the paper. The typical newspaper editor is able to scan and discard individual stories in seconds. At such speeds, there is no time to reflect or to weigh the merits or intrinsic importance of one story over another. If the editor has ideological preferences, these are served instinctively, if at all, rather than deliberately. Papers ordinarily will not save stories left over at the end of the day for the next day's news because newer stories will supersede them. A late-breaking story, therefore, unless it is very unusual or significant, has little chance for publication. Because much of the national news is produced on an East Coast schedule, afternoon stories occurring on the West Coast are often neglected.

In Bagdikian's study, a distaste for the substance of the story or an objection to its ideological slant led editors to reject stories less than 3 percent of the time. Twenty-six percent of stories were rejected because of space shortages. The chief reason for other rejections was lack of newsworthiness. The published newspaper usually contained the same proportions of different types of news as the original pool from which the stories were selected.[35]

Public relations experts and campaign managers know the deadlines of important publications, such as the *New York Times, Wall Street Journal, Time, Newsweek,* and network television news. They schedule events and news releases to arrive in editors' offices precisely when needed and in easy-to-use formats. Public relations firms distribute thousands of releases annually. If these releases are attractively presented and meet newsworthiness criteria, journalists find it hard to resist using them. This is especially true for smaller news organizations that lack adequate resources to produce their own stories. They relish receiving such information subsidies.[36] Powerful elites in the public and private sector make ample use of these opportunities. Even though news organizations discard the bulk of public relations releases, they do use them in a substantial portion of news stories, usually without identifying the sources. If publicists want to stifle publicity that is likely to harm their clients, they can announce news just past the deadlines, preferably on weekends when few newscasts air.

Publications with less frequent deadlines, such as weekly news magazines, have a lot more time to decide which items to publish. That makes it easier to separate the wheat from the chaff. News magazine staffs also have more resources than most daily papers to explore background information and present stories in a context that helps readers to evaluate them. Hence their stories are often far more measured and thought-provoking than corresponding stories in the daily press.

Television news staffs, especially those working for stations that broadcast around the clock, have even less time than newspaper staffs to investigate most stories and far less time to provide background and interpretation. This is why background or investigative stories that appear on television frequently originate in the print media. The problem of insufficient time pertains not only to preparing stories but also to presenting them. The average news story on television and radio takes about a minute to deliver, just enough time to announce an event and present a fact or two. Newscasters may have to ignore complex stories if they cannot drastically condense them.

Print media have space problems as well, but these are less severe than the time constraints that electronic media face. The average newspaper reserves 55 percent of its space for advertising. Straight news stories account for 27 percent of the remaining space, and features account for the rest. Some papers reserve a fixed amount of space for news; others expand or contract the newshole depending on the flow of news and advertising. But whether the paper is a slim eight-page version or five to ten times that size, there is rarely enough space to cover stories as fully as reporters and editors would like.[37]

Besides the need to capsulate news stories, television reporters also seek stories with visual appeal. Events that lack good pictures may not make the cut. Racial violence in South Africa, for example, disappeared worldwide from television news after the government prohibited picture taking. Unfortunately, the most visually appealing aspects of a story may not be the most important. For instance, during political campaigns the

Located in the heart of downtown Atlanta, the world famous CNN Center is the global head-quarters of CNN and Turner Broadcasting. A bank of television monitors lines the center's twenty-four-hour-a-day newsroom.

motorcades, rallies, hecklers, and cheering crowds make good pictures, whereas candidates delivering speeches are visually dull. Television cameras therefore concentrate on the colorful scenes rather than on the speeches. If interesting pictures are flashed on the screen in competition with a speech, they often distract attention from it.

A final constraint on news production is news staffing. For financial and personnel reasons, news outlets favor stories by their own staff. This saves the additional fees that must be paid to freelance journalists. News executives also have personal relationships with their own staff members and do not want to give scarce space and time to strangers in preference to their own employees.

Effects of Gatekeeping

The gatekeeping influences discussed in this chapter give a distinctive character to U.S. news. There are many exceptions, of course, when one looks at individual programs or stories. There are also noticeable differences in emphases among the conservative rural press, more moderate papers in small and middle-sized towns, and the liberal press in major metropolitan centers. The unique conditions of Internet journalism have an even more profound impact on news presentation.[38] Unlike journalists in traditional media who must rigorously prune the lush growth of incoming news stories because time or space is scarce, Internet journalists have abundant time and space and must strain to fill it around the clock. Most newspapers and television operations use their Internet sites to expand stories covered in their traditional media, rather than enhancing the pool of news stories with previously excluded coverage. The news organizations update these stories throughout the day and night, often scooping the printed and broadcast stories that they will later feature in their traditional venues. Most news Web sites also provide links to information that broadens and deepens the story by adding new data or refreshing previously published details. The upshot is more in-depth news at a much faster pace. Despite variations in the news story environment, four features of U.S. news are noteworthy. They fall under the headings of people in the news, action in the news, infotainment news, and support for the establishment.[39]

People in the News

Gatekeeping winnows the group of newsworthy people to a small cadre of familiar and unfamiliar figures. In print and broadcast news, most stories in news magazines and network television news feature familiar people, predominantly entertainers, athletes, and political figures. Fewer than fifty politicians are in the news regularly, and the most popular is the incumbent president. Other people may receive coverage primarily for unusual or remarkable activities, but incumbent presidents receive coverage regardless of what they do. News about leading presidential candidates ranks next; in presidential election years it often outnumbers stories about the president.[40]

A third well-covered group consists of *major federal officials,* such as political leaders in the House and Senate, the heads of major congressional committees, and cabinet members in active departments. Major White House staff members are part of the circle. So are former officials such as secretaries of state and secretaries of defense when asked to comment on the current scene. The Supreme Court is in the news only intermittently, generally when it announces important decisions or during confirmation hearings for Supreme Court justices. Agency heads rarely make the news except when they announce new policies or feud with the president. Some people, however, are regularly in the news regardless of their current political status merely because their names are household words. Members of the Kennedy clan and a host of "experts," such as Federal Reserve chairperson Alan Greenspan, consumer activist Ralph Nader, or civil rights activist Jesse Jackson, are prime examples.

Below the federal level, the activities of governors and mayors from large states and cities are newsworthy if they involve major public policy issues or if the incumbent is unusual because of race, gender, or prior newsworthy activities. Notorious individuals also receive frequent attention if their deeds have involved well-known people. Presidential assassins, mass murderers, or terrorists like Timothy McVeigh and Osama bin Laden fall into this category. Ample coverage also goes to targets of congressional investigations and politicians indicted for wrongdoing in office.

Among the many powerful people rarely covered in the news are economic leaders (such as the heads of large corporations), financiers, and leaders of organized business (such as the National Association of Manufacturers or the U.S. Chamber of Commerce). A few colorful labor leaders, such as George Meany and James Hoffa, have been news figures in the past, but this was probably due more to their personalities than to their jobs. Important military leaders also remain obscure unless they conduct major military operations, such as Gen. Norman Schwarzkopf in the Persian Gulf War or Gen. Colin Powell, who was then his boss. Political party leaders surface during elections but remain in the shadows at other times. Political activists, such as civil rights leaders or the heads of minority parties, or pleaders of special causes, such as right-to-die activist Dr. Jack Kevorkian, come and go from the news scene, depending on the amount of visible conflict they are able to produce. The same holds true for the heads of voluntary associations, such as leaders of antiabortion groups or churches.

Most people never make the news because their activities are not unusual enough to command media attention, although coverage of average citizens has risen slightly in recent years. Ordinary people have their best chance for publicity if they protest or riot or strike, particularly against the government. The next best chance goes to victims of disasters, personal tragedy, and crime and to the actors who brought about their plight. The grisly nature of crimes, disasters, or other human tragedies, rather than the identity of the people involved, determines their newsworthiness. Ordinary people also make the news if their lifestyles or social activities become highly unusual or if their behavior diverges greatly from the norm for persons of their age, gender, and status. Finally, ordinary people make the news in large numbers as nameless members of groups whose statistical profile becomes news or whose opinions have been tapped through polls or elections.

Action in the News

The range of activities reported in the news is limited—conflicts and disagreements among government officials (particularly friction between the president and Congress about economic or foreign policies), violent and nonviolent protest (much of it in opposition to government activities), crime, scandals and investigations, and impending or actual disasters. When the nation is at war, the media report a large number of war stories.

Government policies involving health care reform, energy, or changes in tax rates also provide frequent story material. These stories often highlight the political maneuvers leading to policy decisions rather than the substance of the policy and its likely impact. Government personnel changes, including details about campaigns for office, are another news focus. Finally, two aspects of the ever-changing societal scene receive substantial coverage from time to time: national events such as inaugurations or space adventures, and important social, cultural, or technological developments, such as major efforts to raise the quality of public schools or advances in the fight against such killer diseases as cancer and AIDS.

Infotainment News

Newsworthiness criteria and news production constraints shape U.S. news and its impact, regardless of a particular subject under discussion. Among these constraints, economic pressures to generate large audiences are often paramount. Economist James T. Hamilton has amassed evidence showing that evening news broadcasts are pitched largely to fickle younger viewers who are likely to quit watching if the program does not please them. The upshot is a program mix that is short on hard news and long on infotainment.[41] Comparisons of news story topics show that the shift toward soft news has been dramatic. For example, between 1977 and 1997, soft news increased by an average of 25 percent in all news venues, at the expense of hard news.[42] Many critics inside and outside journalism deplore this turn, claiming that it diminishes citizens' concern about politics and hence weakens democracy. But there is also considerable evidence that the opposite may be true because infotainment news attracts audiences who would otherwise ignore the news altogether.[43]

Novelty and Excitement. When the focus is on attracting young viewers, sensational and novel occurrences often drown out news of more lasting significance that lacks excitement. For instance, a fairly typical newspaper such as the *Chicago Sun Times* devotes nearly twenty times more news to sports than to news about the state's government. Dramatic events, such as airline hijackings or serial murders, preempt more far-reaching consequential happenings. Preoccupation with a single striking event, such as the Clinton impeachment deliberations in 1999, can shortchange coverage of other news, such as a punitive U.S. airstrike against targets in Iraq.

The emphasis on excitement also leads to a stress on the more trivial aspects of serious stories. Inflation becomes a human-interest drama about John and Jane Doe, working-class homeowners who are struggling to pay their mortgage. Journalists are apt to ignore the larger issues involved in inflation unless they can be combined with human-interest aspects. In such cases, dramatization helps because personalized dramatic stories are far more likely to catch audience attention than dry, learned discussions by economic experts.

The search for novelty and entertainment leads to fragmented, discontinuous news that focuses on the present and ignores the past. When breaking news is published in a hurry, it often lacks background that places stories into context. Fragmentation makes it difficult for audiences to piece together a coherent narrative of events. Snippets of news may drive home an easily understandable theme, such as "Washington is in a mess" or "the inner city is decaying," thereby blurring individual news items. A few papers, such as the *Christian Science Monitor,* and a few news programs, such as the *NewsHour with Jim Lehrer,* cover fewer stories so that they can present them in more detail.

Familiarity and Similarity. Young audiences like stories about familiar people and events close to home. That preference leads to circular effects. When familiar people and situations are covered in minute detail, they become even more familiar and therefore even more worthy of publicity. The reverse is also true. Journalists ignore unfamiliar people and events. Celebrities may become objects of prying curiosity. The details of their private lives may take up an inordinately large amount of time and space in the mass media. The death of a beloved entertainment giant like comedian Johnny Carson may command news report and special feature coverage for days or weeks. Tabloids and serious media alike cover such stories at length.

The criteria of newsworthiness used in the United States lead to news that is very parochial compared with news in other countries. Coverage of news about foreign people and cultures is slim, leaving Americans ignorant about important international affairs. When news outlets rarely cover events in distant countries, stories about them require a lot of background if they are to make sense to Americans. To avoid the need for lengthy introductions, U.S. media therefore prefer to cover people from western cultures whose policies are somewhat familiar, such as the English, the Canadians, and the people of western European countries. Foreign news concentrates on situations that are easy to report, which often means focusing on such violent events as revolutions, major disasters, and the like. This type of coverage then conveys the faulty impression that most foreign countries are always in serious disarray.

Conflict and Violence. The heavy news emphasis on conflict and bad news, which is most prevalent in big city media, has three major consequences.[44] The first and perhaps most far reaching is the dangerous distortion of reality. Crime coverage provides examples. Media stories rarely mention that many inner-city neighborhoods are relatively free of crime. Instead, they convey the impression that entire cities are dangerous jungles. This impression may become a self-fulfilling prophecy. In the wake of crime publicity, many people avoid the inner city. They even shun comparatively safe neighborhoods after a single, highly publicized crime. The empty streets then make crime more likely.

Studies of people's perceptions of the incidence of crime and the actual chances that they will be victimized indicate that their fears are geared to media realities. In the world of television drama, the average character has a 30–64 percent chance of being involved in violence; in the real world the average person's chance of becoming a crime victim is a small fraction of that number.[45] In the same way, heavy media emphasis on air crashes and scant coverage of automobile accidents has left the public with distorted notions of the relative dangers of these modes of transportation.

A second consequence is that average people, when presented with clashing viewpoints, often feel confused and find it extremely difficult to determine the truth. They are also left with the disquieting sense that conflict and turmoil reign nearly everywhere. This impression is likely to affect people's feelings toward society in general. They may contract "videomalaise," characterized by lack of trust, cynicism, and fear.[46] Many social scientists believe that such feelings undermine support for government, destroy faith in leaders, produce political apathy, and generally sap the vigor of the democratic process.

The emphasis on conflict may also cause some people to believe that violence is an acceptable way to settle disputes. Even when exposure of the conflict ultimately promotes its resolution, highlighting violence often has adverse effects. Furthermore, the popularity of violent stories has encouraged groups who seek media coverage to behave violently or sensationally to enhance their chances for publicity. The media usually dramatize and oversimplify conflict, picturing it as a confrontation between two clearly defined sides. The reality is murkier. Issues are rarely clear-cut and viewpoints divide in multiple ways, rather than just two. Ample publicity may create enough pressure to bring about settlements that would have been impossible without it.[47]

A taste for conflict is not the same as a taste for controversy, however. Fear of offending members of the mass audience, or annoying prominent critics and business associates, may keep some topics—such as abortion or misconduct by teachers—out of the news, especially network television. When news outlets do report such stories, the treatment is ordinarily bland, carefully hedged, and rarely provocative. In fact, the world that television presents to the viewer often lags behind the real world in its recognition of controversial social changes. The civil rights struggle, women's fight for equality, and changing sexual mores were widespread long before they became common issues on the television screen or received serious attention in the print media. Compared with television, newspapers can afford to be more daring because normally there is no other daily paper in the same market. Besides, the medium is far less visual, and it is much easier for the audience to ignore stories that members find offensive or distasteful.

Neglect of Major Societal Problems. Despite the ascendancy of social responsibility journalism, the constraints of news production still force the media to slight serious persistent societal problems such as alcoholism, truancy, environmental pollution, and the care of preschool children, the elderly, and the disabled. However, the turn toward softer, human-interest oriented news that began in the 1970s has brought greater attention to such stories. When the audience has become bored with a story, media coverage evaporates, even for important stories. The same thing happens when trivial sensational happenings blot out matters of long-range significance that have become "old" news while the sensational stories grab the media's and the public's attention.

Inadequate training of media staff is another reason for unsatisfactory coverage of major stories. Proper appraisal of the merits of health care plans, or prison systems, or pollution control programs requires technical knowledge. As yet, only large news organizations have specialized reporters with expertise in such areas as urban affairs, science, or finance. Moreover, a science reporter can hardly be expected to be an expert in all fields of science. Nor can a reporter skilled in urban problems be expected simultaneously to master all the intricacies of a major city's budget, its transportation system, and its services to juveniles. Because most news organizations throughout the country lack the trained staffs needed to discuss major social and political problems constructively, politicians and all kinds of "experts" can easily challenge the merits of unpalatable media stories.

Support for the Establishment

Gatekeeping also yields news that supports political and social institutions in the United States. Although the media regularly expose the misbehavior and inefficiencies of government officials and routinely disparage politicians, they show respect and support for the political system and its high offices in general. Misconduct and poor policies are treated as deviations that implicitly reaffirm the merit of prevailing norms. News stories routinely embed assumptions that underscore the legitimacy of the current political system. For instance, when police protect a factory from violence by workers, reporters assume that the police are the legitimate guardians of public order engaged in an appropriate government activity. The possibility that workers, rather than capitalists, should own the factories and have a right to wrest them away is never raised. Similarly, stories discussing the plight of homeless children tacitly assume that these young people ought to be living in conventional family units. Journalists rarely consider the fact that other arrangements might be preferable.[48]

The media treat U.S. political symbols and rituals, such as the presidency, the courts, elections, and patriotic celebrations, with respect, enhancing their legitimacy. By contrast, news stories cast a negative light on antiestablishment behavior, such as protest demonstrations that disrupt normal activities, inflammatory speeches by militants, or looting during a riot.[49] Obscenity and profanity in public places usually are edited out of news events. When journalists do include them, they generate floods of complaints about disrespect, prying, and poor taste. This dampens such exposés, at least temporarily.

Explicit and implicit support for the established system, as well as sugarcoating of political reality, sometimes helps and sometimes hurts the public interest. It hurts if faults in the established system and prevailing political ideologies are allowed to persist when publicity might lead to correction. The fear of publicity can also improve behavior from errant public figures. There are, however, situations in which shielding the shortcomings of the political system and even individual misconduct may be helpful. For instance, at times of national or international crises, when the nation's prestige is an important political asset, detrimental stories can severely weaken the country. Similarly, the ability of elected leaders to govern effectively can suffer at the hands of stories focusing disproportionately on failures and slighting successes and by stories dwelling on irrelevant personal issues that diminish a leader's stature.

Generalized support for the establishment and the status quo is not unique to the media, of course.[50] Most institutions within any particular political system go along with it if they wish to prosper. People on government staffs have been socialized to believe in the merits of their political structures. People are socialized throughout their lives to support their country and its policies. They often resent exposés that call into question this comfortable sense of security. Media support for the establishment thus helps to maintain and perpetuate existing respect for it.[51] The media's heavy reliance on government sources and press releases further strengthens establishment support. Official viewpoints tend to dominate the news when reporters must preserve access to government beats or when story production requires government assistance for data collection.[52]

Reporters use government officials routinely to verify information, validating stories by attributing them to "official" sources. The higher the official's level and rank, the better. The assumption that government sources, such as police departments or Department of Agriculture spokespersons or presidential press aides are reliable information sources is, of course, debatable, especially because the particular thrust of a story may put agencies into a good or bad light. Many private groups have complained that the nearly exclusive reliance on government sources deprives them of the chance to publicize their own, in their view more accurate, versions of stories and that the result is one-sided reporting tilted toward support of the establishment.

Appraising News Making

Do newspeople do a good job in selecting the types of news and entertainment categories they cover? Do they allot appropriate time and space to each of these categories? Do they fill them with good individual stories? The answers depend on the standards that the analyst applies. If one contends that news can and should be a mirror of society, then news making leaves much to be desired. By emphasizing the exceptional rather than the ordinary, a few regular beats rather than a wide range of news sources, and conflict and bad news rather than the ups and downs of daily life, the media picture a world that is far from reality. Reality becomes further distorted because the process of shaping news events into interesting, coherent stories often gives these events totally new meanings and significance. This is why critics claim that the news creates reality rather than reports it.[53]

If one shares the belief of many journalists and other elites that the media should serve as the eyes and ears of intelligent citizens who are hungry for news of major social and political significance, one will again find fault with news making. The media devote much space and time to trivia and ignore or report many interesting developments so briefly that their meaning is lost. Often the human-interest appeal of a story or its sensational aspects distract the audience from the story's real significance.[54]

When one measures the media by their professed story formulas, appraisal scores are not high. An analysis of 400 television news reports selected randomly in June 2004 that yielded 312 routine average-length stories showed that only one of seven key story elements (who, what, where, when, why, how, and context) was nearly always covered. Most stories included major factual elements—what actually took place, who was involved, and where and when it happened (Table 4-6). Coverage was less regular when it came to stating why the reported event took place, how it occurred, and in what context. The audience received the facts of what occurred but not the information that would help it grasp the meaning and implications of these facts.

To find fault is easy; to suggest realistic remedies is far more difficult. Few critics would agree on what is noteworthy enough to deserve publication. Gradations and ranks in significance depend on the observer's world view and political orientation. Much of the published criticism of the media appears in polemical publications that take the media to task for omitting the critic's special concerns. But one person's intellectual meat is another's poison. Conservatives would like to see more stories about the misdeeds of the country's enemies and about waste and abuse in social service programs. Liberals complain that the media legitimize big business and the military and neglect social reforms and radical perspectives.

When the media have featured controversial public policy issues, such as the dangers of nuclear energy generation or the merits of a new health care system, or when they cover political campaigns or demonstrations, each side often charges that political bias dictated the choices about inclusion and exclusion of media fare and about the story's focus and tone. A number of content analyses of such events definitely refute the charges of pervasive political bias, if bias is defined as deliberately lopsided coverage or intentional slanting of news. These analyses show instead that most newspeople try to cover a balanced array of issues in a neutral manner and do include at least a few contrasting viewpoints. But given the constraints on the number of sources that can be used and the desire to produce exciting stories that top the competition, the end product is rarely a balanced reflection of all elite viewpoints and all shades of public opinion.[55] Moreover, as mentioned, the prevailing political culture colors everything because it provides the standards by which events are judged and interpreted.

When coverage is unbalanced, as happens often, the reasons generally spring from news making itself rather than from politically or ideologically motivated slanting. For instance, the media covered famine conditions in Somalia because that country was fairly accessible. They ignored similar conditions in Sudan because travel was too difficult there. Journalists report events happening in major cities more fully nationwide than similar events in smaller communities, because the cities are better equipped for news collection and transmission. The New Hampshire presidential primary receives disproportionately heavy coverage because it happens to be the first one in a presidential election year.

TABLE 4-6   Coverage of News Elements in National and Local Broadcasts

News elements	Who	What	Where	When	Why	How	Context	Total number of stories
Events abroad								
Mideast problems	95%	100%	93%	73%	66%	61%	73%	41
Asia politics	100	100	100	100	100	50	100	2
Europe politics	100	100	100	100	100	100	100	3
Natural events								
Weather/nature	62	100	100	69	46	54	46	13
Accidents/safety	76	100	94	100	24	71	24	17
Economic issues								
Economic conditions	100	100	100	100	100	100	0	1
Fiscal policies	100	100	60	60	60	40	80	5
Noneconomic issues								
Local/national government	88	100	65	73	69	58	54	26
Public officials	98	100	79	94	81	45	60	47
Crime/law enforcement	97	100	93	96	45	74	38	73
Other domestic issues	78	100	80	88	55	43	53	40
Private-sector news								
Business	90	100	63	80	73	43	57	30
Health/medical	79	100	64	43	64	50	50	14
Average scores	89	100	84	83	68	61	57	312

SOURCE: Author's research, based on analysis of 400 randomly selected television news stories from June 1 to June 30, 2004. Feature stories and stories briefer than twenty seconds were omitted.

NOTE: Numbers represent the percentage of stories in each group that covers the question.

Press output inevitably represents a small, unsystematic sample of the news of the day. In this sense, every issue of a newspaper or every television newscast is a biased sample of current events. Published stories often generate follow-up coverage, heightening the bias effect. Attempts to be even-handed may lead to similar coverage for events of dissimilar importance, thereby introducing bias.

When news is evaluated from the standpoint of the audience's preference, rather than as a mirror image of society or as a reflection of socially and politically significant events, media gatekeepers appear to be doing well. People like the products of the mass media industry well enough to devote huge chunks of their leisure time to broadcasts and the Internet. Millions of viewers, by their own free choice, watch shows condemned as "trash" by social critics and often even by the viewers themselves. These same people ignore shows and newspaper stories with the critics' seal of approval. Most claim to enjoy broadcast news and to learn important information from it. Media critics may scoff at such accolades, but if an old saying is right that "the voice of the people is the voice of God," the people's voice deserves respect.[56]

Summary

What is news depends on what a particular society deems socially significant or personally satisfying to media audiences. The prevailing political and social ideology therefore determines what type of information journalists will gather and the range of meanings they will give it. News collection is structured through the beat system to keep in touch with the most prolific sources of news.

Beyond the larger framework, which is rooted in the country's current political ideology, overt political considerations rarely play a major part in news selection. Instead, the profit motive and technical constraints of news production are paramount selection criteria. These criteria impose more stringent constraints on television than on print media because television deals with larger, more heterogeneous audiences and requires pictures to match story texts. Unlike newspapers, which rarely have competition in the local market, television must compete for attention with multiple other electronic outlets.

The end products of these various constraints on news making are news media that generally support the U.S. political system but emphasize its shortcomings and conflicts because conflict is exciting and journalists see themselves as watchdogs of public honesty. News is geared primarily to attract and entertain rather than to educate the audience about politically significant events. The pressures to report news rapidly while it is happening often lead to disjointed fragments and disparate commentary. This leaves the audience with the impossible task of weaving the fragments into a meaningful tapestry of interrelated events.

Judged in terms of the information needs of the ideal citizen in the ideal democracy, news is inadequate. This is especially true of television, which provides little more than a headline service for news and which mirrors the world about as much as the curved mirrors at the county fair. The news reflects reality, but it seems badly out of shape and proportion. It is no wonder then that distrust of the media is pervasive and growing as are charges that the news media are politically biased and out of tune with the views of average Americans.[57]

Most Americans only faintly resemble the ideal citizen, and most look to the media for entertainment rather than enlightenment. From that perspective, a different appraisal suggests itself. By and large, U.S. mass media serve the general public about as well as that public wants to be served in practice rather than in theory. News outlets intersperse entertainment with a smattering of serious information. They prefer breadth of coverage over narrow depth. In times of acute crisis, as we shall see in the next chapter, the media can and do follow a different pattern. Serious news displaces entertainment, and the broad sweep of events turns into a narrow, in-depth focus on the crisis. But short of acute crisis, superficiality prevails most of the time.

Notes

1. Pew Research Center for the People and the Press, "How Journalists See Journalists in 2004," http://people-press.org; David H. Weaver and G. Cleveland Wilhoit, with Randy Beam, Bonnie Brownlee, and Paul Voakes, *The American Journalist in the 21st Century*, (Indiana: Indiana University Press, forthcoming).
2. Pew Research Center for the People and the Press, "How Journalists See Journalists in 2004."
3. See Chapter 8.
4. Stuart Kallen, ed., *Media Bias* (San Diego: Greenhaven Press, 2004); Reginald Estoque Ecarma, *Beyond Ideology: A Case of Egalitarian Bias in the News* (Lanham, Md.: University Press of America, 2003). Also see Shelly Rodgers and Esther Thorson, "A Socialization Perspective on Male and Female Reporting," *Journal of Communication* 53 (4): 658–675.
5. Elizabeth Vargas, "People of the Year: Bloggers," *World News Tonight*, December 30, 2004, http://abcnews.go.com/; Eugene Volokh, "You Can Blog, but You Can't Hide," *Chicago Tribune*, December 2, 2004. The Movie Blog makes similar claims and manages to cover costs by selling advertising.
6. Mike Hughlett, "Bloggers Blend Business with Stuff They Like," *Chicago Tribune*, February 20, 2005.

7. Wolfram Peiser, "Setting the Journalist Agenda: Influences from Journalists' Individual Characteristics and from Media Factors," *Journalism and Mass Communication Quarterly* 77 (summer 2000): 243–257.

8. Pippa Norris, *A Virtuous Circle: Political Communications in Postindustrial Societies* (Cambridge: Cambridge University Press, 2000); Kathleen Hall Jamieson and Paul Waldman, *The Press Effect: Politicians, Journalists, and the Stories That Shape the Political World* (New York: Oxford University Press, 2003); Matthew R. Kerbel, *If It Bleeds It Leads: An Anatomy of Television News* (Boulder, Colo.: Westview, 2001).

9. Coverage patterns for prominent stories may set the mold for subsequent reporting, although this did not happen in the O.J. Simpson murder case. Kimberly A. Maxwell, John Huxford, Catherine Borum, and Robert Hornik, "Covering Domestic Violence: How the O.J. Simpson Case Shaped Reporting of Domestic Violence in the News Media," *Journalism and Mass Communication Quarterly* 77 (summer 2000): 258–272.

10. Thomas E. Patterson, "Political Roles of the Journalist," in *The Politics of News, the News of Politics,* ed. Doris Graber, Denis McQuail, and Pippa Norris (Washington, D.C.: CQ Press, 1998), 17–32. For comparative approaches see Daniel C. Hallin and Paolo Mancini, *Comparing Media Systems: Three Models of Media and Politics* (Cambridge: Cambridge University Press, 2004).

11. Theodore L. Glasser, ed., *The Idea of Public Journalism* (New York: Guilford, 1999); Arthur Charity, *Doing Public Journalism* (New York: Guilford, 1996). Public journalism has been primarily a print news movement. But there are converts in television news as well, as discussed in David Kurpius, "Public Journalism and Commercial Local Television News: In Search of a Model," *Journalism and Mass Communication Quarterly* 77 (summer 2000): 340–354.

12. Weaver and others, *The American Journalist.*

13. The question is explored briefly, but poignantly, by Michael Orestes, Tom Bettag, Mark Jurkowitz, and Rem Rieder in "What's News?" *Harvard International Journal of Press/Politics* 5 (summer 2000): 102–113.

14. "Mr. President, Ben Bradlee Calling," *Public Opinion* 9 (September–October 1986): 40.

15. See Dominic L. Lasorsa and Stephen D. Reese, "News Source Use in the Crash of 1987: A Study of Four National Media," *Journalism Quarterly* 67 (spring 1990): 60–63, and sources cited therein. Also see Timothy E. Cook, *Governing with the News: The News Media as a Political Institution* (Chicago: University of Chicago Press, 1998), 91–97; Regina Lawrence, "Accidents, Icons, and Indexing: The Dynamics of News Coverage of Police Use of Force," *Political Communication* 13 (1996): 437–454.

16. Jane Delano Brown, Carl R. Bybee, Stanley T. Wearden, and Dulcie Murdock Straughan, "Invisible Power: Newspaper News Sources and the Limits of Diversity," *Journalism Quarterly* 64 (spring 1987): 45–54; Sharon Dunwoody and Steven Shields, "Accounting for Patterns of Selection of Topics in Statehouse Reporting," *Journalism Quarterly* 63 (autumn 1986): 488–496.

17. S. Robert Lichter, Stanley Rothman, and Linda S. Lichter, *The Media Elite* (Bethesda, Md.: Adler and Adler, 1986), 62. The study is reported on pp. 54–71. Also see Hans Mathias Kepplinger, "Artificial Horizons: How the Press Presented and How the Population Received Technology in Germany from 1965–1986," in *The Mass Media in Liberal Democratic Societies,* ed. Stanley Rothman (New York: Paragon House, 1992), chap. 7.

18. Lasorsa and Reese, "News Source Use in the Crash of 1987."
19. The impact of news stories attributed to highly credible sources is described in Benjamin I. Page, Robert Y. Shapiro, and Glenn R. Dempsey, "What Moves Public Opinion?" *American Journal of Political Science* 81 (March 1987): 23–43. For a negative reaction to the power of anchors, see James Fallows, *Breaking the News: How the Media Undermine American Democracy* (New York: Pantheon, 1996), chap. 1.
20. Peter Braestrup, *Big Story* (Garden City, N.Y.: Anchor Books, 1978).
21. Jacques Steinberg, "Washington Post Rethinks Its Coverage of War Debate," *New York Times*, August 13, 2004.
22. George Gerbner, "Ideological Perspective and Political Tendencies in News Reporting," *Journalism Quarterly* 41 (August 1964): 495–508.
23. For a discussion of the social systems framework for mass communications analysis, see James S. Ettema, "The Organizational Context of Creativity," in *Individuals in Mass Media Organizations: Creativity and Constraint*, ed. James S. Ettema and D. Charles Whitney (Beverly Hills, Calif.: Sage, 1982), 91–106.
24. Joseph N. Cappella and Kathleen Hall Jamieson, *Spiral of Cynicism: The Press and the Public Good* (New York: Oxford University Press, 1997), 33–34.
25. Regina Lawrence, "Game-Framing the Issues: Tracking the Strategy Frame in Public Policy News," *Political Communication*, 17 (2000): 93–114; also see Jim A. Kuypers, *Press Bias and Politics: How the Media Frame Controversial Issues* (Westport, Conn.: Praeger, 2002).
26. "1995 Year in Review," *Media Monitor* 10 (January–February 1996): 3. Also see Everett M. Rogers, James W. Dearing, and Soonbum Chang, "AIDS in the 1980s: The Agenda-Setting Process for a Public Issue," *Journalism Monographs* 126 (April 1991).
27. Chicago police crime reports and *Chicago Tribune* index, 2002.
28. Ibid.
29. Shanto Iyengar and Donald Kinder, *News That Matters* (Chicago: University of Chicago Press, 1987); Shanto Iyengar, *Is Anyone Responsible? How Television Frames Political Issues* (Chicago: University of Chicago Press, 1991).
30. Doris Graber, *Processing Politics: Learning from Television in the Internet Age* (Chicago: University of Chicago Press, 2001), 134–135. Also see Stephen Earl Bennett, Staci L. Rhine, and Richard S. Flickinger, "The Things They Cared About: Americans' Attention to Different News Stories, 1989–2002," *Press/Politics* 9 (1): 75–99.
31. Leon V. Sigal, *Reporters and Officials: The Organization and Politics of Newsmaking* (Lexington, Mass.: Heath, 1973), 119–130. Also see Leon V. Sigal, "Sources Make the News," in *Reading the News*, ed. Robert Karl Manoff and Michael Schudson (New York: Pantheon, 1987), 9–37.
32. Thomas E. Patterson, "Doing Well and Doing Good: How Soft News and Critical Journalism Are Shrinking the News Audience and Weakening Democracy—And What News Outlets Can Do about It," John F. Kennedy School of Government Faculty Research Working Papers Series RWP01–001, December 2000.
33. Walter Lippmann, *Public Opinion* (New York: Free Press, 1965), 229.
34. Ben Bagdikian, *The Information Machines* (New York: Harper and Row, 1971), 99–100.
35. Ibid.; Dunwoody and Shields, "Statehouse Reporting," 488–496.
36. Judy Van Slyke Turk, "Information Subsidies and Media Content: A Study of

Public Relations Influence on the News," *Journalism Monographs* 100 (December 1986): 1–29. Also see Jarol B. Manheim, "The News Shapers: Strategic Communication as a Third Force in News Making," in Graber, McQuail, and Norris, *The Politics of News*, 94–109.

37. See Leo Bogart, "How U.S. Newspaper Content Is Changing," *Journal of Communication* 35 (spring 1985): 82–91; Richard Campbell, Christopher R. Martin, and Bettina Fabos, *Media and Culture*, 4th ed. (Boston: Bedford/St. Martin's, 2005).

38. The content of Web sites sponsored by print and broadcast media is in flux. For one snapshot of Web content on television Web sites, see Sylvia M. Chan-Olmsted and Jung Suk Park, "From On-Air to Online World: Examining the Content and Structures of Broadcast TV Stations' Web Sites," *Journalism and Mass Communication Quarterly*, 77 (summer 2000): 321–339.

39. The first two headings have been adapted from Herbert Gans's study of news magazine and network television news. See Gans, *Deciding What's News* (New York: Pantheon, 1979), 8–31. See also Gaye Tuchman, *Making News: A Study in the Construction of Reality* (New York: Free Press, 1978); and W. Lance Bennett, *News: The Politics of Illusion*, 5th ed. (New York: Longman, 2003).

40. Karen S. Johnson, "The Portrayal of Lame-Duck Presidents by the National Print Media," *Presidential Studies Quarterly* 16 (winter 1986): 50–65. For a broad discussion of the coverage mix at the federal government level, see Stephen Hess, *The Washington Reporters* (Washington, D.C.: Brookings Institution, 1981).

41. James T. Hamilton, *All the News That's Fit to Sell: How the Market Transforms Information into News* (Princeton: Princeton University Press, 2004).

42. Doris Graber, *Processing Politics* (Chicago: University of Chicago Press, 2001).

43. Patterson, "Doing Well and Doing Good," provides citations.

44. Kerbel, *If It Bleeds, It Leads*.

45. George Gerbner, Larry Gross, Michael Morgan, and Nancy Signorielli, "Charting the Mainstream: Television's Contributions to Political Orientations," *Journal of Communication* 32 (spring 1982): 106–107. Small-town newspapers are more apt to highlight the positive, telling what is good rather than what is bad, because conflict is less tolerable in social systems in which most of the leaders constantly rub elbows.

46. "Videomalaise" is Michael J. Robinson's term. See Robinson, "American Political Legitimacy in an Era of Electronic Journalism: Reflections on the Evening News," in *Television as a Social Force: New Approaches to TV Criticism*, ed. Richard Adler (New York: Praeger, 1975), 97–139.

47. Stephen E. Rada, "Manipulating the Media: A Case Study of a Chicano Strike in Texas," *Journalism Quarterly* 54 (spring 1977): 109–113. Also see Gadi Wolfsfeld, "Symbiosis of Press and Protest: An Exchange Analysis," *Journalism Quarterly* 61 (autumn 1984): 550–555.

48. Klaus Bruhn Jensen, "News as Ideology: Economics Statistics and Political Ritual in Television Network News," *Journal of Communication* 37 (winter 1987): 8–27; Bennett, *News*.

49. Gadi Wolfsfeld, "Media, Protest, and Political Violence: A Transactional Analysis," *Journalism Monographs* 127 (June 1991): 1–61.

50. For a strong attack on status quo support, see Edward S. Herman and Noam Chomsky, *Manufacturing Consent: The Political Economy of the Mass Media* (New York: Pantheon, 2002).

51. There is resistance to change, even in entertainment program formats. See Jay G. Blumler and Carolynn Martin Spicer, "Prospects for Creativity in the New Television Marketplace: Evidence from Program-Makers," *Journal of Communication* 40 (autumn 1990): 78–101.
52. A comparison of war movies made with and without Pentagon aid showed that aided movies depicted the military in a more favorable light. Russell E. Shain, "Effects of Pentagon Influence on War Movies, 1948–70," *Public Opinion Quarterly* 38 (fall 1972): 641–647.
53. For a fuller exploration of this issue, see David L. Altheide, *Creating Reality: How TV News Distorts Events* (Beverly Hills, Calif.: Sage, 1976); Tuchman, *Making News*; Mark Fishman, *Manufacturing the News* (Austin: University of Texas Press, 1980); and Bennett, *News*.
54. But sensational news often contains a great deal of information. See C. Richard Hofstetter and David M. Dozier, "Useful News, Sensational News: Quality, Sensationalism, and Local TV News," *Journalism Quarterly* 63 (winter 1986): 815–820; and Matthew A. Baum, *Soft News Goes to War: Public Opinion and American Foreign Policy in the New Media Age* (Princeton: Princeton University Press, 2003).
55. Frederick Fico and Stan Soffin, "Fairness and Balance of Selected Newspaper Coverage of Controversial National, State, and Local Issues," *Journalism and Mass Communication Quarterly* 72 (autumn 1995): 621–633; Neil J. Kressel, "Biased Judgments of Media Bias: A Case Study of the Arab-Israeli Dispute," *Political Psychology* 8 (June 1987): 211–226; and Lichter and others, *The Media Elite*, 293–301. The difficulties of defining "bias" are explained in Stephen Lacy, Frederick Fico, and Todd F. Simon, "Fairness and Balance in the Prestige Press," *Journalism Quarterly* 68 (fall 1991): 363–370. Also see Simon, Fico, and Lacy, "Covering Conflict and Controversy: Measuring Balance, Fairness, Defamation," *Journalism Quarterly* 62 (summer 1989): 427–434.
56. Pew Research Center for the People and the Press, *Trends 2005*, http://people-press.org/commentary/pdf/05pdf.
57. Ibid.

Readings

Callaghan, Karen, and Frauke Schnell, eds. *Framing American Politics*. Pittsburgh: University of Pittsburgh Press, 2005.

Emery, Michael, Edwin Emery, and Nancy L. Roberts. *The Press and America: An Interpretive History of the Mass Media*. 9th ed. Boston: Allyn and Bacon, 2000.

Glasser, Theodore L., ed. *The Idea of Public Journalism*. New York: Guilford, 1999.

Graber, Doris, Denis McQuail, and Pippa Norris. *The Politics of News, the News of Politics*. Washington, D.C.: CQ Press, 1998.

Jamieson, Kathleen Hall, and Paul Waldman. *The Press Effect: Politicians, Journalists, and the Stories That Shape the Political World*. New York: Oxford University Press, 2003.

McChesney, Robert W. *The Problem of the Media: U.S. Communication Politics in the Twenty-First Century*. New York: Monthly Review Press, 2004.

Overholser, Geneva, and Kathleen Hall Jamieson, eds. *Institutions of American Democracy: The Press.* New York: Oxford University Press, 2005.

Schudson, Michael. *Sociology of News.* New York: Norton, 2003.

Van Zoonen, Lisbet. *Entertaining the Citizen: When Politics and Popular Culture Converge.* Lanham, Md.: Rowman and Littlefield, 2004.

Weaver, David H., and G. Cleveland Wilhoit, with Randy Beam, Bonnie Brownlee, and Paul Voakes. *The American Journalist in the 21st Century.* Bloomington: Indiana University Press, forthcoming.

Reporting Extraordinary Events

TERROR! ATTACKED! THE HORROR! DARKEST HOUR! America's Nightmare! Act of War! Those are some of the headlines that heralded the attack on the United States on September 11, 2001.[1] It began at 8:45 a.m. eastern standard time when an American Airlines passenger jet crashed into one of the two 110-story towers at the World Trade Center. Minutes later, at 9:03 a.m., another jetliner slammed into the second tower. By 9:59 a.m. one tower had collapsed; the second tower tumbled at 10:28 a.m. Almost simultaneously, a plane had crashed into the Pentagon in the nation's capital, causing the collapse of several floors. Initial reports about these assaults indicated that thousands had died and even more thousands were wounded, property had been destroyed, and people were evacuating government sites in Washington, D.C., and throughout the country.

What politically significant roles do media play when such extraordinary events occur, and how do they go about playing them? To answer these questions, we will take a close look at four types of crises: war situations, terrorism on U.S. soil, urban rioting fueled by racism, and a major natural disaster. After explaining how media cover such manmade and natural disasters, the discussion will turn to a number of pseudo-crises. These are comparatively normal events that crisis-type coverage elevates to the status of extraordinary.

In times of crisis, the media, particularly radio and television, play a vital support role for crisis control agencies. In addition to reporting news about the event, the media provide crisis workers quick access to the public by allowing them to use media channels personally or through media personnel. Such messages keep endangered communities in touch with essential information and instructions. The messages also allow personnel on the scene, including government authorities, to shape perceptions of the nature and extent of the crisis, its causes, and appropriate remedies. The close collaboration between public officials and journalists raises major philosophical and policy questions. In times of crises, when citizens pay close attention to the media's messages, should public officials have unrestricted and largely unedited access to the public? At such times, should the media concentrate their efforts almost entirely on serving crisis-related needs at the cost of keeping other stories out of the news? Do journalists compromise their role as neutral observers when they become part of the crisis management team? Does the widespread notion that criticism in times of crisis is unpatriotic stifle reporters at a time when the need for dispassionate analysis is greatest?

Four Crises

To answer these questions, we will examine media coverage of four crises that represent typical disasters. They are the war against Iraq in 2003; the terrorism strike on U.S. soil on September 11, 2001; the race riots in Los Angeles that started on April 30, 1992; and the horrendous tsunami that devastated parts of southern Asia in 2004.

War Against Iraq, 2003

On March 20, 2003, a massive force of U.S. troops invaded Iraq, supported by a coalition that included Britain, Australia, and Poland as well as sizable contingents of Iraqi Kurdish militia. The invasion followed an ultimatum that Saddam Hussein, the country's president, and two of his sons must leave the country. The United States, Great Britain, and their allies had issued the ultimatum, which Saddam Hussein defied, because they believed that Hussein and his supporters possessed weapons of mass destruction destined for attacks on their enemies. Repeated requests by the United Nations to surrender these weapons had been denied.

After approximately three weeks of military operations, coalition forces overthrew Hussein's government and occupied the country. On May 1, 2003, President Bush declared the war over. Nonetheless, fighting continued beyond that date in many parts of the country. Investigators found no weapons of mass destruction, leading to charges that U.S. and British leaders had exaggerated the threat posed by Iraq to justify the invasion and depose the hated Hussein. Criticism of the war was widespread among world powers and grew steadily within the United States, where citizens were disturbed that the initially low numbers of casualties increased sharply during the occupation period. Media coverage of the war was intense throughout with a steady flow of blow-by-blow daily reports.

Terrorism in 2001

On the morning of September 11, 2001, terrorists hijacked four U.S. passenger jets and crashed two into the World Trade Center in New York and one into the Pentagon. One plane's mission was aborted when it crashed in the Pennsylvania countryside. The hijacked planes were loaded with fuel for their scheduled flights from the East Coast to California, making them ideal weapons of destruction. Obviously, these attacks were a well-planned, well-coordinated terrorist plot. Federal officials identified terrorists with links to the fugitive Osama bin Laden, believed to be in Afghanistan, as likely perpetrators of the assault.

In the wake of the crashes, thousands of people were missing and presumed dead and many more were injured. The 110-story World Trade Center and its immediate surroundings lay in ruins and the Pentagon suffered substantial damage. The nation's domestic air traffic system shut down temporarily, as did many government and business operations. U.S. military forces at home and abroad went on the highest state of alert and borders with Canada and Mexico were sealed. President Bush, in an address to the nation, denounced the hijackers and pledged that the United States would hunt down and punish all responsible parties and their supporters.[2]

Los Angeles Riots, 1992

On March 3, 1991, after a high-speed chase, several officers of the Los Angeles police stopped an African American motorist for traffic violations. An angry confrontation ensued that ended with the white officers severely beating the motorist. A resident of a nearby apartment building, alerted by the noise, videotaped scenes of the beating. Over the course of the next year, the shocking footage was broadcast thousands of times throughout the nation, creating a widespread consensus among citizens of all races that the police had used excessive force. The repeated airing of the beating kept police brutality and racism, which had long been simmering public issues, near the boiling point.

When news reports informed Americans at the end of April 1992 that an all-white jury had exonerated all but one of the Los Angeles officers on the charges of brutality, protest demonstrations pockmarked the country. In Los Angeles these demonstrations turned into one of the ugliest urban riots in decades, complete with shootings, beatings, massive arson, and looting. Fifty-three people were killed, and more than two thousand were injured. Rioters destroyed property worth millions of dollars, leaving sections of the city an economic wasteland that remains to be fully restored. In the wake of the rioting, the focus of the presidential campaign that year turned to the hitherto neglected problems of urban decay; the alienated, impoverished underclass; and deepening tension among races.[3]

The 2004 Asian Tsunami

Thousands of people died throughout southern Asia in late December 2004 when a powerful underwater earthquake off the coast of Sumatra created a tsunami. Gigantic, hundred-mile-wide waves up to forty feet high crashed into coastlines, destroying everything in their wake. Traveling at speeds up to 500 miles per hour, the tsunami quickly reached coastal areas in Indonesia, Sri Lanka, India, Thailand, Malaysia, the Maldives, and even Somalia, more than 3,000 miles away from the earthquake center. None of the affected countries had warning systems in place to alert their citizens to evacuate low-lying coastal areas. The waves wiped out entire villages, leaving survivors without potable water, food, shelter, or medical care. Millions of people were displaced from their homes. Worldwide relief efforts began almost immediately but had difficulty reaching devastated areas when normal access routes and communication channels had been destroyed. International health authorities feared the outbreak of epidemics in areas where unburied, rotting corpses and polluted water were poisoning the environment. Red Cross and Red Crescent organizations, Doctors without Borders, and other relief organizations with staff and resources near the disaster areas moved in via helicopters and naval vessels as soon as weather conditions permitted. But the devastated area was so vast and the damage so catastrophic that the disaster overwhelmed all efforts to cope with the consequences.

Media Responses and Roles

During crises, the public depends almost totally on the media for news and for vital messages from public and private authorities. The news media are the only institutions equipped to collect substantial amounts of information and disseminate it quickly. Therefore, when people become aware of a crisis, they monitor developments through their radios, television sets, or computer monitors, often round the clock. Portable equipment that does not require connection to electricity sources is particularly important. Televised offerings, especially network and cable news, attract the largest audiences during crises because of their ability to report breaking stories quickly, while newspapers with their slower publication cycles lag behind (Table 5-1).[4]

The audience for crisis information is massive and loyal and generally pleased with the quality of coverage. After the 2001 terrorist attack, 74 percent of the U.S. public claimed to watch news about the event very closely. The figures were 70 percent for the Los Angeles riots and 63 percent for the 2003 Iraq War.[5] When one adds the numbers for people who said that they paid "fairly close" attention, they rise above the 90 percent mark for each crisis. During the 2003 Iraq War, cable news channels, which have become increasingly popular, tripled their audiences, averaging 7 million nightly viewers. Newspapers added roughly 15 percent to their audience during the later stages of the crisis when people were hungry for more in-depth analysis. Television nightly news, though yielding audience to the cable programs, still captured 28 million viewers, way beyond the figures that cable outlets could boast. In fact, those numbers topped primetime entertainment shows like *CSI: Crime Scene Investigation,* with a 27 million audience, and *Friends* with 22 million.[6]

Besides seeking information, the public looks to the media for interpretations of situations. Media personnel are often the first to try to fit breaking events into a coherent story. Official investigations generally come much later. The media also guide the public's actions during a crisis. They direct people to shelters, announce which areas are unsafe to enter, describe purification processes for polluted food and water, and supply news of missing persons or schedules to be maintained by schools and workplaces. News stories also explain what immediate steps government authorities are taking to cope with the crisis.

Stages and Patterns of Coverage

Observers of crisis coverage have identified three stages that merge almost seamlessly and often overlap.

Stage One. During the first stage, the crisis or disaster is announced as having already struck or impending. Reporters, officials, and onlookers rush to the scene. Radio and television stations interrupt regularly scheduled programs with a flood of uncoordinated bulletins announcing the extraordinary event. The stations may preempt the entire program for reports from the scene.

Minutes after the start of the Los Angeles riots, television and radio reporters broadcast live from the scene. They showed buildings on fire and beating and looting scenes, usually without a single police officer within camera range. Later, these broadcasts were blamed for tipping off

TABLE 5-1   Principal Sources of News before and after the September 11, 2001, Terrorist Attack (in percentages)

News source	Before the strike	After the strike	Change
Television	74	90	16
Network news	20	30	10
Local news	26	17	−9
Cable news	34	45	11
Newspapers	45	11	−34
Radio	18	14	−4
Magazines	6	—	−6
Internet	13	5	−8

SOURCE: Adapted from Pew Research Center for the People and the Press, "American Psyche Reeling from Terror Attacks," September 19, 2001, http://people-press.org/reports/print. php3?PageID=32.

NOTE: Two answers were permitted. $N = 1,200$.

rioters about places where they might assault, burn, and loot with impunity. These same stories also helped police find locations where they were sorely needed. Media offices became information collection centers because people phoned them with reports or called them for information. The most important broadcasts at the start of a disaster are messages describing what is happening, directing people to places of safety, summoning police and military units, and coordinating appeals for relief supplies, such as food, blankets, blood donations, and medical equipment.

In the early phase of an event, the number of news broadcasts rises steeply. During all four crisis events broadcast time escalated sharply and audience figures multiplied, especially on twenty-four-hour news outlets. Crisis-related news and interviews replaced many regular programs. News bulletins were issued throughout the day on radio and television. Journalists interviewed a steady stream of eyewitnesses. With little new to report, media rehashed the same facts endlessly. During these types of catastrophes, the initial reports about the disaster reach many people by word-of-mouth through face-to-face or telephone conversations. The news of the attempted assassination of President Ronald Reagan in 1981 illustrates the speed of diffusion of crisis news. The story initially reached a large daytime audience that heard it on radio or television. Then, on average, each person told the news to three other people. More than 90 percent of the U.S. public—over 200 million people—received the news within ninety minutes after the shooting.[7] The rate of diffusion was equally swift for the 2001 terrorist strike because, like the assault on Reagan, it occurred during daytime on a working day when most adults are in touch with their normal information networks.

Rapidity of communication is the most striking characteristic of initial coverage of extraordinary events. Television, radio, and the Internet, helped by satellite technology, can focus the public's attention almost instantaneously on developing situations throughout the world. In many cases news about the extraordinary event replaces most other stories. On September 12, 2001, most major U.S. newspapers, as well as flagship papers around the world, devoted their entire front pages, along with many inside pages, to the terrorist attack. Whatever else happens in the world during crisis periods, regardless of importance, may drop off the radar screen in the affected nations or even worldwide.

During the first stage of crisis, the media are the major sources of information, even for public officials. Media reports coordinate public activities and calm the audience. For example, broadcasts and newspapers in the nations affected by the tsunami carried special reports on "coping with the crisis" right after it struck. The reports gave people tips about temporary housing, health care, emergency food supplies, and ways to deal with damage to their homes.

Next to reaching the disaster site, the chief problem for newspeople during the first stage is getting accurate information. Rumors abound. When the first plane crashed into the World Trade Center in 2001, the media first reported it as an aviation accident. Each subsequent piece of news sparked an explosion of rumors that turned out to be largely untrue or only partly correct. National Public Radio reported that a Palestinian group was claiming responsibility for the assault but warned listeners to bear in mind that government sources had "a history of disinformation and this information may not be correct." [8] The number of dead and the extent of injuries are frequently inflated, although underestimates are also common. Deaths in the 2004 tsunami were initially reported in four digit numbers. The ultimate toll approximated 200,000. Newspeople receive so many conflicting reports that they lack enough time to check accuracy. The unrelenting pressure for fresh accounts often tempts media personnel to interview unreliable sources, who may lend a local touch but confuse the situation by reporting unverified or irrelevant information. [9] When reporters focus only on crisis events, as happened during the Los Angeles riots and the Asian tsunami, they may convey the wrong impression that, for example, the entire city has been left in ruins or that the affected areas have become a barren wasteland. [10] If highly technical matters, such as explosions, structural failures, and nuclear radiation disasters are involved, it may be impossible to present a coherent story, especially when government officials, eager to allay the public's fears and prevent panic, minimize dangers or obscure them by using impenetrable technical jargon.

The pressure for news encourages reporters and public officials alike to speculate about a disaster's causes. At times, these observers spin their own prejudices into a web of scenarios that puts blame for humanmade tragedies or their aftermath on socially outcast groups. For instance, the Los Angeles riots, which occurred during the 1992 presidential campaign, were blamed by Democrats on Republican inattention to urban blight and by Republicans on the welfare programs that had started during the liberal Democratic administration of Lyndon B. Johnson. "Outsiders" in a community (ethnic minorities or political deviants, for example) often become the hapless scapegoats. The racial riots of the 1960s were routinely attributed to "outside agitators" who were depicted as common criminals, bereft of moral scruples and social consciousness.

Stage Two. During the second stage of a crisis, the media try to correct past errors and put the situation into proper perspective. By that time, the chief dimensions of the crisis have usually emerged. For instance, in the Los Angeles riots, the 2001 terror strike, and the 2004 tsunami, the majority of victims and their injuries were known. Repairs and reconstruction plans were in place, and data rather than pure guesses informed damage estimates.

In general, the print media are able to do a more thorough job than are radio and television in pulling together the various events and fitting them into a coherent story. Print media have larger staffs for investigation and more room to present background details that make the events understandable. For instance, in the months preceding the outbreak of the 2003 Iraq War and in the days following its start, major newspapers reviewed the reasons for the hostilities, the cost in human lives and property, and the damage done to America's foreign relations by policy disagreements with traditional allies. They drew much of their information from Web sites that, thanks to ample links, now rival and often surpass newspapers in completeness of coverage of breaking news. As media scholar Al Tompkins put it: "If Vietnam was the 'living room war,' this was the 'real-time war' . . . we were actually seeing the story, not as it recently unfolded, but as it was unfolding." [11] The growing number of citizens who turn to cable television and the Internet for news could sample an assortment of foreign news sources in addition to multiple U.S. venues. Widely available foreign sources included Arab news broadcast by Al Jazeera and Al Arabia, and the *Middle East Times*. Other widely quoted sources were the British Broadcasting Corporation (BBC), various European newspapers, and C-SPAN's nightly sampling of the world's television coverage.

During this second stage, governments and their critics may try to shape political fallout from the event in ways that support their policy preferences. Media presented coverage of the Iraq War, for example, largely through the lens of military operations. Media sanitized the war while appearing to present reality. Television showed a succession of successful military maneuvers recorded by reporters embedded in various units. Military failures and the damage caused by military operations were rarely shown. The political aspects of the situation were largely ignored. The torrent of specific information left journalists little time to interpret the significance of the events they were reporting. Military censorship prevented featuring casualties or showing the arrival of dead soldiers in body bags at Dover Air Force base. During the terrorism and tsunami disasters, political leaders, including the president, earned political plaudits for visiting the afflicted places and expressing sympathy and encouragement as well as announcing emergency aid.

Stage Three. The third stage overlaps with the first two. It involves attempts by media personnel to place the crisis into a larger, long-range perspective and to prepare people to cope with the aftermath. Following the Los Angeles riots, presidential candidates Bill Clinton and George Bush toured the damaged neighborhoods and announced plans for rebuilding. The media also reported about clean-up efforts and restored services, such as mail deliveries and bus transportation. Within days of the assault on the World Trade Center and Pentagon, news stories reported plans for restoring the New York skyline to renewed glory and resuming full operations at the Pentagon. To deal with long-range post-traumatic shock and to sustain morale during prolonged crises, the media describe how some of the hardest-hit victims are coping and give full coverage to healing ceremonies, such as memorial church services or fund-raising concerts and sports events.

Positive and Negative Effects of Coverage

Information about crises, even if it conveys bad news, relieves disquieting uncertainty and calms people. The mere activity of watching or listening to familiar reporters and commentators reassures people and keeps them occupied. It gives them a sense of vicarious participation, of "doing something." To maintain this quieting effect, media personnel may avoid showing gruesome details of the crisis. However, this was not true of Asian tsunami coverage, during which gruesome photographs taken by thousands of amateur witnesses quickly flooded news channels thanks to the ease of computerized transmission. The tide of images generated an unprecedented outpouring of relief donations by people who were touched by the vivid scenes of human suffering.

News stories serve to reassure injured people that their grief and fears are shared. After seeing the same pictures and listening to the same broadcasts, people can discuss a crisis with neighbors, friends, and coworkers and feel mutual support. Watching military briefings on television during the Iraq War, for example, made Americans feel that they were fully informed about the war's progress and that the authorities were in control of the situation. Similarly, scenes of collapsing buildings or city blocks put to the torch during a riot can seem less frightening if the news shows that police, firefighters, ambulances, and medical personnel are on the scene. Watching the mayor or governor tour a disaster site provides further reassurance. Finally, directions conveyed by the media about appropriate behavior save lives and property and ensure that a stricken community continues to function.

Media coverage also can do harm during a crisis, raising serious questions about the responsibility of government and media personnel to consider the societal consequences of freedom to publish. News messages may so disturb people that they panic, endangering themselves and others. For instance, a precipitous mass exodus of frightened people during an impending flood or storm calamity may clog roads and overcrowd shelters; it may lead to injuries and death for those caught beyond the safety of their homes and workplaces. Inflammatory accusations are more likely to be publicized in times of crisis because the exceptionally large demand for news and guidance reduces gatekeepers' vigilance. Pack journalism may run rampant when media pool their stories to provide as much coverage as possible. If news sources or reporters make mistakes, they are spread by all the media. Pictures of violence often produce terrifying multiplication effects. Audiences tend to believe that the violent acts shown are merely a tiny sample. One house on fire or the sight of one victim's body may lead to visions of whole neighborhoods on fire and scores of victims killed. Overreaction may ensue. Police may be ordered to shoot lawbreakers on sight, and citizens may use excessive violence to protect themselves. When perpetrators of crimes are linked to an identifiable ethnic group, there may be a spate of hate crimes targeting members of that group, as happened when the 2001 terror strike was linked to Arab Americans.

Crisis and disaster news frequently attracts crowds of citizens and reporters to a site, impeding rescue and security operations. News coverage of physical disasters routinely draws looters to the scene. During the Los Angeles riots, police reported that the presence of television cameras seemed to escalate the violence. Rioters actually appeared to perform for the cameras. Sights of looters attracted other looters to the scene, particularly when the pictures revealed that no police officers were present. When violence pits government agents against antigovernment groups, as is often the case in terrorist incidents, ample coverage may incite retaliatory terrorism. Extensive media coverage has been called the lifeblood of terrorism because the perpetrators use their assaults to attract attention to their causes and gain sympathy and support. However, usually this turns out to be a false hope because news coverage outs the spotlight on the deeds and neglects the underlying causes.[12] Wide publicity for terrorist acts and heinous crimes (such as airline hijackings, poisoning of food supplies, or serial mass murders) may lead to copycat crimes.

Economic crises, too, can escalate as a result of media images. When prices on the financial markets plunged precipitously on October 19, 1987, media accounts used highly alarming language. *Panic, carnage,* and *nightmare selling* were common descriptive terms. Moreover, the media frequently compared the crash to the 1929 stock market calamity and discussed the Great Depression that followed. Such gloomy news apparently fanned the growing panic and further weakened the markets.[13]

Planning Crisis Coverage

Because media play such a crucial role in keeping communities going during crises, most media organizations have plans to cope with the problems of crisis coverage. This is particularly true for electronic media. The plans generally are more detailed for natural disasters than for civil disturbances because needs are more predictable, and there is greater consensus about objectives. Nevertheless, much remains to be decided on the spur of the moment.[14] Confusion inevitably reigns at the start of a crisis. Contradictory messages are likely to abound until coordination can be arranged. In addition to media-sponsored plans, most stations are tied into the federal Emergency Broadcast System (EBS), a network for relaying news during emergencies.

Crisis coverage planning has two aspects: preparing for crisis routines and deciding how to present ongoing events. Aside from warning people about impending natural disasters and suggesting preparations, plans to forestall crises are rare, probably because the media focus on short-range happenings and because most crises cannot be accurately predicted. Nonetheless, viewers have often blamed the media for neglecting preventive coverage. The Kerner commission in 1968 condemned media silence about the plight of African Americans in the United States for allowing frustrations to build up and explode into race riots in the mid-1960s. In the same vein, the Los Angeles riots of 1992 were blamed in part on inattention by the media and other institutions to the plight of inner cities and their minority residents (Box 5-1). When public approval of the 2003 Iraq War began to sag in reaction to mounting casualties and the failure to find the weapons of mass destruction that had been a major reason for going to war, the public criticized the media's gatekeeping decisions. Why had early

BOX 5-1
Playing the Crisis Blame Game:
The *ExxonValdez* Disaster

When crises strike, blaming becomes big business. Newspeople speculate about who caused the disaster or could have prevented it, as well as who acted imprudently in coping with its aftermath. News stories frame the public's perceptions of the nature of the crisis, its causes and consequences, and the proficiency of the personnel charged with dealing with crisis damage. When blame falls on a business organization, millions and even billions of dollars of restoration and compensation money may be at stake, as well as the reputation and even the survival of the company. How do companies try to influence news framing to avoid harmful publicity?

The Exxon Company's flawed press dealings in coping with oil spill disaster news in Alaska are instructive. The company's oil tanker *Exxon Valdez* ran aground on a reef in Prince William Sound on March 24, 1989, spilling 11 million gallons of crude oil that coated the pristine waters. An estimated 1 million migratory fowl and one-third of the sea otters in the area died, as did seals, sea lions, clams, salmon, and other fish. Alaska's fishery and tourism industries were threatened. Hordes of U.S. and foreign journalists arrived within hours of learning about the environmental tragedy.

Exxon immediately dispatched the Alaska coordinator of its public affairs team to the disaster scene to deal with the media. Media relations experts later called this a mistake, pointing out that major disasters require media access to the highest, most authoritative levels of the company. The coordinator set up a media center in Valdez, a small and remote Alaskan town with limited accommodations and facilities for the large contingent of journalists. That decision also became controversial. Some analysts said that a local office was essential because camera crews had to be near the scene; others argued that the media office should have been in a major city with ample press facilities.

The president of the shipyard from which the tanker hailed served as the official representative of Exxon's management. Unfortunately, he was inexperienced in media relations. His news conferences were debacles, demonstrating how essential media savvy has

(Box continues, next page)

become for business elites who must interact with the press. When Exxon's chief executive officer finally spoke on television, his message was equally ineffective. He calmly discussed the chemicals the company was using to disperse the oil. But he neglected the essential human relations touch when he failed to apologize for the disaster or show emotion about losses. Ten days later, full-page Exxon ads appeared in the press. They expressed the company's deep concerns about the disaster and vowed to clean up the polluted area. Possibly with an eye to discouraging lawsuits, the ads avoided acknowledging responsibility for the spill.

Conducting media relations was exceptionally difficult in this case because many competing information sources were dispatching conflicting messages. Messages came from the U.S. Coast Guard, the Environmental Protection Agency, Alaska state and local officials, and such environmental interest groups as the National Wildlife Federation and Greenpeace. Reporters knew little about oil spills and were trying to simplify a very complex story for a public that knew even less. Blaming all bad happenings on a single villain—Exxon—was the easiest way to go, even though there were many other culprits. With better media relations, Exxon could have shaped the coverage in a more accurate and less damaging way. Exxon should have had well-prepared, top-level personnel available on the scene from the start. It should have issued more-informative, simply written press releases, and it should have soothed the public's anger by acknowledging responsibility for those actions for which it was at fault. A bit more emotion and empathy for others would have evoked more compassion from critics. As one analyst put it, albeit a bit too simply, "if the media had captured, on video and film, the CEO on the site at Prince William Sound holding an oil-covered bird in his hand and looking as if he were crying, the entire story would be told differently today." [1]

1. Kathleen Fearn-Banks, *Crisis Communications: A Casebook Approach* (Mahwah, N.J.: Erlbaum, 1996), 149–150.

opposition to the war received so little publicity? Why had news outlets relegated it to back pages of papers and tail ends of broadcasts while featuring the government's case in favor of war? Would media efforts to undermine the case for war have been a patriotic act or undue interference in the nation's foreign policy? The answer is controversial.[15]

Plans for covering natural disasters are generally predicated on the assumption that people tend to panic and that coverage must forestall this. Stories that are graphic enough to arouse a lethargic population to prepare for the disaster unfortunately may cause panic or denial. Denial seems to be rampant in southern California, where most residents have not taken recommended precautions against earthquakes—such as fortifying buildings and storing emergency supplies—despite frequent warnings.[16] Similarly, when the Department of Homeland Security warns the nation that the danger of a terrorist attack has risen to a higher level, few citizens take suggested precautions. Government officials and newspeople often abstain from warnings about an impending disaster because they fear adverse consequences if the danger does not materialize. The warning may lead to costly, unnecessary preventive measures. That happened in the winter of 1990, when warnings about a 50 percent chance of an earthquake in the New Madrid earthquake zone in the Midwest prompted residents to flee, public services to be shut down, and numerous business events to be canceled. A controversial climatologist had made the predictions. Most people believed the story despite misgivings voiced by seismologists and geologists. Reporters by the hundreds gathered in the "danger zone" ready to report the event, which did not occur.

Reluctance to issue warnings is even greater when civil disorders threaten. Officials and their media mouthpieces assume that broadcasts about civil disturbances will produce panic and copycat effects among the public. Social scientists who study disasters deny that panic and contagion occur frequently.[17] Whether or not these scientists are correct, the important fact is that media personnel have been expecting these reactions and have acted accordingly. That may be changing if coverage of antiglobalization protests becomes typical. Some news coverage of violence during street protests in Seattle in 1999 featured sympathetic stories that depicted the violence as necessary action to stop global corporations from exploiting the public.[18] The fact that favorable publicity was readily available on the Internet may have been a factor in inducing news media to feature more balanced coverage.[19] From the riots of the 1960s, media personnel learned to keep a low profile when violence occurs because the perpetrators are energized by the chance to have their actions publicized. Media personnel accordingly try to act unobtrusively. For example, they avoid bringing identified television trucks into areas where disturbances are taking place. However, such precautions are largely wasted when television reporters broadcast live coverage from the scene.

The media also try to avoid inflammatory details or language in news reports. Milder terms can replace such words as *carnage, holocaust, mob action,* or *massacre.* The general rule during crises is "when in doubt, leave it out." Publicizing interviews with public officials and civic leaders who urge calm behavior and indicate that the situation is under control can soothe tempers. During the Los Angeles riots, Mayor Tom Bradley and Gov. Pete Wilson appeared repeatedly in the media to talk about progress in quieting the city. Rodney King, the victim of the police beating that sparked the disturbances, also made an impassioned appeal for ending the violence. Following the Twin Towers bombing, President Bush and other public and private leaders throughout the country pleaded for ending hate crimes and discrimination against people presumed to have ties to Islamic countries. The leaders failed to consider the high emotional arousal of average Americans in response to the mainstream media's extensive coverage of the activities of extremist groups after September 11 and the constant repetition of the gruesome pictures.[20]

The Problem of News Suppression

In natural as well as human-made crises, suppressing news, either temporarily or permanently, raises major policy questions. How much coverage should the media present immediately, at the risk of telling an inaccurate story, spreading panic, and attracting bystanders and destructive participants to the scene? What facts should be withheld initially or permanently to forestall troublesome reactions? Should live coverage be banned, particularly in civil disturbances, lest it increases the intensity and duration of the crisis? Some news outlets routinely delay live coverage until officials have the situation under control. Others believe that suppression of live coverage will allow the spread of rumors that may be more inciting than judicious reporting of ongoing events. No one knows which of these views is most correct or how different circumstances affect reactions to media coverage of crises.

Deciding whether to suppress coverage becomes particularly difficult when a crisis involves terrorists, prison rioters, assassins of political leaders, or maniacal mass murderers who crave publicity. Live coverage of the crime scene glamorizes their violent acts and may encourage further outrages. "By transforming a killer into a celebrity, the press has not merely encouraged but perhaps driven him to strike again and may have stirred others brooding madly over their grievances to act."[21] As Rep. Edward Feighan, D-Ohio, pointed out after chairing congressional hearings on terrorism and the media, the television age poses new dilemmas for a responsible press. "Terrorism is a new form of symbolic warfare, and the television screen is the battlefield on which these wars will be fought in the future."[22] Even the print media face such dilemmas. The *New York Times* and the *Washington Post* reluctantly agreed in 1995 to publish a lengthy tract by a terrorist. The "Unabomber" had threatened to continue his spree of letter bombings unless the media published his manifesto of complaints against society.

Publicity does play into the hands of individuals willing to spread terror through indiscriminate killings and other heinous deeds. However, if the press fails to cover the terrorist acts or subsequent court actions and penalties, including death sentences, some will accuse it of infringing on the public's right to know, even when the information appears on the Internet. The press also forgoes publishing a dramatic event with wide audience appeal and substantial financial rewards. If the press follows the government's official line in describing terrorists and their motives, it may become a government propaganda tool.[23] If it dwells on either the human strengths or the frightful human frailties of the violent actors, it will be accused of making saints out of villains or villains out of hapless victims of society's malfunctions.

The press faces similar difficult decisions about news suppression during international crises and in time of war. During the Iraq War, the military kept tight control over news stories by inviting journalists to join military units—"embedding" is the technical term—and report the news from an insider's perspective. Reporters' loyalty to their unit and a pledge to abstain from publishing sensitive information served to dull criticism of war activities. Some reporters resented such constraints and ventured forth on their own in defiance of official rules and at the risk of their personal safety. Although their fellow journalists generally approved, the majority of the public did not because it supported wartime censorship as a security measure.[24]

Muted coverage is problematic. It generally leads to presentation of the official story only and suppression of unofficial views. The perspectives of civilian and military public security personnel become paramount and accepted by much of the public.[25] As a result, security aspects are stressed, rather than the causes of violent behavior and the political and social changes, including new public policies, that might prevent future violence. Consider the muted coverage of a tense racial incident that involved murder in a New York City neighborhood. A review of the incident two years later indicated that the media had covered the facts adequately without further inflaming the tense public. But media had also omitted crucial details about mistakes made by former public officials in handling the crisis, largely because these officials had been the main sources of news. These omissions delayed reforms and deepened the community's racial divisions.[26] In terrorist incidents or prison riots, failure to air the grievances of terrorists and prison inmates deprives them of a public forum for voicing their grievances. Their bottled-up anger may lead to more violent explosions. Wartime news suppression by government censorship or reporters' self-censorship out of a sense of patriotism may cover up misdeeds and encourage their repetition.[27]

Some observers contend that muted reporting reduces the potential for arousing hatred and creating unbridgeable conflicts. Delayed coverage, these observers argue, can be more analytical and thus more likely to produce reforms. Others contend that the drama of an ongoing crisis raises public consciousness much better and faster than anything else. People will act to remedy injustice only if the situation is acute. If the crisis has already passed, action may seem pointless. A permanent news blackout will make reforms highly unlikely. Those opposed to muted coverage or news suppression are willing to risk paying a high price in lost lives, personal injuries, imprisonment, and property damage in hopes that immediate, complete coverage will shock the community to undertake basic social reforms. Most American political leaders, as well as most newspeople, have hitherto opted for muting violent conflict rather than bringing it to a head.

Finally, there is the unresolved philosophical question about the wisdom and propriety of news suppression in a free society. The true test of genuine press freedom does not come in times of calm. It comes in times of crisis when the costs of freedom may be dear, tempting government and media alike to impose silence. If a free press is a paramount value, then the die must be cast in favor of unrestrained crisis coverage, moderated only by a muted sense of responsibility of individual journalists.

Covering Pseudo-Crises

Thus far, we have discussed genuinely extraordinary events. But there are many other situations that the press treats like crises because that makes them interesting news stories. These pseudo-crises become front-page news for days on end, generating many hours of live television and radio coverage. In 2004 pseudo-events included extensive coverage of the death of former President Ronald Reagan, biographies of hundreds of couples involved in homosexual marital unions after they became legalized in several U.S. jurisdictions, and a slate of celebrity crime cases featuring business entrepreneur Martha Stewart, sports star Kobe Bryant, and entertainer Michael Jackson.

The scenarios that make up these real-world soap operas cause two serious problems. They exaggerate the significance of events that are not extraordinary, and they crowd out other events that need coverage. For example, coverage of the Stewart, Bryant, and Jackson cases, supplemented by the trial of wife murderer Scott Peterson, equaled the attention

A news crew documents the arrival of Hurricane Frances at Cocoa Beach, Florida, on September 4, 2004.

given to the presidential campaign and to the war in Iraq.[28] Had the media cut back on overblown coverage, they could have filled their newshole with other, more significant, stories.

A brief look at these 2004 news stories should be instructive. The death of former president Reagan was an important event, of course. However, there was no need for pseudo-crisis type reporting; at the time of his death he had been retired for fifteen years. Even though he died on a weekend, which is a comparatively slow time for news, there were other more important stories warranting extensive analysis. They included President Bush's meetings in Europe with major allies, political developments in Iraq, and a lengthy Senate report detailing serious intelligence failures by the CIA. Similarly, when media devoted scarce news space and time to stories about homosexual couples, more significant news was throttled. The fact that same-sex marriages were legalized was important, but the personal circumstances of hundreds of couples were not truly newsworthy.

Turning briefly to the crime cases, Martha Stewart was convicted of lying to federal investigators about a 2001 sale of stock. For this relatively minor law infraction, she was sentenced to serve five months in a minimum security prison and five months in home arrest. The media likely would have ignored this story had the celebrity element been lacking. By contrast, the Bryant and Jackson cases would have made the news because they involved serious accusations: rape in the Bryant case and child molestation in the Jackson case. However, compared to other such crime cases, the coverage was excessive and overblown.

The Peterson case is more unusual. Peterson, a personable young man, was accused of murdering his pregnant wife on Christmas Eve, 2002. As the case progressed, new shocking details emerged and rekindled media interest: the remains of mother and child washed up on San Francisco area beaches, a woman with whom Peterson had an extramarital affair at the time of his wife's murder came forward with incriminating taped testimony, and a disguised Peterson allegedly attempted to flee the country. Whereas the Peterson case became a pseudo-event because the repeated "news pegs" encouraged further coverage, the far more serious case of a Michigan serial killer who had confessed to twelve murders was largely ignored.[29]

Summary

In U.S. political culture, the normal feuds of politics are deferred when major emergencies happen. Although this unwritten rule has been mentioned most often in connection with foreign policy, where "politics stops at the water's edge," it applies as well to the types of domestic crises discussed in this chapter. When life and property are endangered, when sudden death and terror reign, when well-known leaders are assassinated, or when the nation goes to war, the media suspend their normal coverage practices. Instead of playing their adversarial role, the media become teammates of officialdom in attempts to restore public order, safety, and tranquility.

The media perform indispensable functions during crises: they diffuse vital information to the public and officials, interpret events, and provide emotional support for troubled communities. Pocket-size radios and cellular phones are particularly helpful during major disasters because their technical requirements are most adaptable to makeshift arrangements. They can broadcast without regular electric power and they can reach isolated people in remote locations. Round-the-clock radio, television, and Internet news coverage and satellite transmissions from around the world make it possible to observe extraordinary events wherever and whenever they occur.

Because the media play such a large part in public communication during crises, public officials and the community at large are concerned about the quality of their performance. Information gaps, misinformation, and the dissemination of information that worsens the crisis have led to demands for control of the information flow. Many media institutions have formal plans that temporarily set aside the usual criteria for publishing exciting news in the interest of calming the public. The need to plan for crisis coverage is acute. Modern society faces crises of various sorts so frequently that policy makers in the media and in government are remiss when they fail to plan for emergencies. By the same token, they must strive to avoid news distortion and overindulgence in pseudo-crisis coverage when titillating news becomes available.

Muted coverage, particularly during civil disturbances and incidents of political terrorism, may be unwise because it may drown out explicit and implicit messages about unmet societal demands. Moreover, in the Internet age, it has become increasingly difficult to suppress information. As media scholar Robin Brown notes: "The ability of the global communications system to gather and disseminate information has vastly increased. . . . In such an environment it is no surprise that the sensitivity of governments to the media increases. . . . The effects of this will vary from case to case (and from country to country), but it can only increase the interpenetration of war, politics, and the media." [30]

Notes

1. Newseum, "9/11 Terrorist Attacks Front Pages, September 12, 2001," www.newseum.org.
2. Michael Grunwald, "Terrorists Hijack 4 Airliners, Destroy World Trade Center, Hit Pentagon; Hundreds Dead," *Washington Post*, September 12, 2001. Matthew V. Storin, "While America Slept: Coverage of Terrorism from 1993 to September 11, 2001," in *Terrorism, War, and the Press*, ed. Nancy Palmer (Hollis, N.H.: Hollis Publishing Co., 2003), 1–26, analyzes terrorism coverage by the *New York Times* and *Washington Post* from 1993 through 2001.
3. For details of the Los Angeles riots, see "Rage in L.A.," *Chicago Tribune*, May 1, 1992; Erna Smith, *Transmitting Race: The Los Angeles Riot in Television News* (Cambridge: Harvard University Press, 1994).
4. Pew Research Center for the People and the Press, "American Psyche Reeling from Terror Attacks," September 19, 2001, http://people-press.org/reports/print.php3?PageID=32.
5. Pew Research Center for the People and the Press, "Media Report, 1992–2003," http://people-press.org/.

6. Chris Jones, "This Living Room War," *Chicago Tribune,* April 20, 2003. Andrew Glass, "The War on Terrorism Goes on Line," in Palmer, *Terrorism, War, and the Press,* 47–80, analyzes Internet coverage.
7. Walter Gantz, "The Diffusion of News about the Attempted Reagan Assassination," *Journal of Communication* 33 (winter 1983): 56–65.
8. Whitecloud.com, "9/11/01 Events," www.whitecloud.com/events9-11-01.htm.
9. T. Joseph Scanlon, "Media Coverage of Crises: Better Than Reported, Worse Than Necessary," *Journalism Quarterly* 55 (spring 1978): 68–72. Crisis reporting is especially difficult when competing frames regarding causes of the disaster abound. See Frank D. Durham, "News Frames as Social Narratives: TWA Flight 800," *Journal of Communication* 48 (autumn 1998): 110–114.
10. Dennis E. Wenger, "A Few Empirical Observations Concerning the Relationship between the Mass Media and Disaster Knowledge: A Research Report," in *Disasters and the Mass Media: Proceedings of the Committee on Disasters and the Mass Media Workshop* (Washington, D.C.: National Academy Press, 1980), 252–253; Amy Waldman, "Thousands Die as Quake-Spawned Waves Crash onto Coastlines across Southern Asia: Untold Numbers Are Missing in 6 Countries," *New York Times,* December 27, 2004.
11. Quoted in Allan Johnson, "Numbers Don't Lie," *Chicago Tribune,* April 20, 2003.
12. See Storin, "While America Slept."
13. John Corry, "Network News Covers the Stock Market Frenzy," *New York Times,* October 21, 1987; and Alex Jones, "Caution in the Press: Was It Really a 'Crash'?" *New York Times,* October 21, 1987.
14. Private-sector planning for dealing with media in crisis situations is discussed in detail in Kathleen Fearn-Banks, *Crisis Communications: A Casebook Approach,* 2d ed. (Mahwah, N.J.: Erlbaum, 2001).
15. Many authors have wrestled with these questions. Their studies are reviewed in a book review essay by Christopher Hanson, "No Neutral Corner: The American News Media After 9/11," *Journalism and Mass Communication Quarterly* 80 (2003): 731–735.
16. Rodney M. Kueneman and Joseph E. Wright, "News Policies of Broadcast Stations for Civil Disturbances and Disasters," *Journalism Quarterly* 52 (winter 1975): 671.
17. See the report on the work of the Disaster Research Center at Ohio State University in E.L. Quarantelli and Russell R. Dynes, eds., "Organizational and Group Behavior in Disasters," *American Behavioral Scientist* 13 (January 1970).
18. Andrew Rojecki, "Media and the New Post-Cold War Movements," in *Media and Conflict: Framing Issues, Making Policy, Shaping Opinions,* ed. Eytan Gilboa (Ardsley, N.Y.: Transnational Publishers, 2002), 3–24.
19. Melissa A. Wall, "The Battle in Seattle: How Nongovernmental Organizations Used Websites in Their Challenge to the WTO," in Gilboa, *Media and Conflict,* 25–44.
20. Barbie Zelizer and Stuart Allen, eds. *Journalism after September 11* (New York: Routledge, 2002); also Brigette L. Nacos, *Mass Mediated Terrorism* (Lanham, Md.: Rowman and Littlefield, 2002).
21. *New Yorker,* August 15, 1977, 21.
22. Edward F. Feighan, "After the Hostage Crisis, TV Focuses on Itself," *New York Times,* August 19, 1985.
23. Alex P. Schmid and Janny de Graaf, *Violence as Communication: Insurgent Terrorism and the Western News Media* (Beverly Hills, Calif.: Sage, 1982), 98. For an

analysis of the symbiotic relationship of media and sources of crisis news, see Gadi Wolfsfeld, "Symbiosis of Press and Protest: An Exchange Analysis," *Journalism Quarterly* 61 (autumn 1984): 550–555; Regina G. Lawrence, "Icons, Indexing, and Police Brutality: An Exploration of Journalistic Norms" (paper delivered at the annual meeting of the International Communication Association, 1995).

24. Pew Research Center for the People and the Press, "Terror Coverage Boosts News Media Images," November 18, 2001, http://people-press.org/reports/display.php3?PageID=143.

25. Douglas M. McLeod and Benjamin H. Detenter, "Framing Effects of Television News Coverage of Social Protest," *Journal of Communication* 49 (summer 1999): 3–23.

26. William Glaberson, "Press Has Blind Spots, Too," *New York Times,* July 22, 1993.

27. For a fuller discussion, see Storin, "While America Slept."

28. Bryant Robinson, "ABC News: The Year in Infamous Criminal Cases," December 28, 2004, http://abcnews.go.com/US/print?id+349539.

29. Ibid.

30. Robin Brown, "Clausewitz in the Age of CNN: Rethinking the Military-Media Relationship," in *Framing Terrorism: The News Media, the Government, and the Public,* ed. Pippa Norris, Montague Kern, and Marion Just (New York: Routledge, 2003), 43–58.

Readings

Biel, Steven, ed. *American Disasters.* New York: New York University Press, 2001.

———. *Disasters and the Mass Media: Proceedings of the Committee on Disasters and the Mass Media Workshop.* Washington, D.C.: National Academy of Sciences, 1980.

Fearn-Banks, Kathleen. *Crisis Communications: A Casebook Approach.* 2d ed. Mahwah, N.J.: Erlbaum, 2001.

Lawrence, Regina G. *The Politics of Force: Media and the Construction of Police Brutality.* Berkeley: University of California Press, 2000.

Nimmo, Dan, and James E. Combs. *Nightly Horrors: Crisis Coverage in Television Network News.* Knoxville: University of Tennessee Press, 1985.

Norris, Pippa, Montague Kern, and Marion Just, eds. *Framing Terrorism: The News Media, the Government, and the Public.* New York: Routledge, 2003.

Palmer, Nancy, ed. *Terrorism, War, and the Press.* Hollis, N.H.: Hollis Publishing Co., 2003.

Peri, Yoram, ed. *The Rabin Assassination and the Israeli Public.* Stanford: Stanford University Press, 2000.

Singer, Eleanor, and Phyllis M. Endreny. *Reporting on Risk: How the Mass Media Portray Accidents, Diseases, Disasters, and Other Hazards.* New York: Russell Sage Foundation, 1993.

Walters, Lynne Masel, Lee Wilkins, and Tim Walters. *Bad Tidings: Communication and Catastrophe.* Hillsdale, N.J.: Erlbaum, 1989.

c h a p t e r   s i x

The Media as Policy Makers

IN HIS 1931 AUTOBIOGRAPHY, LINCOLN STEFFENS, who has been called "America's greatest reporter," tells how a history professor introduced him to an audience as "the first of the muckrakers." Steffens corrected the professor. "I had to answer first that I was not the original muckraker; the prophets of the Old Testament were ahead of me, and to make a big jump in time so were the writers, editors, and reporters (including myself) of the 1890s who were finding fault with 'things as they are' in the pre-muckraking period." [1]

Steffens was right. Public exposés of evil and corruption in high places have been common throughout recorded history. They rest on the assumption that exposure will shame the wrongdoers and lead to public condemnation of their deeds and possibly punishment. Reforms may ultimately ensue.[2] Exposés have always been and always will continue to be an important feature of social responsibility journalism in America. They are a major part of the deliberate manipulation of the political process mentioned in Chapter 1 as one of the media's important functions.

In this chapter we will examine muckraking to show how it really works, with particular attention paid to the role of public opinion. Agenda building is another media strategy for manipulating politics that merits examination in situations like leadership crises driven by political scandal; the development of science policy, such as regulations affecting global warming; and the support of interest group goals. We will also assess the political impact of nationally broadcast factual and fictional documentaries. The chapter ends with reflections on the responsibility of newspeople to refrain from questionable methods in their zeal to reform society.

The Ethics of Melding Political Activism with Journalism

Like other manifestations of the social responsibility orientation, manipulative journalism raises philosophical, ethical, and news policy questions. Does muckraking create a witch-hunting climate that intimidates officeholders and deters capable people from careers in politics? Do newspeople lose credibility and jeopardize important professional values, such as objectivity and neutrality, when they try to influence the events that they report? Where can media audiences turn for a reasonably unbiased view of the complexities of political life if the media are partisans? Claims by newspeople that their political activities reflect the wishes of their audiences are questionable as long as the selection and activities of journalists are not subject to control by the publics that they claim to represent. In fact, public opinion polls show mixed rates of approval for many tactics of investigative journalism.[3]

Despite these concerns, the role of the journalist as political actor is popular. The rapid spread of civic journalism to newspapers, television, and radio stations in such cities as Chicago, Boston, Miami, Minneapolis, Charlotte, and Wichita is one example.[4] Practitioners of civic journalism explore the political concerns of their audiences by arranging town meetings, focus groups, and interviews. When the journalists have identified community problems, they try to find solutions. Journalists also become participants in politics when they write stories that support a specific politician's policy agenda. Collaboration may begin when politicians leak newsworthy information to journalists. Rather than attempting reforms on their own, these politicians hope to enlist media cooperation to gain their ends. Similarly, citizens routinely contact the media with problems related to public affairs, hoping that media publicity will spur government action. Just as the media have taken over many functions formerly performed by political parties during election times, so too have they assumed many of the ombudsman, reform, and law enforcement functions traditionally performed by other institutions in society. Whether this is the cause or consequence of the weakening of these other institutions is a hotly debated question.

Manipulative Journalism in Perspective

The extent of the efforts of newspeople to participate in policy making has fluctuated as philosophies of news making have changed. The turmoil of the 1960s, which raised the public's social consciousness; the

Watergate scandal, which forced President Richard Nixon to resign in 1974; and the shift toward advocating a social responsibility ethic in journalism schools raised manipulative journalism from a position of disdain in the early 1900s to one of high esteem in the closing decades of the twentieth century. Approval of these journalistic practices, while not unanimous, has been widespread, especially in elite media circles. Reporters and media institutions whose investigations have led to important social and political reforms frequently win plaudits as well as prestigious prizes for high journalistic achievement.

Independent investigative organizations that collaborate with media sleuths have flourished as well. The nonprofit, foundation-subsidized Center for Investigative Reporting, established in San Francisco in 1977, is an example. The center uses freelance reporters who collectively conduct investigations and who can be hired by various media to undertake projects that cannot readily be handled internally. The Better Government Association in Chicago is one of many local institutions doing investigative work within a particular city or state. Investigative Reporters and Editors, a national organization, has been teaching its approaches to mainstream journalists. The Nieman Foundation for Journalism at Harvard University holds annual conferences to improve watchdog journalism.[5]

Collaboration between independent watchdog organizations and the media is mutually beneficial. When the Center for Investigative Reporting and CNN collaborated in scrutinizing problems with the nation's crime laboratories, publication of significant findings was assured, making it likely that the center would reach its goals: corrective actions.[6] Tapping into media resources also helps cover the costs of complex investigations that can run into hundreds of thousands of dollars. This added financial support can be crucial. The media, in turn, gain collaborators who are skilled in investigating public issues and who often have excellent connections in government and in the community. The prestige and credibility of watchdog organizations may also enhance the credibility of jointly issued reports, such as the CNN special report on flawed forensic laboratory procedures.

The substance and style of most investigative stories reflect three major media objectives. The first objective is to produce exciting stories that will appeal to audiences. The second goal is to gain praise from the journalism profession. In addition to these routine journalistic goals, many reporters want a third result, to trigger political action or be part of it. Even when political consequences are not initially envisioned, most reporters feel highly gratified when their stories lead to actions that accord with their political and social preferences.

The line between deliberate attempts to produce political changes and incidental sparking of reforms is often too fine to distinguish. For

Lincoln Steffens (1866–1936) was a prominent investigative journalist who exposed corrupt relations between government officials and the business community.

example, when the media follow up on a report of a series of deaths in nursing homes and discover and describe deplorable conditions that led to these deaths, is this a case of muckraking designed to manipulate political events and bring about reform? Or does the idea that reform is needed arise naturally and purely incidentally from a routine news story? Was Lincoln Steffens telling the truth when he claimed that he did not intend to be a muckraker?[7] Could he have specialized in writing sensational exposés of corruption in state and local government and in private business for the sheer joy of delving into the muck, with no thought given to reforms that might follow in the wake of his stories?

From the standpoint of the political reformer, it may not matter whether reform was an intended or unintended byproduct of investigative reporting. The distinction matters to newspeople, however, because it raises controversial issues about the proper role of journalism in U.S. society. Journalists, even when they favor social responsibility journalism in the abstract, do not like to admit that they wrote their stories intending to produce social and political reforms. Moreover, they do not call attention to the fact that they often carefully select their sources to support their investigative goals.[8]

Muckraking Models

Investigative journalism leads to political action in three ways. Journalists may write stories about public policies in hopes of engendering a massive public reaction that will lead to widespread demands for political remedies.[9] They may write stories to arouse political elites who are officeholders or who have influence with officeholders. These elites, eager to forestall public criticism, may then attempt to resolve the problems, often even before a media report is published. Finally, action may ensue from direct collaboration between investigative journalists and public officeholders who coordinate news stories and supportive political activities.[10]

In each case, muckraking may take the form of one of three models: the simple muckraking model, the leaping impact model, and the truncated muckraking model. Social scientists Harvey Molotch, David Protess, and Margaret Gordon and their coworkers identified and tested these models in typical muckraking situations—sensational exposés of corruption usually involving high-status individuals.[11]

The simple muckraking model presented schematically below begins when journalists decide to investigate a problematic situation, and the investigation leads to published news that stirs public opinion. An aroused public then mobilizes policy makers who solve the problem.

Journalistic investigation	→	Publication	→	Public opinion	→	Policy initiatives	→	Policy consequences

When some elements in the model are skipped entirely, it becomes a leaping impact model. For instance, following the investigation and publication of a story, officials may act without pressure from public opinion. Journalistic investigations may have policy consequences even when no reports about the investigation have surfaced because officials often act to forestall adverse publicity.

In the truncated muckraking model, the sequence is aborted at some point so that the investigation fails to lead to corrective policies. This happens when the evidence that journalists discover is insufficient or too risky to publish because it may lead to costly lawsuits or damaging retaliation by compromised individuals or organizations. Such considerations have come into play in investigations of major tobacco companies and racketeering operations. In many instances, published stories do not stir public opinion. If the public is aroused, public officials may still fail to act, or policy initiatives may not lead to any symbolic or substantive results.

Several examples of muckraking will illustrate these models. Most of the examples come from intensive studies of muckraking conducted by scholars who had arranged to be alerted to forthcoming media exposés. This enabled them to interview citizens and policy makers concerned with the issues under investigation, both before and after publication of the stories. The impact of the story could then be assessed far more accurately than is usually possible when stories come as a surprise and permit assessment only after the fact. Scholars monitored changes in public policy for several months following the exposés and judged the journalists' motives and methods in conducting the investigations.[12]

Simple Muckraking

A story about shocking conditions in school cafeterias in Washington, D.C., in June 2003 illustrates simple muckraking. Reports from *Inside Edition,* a television news magazine, reported that they had found dead mice, rodent droppings, and broken refrigerators, freezers, and garbage disposals in two out of three schools the show had investigated. An aroused public demanded action. Public school officials promised repairs and reforms. But a follow-up investigation in September 2003 showed little progress.[13]

Modest outcomes are typical in situations that reflect the simple muckraking model. Media-aroused public opinion rarely is a strong force for change. Why? Many Americans are complacent or cynical about the political status quo. It is therefore difficult to spur them to take action on public problems, even those directly affecting them. For example, extensive efforts to arouse public concern about obesity and the need for avoiding fattening foods have proved largely futile.[14] Politicians accordingly may feel safe in ignoring swells in public opinion, believing that they involve relatively few people and that the issues will soon subside when new situations capture the public's fancy.

On the other end of the interest spectrum, investigative stories may be about an issue that is already a matter of great concern to the public. Although the investigative story confirms that concern, it does not push the public across the barrier of reluctance to press for political action. For example, a five-part newspaper series in the *Chicago Sun-Times*—"Rape: Every Woman's Nightmare"—dealt with the incidence and consequences of rape in the Chicago area. Interviews conducted prior to the series had shown that the public was already greatly concerned about the problem.

The series enhanced that concern but did little to spur new crime-fighting measures. However, the rape series heightened the sensitivity of newspaper staffs to the problem. The number of stories in the *Sun-Times* about rape more than doubled, and coverage became more insightful.[15] Such consequences are unexpected and, because they do not entail the government action specified in the model, are rarely recorded as muckraking triumphs.

Although it is difficult for the media to arouse public opinion, it does happen, as the school cafeteria case demonstrates. The elements that aroused the public in that instance included an emotional issue—the health of school children in the audience's locality—a graphic report showing pictures of unsanitary conditions on school grounds, and pictures of responsible public officials. When such a story captures people's interest, and they have little prior knowledge about the situation, they may learn much and become highly concerned. Still, major corrective government action remains unlikely, especially if it involves high costs for which no funds are readily available.[16]

Leaping Impact Muckraking

A media exposé called "Arson for Profit" that ABC aired on its *20/20* program exemplifies the leaping impact model. The investigation indicated that a group of real estate owners had instigated extensive fire damage in Chicago's Uptown neighborhood. The group bought dilapidated buildings, insured them heavily, and then burned them down to collect the insurance. Following the exposé, community leaders voiced concern but failed to act. Nevertheless, the arson stopped because the perpetrators feared further public exposure. Fires declined by 27 percent in the afflicted neighborhood, representing the first decline in five years. Insurance payments for arson also dropped by more than 20 percent in the year following the arson stories. No other metropolitan area showed comparable drops. The Illinois legislature responded belatedly with very minor policy reforms. There were no criminal indictments of the parties implicated in the insurance fraud. This story illustrates the leaping impact model because publication of the story linked directly to correction of the problem, even without elite action and the pressures of public opinion.

Leaping impact is most common when newspeople and public officials openly collaborate. Such coalition journalism may be initiated by media or government personnel, or it may arise by chance. Journalists are eager to involve government officials in investigative stories because the presence of these officials lends credibility and increases the chances of substantial policy consequences. Although working in coalition with government officials may jeopardize the media's zealous pursuit of the watchdog role, it gets results.

The events following an NBC *Newsmagazine* story, "The Home Health Hustle," that exposed fraud and abuse in home health care programs, provide a good example of coalition journalism. Public opinion polls showed that the broadcast aroused the concerns of many viewers who previously had been unaware of problems with these programs. But public opinion apparently was not instrumental in the decision of Congress to introduce appropriate reform legislation. In the fashion of the leaping impact models, legislative results seemed to flow directly from collaboration between investigative reporters and members of the U.S. Senate that preceded airing of the story by several months.

Journalists had met with officials of the Senate's Permanent Subcommittee on Investigations to plan hearings on home health care fraud and to coordinate their broadcasts with the Senate's activities. The hearings were then announced during the broadcast. Senators subsequently credited media personnel with major contributions to the investigation of home health care fraud. However, it is uncertain to what degree the knowledge that television would feature the story spurred the senators to collaborate with the media. The combined investigative activities of the media and the Senate ultimately led to a number of proposals for corrective legislation. Still, in the end, the bills failed to pass. Aside from the effects of increased vigilance by public officials and home health care consumers, no major changes could be directly linked to the investigative stories.[17]

In the same way, when the rape series appeared in the *Chicago Sun-Times,* newspeople had already alerted policy makers about the issue. This permitted the policy makers to time announcements of previously planned measures, such as creation of a rape hotline, to coincide with the investigative series. When a story about unnecessary and illegal abortions in state clinics was about to break in Illinois, the governor immediately associated himself with the media investigators prior to publication. This made it possible to make reform proposals part of the original story. It also enhanced the governor's image as an effective leader.

Truncated Muckraking

The Mirage investigation illustrates the truncated muckraking model. The *Chicago Sun-Times* and CBS's *60 Minutes* program conducted the investigation jointly, with the help of Chicago's Better Government Association, a civic watchdog organization. Hoping to demonstrate extensive graft in Chicago's regulatory agencies, the partners in the investigation opened a bar in the city, appropriately named the Mirage. The bar was wired to record transactions between its personnel and city officials. It took little time to gather ample evidence of bribery and fraud.[18]

Public opinion polls recorded that many citizens were outraged when they learned about the illegal transactions. But they did not pressure public officials for reforms to prevent similar graft in the future. The situation ended with the arousal of public opinion, but the elite were not moved to action and there were no corrective measures. The failure to produce a correction does not necessarily mean that officials totally ignored the story. Symbolic responses in such circumstances are common. Politicians promise reforms or further studies of the problem, including public hearings, but no action follows. At other times, policy makers may punish individual offenders but do nothing to correct the underlying situation.[19]

The Minor Role of Public Opinion

These examples of muckraking suggest that the major role attributed to public opinion in producing political action is greatly exaggerated. More often than not, the media fail to arouse the public, even when investigative stories are written to produce public excitement. When stories do agitate the public, usually little happens ultimately. Politicians and journalists have learned that public anger is short-lived. It can be safely ignored or channeled to support reform movements that are already under way. Corrective action is more likely to come when publicity-shy wrongdoers mend their ways, when the stories arouse elites, or when journalists and political elites have arranged to collaborate. It also helps when follow-ups on the story appear in different media and over time.

Even though publicity rarely causes a tidal surge of public opinion, fear that it might do so makes the media more successful than other pressure groups in gaining their objectives. Because public opinion is in fact largely irrelevant in generating political reforms, the media's claim that they are handmaidens to the democratic process becomes highly questionable. In fact, the media are using the façade of public opinion support to enhance their already powerful position as political movers and shakers.

The Muddying of Public Figures

Stories about President Bill Clinton's philandering, civil rights leader Jesse Jackson's out-of-wedlock daughter, President George W. Bush's drunken driving conviction, and charges that Trent Lott, the Senate Republican leader, had made racially insensitive remarks at a birthday party—all of these are part of the epidemic of mudslinging that mars the nation's political landscape.[20] In each case the media endlessly examined, interpreted, and judged incidents in the lives of these individuals, often regardless of the story's significance, truth, or private nature (Box 6-1). It is true that these people are important political figures. Although the U.S. press is entitled to probe the lives and reputations of such public persons, and the U.S. public has a right to know about matters that are politically relevant, there is wide-spread agreement that the press is often overzealous in such investigations and destroy reputations needlessly. Blogging has heightened the pace. The Trent Lott story, for instance, first appeared in the bloggosphere and then gained notice from the mainline press, as now happens regularly.

Political scientist Larry Sabato, who refers to mudslinging episodes as "feeding frenzies," puts the blame on the increasingly stiff competition among media for attention and on the need for round-the-clock radio and television enterprises to fill long hours with emotional audience bait.

> In such situations any development is almost inevitably magnified and over-scrutinized; the crush of cameras, microphones, and people combined with the pressure of instant deadlines and live broadcasts hype events and make it difficult to keep them in perspective. When a frenzy begins to gather, the intensity grows exponentially. Major newspapers assign teams of crack reporters and researchers to the frenzy's victims. . . . Television news time is virtually turned over to the subject of the frenzy.[21]

At times newspeople bully politicians and other public figures into action by threatening to publicize stories that these targets would prefer to conceal. Threats about unfavorable coverage can have major political consequences. Politicians often act or refrain from acting because they know that newspeople might publish damaging information. They especially dread adverse publicity from influential columnists.

Attack journalism raises a number of important ethical and political issues. From the perspective of the people whose reputations and careers are dragged through the mud and often ruined, attack journalism raises questions about the rights of privacy of public figures and the ethics of journalists who publish such stories even when the subject matter is considered to be politically insignificant. Some journalists justify focusing on such incidents by claiming that they illuminate the individual's character. But many others admit that they are merely jumping on the bandwagon of competition. They argue that if others exploit the story, they must feature it as well. That is hardly the epitome of ethical behavior.

Beyond injury to individual public figures, there are broader consequences. The risk of having long past or more recent indiscretions exposed to public view or having offhand remarks elevated into major pronouncements sharply reduces the pool of people willing to make their careers in politics. Many talented people are likely to prefer the safety of private life over the merciless glare of unstoppable publicity in the public sector. "Gotcha" journalism also contributes to the public's growing cynicism about politics and politicians and erodes its respect for the news profession. Finally, the extraordinary amount of media time and space devoted to

BOX 6-1
 Can Watchdog Journalism Survive?

Watchdog journalism is a hallowed tradition in the United States that has contributed to curbing government and business excesses. In the years since the 2001 terrorism strike on U.S. soil, for example, it has led to scrutiny of the way the government dealt with terrorism suspects incarcerated without trial in detention camps in Cuba. It has sparked investigations of deceptive accounting practices in numerous major corporations, such as Enron in 2003, and to the passage of reform legislation. Investigative journalism also contributed to bringing priests to justice for sexually molesting children.

Proliferation of tabloid journalism and of blogging unfortunately has vastly increased abuses of the watchdog role, undermining the public's high regard for investigative journalism. Media audiences have become disgusted with the never-ending stream of scandals and rumors that mostly concern misbehaviors in the private lives of prominent Americans. The public has tired of innuendo that smears reputations and sleazy stories that dig into events that deserve to remain buried.

The costs of watchdog journalism have also grown, putting a strain on slender news production budgets. Painstaking investigations require countless interviews to elicit and verify facts and make sure that the initial reports about wrongdoing are meritorious rather than mere grudge fights or ego-trips based on misconstrued, distorted, or false information. Investigative reporters must check with legal counsel to lessen the chances of costly lawsuits for libel or damages caused by misrepresentation. Journalists must also deal with the counterefforts by powerful targets of investigation who hire public relations firms to challenge investigative reports before and after publication. In large bureaucracies, like the Pentagon, journalists must get around the top brass and their public relations team to interview the troops in "distant trenches" and get the real story. Besides managing production costs, reporters must sense when a story is likely to appeal to their editors and audiences, and when it is useless to prepare for a crusade for which there are few followers. Nonetheless, this major journalistic activity remains essential to a vigorous democracy; to retreat now would be tragic when new worldwide concentrations of power are mushrooming and corruption looms more menacingly than ever.

What can journalists do to revive full respect for their investigations? To restore the public's faith, watchdog journalists must focus on serious political, economic, or social concerns, preferably matters where public action can repair or forestall major problems that affect a large number of people. Journalists must be willing to take on all types of wrongdoers, even if this requires alienating advertisers. It should not matter, for instance, that stories about lax security in theme parks or price gouging by pharmaceutical companies involve business giants. Notwithstanding the important objectives of muckraking, journalists must shun illegal investigative means, such as unauthorized wiretaps, spy cameras, or ruses that constitute entrapments. Reporters should avoid anonymous sources, although that is often hard to do when accusers insist on anonymity. Shrouded sources make it hard for audiences to judge credibility and biases. Investigative stories should always be based on multiple sources because no single source knows everything.

Following such rules does not mean that all watchdog journalism will be well conducted and successful. Even the best watchdog occasionally barks at the wrong time and target. Journalists must understand and accept that; so must their audiences.

SOURCE: The information presented here is based on reports from the Nieman conferences on watchdog journalism held annually since 1998 and on reports published in the *Columbia Journalism Review*. See www.nieman.harvard.edu and www.cjr.org.

mudslinging frenzies comes at the expense of other, more worthwhile news that may never be published. The old Greek admonition "everything in moderation" is relevant. Whenever attack journalism seems appropriate, the media should practice it. But there is never a need for feeding frenzies of journalists in sorry exhibitions of pack journalism.

Beyond Muckraking: Journalists as Political Actors

Direct media intervention in the government process may take a number of forms other than muckraking. Three types of situations are typical: media acting as surrogates for public officials, media acting as mouthpieces for government officials or interest groups, and media deliberately slanting stories to serve a political purpose.

Acting as Surrogates

News personnel occasionally act as surrogates for public officials by actively participating in an evolving situation, such as a prison riot or a diplomatic impasse. The outcome may then significantly shape government action. News anchor Walter Cronkite's influence on relations between Egypt and Israel in 1977, when he served as a go-between to get the parties to the peace table, is a famous example of diplomacy conducted by a journalist. So were the efforts by CNN reporters stationed in Baghdad during the 1991 Persian Gulf War to broker an end to hostilities and the activities of British and Irish media in 1994 to facilitate dialogue between their governments and the Irish Republican movements.[22] Individual journalists, including media celebrities, are often instrumental in moving crises from obscurity to the political action agenda. Examples are genocide in Bosnia in 1995 and in the Sudan's Dafur region in 2004.[23] More commonly, reporters spark investigations of illegal activities by alerting law enforcement officials. For example, a Chicago television station alerted city officials to the illegal storage of hazardous and flammable chemical waste on the campus of the University of Chicago. Hours later, city fire officials inspected the scene and cited the university for numerous fire code violations.[24]

To prevent impending tragedies and solve existing cases, journalists have also become involved in broadcasts about kidnapped children and in crime-stopper programs that feature reenactments or recountings of unsolved crimes. The programs use media stories, coupled with financial rewards, to elicit information from citizens that may help solve the crime. The programs are featured in thousands of communities in the United States and Canada and have helped to clear up thousands of felony cases.[25] In fact, the FBI credits such programs with facilitating the capture of up to 30 percent of the criminals on its most wanted list.[26]

Acting as Mouthpieces

A far more common form of interaction occurs when the media become mouthpieces for government officials or interest groups, either because they believe in their causes or in return for attractive stories and other favors. This type of interaction often involves leaks. Government officials who are disgruntled with current policies or practices for personal, professional, or political reasons may leak information to sympathetic journalists to enlist their support. Journalists may cooperate and publish the allegations, or they may investigate the situation, often with the cooperation of the individuals who leaked the information.

When newspeople and officials collaborate, the boundary between ordinary reporting and manipulative journalism can blur. It is difficult to tell when one merges into the other because a correct diagnosis of manipulative journalism requires establishing motives. In many instances, newspeople act as political partisans who use their powers of publicity to foster pet causes. When the *Philadelphia Inquirer* received a tip from a congressional committee staff member about shoddy treatment of kidney dialysis patients, the paper rushed to the aid of the patients. It was clear from the start that dialysis providers and a negligent federal government would be the outright villains in the news stories.[27] In other cases, the main objective in publicizing leaked information is mercenary. Newspeople put their services at the command of anyone who promises to be a fertile source for future news or who can provide an attractive publishable story. Television networks are particularly eager for exciting scoops during "sweeps," when rating services check audience size to determine advertising pricing. Larger audiences mean higher prices.

Public officials and political interest groups often exploit the media's access to the public to attain their political objectives. The *New York Times* and the *Washington Post* agreed in 1995 to publish a terrorist's lengthy political ramblings to forestall further lethal bombings. The newspapers acted at the request of Attorney General Janet Reno, who feared another terrorist attack by the crazed "Unabomber." Reno's office also hoped that someone would recognize the writing style or handwriting and thus identify the terrorist.[28] Similarly, the media were accused of playing the game of Miami's Cuban refugee community when they lavished coverage on six-year-old Elian Gonzalez, who had been rescued after a refugee boat had been shipwrecked. The Cuban youngster's Miami relatives wanted the boy to remain in the United States rather than allowing him to return to his father in communist Cuba.

Although the media are often quite willing to publish stories in compliance with government wishes when they believe that the story serves a good purpose, they are loath to become unwitting government tools. In 1986, for example, officials of the Reagan administration were suspected of spreading false information about Libya in an attempt to forestall terrorist attacks. When rumors about the administration's deception surfaced, news executives expressed outrage. The comment of Roone Arledge, president of ABC News, was typical of the general reaction when he called it "despicable to tinker with the credibility of one of our most sacred and basic institutions, the press, for whatever reason." [29]

Acting as Chief Framers

Finally, the media can shape political action by framing—reporting the news from a particular perspective so that some aspects of the situation come into close focus and others fade into the background. How much control journalists have over framing varies widely, from merely reporting the frames chosen by regular beat sources or special pleaders to choosing sources who share the frame preferences of journalists to expressing their own frame choices in editorials and editorialized news. Journalists tend to exercise least control over the framing of uncontroversial news coming from official sources and most control over the framing of news about unexpected events or events unearthed by journalists through their own efforts.

Developments in an ongoing story also influence the evolution and choice of frames. Table 6-1 shows the types of frames used in 841 stories about stem cell research in the *New York Times* and *Washington Post* from 1975 through 2001. Frames describing new scientific developments were most prominent initially. Once the public learned that stem cells would come from human embryos, frames related to ethics and morality and to strategies and conflict leaped to the fore. For the entire period, the most widely used major frames were political strategies and conflict (29 percent), new research findings (20 percent), and regulation issues (16 percent). For minor themes, the top three were information about the scientific and medical background of the issue (29 percent), ethics and morality questions (27 percent), and regulation issues (27 percent).

When it comes to influencing debate and action on public policies, journalists' decisions are extraordinarily important if they relate to framing issues either in terms of the substance of the policy or the strategies used in battles about the policy. For example, welfare reform stories in 1996 in the *New York Times,* the *Washington Post,* the *Los Angeles Times, Time, Newsweek,* and *U.S. News and World Report* focused on the substance of proposed reforms in 47 percent of the stories and on the strategy of passing reform legislation in 41 percent. Both frames were used simultaneously in 12 percent of the stories. Scholars contend that the predominance of the strategy frame in most public policy stories marginalizes the substance of political issues and prevents political leaders from explaining policy substance to the public prior to the adoption of laws. Lack of intelligent public dialogue about public policies is one of the damaging consequences of such framing. Public cynicism is another.[30]

Agenda Building

In many instances, the media create the climate that shapes political action. This makes them major contributors to agenda building. The process goes beyond agenda setting. The media set the public agenda when news stories rivet attention on a problem and make it seem important to many people. The media build the public agenda when they create the political context that shapes public opinions. Agenda building often occurs around a precipitating event; such was the case with the beat-

TABLE 6-1   Framing Categories for Stem Cell Research
(percentage of newspaper stories featuring the theme)

Framing category	Major theme	Minor theme
Political strategy and/or conflict involving government and interest groups	29	16
New research findings and clinical trials	20	4
Regulatory framework for stem cell research; jurisdiction and oversight	16	27
Scientific and medical background of stem-cell-related research	15	29
Ethics or morality of stem-cell-related research, bioethicists' perspectives	15	27
Scientific and technical controversies about merits of various research plans	9	25
Market/economic aspects of stem cell research applications; competition	5	6
Anecdotes about specific actual or potential stem cell transplant patients	5	2
Patenting, property rights, ownership, and access to stem cell lines	2	6
Public opinion and public support; poll results	1	4
Reactions of average people outside research community and federal bureaucracy	1	1

SOURCE: Adapted from Matthew C. Nisbet, Dominique Brossard, and Adrianne Kroepsch, "Framing Science: The Stem Cell Controversy in an Age of Press/Politics," *Press/Politics* 8 (2): 11–35.

NOTE: $N = 841$ articles from the *New York Times* and *Washington Post*, 1975–2001.

ing of an African American motorist assaulted by police officers in Los Angeles. The incident became a news icon for dwelling at length on the issues of police brutality and racism and turning them into a major focus of public policy.[31]

Constructing Political Climates

The breakup of the Soviet Union is another telling case of agenda building. In 1990, during the annual May Day parade, Soviet television covered the festivities for the nation, as was usual. Camera operators had been told to stop filming if protesters against the government appeared. Mikhail Gorbachev, the country's leader, did not wish scenes of unrest to be broadcast. He had given protest groups permission to march to symbolize that he was a more liberal leader than his predecessors. But the television cameras kept filming when protesters came into view carrying banners that asked Gorbachev to resign, condemned the Communist Party and the Secret Service (KGB), proclaimed the end of the Red Empire, praised the secession of Lithuania, and carried images of Christ. The huge, nationwide audience watched—for the first time since the advent of communism—a vivid demonstration of opposition to the government. The broadcast demonstrated that the country was no longer united behind the leadership and that the voices of protest could make themselves heard. In the view of many observers, this televised humiliation built the agenda for the collapse of the Soviet empire.[32]

Newspeople have been criticized for rarely stirring up controversies when established elites agree on matters of public policy.[33] In the absence of conflicting reports, it may seem that no one opposes the policy even when that is not so. When an issue becomes controversial among political elites, the media frequently zero in on it. Thereby, they "supply the context that . . . gives people reasons for taking sides and converts the problem into a serious political issue. In this sense the public agenda is not so much set by the media as built up through a cycle of media activity that transforms an elite issue into a public controversy." [34] The agenda-building role of the media in policy making is symbiotic. The media perform essential steps, but ultimate success hinges on major roles played by other political actors as well.

Molotch, Protess, and Gordon make this clear in the conclusion of their study of the role of investigative journalism in the Watergate scandal during the Nixon presidency. The resolution of the issue was not, as popularly believed, a triumph for unaided media power:

> We therefore disagree with those who would assign "credit" for the Nixon exposures to the media just as we would disagree with those who would assign it to the Congress. Nor should the credit go, in some acontextual, additive sense, to both of these sectors. Instead, the Watergate "correction" was the result of the ways in which news of the Nixon scandals fit the goals and strategic needs of important media and policy actors. All of these actors, each with some degree of "relative autonomy" . . . are part of an evolving "ecology of games," . . . part of a "dance" . . . in which actors have, by virtue of their differential skills and status positions, varying access to participate. Because they so continuously anticipate each other's moves, their activities are, as a matter of course, mutually constituted.[35]

Sociologists Gladys and Kurt Lang reached similar conclusions. Their study of the role of the media in Watergate traces the precise part played by the media in this "ecology of games" that creates political agendas. A look at the steps makes it clear that there is ample opportunity and often strong temptation for newspeople to guide agenda building deliberately.

Agenda building begins when newspeople decide to publish a particular story. In most instances this is a matter of free choice because few stories are so blatantly significant that omission is unthinkable. The second decision concerns the degree of attention to be given to the story. This is the point where ordinary agenda-setting activities can most readily turn into deliberate agenda building. If newspeople determine that a story should become prominent, they must feature it conspicuously and repeatedly to arouse the attention of the elite media, including national television, and the attention of political elites. The Watergate story, for instance, received extensive and sustained publicity in the *Washington Post* before it finally gained nationwide publicity.

Capturing national attention usually requires several other media-controlled steps. Media must put issues into an interpretive frame that will interest the media's audiences. For instance, as long as the media framed Watergate as an election campaign story, media audiences discounted it as just another partisan squabble. Once the media, with the aid of members of Congress, were able to depict it as an issue of pervasive corruption and dishonesty at the highest levels of government, it generated widespread concern. Without this climate of public concern, severe penalties for the Watergate offenders, including President Nixon, would never have been acceptable. In the course of putting issues into a conceptual framework, language becomes an important tool. When newspeople and politicians switched from writing and talking about the Watergate "caper" or the "bugging incident" and began to discuss the Watergate "scandal" and "tragedy," a once trivial incident became a very serious matter.

The particular sources that journalists choose to cite for their story are important. Skewing inevitably takes place when one human source, rather than another, provides information and interpretation. When major public policy issues are at stake, media audiences judge the merits of various options by the credibility of the proponents. The Watergate crisis justified drastic action, like impeachment of the president, only after the media featured prominent Republicans and members of the judiciary who acknowledged the gravity of the issues and the need for a massive investigation.

Most agenda building does not concern momentous political events like the fall of the Soviet Union or Watergate. A more typical example occurred in 2004 when the *Chicago Sun-Times* published a brief story about four Chicago building inspectors accused of falsifying their work histories. Normally the city resolves such cases by levying small fines of $500 or less. But in the wake of the publicity, city authorities initiated a policy of vigorous prosecution of such offenses. It filed lawsuits against the offenders and reinspected the buildings where they had worked. It also decided to investigate the city's hiring practices. The incumbent building commissioner had to institute major reforms in hiring procedures to save his job. All these developments yielded ample news stories and kept interest in the story alive.[36]

Constructing Climates for Science Policies

Media agenda building is not limited to political scandals but includes many other issues. Two of particular importance for U.S. political life are science policy and social movements.

Government support and regulation of science operations became highly controversial U.S. public policy issues in the twentieth century.[37] Two environmental issues provide particularly interesting examples. The first one has been called the great greenhouse debate about the threat of global warming.[38] Researchers tracked media coverage of the global warming controversy over eight years from 1985 to 1992 in television network evening newscasts and the *New York Times,* the *Washington Post,* the *Wall Street Journal, Time, Newsweek,* and *U.S. News and World Report.* Coverage was minimal at first, totaling only twenty-five stories from 1985 through 1987 in all the media combined—not enough to arouse government and public concern. Coverage soared in 1989 and 1990, when the first Bush administration sought to defuse growing worldwide pressures for governmental action by expressing doubts about the seriousness of the situation. With the media taking their cues from the science community, the thrust of their coverage indicated otherwise. By a margin of nearly nine to one, news coverage suggested that global warming was indeed a major problem that required preventive government action throughout the world. News stories also focused the public's attention on specific remedies, such as controlling carbon dioxide emissions, halting or reversing deforestation, and conserving energy. In the end, the media's efforts to create a climate favoring stricter control laws faltered because the science community disagreed about the ability to keep global warming in check through various government regulation programs. Coupled with the strongly expressed resistance of the Bush administration to major control measures—which could not be ignored by the media—the earlier climate for controls became far less friendly.

The second tale concerns cancer-causing agents in the environment, which, unlike global warming, have been a topic of government attention for some time. The main issues related to identifying the most dangerous pollutants that required regulation. One would expect that experts in the field of environmentally caused cancers would be the dominant voices that the media would quote, but that is not always the case. When journalists select "expert" opinions to quote, they often find that frontline researchers are so deeply involved in their scientific pursuits that they do not wish to talk to the media. When they do, their stories often lack punch because scientists hedge their claims, believing that no truth is absolute. This is why reporters often turn to less well qualified sources who are willing and able to express their views strongly and without caveats. Activists, such as spokespersons for environmental groups, make good storytellers. Reporters may also have their own views about environmental and other dangers and seek out spokespersons who share their views, especially if they think that most of their audience agrees or has no opinion. News opposing nuclear power plants is an example. It dominated because few journalists bothered to get stories that supported views that they themselves deemed undesirable.[39]

In the case of carcinogens in the environment, ABC, CBS, and NBC television, the three major newsmagazines, and the *New York Times,* the *Washington Post,* and the *Wall Street Journal* paid more attention to man-made chemicals than to any other cancer agent, including tobacco, in the twenty years from 1972 to 1992.[40] If judgment is made on the number of stories devoted to each carcinogen, the dangers of tobacco were ranked roughly on a par with those of such food additives as dyes, preservatives, and sweeteners and such reproductive hormones as birth control pills. By contrast, experts rated smoking, overexposure to sunlight, and diet as prime causes of cancer and downplayed the role of food additives and preservatives.

In fact, half or more of cancer experts believed that the media distorted the dangers of particular carcinogens in nine out of eleven areas (Figure 6-1). Media coverage got its best ratings—albeit only 60 percent or less approval—in rating the dangers of sunlight and tobacco. It got its worst ratings (less than 39 percent approval) on naturally occurring chemicals in food and food additives, nuclear plants, pollution, pesticides, household chemicals, and dietary choices. Chemicals in the workplace and radon received rankings of "fairly stated" by 42 percent and 50 percent of the scientists, respectively. Given that news stories, particularly in the key media examined for this study, provided the agenda-building context in which government actions and public opinion flourish, it is a worrisome finding that the media may stray widely from scientific opinions in matters of great public concern. The potential for major damage is great because the needed protective measures may be thwarted.

Studies show that media coverage of scientific controversies influences public opinion. For example, when the media cover stories about controversial new technologies or medical treatments, public opposition to the highlighted developments is common, even when the coverage is not particularly hostile. When media coverage of the controversy diminishes,

FIGURE 6-1   How Scientists Rate Media Portrayals of Cancer Risks

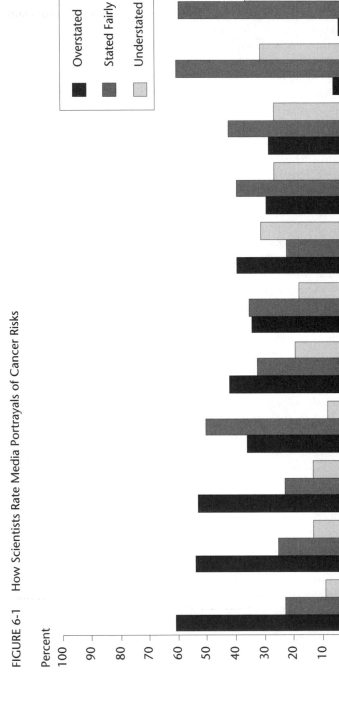

SOURCE: *Media Monitor* 7, no. 8 (November/December 1993): 4.

[a] Naturally occurring.

opposition diminishes as well. The public, it seems, opts against scientific advances when media raise doubts about their safety. People are especially sensitive to heavily negative safety reports. Political elites, in turn, often are loath to challenge scientific findings that the media have labeled as "expert" opinion or to take actions that may alarm the public.[41]

Similar concerns have arisen about stories in other fields of science. Although some of the coverage is excellent, many stories are flawed. Only a few scientists, distinguished by their controversial positions on public issues, are steady sources for news about new drugs, new medical procedures, and various aspects of genetic engineering. The rest of the scientific community has largely excluded itself, often by choice and sometimes because of its disdain for popularized stories. In the same way, science reporters have scrutinized only a few potentially risky technologies; the media's choices of which industries to cover are haphazard or mirror the interests of effective pressure groups. The media have ignored many other scientific topics and thereby kept them off the public agenda, even though they address significant public health and safety issues. In fact, omissions may be a far more serious problem than the fact that most media reports contain minor and major errors of emphasis or fact because it is difficult to simplify highly technical matters. But science coverage is improving with the addition of weekly science sections in many newspapers.[42]

Nourishing Social Movements and Interest Groups

Just as the media regularly boost selected public policy issues, so too can they promote selected groups that are working for public causes. Whenever a group needs wide publicity to reach its goals, journalists' decisions to grant or withhold publicity become crucial for the group's success. Although journalists make most decisions about coverage without explicit political motivations to boost a movement or suppress it, many times the sympathies of newspeople for particular causes guide their choices of news content. This happened in the 1960s with Students for a Democratic Society (SDS), a "New Left" movement. The story is particularly interesting because it demonstrates that attention from sympathetic newspeople may boomerang and produce unintended, highly destructive consequences.

SDS had received little media attention for its activities on U.S. campuses until *New York Times* reporter Fred Powledge wrote a long, supportive story in 1965, some five years after the birth of the movement.[43] Coverage by a national news medium amounted to symbolic recognition that student radicalism had become an important political issue. When SDS sponsored a march on Washington, D.C., to protest the Vietnam War in the spring of 1965, the event received nationwide coverage. Although many newspeople sympathized with the left-liberal reforms advocated by SDS, they focused their stories on the movement's most radical leaders and goals, risking alienating the public. The framing produced exciting news but misled media audiences, including SDS members, about the peaceful nature of the movement. The radicals singled out by the media as spokespersons for the organization became celebrities who attracted new Leninist and Maoist members, who then took over the leadership of the organization and turned it away from its long-range reformist goals to short-range and violent antiwar activities.

Sociologist Todd Gitlin contends that the media's decision in 1965 to give wide publicity to SDS ultimately destroyed the movement and with it much of the power of the New Left. In his vivid metaphor, the media spotlight became a magnifying glass that burned everybody to a crisp. Powledge's efforts to bestow legitimacy on the movement through *New York Times* stories had failed totally. As is often true in agenda building, political forces other than the media contributed to the turn of events. Radicalization of the SDS movement was also enhanced by the Johnson administration's escalation of the Vietnam War and by the growing alienation from mainstream society that the involvement produced among many Americans.[44]

Of course, many movements, interest groups, and lobbies have been helped by media coverage if they did not deviate too far from mainstream values. Media publicity has legitimized consumer organizations and environmentalist groups in the eyes of the public and the eyes of public officials.[45] The media also were instrumental in legitimizing the civil rights movement. The media framed civil rights protesters as victims of racism rather than as troublemakers and lawbreakers, as their opponents would have preferred. Sympathetic nationwide coverage of freedom marches and of battles fought for civil rights in Little Rock, Arkansas; Selma, Alabama; and Oxford, Mississippi, prepared lawmakers and the nation for passage of the Civil Rights Act in 1964 and the creation of public agencies to implement its mandates.

There seems to be a pattern in the role played by media on behalf of successful social movements.[46] Legitimization of the incipient movement begins with favorable coverage by a few sympathetic journalists. Undisputed media praise then attracts support for the movement among segments of the public. In this favorable climate, the growing movement becomes strong and legitimate enough to make political demands and engage in protest activities. In response, opposing voices speak out in the hitherto silent mainstream media. They come too late, however, to stop the success of the movement in the legislative arena and among important groups within the public.

Protest groups are active partners in the agenda-building game. If they consider publicity essential to the success of their causes, as most of them do, they may initiate contacts with potentially sympathetic journalists and create newsworthy events to showcase their objectives. The environmental protection organization Greenpeace, for example, arranges photo opportunities showing gruesome details of whale hunts and invites the media to attend. Attracting sustained media attention hinges on the status and goals of the group and its perceived social and political legitimacy; the newsworthiness of its story, judged by the usual criteria; and the consonance of the group's ideology with the journalists' inclinations.[47] Greenpeace has been highly successful on all of these scores. As exchange theory predicts, journalists exchange their ability to bestow publicity for the group's ability to supply newsworthy stories.

Low-status organizations whose goals encompass routine human concerns are least likely to attract helpful publicity. Political scientist Edie Goldenberg studied the attempts of four citizens' groups in Massachusetts to attract newspaper coverage to the problems of welfare mothers, senior citizens, low-income tenants, and people treated unfairly by the courts. She found that these groups had little success and concluded, "There is bias in the system that consistently favors some and neglects others." The favored groups are "haves," those who possess the resources to make and maintain contact with the press and to arrange their operations so that they complement the needs of the press. The unfavored ones are those "most in need of press attention in order to be heard forcefully in the political arena" yet "least able to command attention and . . . least able to use effectively what few resources they do control in seeking and gaining press access." Goldenberg warns, "If intensely felt interests go unarticulated and therefore are unnoticed and unaffected by policy makers, one important aspect of rule of, for, and by the people is weakened."[48] In the eyes of social critics such as Goldenberg, a free press must use its agenda-building powers to benefit all segments of society.

Documentaries and Docudramas

To influence public policy, newspeople are not limited to straight news and feature stories. Fictional productions, such as docudramas shown to millions of viewers on primetime national television, are another tool. Docudramas are especially compelling because they reconstruct events in highly dramatic, emotional ways. The viewer cannot tell which part of the story is real and which part is dramatic frosting.[49]

The political motivations leading to the production and display of many documentaries and docudramas are obvious. As communications scholar Oscar Gandy has pointed out, "Too frequently to be mere coincidence, serial dramas, or the made-for-television movies we describe as docudramas, have been aired simultaneously with the discussion of related issues in Congress." [50] An example of a widely publicized docudrama that coincided with related political events was "The Day After," a two-hour ABC dramatization of a nuclear attack on Kansas City and its aftermath. It aired on Sunday, November 20, 1983, following an extensive prebroadcast advertising campaign by the network that included an eight-page viewer's guide. Scenes of burned bodies, people rotting from radiation sickness, smoldering rubble, and survivors reduced to preying on each other were part of the episode.

At the time of broadcast, nuclear weapons policy was in the limelight. The Reagan administration was seeking support in the United States and in Europe for deploying U.S. missiles in European NATO countries. Antinuclear groups at home and abroad were working feverishly to stop the deployment. ABC aired the docudrama a few days before the West German legislature was to approve the decision to place the missiles. The station made excerpts of the docudrama available to German television.

Supporters of missile deployment feared that the program would lead to massive public demonstrations designed to force a change in nuclear deployment policies. Throughout the furor raised by the broadcast, ABC denied that the timing had been politically motivated. What then was the political impact of "The Day After," which was viewed by more than 100 million people in homes, schools, churches, and town halls? [51] The broadcast energized antinuclear groups and aroused fears in pronuclear groups that "The Day After" might generate defeatist attitudes among Americans. Contrary to expectations, public opinion polls after the broadcast did not show massive shifts of public attitudes about nuclear missile policies. In Europe, where people had predicted immediate drastic political consequences, the missiles were deployed without major obstacles. A number of analysts ascribed the lack of impact to flaws in the docudrama, which left the reasons for the nuclear attack uncertain and failed to deal squarely with nuclear policy issues. Others felt that the public had gained knowledge and awareness from the film but had learned to distance itself psychologically from fictional disasters.

Whereas the apparent consequences of "The Day After" were less than expected, other docudramas as well as full-length motion picture versions of historical events may be more compelling. *J.F.K.*, a 1991 movie docudrama, suggested that President Kennedy's assassination sprang from a massive conspiracy that involved the White House, the CIA, and the FBI, among others. Polls subsequently showed that numerous viewers accepted the film's premises. [52] Docudramas like *Schindler's List*, which dealt with Jewish refuges escaping the Nazi holocaust; *Mississippi Burning*, which portrayed atrocities in the civil rights struggle; *DC 9/11,* which described the Bush administration's management of the terror attack crisis; and *Fahrenheit 9/11,* which condemns the 2003 war against Iraq as a nefarious plot of the Bush administration, shape people's images of the nature and significance of these events even when the producers disclaim historical accuracy. This potential impact and the associated media coverage and public discussions of these primetime presentations obligate a responsible press to take greater pains to present all sides of an issue and to be accurate in its depiction, even in fictional programs.[53]

Methods: Fair and Foul

The fairness and accuracy of news presentations and the appropriateness of news-gathering techniques become important issues when one considers that the media, in combination with other political actors, create the political reality that sets the context for political action.[54] It is a serious matter, therefore, when the media are accused of frequently resorting to improper methods.

Confirming Prejudgments

An incident during the 2004 presidential campaign illustrates concerns about the legitimacy of some media tactics.[55] CBS *Evening News* and *60 Minutes* broadcast a story about President Bush's National Guard service in the early 1970s that suggested he did not fulfill his obligations. Purportedly, he escaped penalties for his neglect of duty thanks to powerful political connections. His privileged status allegedly helped him get a lieutenant's commission in the National Guard. The report relied heavily on documents from the files of Bush's squadron commander. When the authenticity of the documents was questioned because they had been inadequately checked, all confirmation efforts failed.

The network and anchor Dan Rather initially defended their story. When it became clear that the story drew on flawed sources, CBS appointed a panel of prestigious experts to investigate what had gone wrong. The panel had full access to the network's records. Its findings are a laundry list of major sins that journalists in high-quality media should never commit. The cardinal sin was failure to seek professional help to check the authenticity of the documents at the heart of the story. Misleading statements in the broadcast that suggested that the network had properly checked the story compounded this sin. Moreover, in CBS's haste to publish the story ahead of its competitors, it had failed to check the controversial background of the source who had supplied the documents, claiming that he received them from an unidentified person. The station made no effort to verify the identity of that person so that reliability could be established. Nor was evidence presented that the documents had actually come from the files of Bush's squadron commander, as claimed.

When journalists are reporting important allegations, professionalism requires comparing incriminating information first with other sources to detect discrepancies. In this case, Rather and his coworkers should have examined official National Guard records. They did not. CBS should have interviewed guardsmen from the unit who might have offered corroborating or disconfirming information. Again, in the haste to publish and in the obvious absence of any desire to examine information that might favor Bush, reporters did not.

When viewers raised questions about the accuracy of the broadcast after the initial airing of the story, CBS brushed them aside without checking whether they had merit. The spokespersons defending the report were individuals involved in its production, rather than impartial examiners. CBS again claimed falsely that the authenticity of the story had been adequately checked and that its sources were totally reliable.

The panel did absolve Rather of the charge that the distortions were politically motivated because Rather and many members of his team disliked the president intensely and were eager to believe stories that discredited him. However, motivations are hard to prove. In a somewhat similar case involving a CBS documentary that alleged misbehavior by General William C. Westmoreland, an internal report showed that the producers of the documentary believed in Westmoreland's guilt from the very start and constructed the story to support their preformed conclusions.[56]

The upshot of the Bush story incident was an apology by the network and anchor Dan Rather's announcement that he would resign from his post within a few months. Several high-level CBS journalists resigned or were fired. It is difficult to tell whether the story damaged President Bush in the election. Had he lost, many would have speculated about the influence of the National Guard stories. The incident did show that there is little disagreement about the standards of fairness and accuracy that should be applied in broadcasts about important public issues. But—and this is the disturbing aspect—these standards continue to be breached all too often. Such breaches raise questions about the sense of responsibility of high-level media personnel when important public matters are at stake. Are the media, especially the influential electronic media, taking sufficient care to keep the preconceptions of media personnel out of stories?

With investigative journalism growing in popularity, the problem of inaccurate reports has mounted. In 1989, for instance, charges surfaced that a freelance photographer had faked and restaged battle scenes in film used in CBS newscasts and documentaries about the war in Afghanistan. Scenes of sabotaging electric supply lines for Kabul, the capital of Afghanistan, allegedly were reenacted days after the event. The photographer misstated the location of refugees to make the story more dramatic, and he misidentified a Pakistani jet as a Soviet plane.[57] In 1993 NBC's *Dateline* program showed how easily General Motors pickup trucks with sidesaddle gas tanks burst into fire after collision. The problem was that production crews had taped toy rockets to the underside of a truck and had tampered with its gas cap to make sure that the explosion would take place on cue. Caught red-handed in a major deception, NBC quickly settled a suit brought by General Motors.[58]

In many instances, inaccurate reports have permanent economic, professional, and social consequences for the individuals and institutions whose stories are told. The National Guard stories could have cost President Bush reelection. In a case involving the Kaiser Aluminum and Chemical Corporation, business losses could have run into millions of dollars. An investigative report had erroneously accused the company of knowingly selling dangerous household electrical wiring under false pretenses. Successful libel suits can recoup a portion of the damage, but they fall short of fully restoring damaged reputations. This is why careless or biased publicity has become a deep concern for civil libertarians. If networks permit rebuttals to misinformation in interpretive stories, the rebuttals are treated as opinion pieces rather than straight news and therefore are subject to editorial control.

Entrapment

Serious ethical issues arise also when newspeople undertake undercover operations or create bogus enterprises to entrap potential and actual wrongdoers. The story told earlier about the Mirage tavern, set up to elicit and record bribery by city officials, illustrates the practice. So does the preparation of NBC's program "Cataract Cowboys" in 1993. NBC's investigative team wanted to tell a story about unnecessary cataract surgeries.[59] When several Florida eye clinics turned down requests by healthy undercover reporters for eye surgery, the producers staged a partly successful entrapment. One "patient," whose requests for surgery had been denied initially, telephoned the clinic to schedule an appointment. The filmed report of her return to the clinic notes that she "was only a few tests and a half-hour away from surgery." The report neglected to mention that the presurgery tests might have forestalled the surgery and therefore did not constitute evidence of malpractice.

Canadian media set a far more massive crime trap to expose organized crime in North America. The investigation resulted in a three-and-a-half hour documentary broadcast by the Canadian Broadcasting Company (CBC). CBC reporters and agents planted inside organized crime circles used hidden microphones and cameras to obtain dramatic film footage of gangsters discussing their activities. In one instance, a reporter arranged several meetings with a woman suspected of helping gangsters to buy real estate in Atlantic City. The reporter pretended to represent a crooked Italian real estate investor. All of these meetings where illegal deals were arranged were audiotaped and some parts were filmed.[60]

Sting operations like these raise serious civil liberties issues at best, even when regular law enforcement agencies conduct them under the watchful eyes of the courts. Concerns about protecting the rights of suspects are even greater when the sleuths are journalists acting without an official mandate and without supervision by a responsible public body.[61] Quite aside from civil liberties issues, sting operations raise fundamental questions about the proper functions of the press. Should its watchdog role be carried to the point where it becomes a quasi-police force, tracking down selected offenders whenever a good story promises to be the likely reward?

Summary

In this chapter we examined direct involvement by journalists in the affairs of government. The chapter began with an analysis of muckraking, comparing reality to a series of models of the process. The media's power to arouse public opinion with exposés of corruption is far less than is popularly believed. Even if the public becomes highly concerned, political action is not guaranteed. It is a mistaken belief that exposés commonly produce reforms because an aroused public pressures for political action. The most propitious road to reform is via direct liaisons between newspeople and government officials. When officials provide story leads in areas in which they would like to produce action, or when newspeople can interest officials in taking action on issues that have come to the media's attention, successful political activities are apt to occur. On rare occasions the media are also able to produce action by participating in political negotiations or by using the club of potential unwanted publicity to force officials to act.

The Watergate scandal illustrates how political action can emerge from the interplay of various political institutions. The media, through a series of agenda-building steps, created the climate in which it became possible to force the resignation of a president. Agenda-building examples from science policy and from interest group politics demonstrate the media's impact on developments in these fields. The media serve as catalysts that precipitate the actions of other elements within the society. They enhance the influence of some political forces and weaken others, but the ultimate outcome is often beyond their control.

The media's public policy making roles influence U.S. politics in general as well as the lives of many individuals and institutions. How sensitively and accurately they are performed therefore become matters of grave concern. News gathering and news production frequently are seriously flawed, even when media institutions profess to believe in high standards. How often the ethics and standards of the profession are violated, and what the costs are to people caught in the net of inaccurate publicity, are matters for conjecture.

At the heart of most instances when newspeople become actively involved in politics lies the desire to produce exciting news stories. This is not surprising. Journalism requires telling stories that will attract audiences. That journalists are tempted to be good storytellers above all, even at the expense of other goals, should give pause to those who advocate that journalists should play the political game actively and regularly. One must ask whether journalists' professional standards equip them to guide politics wisely and well. To put it another way: When issues are put on the crowded political agenda, should their newsworthiness be the controlling factor? If the answer is no, then massive participation by the media in policy making may be quite troubling.

Notes

1. Lincoln Steffens, *The Autobiography of Lincoln Steffens* (New York: Harcourt Brace, 1931), 357.
2. See Larry J. Sabato, *Feeding Frenzy: How Attack Journalism Has Transformed American Politics* (New York: Free Press, 1991), chap. 2; David L. Protess , Fay Lomax Cook, Jack C. Doppelt, James S. Ettema. Margaret T. Gordon, Donna R. Leff, and Peter Miller, *The Journalism of Outrage: Investigative Reporting and Agenda Building* (New York: Guilford Press, 1991), chap. 2.
3. David Weaver and LeAnne Daniels, "Public Opinion on Investigative Reporting in the 1980s," *Journalism Quarterly* 69 (spring 1992): 146–155. Ethical reporting guidelines for journalists are laid out in Bruce J. Evenson, *The Responsible Reporter* (Northport, Ala.: Vision Press, 1995). Also see Louis A. Day, *Ethics in Media Communications,* 4th ed. (Belmont, Calif.: Wadsworth, 2003).
4. The pros and cons of public journalism as well as the relevant literature are examined in a collection edited by Theodore L. Glasser, *The Idea of Public Journalism* (New York: Guilford Press, 1999); and by John C. Merrill, Peter J. Gade,

and Frederick R. Blevens, *Twilight of Press Freedom: The Rise of People's Journalism* (Mahwah, N.J.: Lawrence Erlbaum Associates, 2001).

5. David L. Protess, *Muckraking Matters: The Societal Impact of Investigative Reporting,* Institute for Modern Communications Research Monographs Series (Evanston: Northwestern University, 1987), 13. The public's changing views about investigative journalism are traced in Lars Willnat and David Weaver, "Public Opinion on Investigative Reporting in the 1990s: Has Anything Changed Since the 1980s?" *Journalism and Mass Communication Quarterly,* 75, no. 3 (1998): 449–463. The Nieman Watchdog conference reports are available on the foundation's Web site at www.nieman.harvard.edu. For an anthology of muckraking throughout U.S. history see Judith Serrin and William Serrin, *Muckraking! The Journalism that Changed America* (New York: New Press, 2002).

6. Ken Shiffman and Robin Mejia, "Reasonable Doubt: Can Crime Labs Be Trusted?" CNN, January 9, 2005, www.muckraker.org.

7. Steffens, *Autobiography,* 357.

8. Protess and others, *Journalism of Outrage,* 214–227.

9. How investigative stories differ from other forms of journalism is described by Matthew C. Ehrlich, "The Journalism of Outrageousness: Tabloid Television News vs. Investigative News," *Journalism and Mass Communication Monographs* 155 (February 1996).

10. Eytan Gilboa, "Media Diplomacy: Conceptual Divergence and Application," *Harvard International Journal of Press/Politics* 3, no. 3 (1998): 56–76, makes a similar distinction.

11. Harvey L. Molotch, David L. Protess, and Margaret T. Gordon, "The Media-Policy Connection: Ecologies of News," in *Political Communication Research: Approaches, Studies, Assessments,* ed. David L. Paletz (Norwood, N.J.: Ablex, 1987), 26–48. Protess and others model the process somewhat differently in their more recent *Journalism of Outrage.* But the earlier version seems more explicit.

12. Protess and others, *Journalism of Outrage,* chaps. 3–6 detail six investigations.

13. *Inside Edition,* "Unsanitary Conditions Found at Washington DC School Cafeterias, Inside Edition Reports," September 10, 2003, www.insideedition.com.

14. Regina G. Lawrence, "Framing Obesity: The Evolution of News Discourse on a Public Health Issue," *Press/Politics* 9 (3): 56–75 discusses how the issue has been presented to the public.

15. Protess and others, *Journalism of Outrage,* chap. 4.

16. Often the chief point of a program is simply to alert the public to a problem; immediate action may not be expected.

17. Protess and others, *Journalism of Outrage,* chap. 3.

18. The full story is told in Zay N. Smith and Pamela Zekman, *The Mirage* (New York: Random House, 1979).

19. Protess and others, *Journalism of Outrage,* 240–244.

20. Larry J. Sabato, Mark Stencel, and S. Robert Lichter, *Peepshow: Media and Politics in an Age of Scandal* (Lanham, Md.: Rowman and Littlefield, 2000), discuss many cases of scandal reporting along with guidelines that media should follow in publishing or ignoring such incidents.

21. Sabato, *Feeding Frenzy,* 53.

22. Philip Seib, *Headline Diplomacy: How News Coverage Affects Foreign Policy* (Westport, Conn.: Praeger, 1997), 108–111; Kirsten Sparre, "Megaphone Diplomacy in the Northern Irish Peace Process," *Press/Politics* 6, no. 1 (2001): 88–104.

23. Yaeli Bloch and Sam Lehman-Wilzig, "An Exploratory Model of Media-Government Relations in International Crises: U.S. Involvement in Bosnia 1992–1995," in *Media and Conflict: Framing Issues, Making Policy, Shaping Opinion,* ed. Eytan Gilboa (Ardsley, N.Y.: Transnational Publishers, 2002), 153–174; Piers Robinson, "Global Television and Conflict Resolution: Defining the Limits of the CNN Effect," in Gilboa, *Media and Conflict,* 175–192

24. Protess and others, *Journalism of Outrage,* 134–135.

25. Greg Cima, "Fighting Crime: Crime Stoppers Program Connects Police with Community, Media," February 13, 2005, www.pantagraph.com; Stefan Lovgren, " 'CSI Effect' is Mixed Blessing for Real Crime Labs," National Geographic News, September 23, 2004, http://news.nationalgeographic.com.

26. Michael Killian, "New FBI TV Series Will Seek Viewer Help in Nabbing Criminals," *Chicago Tribune,* February 5, 1988.

27. Protess and others, *Journalism of Outrage,* 179–180.

28. Tim Jones and Gary Marx, "Unabomber Has Media in a Bind," *Chicago Tribune,* September 20, 1995.

29. Robert D. McFadden, "News Executives Express Outrage," *New York Times,* October 3, 1986.

30. Regina G. Lawrence, "Game-Framing the Issues: Tracking the Strategy Frame in Public Policy News," *Political Communication* 17, no. 2 (2000): 93–114; and Joseph N. Cappella and Kathleen Hall Jamieson, *Spiral of Cynicism* (New York: Oxford University Press, 1997), chaps. 3, 8.

31. Regina Lawrence, "Managing Meaning: Media, Officials, and Police Brutality" (Ph.D. diss., University of Washington, 1996).

32. Ellen Mickiewicz, *Opening Channels* (New York: Oxford University Press, 1996).

33. W. Lance Bennett, "Toward a Theory of Press-State Relations in the United States," *Journal of Communication* 40 (spring 1990): 103–125; George A. Donahue, Phillip J. Tichenor, and Clarice N. Olien, "A Guard Dog Perspective on the Role of Media," *Journal of Communication* 45, no. 2 (spring 1995): 115–132.

34. Gladys Engel Lang and Kurt Lang, *The Battle for Public Opinion: The President, the Press, and the Polls during Watergate* (New York: Columbia University Press, 1983), 58.

35. Molotch, Protess, and Gordon, "The Media-Policy Connection," 45, citing Peter Dreier, "The Position of the Press in the U.S. Power Structure," *Social Problems* 29 (February 1982): 298–310; also see Gadi Wolfsfeld, "Media Protest and Political Violence: A Transactional Analysis," *Journalism Monographs* 127 (June 1991); William A. Gamson, *The Strategy of Social Protest,* 2d ed. (Belmont, Calif.: Wadsworth, 1990); and Clarice N. Olien, Phillip J. Tichenor, and George A. Donahue, "Media Coverage and Social Movements," in *Information Campaigns: Balancing Social Values and Social Change,* ed. Charles T. Salmon (Beverly Hills, Calif.: Sage, 1989), 139–163.

36. Fran Spielman, "Fired Inspectors Face City Lawsuits," *Chicago Sun Times,* January 8, 2005.

37. Oscar H. Gandy, *Beyond Agenda Setting: Information Subsidies and Public Policy* (Norwood, N.J.: Ablex, 1982), 149–162. Also see Matthew C. Nisbet, Dominique Brossard, and Adrianne Kroepsch, "Framing Science, the Stem Cell Controversy in an Age of Press/Politics," *Press/Politics* 8 (2): 11–35; Debra E. Blakely, "Social Construction of Three Influenza Pandemics in the New York Times," *Journalism and Mass Communication Quarterly,* 80 (2003): 884–902.

38. The title and the information that follows come from "The Great Greenhouse Debate," *Media Monitor* 6, no. 10 (December 1992): 1–6.
39. Stanley Rothman and S. Robert Lichter, "Elite Ideology and Risk Perception in Nuclear Energy Policy," *American Political Science Review* 81 (June 1987): 383–404. For a more general discussion of the problem of sources of science information, see Hans Mathias Kepplinger, "Artificial Horizons: How the Press Presented and How the Population Received Technology in Germany from 1965–1986," in *The Mass Media in Liberal Democratic Societies,* ed. Stanley Rothman (New York: Paragon House, 1992), 147–176.
40. The information about this case comes from "Is Cancer News a Health Hazard? Media Coverage vs. 'Scientific' Opinion on Environmental Cancer," *Media Monitor* 7, no. 8 (November–December 1993): 1–5.
41. Patrick Leahy and Alan Mazur, "The Rise and Fall of Public Opposition in Specific Social Movements," *Social Studies of Science* 10 (1980): 191–205; and Alan Mazur, "Media Coverage and Public Opinion on Scientific Controversies," *Journal of Communication* 31 (spring 1981): 106–115.
42. Renate G. Bader, "How Science News Sections Influence Newspaper Science Coverage: A Case Study," *Journalism Quarterly* 67 (spring 1990): 88–96; Eleanor Singer, "A Question of Accuracy: How Journalists and Scientists Report Research on Hazards," *Journalism Quarterly* 40 (fall 1990): 102–116.
43. Todd Gitlin, *The Whole World Is Watching: Media in the Making and Unmaking of the New Left* (Berkeley: University of California Press, 1980), 25–26.
44. For models of the roles played by the media in fostering social movements, see Kevin M. Carragee, "News and Ideology," *Journalism Monographs* 128 (August 1991); Wolfsfeld, "Media Protest and Political Violence"; and Gamson, *The Strategy of Social Protest.*
45. Laura R. Woliver, *From Outrage to Action: The Politics of Grass-Roots Dissent* (Urbana: University of Illinois Press, 1993).
46. Hans Mathias Kepplinger and Michael Hachenberg, "Media and Conscientious Objection in the Federal Republic of Germany," in Paletz, *Political Communication Research,* 108–128. Also see Fay Lomax Cook and Wesley G. Skogan, "Convergent and Divergent Voice Models of the Rise and Fall of Policy Issues," in *Agenda Setting: Readings on Media, Public Opinion, and Policymaking,* ed. David L. Protess and Maxwell McCombs (Hillsdale, N.J.: Erlbaum, 1991), 189–206.
47. Wolfsfeld, "Media Protest and Political Violence," 8–10.
48. Edie Goldenberg, *Making the Papers* (Lexington, Mass.: Heath, 1975), 146–148.
49. The potential impact of docudramas is discussed by William C. Adams, Allison Salzman, William Vantine, Leslie Suelter, Anne Baker, Lucille Bonvouloir, Barbara Brenner, Margaret Ely, Jean Feldman, and Ron Ziegel, "The Power of *The Right Stuff*: A Quasi-Experimental Field Test of the Docudrama Hypothesis," *Public Opinion Quarterly* 49 (fall 1985): 330–339. Also see Alan Rosenthal, ed., *Why Docudrama? Fact-Fiction on Film and TV* (Carbondale, Ill.: Southern Illinois University Press, 1999).
50. Gandy, *Beyond Agenda Setting,* 88.
51. Sally Bedell Smith, "Film on a Nuclear War Already Causing Wide Fallout of Partisan Activity," *New York Times,* November 23, 1983.
52. Bernard Weinraub, "Hollywood Wonders if Warner Brothers Let 'J.F.K.' Go Too Far," *New York Times,* December 24, 1991; Jack R. Payton, " 'J.F.K'.'s Premise Is Full of Holes—But So Was Warren Report," *Chicago Tribune,* December 24, 1991.

53. For a discussion of the subtle yet significant consequences that are often missed, see Stanley Feldman and Lee Sigelman, "The Political Impact of Prime-Time Television: 'The Day After,' " *Journal of Politics* 47 (May 1985): 556–578.

54. For a full discussion of the role of the media as political actors, see Timothy E. Cook, *Governing with the News: The News Media as Political Institutions* (Chicago: University of Chicago Press, 1998); and Maxwell McCombs, *Setting the Agenda: the Mass Media and Public Opinion* (Cambridge: Polity Press, 2004).

55. The account is based primarily on Bill Carter, "Post-Mortem of a Flawed Broadcast," *New York Times,* January 11, 2005.

56. Richard Bernstein, "CBS Releases Its Study of Vietnam Documentary," *New York Times,* April 27, 1983.

57. Bill Carter, "The Larger Issues Behind the Dan Rather Case," *New York Times,* October 4, 1989.

58. Pat Widder, "Playing with Fire: Blur of Fact and Fiction Costs NBC," *Chicago Tribune,* February 11, 1993.

59. Walter Goodman, "What's News Worthy Is in the Eye of the Beholder," *New York Times,* August 30, 1993.

60. Andrew H. Malcolm, "TV Film Links to Mob in Toronto," *New York Times,* March 28, 1979.

61. Louis A. Day, *Ethics in Media Communications,* 4th ed. (Belmont, Calif,: Wadsworth, 2003), chaps. 4, 9.

Readings

Cappella, Joseph N., and Kathleen Hall Jamieson. *Spiral of Cynicism.* New York: Oxford University Press, 1997.

Day, Louis A. *Ethics in Media Communications.* 4th ed. Belmont, Calif.: Wadsworth, 2003.

Graber, Doris, Denis McQuail, and Pippa Norris, eds. *The Politics of News, the News of Politics.* Washington, D.C.: CQ Press, 1998.

Lang, Gladys Engel, and Kurt Lang. *The Battle for Public Opinion: The President, the Press, and the Polls during Watergate.* New York: Columbia University Press, 1983.

Merrill, John C., Peter J. Gade, and Frederick R. Blevens. *Twilight of Press Freedom: The Rise of People's Journalism.* Mahwah, N.J.: Erlbaum, 2001.

Miljan, Lydia, and Barry Cooper. *Hidden Agendas: How Journalists Influence the News.* Vancouver, BC: UBC Press, 2003.

Sabato, Larry J., Mark Stencel, and S. Robert Lichter. *Peepshow: Media and Politics in an Age of Scandal.* Lanham, Md.: Rowman and Littlefield, 2000.

Serrin, Judith, and William Serrin. *Muckraking! The Journalism That Changed America.* New York: New Press, 2002.

Smith, Rebecca, and John R. Emshwiller. *24 Days: How Two Wall Street Journal Reporters Uncovered the Lies That Destroyed Faith in Corporate America.* New York: HarperBusiness, 2003.

Steffens, Lincoln. *The Autobiography of Lincoln Steffens.* New York: Harcourt Brace, 1931.

Media Influence on Attitudes and Behavior

DO ADULTS LEARN FROM MEDIA EXPOSURE? More than half say they do.[1] This is why the Centers for Disease Control and Prevention (CDC) encourages media enterprises to include health messages in their programs. Accordingly, CDC worked with the producers of the popular daytime soap opera *The Bold and the Beautiful* to produce a subplot about HIV. In August 2001 millions of the show's viewers watched an attractive young Hispanic man who was HIV positive tell his doctor that he had encouraged his fiancée and other female sex partners to be tested for the virus. During this and a subsequent similar episode, the CDC's national sexually transmitted disease and AIDS hotline toll-free phone number appeared on screen, along with a message by the show's HIV-positive character to call the number for information about HIV and AIDS. During the thirty-minute show and within the adjacent hour, a tidal wave of calls overwhelmed the hotline phones. Many of the callers, who included a large number of African American women, told interviewers that they had first learned about the hotline from the soap opera episode. More than half alleged that the episode had inspired them to make lifestyle changes to protect their health.[2]

How representative is that example? Do media stories really shape the thinking and behavior patterns of countless Americans? Are people's values and attitudes about social and political issues influenced substantially by what they read and see? Do desirable and undesirable behaviors in television fiction and news programs produce imitations in real life? How much do people learn from the media and what do they learn?

We will examine these questions, beginning with the shaping of attitudes that occurs as an unintended byproduct of media exposure. Aside from programs directed at children, journalists usually do not try to teach political attitudes and values to their audiences, nor do people try to learn them. Rather, exposure to individual, dramatic events or to the incremental impact of the total flow of information over prolonged periods leads to "incidental" learning about the political world. We also will consider the ways in which people choose the media to which they pay attention and the sorts of things they learn. Finally, we will address the question posed at the start: to what degree does exposure to the mass media influence behavior in politically and socially significant ways?

Differential Effects of Print and Broadcast News

Most Americans are exposed to the combined effects of print and broadcast media either directly or indirectly through contact with people who tell them what they have heard or seen or read. We may know that President Bush selected an African American woman, Condoleezza Rice, as his secretary of state. We may feel reassured or disturbed by the appointment and may believe that it is either good or bad to have a woman in that position. But which of these thoughts and feelings come from television, newspapers, conversations, or a combination of media? It is nearly impossible to disentangle such strands of information.[3]

Each medium, however, does make unique contributions to learning. For example, television, because of its visuals, is especially powerful in transmitting realism and emotional appeal. Print media excel in conveying factual details. Because most tests of learning from the media focus on the kinds of facts that print media emphasize, they are generally credited with conveying more knowledge than audiovisual media do.[4] Television bashing is popular when social critics search for a scapegoat for the ills of society.[5] The critics downplay the learning opportunities provided by seeing events unfold on the television screen. Media scholar Neil Postman, for example, warns that massive use of television will turn the United States into a nation of dilettantes who avoid serious thinking because television trivializes the problems of the world.[6] Rod Hart calls it a "seductive" medium that turns people into passive watchers of the political scene, rather than active participants.[7]

The claim that audiences who are print—rather than television—reliant are better informed and that this proves the superiority of print news must be put into the appropriate context. As a group, print-reliant people differ from those who depend mostly on television in ways that make factual learning easier. Print aficionados generally enjoy higher socioeconomic status and better formal education. Their mid- and upper-level jobs provide above-average incentives for learning the factual details by which social scientists judge citizens' knowledge.[8] Attitudes toward the media matter as well. Most people view print media as sources of information, whereas people view electronic media as sources of entertainment. These differences, rather than the nature of each medium, may explain some of the differences in the effects of different types of media. Television becomes the most instructive medium if one tests for information that is best conveyed audiovisually, such as impressions of people and the inferences they engender or comprehension and long-term memory for dramatic events.[9] Television is also the most readily comprehensible medium for millions of people with limited education. That includes the 23 million U.S. adults who are functionally illiterate and, therefore, almost entirely beyond the reach of print media. What the poorly educated learn about politics from television may be fragmentary and hazy, but it represents a quantum leap over the knowledge available to pretelevision-age generations.

Television's greatest political impact, compared with that of other media, springs from its ability to reach millions of people simultaneously with the same images. Although the traditional networks lost more than half of their nightly news viewers in the closing decade of the twentieth century, they remain kings of the information market by a wide margin.[10] Televised events still are experiences shared nationwide. Millions of Americans saw the aftermath of the September 11, 2001, terrorist attack and the models of the reconstructed neighborhoods on television. They watched U.S. troops fight the 1991 Persian Gulf War and joined in vicarious visits to the Vatican during the Papal transition in 2005. They saw the unfolding of the Clinton impeachment trial in 1998 and 1999 and the counting of disputed ballots in Florida following the 2000 presidential election. U.S. print media have never equaled the reach of television and the power that flows from it, including the power to shape collective memories.[11]

In short, the research on the differential effects of media reveals that different types present stimuli that vary substantially in nature and content. It would be surprising, therefore, if their impact were identical, even when they deal with the same subjects. However, "there is no evidence of *consistent* significant differences in the ability of different media to persuade, inform, or even to instill an emotional response in audience members."[12] Because current research does not provide adequate answers about the precise effects of these stimulus variations and about the processes by which individuals mesh a variety of media stimuli, we will focus on the end product—the combined influence of all print and electronic media stimuli on mass audiences.

The Role of Media in Political Socialization

Political socialization—learning about political life and internalizing its customs and rules—affects the quality of interactions between citizens and their government. To operate smoothly, political systems need the support of most of their citizens, who must be willing to abide by the laws and to sustain government through performing duties such as voting, paying taxes, or serving in the military. Citizens are more likely to support their government if they are convinced of its legitimacy and capability, and if they feel strong emotional ties to it.

Childhood Socialization

Political socialization starts in childhood. Children usually learn basic attitudes toward authority, property, decision making, and veneration for political symbols from their families and other early childhood caretakers. When they enter the more formal school setting, teaching about political values becomes quite systematic. At school, children also learn new factual information about their political and social world, much of it based on information from mass media.[13]

Children's direct contacts with the media are equally abundant.[14] Millions of babies watch television. In the winter, young children in the United States spend an average of thirty-one hours a week in front of the television set—more time than in school. Between the ages of twelve and seventeen, the weekly number of hours spent viewing television drops to twenty-four. Eighty percent of the programs children see are intended for adults and show incidents that differ substantially from those in the child's immediate environment. Children watch military combat, funerals, rocket launchings, courtships, seductions, and childbirth. If they can understand the message, the impact is potentially powerful because children are primed for learning and are apt to take such presentations at face value.

When asked for the sources of information on which they base their attitudes about the economy or race, or about war and patriotism, high school students mention the mass media far more often than they mention their families, friends, teachers, or personal experiences.[15] Youngsters who are frequent media users gain substantial information from the media. Compared with infrequent users, they show greater understanding and support for basic American values such as the importance of free speech and the right to equal and fair treatment.[16]

The finding that mass media strongly influence socialization runs counter to earlier socialization studies that showed parents and teachers as the chief socializers. Several reasons account for the change. The first is the pervasiveness of television, which exposes even the youngest children to images of the world displayed by the mass media. The second reason involves deficiencies in measurement. Much of the early research discounted all media influence unless it came through direct contact between the child and the media. That excluded indirect media influence, such as contacts with parents and teachers who conveyed media information to the child. Finally, research designs have become more sophisticated. In the early studies, children were asked to make their own general appraisal of learning sources. A typical question might be, "From whom do you learn the most: your parents, your school, or newspapers and television?" The questions used in recent studies have been more specific, inquiring first what children know about particular subjects, such as immigration or nuclear energy, and then asking about the sources of their information. In nearly every case the mass media are named as the chief sources of information and evaluations.

What children learn from the mass media and how they evaluate it depends heavily on their stage of mental development. According to child psychologist Jean Piaget, children between two and seven years of age do not detect the connections among various phenomena or draw general conclusions from specific instances. Many of the lessons presumably taught by media stories therefore elude young children. Complex reasoning skills develop fully only at the teenage level. Children's interests in certain types of stories also change sharply with age, as do their attention and information-retention spans.[17] Most children strongly support the political system during their early years but often become disillusioned about authority figures during their teenage years. Their skepticism diminishes as they finish their education and enter the workforce. What role the media play in this transformation is unclear.[18] Knowledge is also slim about children's and adolescents' imitation of behavior depicted by media stories, the duration of memories, and the persistence of media effects on learning, behavior, and social relationships.[19]

Adult Socialization

The pattern of heavy reliance on media exposure for political news continues into adulthood, though it has been declining sharply in recent decades. For instance, 70 percent of senior citizens read a newspaper regularly in 1991. That dropped to 59 percent in 2002. In that year, only 25 percent of adults younger than thirty were regular readers. The average American adult spends twenty-eight minutes daily watching television news, sixteen minutes listening to radio news, and fifteen minutes reading a newspaper. Of course, total time spent watching and listening to non-news offerings is much greater, although it has been slipping as well.[20]

This massive exposure to news and to political information embedded in entertainment programs contributes to the lifelong process of political socialization and learning.[21] The mass media form

> the mainstream of the common symbolic environment that cultivates the most widely shared conceptions of reality. We live in terms of the stories we tell, stories about what things exist, stories about how things work, and stories about what to do. . . . Increasingly, media-cultivated facts and values become standards by which we judge.[22]

Once people have formed their basic attitudes toward the political system, these attitudes usually stabilize so that later learning largely supplements and refines earlier notions. The need to cope with information about new events and shifting cultural orientations force the average person into continuous learning and gradual readjustments, although the basic value structure generally remains intact, even when attitudes are modified.[23] However, major personal or societal upheavals may lead to more or less complete resocialization and revised political ideas.

People learn about political norms, rules, values, events, and behaviors largely from fictional and factual mass media stories. Personal experiences are severely limited compared with the range of experiences the media offer to us directly or indirectly about the social order and political activities. An accident report, for example, besides telling what happened, may suggest that police and fire forces respond too slowly and that emergency facilities in the local hospital are inadequate. When societal problems such as poverty or pollution are framed as discrete events and reflect just one family's starvation or a particular oil spill, attention is likely to be focused on individual solutions, obscuring the larger societal problems.[24] Soap operas on radio and television may persuade audiences that most politicians are corruptible—after all, the majority of those shown on television are.[25] In fact, fictional stories are the most widely used sources for political information. Surveys show that only one-half to two-thirds of the adult television audience regularly exposes itself to explicitly political news.[26]

People's opinions, feelings, and evaluations about the political system may spring from their own thinking about facts supplied by the media; from attitudes, opinions, and feelings explicitly expressed in news or entertainment programming; or from a combination of the two (Box 7-1).[27] When audiences have direct or vicarious experiences to guide them, and particularly when they have already formed opinions grounded firmly in their personal values, they are least likely to be swayed by the media. Many people who use the media for information and as a point of departure for formulating their own appraisals nonetheless reject or ignore attitudes and evaluations that media stories supply explicitly or implicitly.[28] For

BOX 7-1
How Democracy Gets by on a Soft News Diet

Most Americans don't worry about problems of public life except when the country seems to be in serious trouble. During calmer times, average Americans focus on daily life, their families, their jobs, and their neighborhoods. Most people are busy, pressured for time, and hungering for brief escapes from the daily rat race. That is why light entertainment rather than the serious but unattractive political fare we know as "hard" news is so attractive. Hard news may be good for the public's civic health, but it is more often praised by elites than consumed by them or their fellow citizens.

Pundits blame media tycoons for catering to the public's penchant for "soft" news and light entertainment instead of supplying the hard news that citizens allegedly need to fulfill their civic obligations. The right to use the nation's airwaves, the critics charge, carries with it the obligation to serve the public interest, which is not equivalent to what the public finds interesting or what media tycoons find profitable. Such criticism implies that the media must offer average Americans the stories that elites think audiences need, and that they must discourage audiences from tasting the forbidden fruit of low-brow media fare by making less of it available.

That stance reveals a profound dilemma. Citizens in a democracy do need to be well informed. But they also should be able to enjoy the right to freely choose the information that best suits their needs and tastes.

The resolution of the dilemma of clashing needs is twofold. Most important, there is ample evidence that soft news addiction has not kept the public from maintaining adequate civic knowledge. Over a lifetime average Americans do learn a great deal about important aspects of politics, the economy, and social issues. During times of political turmoil, the audience for hard news triples and quadruples. It then becomes clear that V.O. Key, the renowned scholar of public opinion, was right when he argued persuasively in the 1960s that "voters are not fools"—no matter the harsh views of academic critics.

The other part of the resolution hinges on needed reforms in hard news production and presentation. Audiences are attracted to entertainment and soft news stories because they tend to be exciting, emotionally involving, titillating, and—yes—are easy to understand. To compete effectively requires imbuing hard news with many of the characteristics of the most appealing entertainment fare. If journalists can make hard news stories as easy to understand and as compelling to watch as the best of the entertainment shows, the ranks of hard news consumers will swell. Jon Stewart's *Daily Show* on Comedy Central is an example. It proves that serious commentary can be entertaining and can appeal to large audiences, including normally elusive young citizens. It also demonstrates that fresh approaches are possible and thereby challenges the journalism community to reinvent itself to meet the needs of the twenty-first century.

example, the public gave little credence to the widely publicized predictions by media pundits that proof of President Clinton's affair with White House intern Monica Lewinsky would end the Clinton presidency.

People are prone to accept newspeople's views about national and international issues absent personal experience or guidance from social contacts. Even when people think they are forming their own opinions about familiar issues, they often depend on the media more than they realize. Extensive television exposure has been shown to lead to "mainstreaming," making people's outlook on political life "congruent with television's portrayal of life and society." [29]

The media's persuasiveness does not mean that exposure is tantamount to learning and mind changing. Far from it. Two-thirds of the people generally do not know their newspaper's preferred position on specific economic, social, and foreign policy issues.[30] Most media stories are promptly forgotten. Stories that become part of an individual's fund of knowledge tend to reinforce existing beliefs and feelings. Acquisition of new knowledge or changes in attitude are the exception rather than the rule. Still, they occur often enough to be significant.

Patterns in Socialization

Race, ethnicity, gender, age, income, education, region, and city size generate differences in habits of newspaper reading, radio listening, and television viewing. For instance, blacks and Hispanics rely more on television than whites, and women are the primary audience for daytime television. Age has a bearing on newspaper reading, with older people reading more than younger ones. Southerners listen to much less radio than northerners. Program preferences vary as well. Women ages fifty and older are the heaviest viewers of television news, followed by men fifty and older. Twelve- to seventeen-year-olds are the lightest news watchers. Men far exceed women in following sports coverage, whereas women spend more time watching television drama.

Differences in media-use patterns are particularly pronounced among income levels in part because the most meaty news media cater primarily to the interests of the wealthier segments of the public. High-income families, who usually are better educated than poor families, use print media more and television less than the rest of the population. Upper-income people also use a greater variety of media than lower-income groups. Being better informed helps the information-rich maintain and increase their influence and power in U.S. society.[31]

Although different media exposure and use patterns offer a partial explanation for knowledge and attitude differences, the notion of vastly different communications environments for various population groups should not be carried too far. The bulk of media entertainment and information is similar throughout the country and is shared by all types of audiences. In Chapter 4 we saw that the news media cover basically the same categories of stories in the same proportions. Specific stories vary, of course, depending on regional and local interests. Newspapers on the West Coast are more likely to devote their foreign affairs coverage to Asian affairs than are newspapers on the East Coast, which concentrate on Europe and the Middle East. Tabloids put more stress on sensational crime and sex stories than do elite papers such as the staid *New York Times*. Nevertheless, news sources everywhere provide a large common core of information and interpretation that imbues their audiences with a shared structure of knowledge and basic values. Although audience predispositions, like party affiliation or religious orientation, produce wide disparities of views on many issues despite shared news, a broad consensus remains on the basic principles that undergird U.S. democracy.

Choosing Media Stories

General patterns of media use do not reveal *why* people pay attention to specific stories, but a number of theories help explain this.

Uses and Gratifications Theories

One of the most widely accepted news-choice theories is the "uses and gratifications" approach. Put simply, proponents of this approach contend that individuals ignore personally irrelevant and unattractively presented messages. They pay attention to the kinds of things that they find useful and intellectually or emotionally gratifying if time and effort constraints permit it.[32]

Media scholar Lance Bennett groups uses and gratifications into three broad categories: curiosity and surveillance, entertainment and escape, and social and psychological adjustment.[33] For instance, people pay attention to stories that help them decide how to vote or to participate in protest demonstrations. They use the media to gain a sense of security and social adequacy from knowing what is happening in their political environment. People feel gratified if the media reinforce what they already know and believe. They also use the media to while away time, reduce loneliness, participate vicariously in exciting ventures, and escape the frustrations of everyday life.[34] People from all walks of life are most likely to view primetime programs that are action filled, humorous, and relaxing.

They are least likely to choose educational programs, particularly when these presentations involve complex political analysis.[35]

Of course, there is no guarantee that people will attain the gratifications they seek. In fact, media may produce anxieties and fears as well as hatred and alienation. When a long strike in Israel shut down radio and television in 1987, the public reacted with relief rather than dismay. Israeli philosopher David Hartman gave this explanation:

> When television and radio become the prisms through which you look at reality, you come away saying, "What an ugly place this is." But when you take away those prisms and people's perceptions of reality are derived exclusively from their own daily experiences, which are for the most part prosaic, they inevitably become more relaxed and stable.[36]

Table 7-1, based on interviews with a national sample of adult Americans, indicates how many news consumers claim that they regularly pay a lot of attention to one of the thirteen categories of news about which they were questioned. The topics that attract attention from the largest numbers of people presumably supply the broadest array of gratifications. The responses vary somewhat depending on the type of news medium that the respondent uses most often. But the differences are relatively small in all categories except for international news and news from the nation's capital. However, national data tend to mask the fact that special subcultural needs may lead to significant variations in gratification patterns. For instance, a Jewish person may be particularly eager to receive news from the Middle East and other places that concern Israel. A person of Polish ancestry may look for news about political developments in Poland. Women who favor increased job opportunities for women are apt to notice stories about women's expanding presence in the business world.

What people actually select depends very much on their lifestyles and the context in which they are exposed to information. What is useful and gratifying in one setting may be less so in another. When people change their lifestyles, like retiring from full-time employment or transitioning from a desk to a travel job, media patterns may change drastically to bring about closer accord with the people encountered in the new setting.[37]

Besides knowing the kind of news that attracts various audiences, it is also important to know why people ignore a lot of available news. Table 7-2 reports journalists' appraisal of why the public finds news less useful and less gratifying than in prior decades. It sheds light on some of the reasons for the sharp and continuing decline in news consumption that raises serious concerns about the status of civic knowledge and the health of the journalistic enterprise. The table suggests that the problem can be summed under three headings: The news is not geared well enough to people's

TABLE 7-1   Regular Audiences' News Preferences, April 2004
(percentage who follow each topic "very closely")

News topics regular audiences view closely	Paper	Network	Cable	Local	*News Hour*	Late night	Internet
Crime	37	41	41	39	35	44	32
Own community	36	38	34	35	31	34	27
Health	31	38	34	32	33	32	25
Sports	29	20	28	27	26	35	30
International	30	33	37	25	49	32	35
People/events in D.C.	32	36	42	28	46	29	36
Local government	30	33	30	29	33	28	24
Religion	22	25	25	23	21	20	16
Science/technology	19	18	20	16	33	23	25
Entertainment	15	14	15	16	16	28	16
Business/finance	19	18	19	16	22	16	21
Consumer	17	20	19	16	27	17	16
Culture and the arts	13	10	10	10	25	17	14

SOURCE: Adapted from Pew Research Center for the People and the Press, "News Audiences Increasingly Politicized," June 8, 2004, http://people-press.org.

NOTE: Topics are listed in rank order of overall popularity. *News Hour* refers to *News Hour with Jim Lehrer.* "Late night" is based on data from *Larry King Live* and the *O'Reilly Factor.*

needs; it is not enjoyably presented; and there are other venues and ventures that are more useful and gratifying.

Other Selective Exposure Theories

Failure to pay attention to news may also spring from psychological factors. According to cognitive balance theories, people avoid information that disturbs their peace of mind, offends their political and social tastes, or conflicts with information, attitudes, and feelings they already hold. Social scientists explain selective exposure by pointing out that people are uncomfortable when exposed to ideas that differ from their own or that question the validity of their ideas. To avoid discomfort, people ignore discordant information. Selectivity reduces the already slim chances that exposure to different views will alter an individual's established beliefs, attitudes, and feelings. Selective exposure therefore helps to explain the considerable stability that exists in orientations, such as party allegiance or foreign policy preferences.

Scholars now believe that selective exposure occurs to a lesser extent than was thought initially. Many people find it too bothersome to avoid news they dislike, particularly when using electronic media. When televi-

TABLE 7-2   Reasons for Lessening Attention to News Stories: Journalists'
Appraisals, 2004 (in percentages)

| Reason for audience loss | National | | Local | | |
	Print	Broadcast	Print	Broadcast	Internet
News not meaningful for average Americans	54	23	54	43	52
News too serious for public tastes	30	30	19	29	24
News overdoes sensational stories and scandals	25	50	33	54	37
News is too boring and static for fast-paced society	17	13	33	11	31
News is too repetitive; same stories reappear	41	44	39	50	38
Specialized news outlets match public's need better	44	47	40	44	55
Americans have more pressing priorities	52	40	58	42	55

SOURCE: Adapted from Pew Research Center for the People and the Press, "Bottom-Line Pressures Now Hurting Coverage, Say Journalists," May 23, 2004, http://people-press.org.

NOTE: Based on a survey of 547 journalists. Respondents were drawn from national and local media samples representing a cross-section of news organizations and their personnel. Interviews were conducted March 10–April 20, 2004.

sion news programs carry stories that are objectionable to a viewer, there is no easy way to screen out the undesired stories and continue to watch the rest of the broadcast. Many people are actually curious about discrepant information or pride themselves on being open minded and receptive to all points of view. For instance, Democrats may want to hear what Republicans are saying to find out how the opposition is stating its case. They may also want to determine what counterarguments they need to formulate. Many people actually enjoy hearing news that contradicts their own ideas so that they can refute what they hear. Apparently exposure to discrepant information is not as universally painful as previously thought. Besides, people often fail to notice that stories diverge in major ways from their own views.[38]

Much of the evidence for selective exposure comes from settings in which available media supported the preferences of the audience. No choice was necessary; selection was de facto rather than deliberate. For example, unionized workers with friends and associates who are also in unions may encounter a lot of prounion information at home and at work. In fact, antiunion information may be unavailable. Genuine rather than de facto selective exposure does occur, of course, but it operates more like a preference for congenial news rather than a total exclusion of displeasing information.

Agenda-Setting Theories

If personal needs and pleasures entirely determined choices of news items, news selection patterns would show infinite variations. This is not the case. Similarities in the political environment of average Americans and social pressures produce common patterns in the selection of news, although polarization along ideological lines is on the rise. For example, conservatives have been flocking to Fox News while liberals choose CNN. In those areas where the political orientations of these two venues differ, their audiences' opinions reflect the cleavages.[39] As previously mentioned, gatekeeping practices largely account for the similarity in news supply, which is a powerful unifying force. Media also tell people in fairly uniform fashion which individual issues and activities are most significant and deserve to be ranked highly on the public's agenda of concerns.[40] Importance is indicated through cues such as banner headlines, front-page placement in newspapers, or first-story placement on television. Frequent and ample coverage also implies significance.

Many people readily adopt the media's agenda of importance, often without being aware of it, rather than selecting or rejecting news on the basis of what is personally gratifying or displeasing. We look at the front page of the newspaper and expect to find the most important stories there. We may watch the opening minutes of a telecast eagerly and then allow our attention to slacken. As a result, agenda setting by the media leads to uniformities in exposure as well as in significance ratings of news items. When the media make events seem important, average people as well as politicians discuss them and form opinions. This enhances the perceived importance of these events and ensures even more public attention and, possibly, political action.

Numerous studies confirm the agenda-setting influence of the media.[41] When people are asked which issues are most important to them personally or to their communities, their lists tend to correspond to cues in the news sources that they use in their communities. However, agenda setting varies in potency. Audiences follow media guidance but not slavishly. Past and current experiences, conversations with others, and independent reasoning provide alternatives to media guidance.[42] Comparisons of media agendas with public opinion polls and reports about political and social conditions show that media guidance is most important for new issues that have not been widely discussed and for issues beyond the realm of personal experience.[43] The need for raw material for conversation with friends and associates is a particularly strong force when people select stories. Prominent media coverage does ensure that an issue will be noticed, but it does not guarantee that the audience will assign it the same relative rank of importance that media have indicated. Likewise, people will note information that is useful or gratifying to them, even if it is on the back pages, receives minuscule headlines, or is briefly reported at the tail end of a newscast.[44]

How People Learn

How do audiences interpret the stories that they have selected? The early models that depicted a straight stimulus–response relationship have been disproven. There is no "hypodermic effect": the media do not inject information unaltered into the minds of audiences. Rather, the images that media convey stimulate perceptions in audience members that reflect the media stimuli as well as each individual's perceptual state at the time he or she receives the message.

Blending New and Old Information

From childhood on, people develop ideas and feelings about how the world operates. When these ideas relate to politics, they are usually grounded in information drawn from the mass media. Cognitive psychologists call these mental configurations by various names, including *schemas* and *scripts*.[45] They serve as organizing devices that help people assimilate new information. As journalist Walter Lippmann explained it:

> For the most part we do not first see, and then define, we define first and then see. In the great blooming, buzzing confusion of the outer world, we pick out what our culture has already defined for us, and we tend to perceive that which we have picked out in the form stereotyped for us by our culture.[46]

For example, media crime stories and statistics have conditioned most Americans to consider African Americans as more likely perpetrators of violent crimes. Numerous experiments accordingly show that whites often mistakenly identify a black person as wielding a murder weapon even when pictures they viewed earlier show a white assailant.[47] Their image is "perceiver determined" which means that it is shaped by what they already believe, rather than "stimulus determined," which means that the image reflects the actual stimulus that their senses have absorbed. Research shows that images of political candidates are largely perceiver determined for those aspects for which the audience already has developed complex schemas. For instance, people assume that Democratic presidential candidates will pursue policies typically associated with Democrats. They read or view the news in that vein, picking up bits of information that fit while rejecting, ignoring, or reinterpreting those that do not fit. The same is likely to hold true for information about big business or labor unions, the pope, or England's queen. Average Americans are likely to interpret big business and big labor news negatively. Similarly, if reports about the pope or Queen Elizabeth permit a choice between favorable and unfavorable interpretations, the favorable image is apt to prevail.

Information about aspects of events or people not widely known or stereotyped leads to stimulus-determined images. How the media frame these political issues and depict people largely determines what the audience perceives. The personalities of newcomers to the political scene, assessments of their capabilities, and appraisals of the people with whom they surround themselves, for example, usually are stimulus determined.[48] Likewise, when the media describe present-day China, when they cast doubt on the safety of nuclear energy production, or when they praise the merits of a newly developed drug, they create images that are apt to dominate people's schemas.

Numerous studies show that political elites and other well-informed people have developed exceptionally large arrays of schemas allowing them to absorb many stories that are beyond the reach of the poorly informed.[49] They even are more physically stimulated by new information and therefore are more likely to remember it.[50] The knowledge gap between the privileged and underprivileged widens as a result. Those with the least political knowledge are likely to remain politically unsophisticated and impotent. The knowledge gap between the information rich and the information poor also makes mutual understanding of political views more difficult.

Transient Influences

Many transitory factors impinge on news processing. People are intermittently attentive or inattentive and inclined or disinclined to learn. Up to half of television viewers eat dinner, wash dishes, read, or talk on the telephone while watching television. Examination time at school, illness in the family, or the year-end rush at work may preempt the time normally devoted to media. Researchers cannot predict the effect of media messages without knowing the group context in which exposure or conversation took place. For instance, if one watches or talks about a presidential inauguration with friends who are making fun of the way the president talks and acts, the occasion loses its solemnity and becomes banal. How a person interacts with information also depends on the format of that information. If news reports present conflicting facts or opinions, if they are overly long or overly short, if they are repetitious, dull, or offensive, their effect is apt to be diminished. Moreover, the total communications matrix affects the influence of its parts so that the impact of print news may be blunted by prior presentations on television and radio that have removed the edge of novelty.[51]

Source credibility and appeal are other significant factors in news processing. People find television news more believable than comparable print news because viewers tend to trust news anchors; seeing them on their living room television screens makes them familiar and trustworthy. Partisanship, too, plays an important role in source appraisal. It may cast a rosy glow over fellow partisans and a pall over the opposition.

Learning Effects: Knowledge and Attitudes

What kinds of politically relevant knowledge, attitudes, feelings, and actions spring from people's contacts with the media? Because of the limitations of measuring instruments, the answer to this question is difficult. In Chapter 1 we pointed out the impossibility of isolating media influence when it is one of many factors in a complex environment. For example, a sample of citizens who were asked during the Reagan years why their worries about nuclear war had increased cited the following mixture of reasons: increased media coverage (52 percent); Reagan administration policies (19 percent); new weapons/new technology/proliferation (19 percent); unrest in developing countries (13 percent); East–West tensions (11 percent); Soviet belligerence (4 percent); children/grandchildren's lives (4 percent); other reasons (2 percent); don't know/no answer/can't explain (5 percent).[52] Although these answers tell us which factors played a role, and how many audience members mentioned them, they do not indicate the precise impact of each factor. Until researchers can trace an individual's mental processes and isolate and appraise the significance of each of the components that interact and combine to form mental images, media's influence on knowledge and attitudes cannot be fully assessed. Nor can researchers understand completely just what is learned from media.

Measurement Problems

Research up to now has focused on very small facets of learning, such as testing what specific facts individuals learn about political candidates or about a few public policies. Even within such narrow areas, testing has been severely limited. It has zeroed in on the memorization of factual details from stories rather than on total knowledge gains. For instance, election coverage of a presidential candidate teaches more than facts about the candidate. It may also inform the audience about the role played by White House correspondents in campaign coverage and about living conditions in other cities. Such knowledge gains from the story, however important they may be, are usually overlooked. Much learning may even be subconscious. People may be unaware that they have learned something new and may not mention it when asked what they have learned. At times people may temporarily forget new information, only to have it reenter consciousness a short while later.[53]

Although many assumptions about learning that seem intuitively correct remain untested, they are widely accepted as true. Accordingly, news reports and dramatic television programs presumably teach audiences how lawyers or police officers or hospitals conduct their business, and people deduce important social lessons from specific news stories. For instance, media researcher Joshua Meyrowitz argues that television has radically changed social roles by stripping them of mystery and holding them up to continuous public scrutiny. Women working in the home who were previously isolated have learned about the attractive roles open only to males in U.S. society, and the successes and failures of the women's movement have affected the behavior of these women. Television allows children to experience the adult world long before they are physically and emotionally prepared to cope with these experiences. In the age of television, political heroes have become ordinary mortals, and authority figures are no longer respected solely because of the mystery of social distance.[54]

We believe that adults as well as children often model their behavior after characters they encounter in the media. We assume that unfavorable stereotypes will hurt the self-esteem of the groups so characterized. Therefore, we urge newspeople to present traditionally adversely stereotyped groups—people with disabilities, gays and lesbians, or people of color—in a better light. Although there is every reason to believe that such effects are quite common, most of them remain unmeasured.

An important exception has been the Cultural Indicators project conducted since the mid-1960s at the University of Pennsylvania's Annenberg School of Communications. Using "cultivation analysis," the investigators have studied trends in the dramatic content of network television and the conceptions of social reality produced in viewers. Their findings confirm that people who watch television for more than four hours daily see the world as television paints it and react to that world rather than to reality more than do their demographic counterparts who watch much less television. For instance, heavy viewers exaggerate the dangers of becoming a crime victim.[55] They fear crime more and are more distrustful and suspicious than are light viewers. They also are generally more pessimistic and tend to gravitate toward the middle-of-the-road mainstream politics depicted on television.

Like most research on mass media effects, these findings have been challenged on the ground that factors other than mass media exposure account for the results. The characteristics of viewers rather than their exposure to television may be responsible for their images of the world and their addiction to television. The technical aspects of the Cultural Indicators project have also been challenged. Such scientific controversies indicate that research on mass media effects needs a lot more refinement.

This holds true, too, for a number of experimental studies that have found, for example, that television news coverage of specific events "primes" audiences to appraise politicians in light of these events. Consequently, their political perspectives narrow so that single phenomena deflect attention from the broader context.[56] Until such findings have been tested in natural settings to appraise under what conditions and for what length of time they apply, they must be considered tentative. For example, it is not surprising that experiments indicate that a president's popularity ratings fare better when the audience has been primed with questions about his political successes rather than his failures.[57] But thus far, experiments have failed to tell us how long the priming effects persist in natural situations and their likely political impact.

A neglected research sphere concerns forgetfulness. Much that is learned from the media is evanescent. When Balkan leaders are charged with war crimes or the mayor of New York becomes involved in a nasty divorce battle, the salient names and facts are on many lips, but after the events have passed, this knowledge evaporates rapidly. How rapidly seems to depend on several factors, most importantly people's ability to store and retrieve information. After three months of inattention, ordinary stories are hard to recall, even by people with good memories. If media periodically revive stories with follow-ups or with closely related stories, memory becomes deepened and prolonged. In fact, the media have rehearsed a few crucial incidents so often that they have become permanent memories. The Great Depression, World War II, the assassination of President Kennedy, and the horrors of the 2001 collapse of the World Trade Center towers are examples.[58]

Factual Learning

Given these limitations on initial learning and on remembering, what can be said about the extent of political learning from the mass media?

Average people are aware of an impressive array of politically important topics that the media have covered. However, they do not master many details. They recognize information if it is mentioned to them but fail to recall it without such assistance.[59] When John Robinson and Dennis Davis tested recall of specific facts mentioned in thirteen television news stories within hours of viewing, accuracy scores hovered around 40 percent, with only minor differences among age groups. Education and prior information levels produced the largest variations in scores, with the best informed scoring 13.8 percentage points higher than the poorly informed; 11.2 percentage points separate the scores of college graduates and people who terminated their education in grade school.

Many people are shocked by low recall scores because they believe that stories cannot be fully understood without memorizing factual details. For example, political scientists Scott Keeter and Cliff Zukin titled their study of voter knowledge gains during the 1976 and 1980 presidential elections *Uninformed Choice* because recall scores were low. Keeter and Zukin argued that most citizens are too uninformed to make intelligent political choices.[60] Such judgments may be unduly harsh, because these studies gauge knowledge solely by a citizen's ability to recall facts like the names of prominent officeholders and figures about the length of their terms of office or the growth rate of budget deficits. These factual information tests are inadequate for judging political knowledge and competence. What really matters is that citizens understand what is at stake in major political issues and what policy options are available for coping with problems. An extensive repertoire of factual detail is not essential for that. As media scholar Michael Schudson puts it: "There's a difference between the 'informational citizen,' saturated with bits and bytes of information, and the informed citizen, the person who has not only information but a point of view and preferences with which to make sense of it." [61]

Are people aware of major political issues and their significance? Are they able to place them in the general context of current politics? When researchers ask these genuinely important questions, the picture of the public's political competence brightens considerably. People may not remember the content of political speeches very well, but, as mentioned already, they are aware of a wide range of current issues. Moreover, when interviewers probe for understanding, rather than for knowledge of specific facts, they often discover considerable political insight. For instance, people who cannot define either *price deregulation* or *affirmative action* may still have fairly sophisticated notions about these matters. They know about government price controls on some goods and services and fully understand the burdens that minorities face in finding a job.[62]

Learning General Orientations

Some media stories leave the audience with politically significant feelings that persist long after facts have faded from memory. Although many details of the 2001 terrorist strike have faded in memory, Americans still retain vivid feelings of horror, sympathy, and grief. News may leave people with generalized feelings of trust or distrust even when it etches few facts into people's memories. For instance, prominently featured stories of serious corruption in government may lower the public's esteem for the integrity of government. People who read newspapers that are severely critical of government actions express significantly less trust in government than do those exposed to favorable views. People who have not gone beyond grade school seem to be particularly susceptible to erosion of trust in the wake of mass media criticism.[63] Cynical people, in turn, tend to participate less than others in such civic activities as voting and lobbying.[64]

As political scientist Murray Edelman has noted, news stories may make people quiescent because they become fearful of interfering with crucial government actions or else complacent about the need for public vigilance. Fear that dissension weakens the government may decrease tolerance for dissidents. Edelman also warns that political quiescence has significant downsides. It may lead to acceptance of faulty public policies, poor laws, and ineffective administrative practices.[65]

On a more personal level, millions of people use the media to keep in touch with their communities. Their contacts help to counter feelings of loneliness and alienation because information becomes a bond among individuals who share it.[66] The models of life depicted by the media create wants and expectations as well as dissatisfactions and frustrations. These feelings may become powerful stimulants for social change for the society at large or for selected individuals within it. Alternatively, the feelings may bolster support for the political status quo and generate strong resistance to change. Whether media-induced orientations and actions are considered positive, negative, or a mixture of both depends, of course, on one's sociopolitical preferences.

Deterrents to Learning

Lack of interest in politics and distaste for media offerings, as well as deficiencies in the supply of information, deter many people from keeping up with politics. Rather than discussing politics, which they see as a sensitive topic, they prefer to talk about sports, or the weather, or local gossip. In fact, as the level of abstract, issue-oriented content of political news rises, the attentive audience shrivels. People scan the news for major crises without trying to remember specific facts. However, when they sense that events will greatly affect their lives, or when they need information for their jobs or for social or political activities, political interest and learning perk up quickly and often dramatically.[67] For example, media coverage of the postelection-day dispute about the outcome of the 2000 presidential election fired up public interest that had smoldered during the campaign. The postelection events received more public attention in five weeks than the entire primary campaign had received during a five-month span.[68] A similar sharp rise in public attention to news followed the 2001 terrorist attack and the 2004 tsunami.

Widespread public interest in most political crises flares up like a straw fire and then dies quickly. Attention spans for news are erratic and brief, even though most Americans believe that, as good citizens, they ought to be well informed about political news and feel guilty, or at least apologetic, if they are not. The alienation of many population groups from the media further inhibits learning. Many white ethnics, such as Polish Americans or Italian Americans, and police and union members, for instance, consider most mass media hostile. They often believe that the media lie and distort when they cast police as trigger-happy oppressors of the disadvantaged or unions as corrupt and a barrier to economic progress. Public opinion polls in recent decades show considerable erosion of public confidence in the trustworthiness of the media in general. The media now rank near the bottom of trustworthiness, along with Congress and the legal profession.[69]

How the media present information also affects learning. The media bombard the public daily with more news than it can handle. Most of the news is touted as significant even though much is trivial. The constant crisis atmosphere numbs excitement and produces boredom. Audiences are not likely to try hard to learn a wealth of factual information that does not interest them. Moreover, "happy talk" television news formats and exciting film footage encourage the feeling that news is a lighthearted diversion.

The presentation of stories in disconnected television snippets complicates the task of making sense out of news stories and integrating them with existing knowledge. This is especially true when stories are complex, as is true of most reports about controversial public policies. People who feel that they cannot understand what is happening are discouraged from spending time reading or listening. Learning also suffers when media present conflicting stories and interpretations without giving guidance to the audience. Journalists may do this to avoid accusations of unacceptable editorializing. If people watch several newscasts, hoping for an enriched news diet, they find that roughly half the material is repetitive. Even within a single newscast a large proportion of every story is rehashed background information that puts the story into perspective for viewers who are seeing it for the first time.

The internal structure of television newscasts also impedes learning. More than 80 percent of all news stories take up less than two-and-a-half minutes, yet they are crammed with information that people cannot possibly absorb in that time. In addition to an abundance of pictures, the average news story contains three verbal statements for every two pictorial scenes (Table 7-3). Viewers must absorb an average of eighteen factual statements and eleven picture scenes per story for each of the fifteen to eighteen stories in a typical newscast. That amounts to 324 statements and 198 pictures compressed into twenty-two minutes of news exposure. Furthermore, most news programs tightly package disparate items without the pauses that are essential for viewers to absorb information. Hence, it is not surprising that half the audience after the lapse of a few hours cannot recall a single item from a television newscast. Distracting activities that viewers combine with watching television enhance the problem.

Despite all of the deterrents to learning, Americans still learn a lot about politics over a lifetime. Their primary and secondary education usually does a good job of socializing them into the U.S. system. They may be disappointed and cynical about particular leaders or policies, but relatively few individuals question the legitimacy of the government, object to its basic philosophies, or reject its claims to their support. If one believes in the merits of the system, this finding is, indeed, cause for satisfaction with current political socialization. In this light, the dire predictions about television-induced deterioration of political life and rampant political alienation among citizens have not materialized.[70] If the U.S. population becomes more eager to learn about politics, and if the media improve political reporting, then knowledge levels could rise sharply. However, because television has become the main provider of information, knowledge tests need to be restructured so that they reflect the unique contributions made by audiovisuals to comprehending the world.

Learning Effects: Behavior

Because the media shape people's knowledge, attitudes, and feelings, they obviously can influence behavior. Two areas that have long been of great political concern illustrate the extent of behavioral effects: imitation of crime and violence, particularly among adolescents, and stimulation of economic and political development in underdeveloped regions. In Chapter 8 we will discuss the effects of media coverage on voting behavior and in Chapter 11 the effect of the media on the conduct of foreign affairs.

TABLE 7-3   Network Television News Characteristics

Story characteristic	Percentage of total stories
Length (seconds)	
Less than 60	37
61–150	45
151–200	16
200+	2
Average picture exposure (seconds)	
0–5	55
6–10	39
11–20	4
20+	2
Number of pictures	
0–5	36
6–10	15
11–20	45
21+	4

SOURCE: Author's research based on a sample of 143 news stories from early evening newscasts on ABC, CBS, and NBC, June 1–30, 2004.

Crime and Violent Behavior in Children

Many social scientists believe that violence and crime portrayed in the media, particularly on television, lead to imitation, especially by children and young adults. Researchers have thoroughly investigated the possible link between television exposure and deviant behavior. The surgeon general's office has produced a bookshelf full of information on the topic since the 1970s.[71] Congressional committees have spent countless hours listening to conflicting testimony by social scientists about the impact of television violence. Violence in the media has been an issue in campaigns, such as the 2000 presidential contest. Meanwhile, the amount of violent content, particularly in fictional programs, has escalated, though numbers vary widely depending on the definition of violence. A 1996 study that defined violence broadly as "any overt depiction of the use of physical force or the credible threat of such force intended to physically harm an animate being or group of beings" found most violence on premium cable channels. On HBO and Showtime, 85 percent of programming contained violence. The rate was 59 percent for basic cable channels and 44 percent for broadcast television.[72]

What have studies of the impact of television violence revealed? Despite the strong inclination of many of the researchers to find that crime fiction causes asocial behavior, the evidence is inconclusive because multiple other factors influence behavior and cannot be ruled out. Some children do copy violent behavior, especially when they have watched aggression that was left unpunished or was rewarded and when countervailing influences from their parents and their teachers are lacking.[73] But aside from imitating television examples when tempted to do so, very few children become violent after exposure to violence in the mass media. Most children lack the predisposition and usually the opportunity for violence, and most do not live in an environment that encourages asocial behavior.[74] A number of studies have tracked the behavior of children exposed to a great deal of violence on television during their early years. As adults, these individuals display a higher incidence of asocial behaviors. Still, that does not point definitively to television as the cause given the complexity of the environments that mold children and young adults.[75]

Other confounding factors in assessing the impact of television on children are age-linked comprehension differences. Younger children may not be able to comprehend many of the events presented by the media in the same way that adolescents do. The complex social reasoning that adults often ascribe to even young children does not develop until youngsters reach their teenage years. Several studies of children in preschool and early grade school suggest that much of what adults consider to be violent does not seem so to children. Cartoon violence is an example.[76] Therefore, many of the programs that adults consider glorifications of violence may actually suggest quite different things to children.

The proportion of preadolescents and adolescents in the United States who are prone to imitate crime is not known. However, the wide dispersion of television throughout U.S. homes makes it almost certain that the majority of children susceptible to imitating violence will be exposed. Even if the actual number of highly susceptible preadolescents and adolescents is tiny and statistically insignificant, the social consequences can be profound. Such considerations prompted Congress to mandate in the Telecommunications Act of 1996 that television sets should include a "V-chip" to enable adults to block violent television programs from transmission to their homes. The device has not been used extensively, and probably least often in the kinds of homes where the most vulnerable youngsters are likely to live, considering the correlation between child delinquency and flawed home environments.

Behavior Change in Adults

What about imitation of socially undesirable behavior by adults? The same broad principles apply. Imitation depends on the setting at the time of media exposure and on the personality and attitudes that viewers bring to a situation. Widespread societal norms seem to be particularly important. For instance, the 1986 report of the Attorney General's Commission on Pornography noted that exposure to aberrant sexual behavior led to comparatively little imitation. In fact, there was some evidence that greater availability of obscene and pornographic materials reduced sex crimes and misdemeanors because vicarious experiences substituted for actual ones.[77] By comparison, there was a great deal more evidence that exposure to criminal behavior encourages imitation. The difference may be more apparent than real, however, because crime is more likely to be reported, whereas sexual perversions usually remain hidden.

In sum, the precise link between exposure to media images and corresponding behavior remains uncertain. Attempts by government bodies to regulate media offerings that might stimulate undesirable behavior therefore lack a firm scientific basis. Even if that hurdle could be overcome, it is questionable whether a democratic society should attempt to manipulate the minds of its citizens to protect them from temptations to violate social norms. It seems best to leave control of the content of entertainment programs to widely based informal social pressures. The question of whether social pressures should be allowed to interfere with reporting real-world violence poses even more difficult dilemmas. The possibly adverse effects on behavior must be balanced against the need to keep informed about the real world.

Socioeconomic and Political Modernization

The potential of the media to guide people's behavior has led to great efforts to use the media as tools for social and political development. The results have been mixed; there have been some successes and many failures.

Psychic Mobility. The hope of using the media to bring about industrialization, improved social services, and democratization ran very high in the decades following World War II. A personality characteristic that political scientist Daniel Lerner labeled "empathic capacity" was called the key to human and material development. The idea behind this theory was that when the media present new objects, ideas, and behaviors, audiences presumably empathize with what is happening in the story and try to imitate it. For instance, when the media show how slum dwellers have built new housing, or how flood victims have purified their polluted water supply, audience members apply the information to their own lives.

Crediting the media with a major role in modernization and democratization rests on three assumptions. First, the mass media can create interest and empathy for unfamiliar experiences. Second, the mass media can provide graphic audiovisual examples of new practices, which audi-

Middle school students in Allentown, Pennsylvania, are using computers to learn about steering robots.

ences can readily understand and copy. Third, development, once started, encourages people to increase their knowledge and skills. Where formal education is not readily available, the media provide information and enhance the capacity to learn. Progress in urbanization, industrialization, living standards, and political advancement that has followed the spread of media to many formerly information-deficient regions is cited as proof that the assumptions are correct.[78]

Psychological Barriers to Modernization. Although many technologically and politically underdeveloped regions have shown measurable progress, with the media apparently serving as catalysts, social and political change has been far slower and more sporadic than development theorists expected. Many psychological and physical obstacles have stood in the way, including outright hostility by individuals or communities to change and unwillingness to alter long-established patterns. Mass media may actually become a negative reference point when people condemn the lifestyles the media depict. In fact, various fundamentalist groups around the world have mobilized to censor mass media offerings and stop social and political innovations.

People who are not overtly hostile to change still may be totally uninterested in altering their lifestyles. To persuade them to adopt innovations may require the intervention of a trusted person, such as a priest, a health care provider, or a family member. The influence of the mass media then becomes a "two-step flow" that moves from the media to opinion leaders and then to their followers.

Adoption of Changes. Although it is difficult to use the mass media to change people's basic attitudes and ingrained behaviors, many mass media campaigns have succeeded. Five steps are important. First people must become aware of the possibility for change. Here the media are especially helpful. Radio can inform people about new energy-saving devices or new child-rearing methods. Television and movies can show new technologies and new styles of political participation. Second is understanding how to accomplish the suggested changes. For example, people may be aware that public assistance is available, but they may not know how to apply for it. Mass media usually fail to supply detailed information. On average, only one-third of all stories that might inspire action, such as environmental protection or energy conservation, contain information about implementation.[79] Unless this gap is filled, the chain leading to the adoption of innovations is broken.

Third is evaluation. People assess the merits of the innovation and decide whether they want to adopt it. Innovations often fail to take root because prospective users reject them as bad, inappropriate, too risky, or too difficult. Media messages alone may not be persuasive enough. It may also be crucial to have a trusted person urge or demonstrate adoption of the innovation. Fourth is trial. The effect of the media in getting people to try innovations is limited. Factors beyond media control are more important, such as social and financial costs of the change as well as the audience's willingness to change. In general young men are most receptive to innovations; older people are most skeptical and cautious. Fifth is adoption. The media contribute most to this phase by encouraging people to stick with the changes that they have made part of their life and work styles. For example, adoption of birth control practices is useless unless their use is continuous. The same holds true for many health and sanitation measures or improved work habits. To ensure persistence, mass media must cover a topic regularly, stressing long-range goals and reporting progress.

Predicting which media campaigns designed to reform behavior will succeed and which will fail is difficult.[80] Douglas S. Solomon, who studied health campaigns conducted by private and public institutions, believes that four factors account for success or failure. To succeed, campaigns must set well-specified, realistic goals that are tailored to the needs of various target groups. They must carefully select appropriate media and media formats and present them at key times and intervals. Messages must be properly designed for greatest persuasiveness. There also must be continuous evaluation and appropriate readjustments.[81]

Above all, the success of the mass media in bringing about change hinges on the receptivity for reforms. Ongoing efforts to use the media to modernize developing areas, to turn former communists into democratic citizens, or to bring socially helpful information to individuals who are poor, elderly, and handicapped must concentrate on identifying the specific circumstances most likely to bring success. Responding to requests initiated locally rather than designing information campaigns from the outside, and integrating local traditions into new approaches, seem to hold the most promise.[82]

Summary

The mass media play a major role in political socialization and in learning and accepting the beliefs, norms and rules that govern political life. Contrary to earlier findings that indicated limited impact, the media are very influential in this process. Consequently, they represent a tremendously powerful political force.

However, the impact of the media on political socialization and other aspects of political learning varies, depending on people's lifestyles and circumstances. Psychological, demographic, and situational factors influence perceptions as does the manner of news presentation and framing. Although many factors contribute to diversity in socialization and learning, there are powerful unifying forces as well. Most Americans are exposed to similar political information and develop roughly similar outlooks on what it means (and ought to mean) to be an American both politically and socially.

Various theories explain why and how individuals select their information sources, process the available information, and commit facts and opinions to memory. Overall, memory for specific facts presented by the media is quite spotty because most people forget the details after they have drawn conclusions from them. Through repeated exposure to news over time, many people become aware of significant political problems and appreciate their basic significance. Equally important, exposure to the media can produce a range of politically relevant moods, like apathy, cynicism, fear, trust, acquiescence, or support. These moods condition participation in the political process, which may range from total abstinence to efforts to overthrow the government by force.

The media may also produce or retard behavior that affects the quality of public life. We assessed the role of the media in fostering socially undesirable behaviors, especially crime and violence. We also explored the ways in which the media influence the political and social development of various population groups. The media are most successful in informing people and creating initial attitudes. They are least effective in changing established attitudes and ingrained behaviors.

Given the many largely uncontrollable variables that determine media influence, concerted efforts to manipulate media content to foster societal goals are risky at best. They could set dangerous precedents for inhibiting the free flow of controversial ideas or for using the media as channels for government propaganda.

Notes

1. Pew Center for the People and the Press, "Trends, 2005: More Voices, Less Credibility," January 25, 2005, http://www.people-press.org/.
2. The facts of the story are presented in May G. Kennedy, Ann O'Leary, Vicki Beck, Katrina Pollard, and Penny Simpson, "Increases in Calls to the CDC National STD and AIDS Hotline Following AIDS-Related Episodes in a Soap Opera," *Journal of Communication* 54 (2004): 287–301.
3. Impact differences between print and electronic media are discussed in W. Russell Neuman, Marion R. Just, and Ann N. Crigler, *Common Knowledge: News and the Construction of Political Meaning* (Chicago: University of Chicago Press, 1992); The political impact of conversations is addressed in Katherine Cramer Walsh, *Talking about Politics: Informal Groups and Social Identity in American Life,* (Chicago: University of Chicago Press, 2004). For the view that differences in media modality are very important, see Patricia Moy and Michael Pfau, *With Malice Toward All? The Media and Public Confidence in Democratic Institutions* (Westport, Conn.: Praeger, 2000).
4. Michael X. Delli Carpini, and Scott Keeter, *What Americans Know about Politics and Why It Matters* (New Haven: Yale University Press, 1996).
5. Robert D. Putnam, *Bowling Alone: The Collapse and Revival of American Community* (New York: Simon and Schuster, 2000); Pippa Norris, "Does Television Erode Social Capital? A Reply to Putnam," *PS: Political Science and Politics* 29 (1996): 474–480; Pippa Norris, *Digital Divide: Civic Engagement, Information Poverty, and the Internet Worldwide* (Cambridge, U.K.: Cambridge University Press, 2001).
6. Neil Postman, *Amusing Ourselves to Death: Public Discourse in the Age of Show Business* (New York: Viking Penguin, 1985); Roderick P. Hart, *Seducing America: How Television Charms the Modern Voter* (New York: Oxford University Press, 1994). For a good discussion of the differences between the effects of print and television news on people's behavior, see Joshua Meyrowitz, *No Sense of Place: The Impact of Electronic Media on Social Behavior* (New York: Oxford University Press, 1985), 94–106.
7. For a succinct discussion of the controversy about the scope of learning from television, see Jan E. Leighly, *Mass Media and Politics: A Social Science Perspective* (Boston: Houghton Mifflin, 2004), chap. 6.

8. The advantages of learning from audiovisuals are detailed in Doris A. Graber, *Processing Politics: Learning from Television in the Internet Age* (Chicago: University of Chicago Press, 2001).
9. Graber, *Processing Politics,* chap. 3.
10. Pew Center for the People and the Press, "Trends, 2005."
11. The importance of collective memories is spelled out in Yoram Peri, "The Media and Collective Memory of Yitzhak Rabin's Remembrance," *Journal of Communication* 49, no. 3 (summer 1999): 106–124.
12. W. Russell Neuman, *The Future of the Mass Audience* (New York: Cambridge University Press, 1991), 99 (emphasis added). Zhongdang Pan, Ronald E. Ostman, Patricia Moy, and Paula Reynolds, "News Media Exposure and Its Learning Effects during the Persian Gulf War," *Journalism Quarterly* 71, no. 1 (spring 1994): 7–19.
13. Dhavan V. Shah, "Civic Engagement, Interpersonal Trust, and Television Use: An Individual-Level Assessment of Social Capital," *Political Psychology,* 19 (1998): 469–496; Eric M. Uslaner, "Social Capital, Television, and the 'Mean World': Trust, Optimism, and Civic Participation," *Political Psychology* 19 (1998): 441–467.
14. Bruce Watkins, "Television Viewing as a Dominant Activity of Childhood: A Developmental Theory of Television Effects," *Critical Studies in Mass Communication* 2 (1985): 323–337. Average high school graduates have spent 15,000 hours watching television and 11,000 hours in the classroom. They have seen 350,000 commercials.
15. David O. Sears and Nicholas Valentino, "Politics Matters: Political Events as Catalysts for Pre-Adult Socialization," *American Political Science Review* 91 (1997): 45–65; David O. Sears and Carolyn L. Funk, "Evidence of the Long-Term Persistence of Adults' Political Predispositions," *Journal of Politics* 61 (1999): 1–28; and Gina M. Garramone and Charles K. Atkin, "Mass Communication and Political Socialization: Specifying the Effects," *Public Opinion Quarterly* 50 (spring 1986): 76–86.
16. Suzanne Pingree, "Children's Cognitive Processes in Constructing Social Reality," *Journalism Quarterly* 60 (fall 1983): 415–422. Also see Jack Demaine, ed., *Citizenship and Political Education Today* (New York: Palgrave Macmillan, 2005).
17. Jean Piaget, *The Language and Thought of the Child,* 3d ed. (New York: Harcourt Brace, 1962). See also Pamela Johnston Conover, "Political Socialization: Where's the Politics?" in *Political Science: Looking to the Future; Political Behavior,* vol. 3, ed. William Crotty (Evanston: Northwestern University Press, 1991), 125–152.
18. A study of primetime values on television showed that fewer than 4 percent featured citizenship values, such as patriotism or citizen duties. Gary W. Selnow, "Values in Prime-Time Television," *Journal of Communication* 40 (summer 1990): 69.
19. Robert Kubey, "Media Implications for the Quality of Family Life," in *Media, Children, and the Family,* ed. Dolf Zillmann, Jennings Bryant, and Aletha C. Huston (Hillsdale, N.J.: Erlbaum, 1994), 61–70.
20. Pew Center for the People and the Press, "Trends, 2005."
21. Matthew A. Baum, *Soft News Goes to War: Public Opinion and American Foreign Policy in the New Media Age* (Princeton, N.J.: Princeton University Press, 2003) explains the important role played by soft news in informing the public. Pew Center for the People and the Press, "Trends, 2005."

22. George Gerbner, Larry Gross, Marilyn Jackson Beeck, Suzanne Jeffries Fox, and Nancy Signorielli, "Cultural Indicators: Violence Profile No. 9," *Journal of Communication* 28 (summer 1978): 178, 193. See also George Gerbner, Larry Gross, Michael Morgan, and Nancy Signorielli, "Political Correlates of Television Viewing," *Public Opinion Quarterly* 48 (summer 1984): 283–300. The media's role in shaping social attitudes is discussed in Benjamin I. Page and Robert Y. Shapiro, *The Rational Public* (Chicago: University of Chicago Press, 1992), 35.

23. The importance of preadult political learning for subsequent political orientations is discussed in Paul Allen Beck and M. Kent Jennings, "Pathways to Participation," *American Political Science Review* 76 (1982): 103–110. Also see Doris A. Graber, *Processing the News: How People Tame the Information Tide*, 2d ed. (Lanham, Md.: University Press of America, 1993), 184–188, 210–213; and Graber, *Processing Politics*, chap. 2.

24. Shanto Iyengar, *Is Anyone Responsible? How Television Frames Political Issues* (Chicago: University of Chicago Press, 1991), 136–143.

25. Stanley Rothman, S. Robert Lichter, and Linda Lichter, "Television's America," in *The Mass Media in Liberal Democratic Societies*, ed. Stanley Rothman (New York: Paragon House, 1992), 221–266.

26. Paula M. Poindexter, "Non-News Viewers," *Journal of Communication* 30 (fall 1980): 58–65; and Michael X. Delli Carpini, and Bruce A. Williams, "Constructing Public Opinion: The Uses of Fictional and Nonfictional Television in Conversations about the Environment," in *The Psychology of Political Communication*, ed. Ann N. Crigler (Ann Arbor: University of Michigan Press, 1996), 149–175.

27. For examples of various types of general and specific information supplied by entertainment programming, see Gary W. Selnow, "Solving Problems on Prime-Time Television," *Journal of Communication* 36 (spring 1986): 63–72; G. Ray Funkhouser and Eugene F. Shaw, "How Synthetic Experience Shapes Social Reality," *Journal of Communication* 40 (summer 1990): 75–87; W. James Potter and William Ware, "The Frequency and Context of Prosocial Acts on Primetime TV," *Journalism Quarterly* 66 (summer 1989): 359–366, 529.

28. Graber, *Processing the News*, 90–93.

29. Gerbner, and others, "Political Correlates," 286.

30. Donald L. Jordan, "Newspaper Effects on Policy Preferences," *Public Opinion Quarterly* 57 (1993): 191–204; and William Schneider and A.I. Lewis, "Views on the News," *Public Opinion* 8 (August–September 1985): 5–11, 58–59.

31. However, the benefits derived from the use of a particular medium vary for demographic groups. For example, while use of local news media coincides with civic participation for most audiences, this does not hold true for African Americans. Their civic participation is encouraged more by interpersonal networks. Teresa Mastin, "Media Use and Civic Participation in the African-American Population: Exploring Participation Among Professionals and Nonprofessionals," *Journalism and Mass Communication Quarterly* 77, no. 1 (2000): 115–127.

32. Karl Erik Rosengren, Lawrence A. Wenner, and Philip Palmgreen, eds., *Media Gratifications Research: Current Perspectives* (Beverly Hills, Calif.: Sage, 1985). Also see Gina M. Garramone, "Motivation and Political Information Processing: Extending the Gratifications Approach," in *Mass Media and Political Thought*, ed. Sidney Kraus and Richard Perloff (Beverly Hills, Calif.: Sage, 1985), 201–222; David L. Swanson, "Gratification Seeking, Media Exposure, and Audience Interpretations: Some Directions for Research," *Journal of Broadcasting and Electronic Media* 31 (1987): 237–254.

33. W. Lance Bennett, *News: The Politics of Illusion,* 5th ed. (New York: Longman, 2003), chap. 7; and Charles Atkin, "Information Utility and Selective Exposure to Entertainment Media," in *Selective Exposure to Communication,* ed. Dolf Zillman and Jennings Bryant (Hillsdale, N.J.: Erlbaum, 1985), 63–92.

34. Michael Morgan, "Heavy Television Viewing and Perceived Quality of Life," *Journalism Quarterly* 61 (fall 1984): 499–504; Philip Palmgreen, Lawrence A. Wenner, and J.D. Rayburn II, "Relations between Gratifications Sought and Obtained: A Study of Television News," *Communication Research* 7 (April 1980): 161–192; Robert W. Kubey, "Television Use in Everyday Life: Coping with Unstructured Time," *Journal of Communication* 36 (summer 1986): 108–123.

35. Neuman, *Future of the Mass Audience,* 122.

36. In Thomas L. Friedman, "No TV? Israel Is Savoring the Silence," *New York Times,* November 6, 1987.

37. Graber, *Processing the News,* 133–136. See also Stuart H. Schwartz, "A General Psychographic Analysis of Newspaper Use and Life Style," *Journalism Quarterly* 57 (fall 1980): 392–401; also see William D. Wells, *Life Style and Psychographics* (Chicago: American Marketing Association, 1974).

38. The literature is reviewed in Zillman and Bryant, *Selective Exposure to Communication.*

39. Pew Center for the People and the Press, "Trends, 2005."

40. For a discussion of replacement of older issues by newer ones, see Hans-Bernd Brosius and Hans Mathias Kepplinger, "Killer and Victim Issues: Issue Competition in the Agenda-Setting Process of German Television," *International Journal of Public Opinion Research* 7, no. 3 (1995): 211–231.

41. Maxwell E. McCombs, *Setting the Agenda: The Mass Media and Public Opinion* (Cambridge, U.K.: Polity Press, 2004); Shanto Iyengar and Donald R. Kinder, *News That Matters: TV and American Opinion* (Chicago: University of Chicago Press, 1987); Benjamin I. Page and Robert Y. Shapiro, *The Rational Public: Fifty Years of Trends in Americans' Policy Preferences* (Chicago: University of Chicago Press, 1991); and Wayne Wanta, *The Public and the National Agenda* (Mahwah, N.J.: Erlbaum, 1997).

42. Diana Mutz, *Impersonal Influence: How Perceptions of Mass Collectives Affect Political Attitudes* (Cambridge, U.K.: Cambridge University Press, 1998); Robert Huckfeldt and John Sprague, *Citizens, Politics, and Social Communication: Information and Influence in an Election Campaign* (Cambridge, U.K.: Cambridge University Press, 1995).

43. Christine R. Ader, "A Longitudinal Study of Agenda Setting for the Issue of Environmental Pollution," *Journalism and Mass Communication Quarterly* 72, no. 2 (summer 1995): 300–311; Behr and Iyengar, "Television News"; and Michael B. MacKuen and Steven L. Coombs, *More than News: Media Power in Public Affairs* (Beverly Hills, Calif.: Sage, 1981).

44. The importance of personal and contextual factors in news selection and evaluation is discussed in Lutz Erbring, Edie Goldenberg, and Arthur Miller, "Front-Page News and Real World Cues: Another Look at Agenda-Setting by the Media," *American Journal of Political Science* 24 (February 1980): 16–49; and David B. Hill, "Viewer Characteristics and Agenda Setting by Television News," *Public Opinion Quarterly* 49 (fall 1985): 340–350. Also see Walsh, *Talking About Politics.*

45. Graber, *Processing the News,* 27–31, and for details on learning processes, chaps. 7–9. Also see Robert H. Wicks, "Schema Theory and Measurement in Mass Communication Research: Theoretical and Methodological Issues in

News Information Processing," *Communication Yearbook* 15 (Newbury Park, Calif.: Sage, 1991), 115–154. An excellent discussion of processing of audiovisual information research, including a lengthy bibliography, is presented by Annie Lang, "The Limited Capacity Model of Mediated Message Processing," *Journal of Communication* 50, no. 1 (2000): 46–70. How learning goals affect processing is reported by Li-Ning Huang, "Examining Candidate Information Search Processes: The Impact of Processing Goals and Sophistication," *Journal of Communication* 50, no. 1 (2000): 93–114.

46. Walter Lippmann, *Public Opinion* (New York: Harcourt Brace, 1922), 31.

47. See, for example, Mary Beth Oliver, "Caucasian Viewers' Memory of Black and White Criminal Suspects in the News," *Journal of Communication* 49, no. 3 (1997): 46–60, and references cited there; and Robert M. Entman and Andrew Rojecki, *The Black Image in the White Mind: Media and Race in America* (Chicago: University of Chicago Press, 2001).

48. Shanto Iyengar, "Television News and Citizens' Explanations of National Affairs," *American Political Science Review* 81 (September 1987): 815–831. The impact of stereotyped beliefs on public policy is discussed in detail in Martin Gilens, *Why Americans Hate Welfare: Race, Media, and the Politics of Antipoverty Policy* (Chicago: University of Chicago Press, 1999).

49. Vincent Price and John Zaller, "Who Gets the News? Alternative Measures of News Reception and Their Implications for Research," *Public Opinion Quarterly* 57, no. 1 (1993): 133–164; and Cecilie Gaziano, "Forecast 2000: Widening Knowledge Gaps," *Journalism and Mass Communication Quarterly* 74, no. 2 (1997): 237–264. For evidence of shared reactions to television programs, irrespective of educational level, see W. Russell Neuman, "Television and American Culture: The Mass Medium and the Pluralist Audience," *Public Opinion Quarterly* 46 (winter 1982): 471–487.

50. Maria Elizabeth Grabe, Annie Lang, Shuhua Zhou, and Paul David Bolls, "Cognitive Access to Negatively Arousing News: An Experimental Investigation of the Knowledge Gap," *Communication Research* 27, no. 1 (2000): 3–26.

51. Larry L. Burriss, "How Anchors, Reporters, and Newsmakers Affect Recall and Evaluation of Stories," *Journalism Quarterly* 64 (summer/fall 1987): 514–519. The impact of framing on the perception of the legitimacy of social protest is discussed in Douglas M. McLeod and Benjamin H. Detenber, "Framing Effects of Television News Coverage of Social Protest," *Journal of Communication* 49, no. 3 (1999): 3–23; also see Annie Lang, "The Limited Capacity Model of Mediated Message Processing," *Journal of Communication* 50, no. 1 (2000): 46–70; William L. Buscemi, "Numbers? Borrinnnggg!!!" *PS: Political Science and Politics* 30, no. 4 (1997): 737–742; and Patti M. Valkenburg, Holli Semetko, and Claes H. de Vreese, "The Effects of News Frames on Readers' Thoughts and Recall," *Communication Research* 26, no. 5 (1999): 550–569.

52. Michael A. Milburn, Paul Y. Watanabe, and Bernard M. Kramer, "The Nature and Sources of Attitudes toward a Nuclear Freeze," *Political Psychology* 7 (December 1986): 672.

53. An overview of hypermnesia research is presented in Robert H. Wicks, "Remembering the News: Effects and Message Discrepancy on News Recall over Time," *Journalism and Mass Communication Quarterly* 72, no. 3 (fall 1995): 666–682.

54. Meyrowitz, *No Sense of Place.*

55. The chances of becoming a crime victim are small in real life, but in television life they are 30–64 percent. See Gerbner and others, "Cultural Indicators," 106–107.

For a critique of the work of Gerbner and his associates, see W. James Potter, "Cultivation Theory and Research: A Methodological Critique," *Journalism Monograph* 147 (October 1994). James Shanahan and Michael Morgan, *Television and Its Viewers: Cultivation Theory and Research* (Cambridge, U.K.: Cambridge University Press, 1999), lays out the pro and con arguments of the cultivation research program. Exposure to news about actual crime predicts salience of crime better than does personal exposure to crime. Edna F. Einsiedel, Kandice L. Salomone, and Frederick P. Schneider, "Crime: Effects of Media Exposure and Personal Experience on Issue Salience," *Journalism Quarterly* 61 (spring 1984): 131–136.

56. Iyengar, *Is Anyone Responsible?*; Iyengar and Kinder, *News That Matters.*

57. An example of corroborative research is Jon A. Krosnick and Donald R. Kinder, "Altering the Foundations of Support for the President through Priming," *American Political Science Review* 84 (June 1990): 497–512.

58. John Stauffer, Richard Frost, and William Rybolt, "The Attention Factor in Recalling Network Television News," *Journal of Communication* 33 (winter 1983): 29–37. Also see Graber, *Processing Politics*, 25–30.

59. Graber, *Processing the News,* chap. 2; Teun A. Van Dijk, *News as Discourse* (Hillsdale, N.J.: Erlbaum, 1988), 139–174; and John P. Robinson and Mark R. Levy, *The Main Source: Learning from Television News* (Beverly Hills, Calif.: Sage, 1986), 57–175. Also see Samuel Popkin and Michael A. Dimock, "Political Knowledge and Citizen Competence," in *Citizen Competence and Democratic Institutions,* ed. Stephen L. Elkin and Karol Edward Soltan (University Park: Pennsylvania State University Press, 1999), 117–146.

60. Scott Keeter and Cliff Zukin, *Uninformed Choice: The Failure of the New Presidential Nominating System* (New York: Praeger, 1983). But see Arthur Lupia and Mathew D. McCubbins, *The Democratic Dilemma: Can Citizens Learn What They Need to Know?* (New York: Cambridge University Press, 1998). Also see Delli Carpini and Keeter, *What Americans Know about Politics and Why It Matters.*

61. Michael Schudson, *The Power of News* (Cambridge: Harvard University Press, 1995), 27.

62. V.O. Key, with the assistance of Milton C. Cummings Jr., reached the same conclusion in *The Responsible Electorate* (Cambridge: Harvard University Press, 1965), 7. Also see Page and Shapiro, *The Rational Public,* 383–390, regarding the wisdom inherent in public opinion and Daniel R. Anderson, "Educational Television Is Not an Oxymoron," *Annals of the American Academy of Political and Social Science* 557 (May 1998): 24–38.

63. Arthur H. Miller, Edie N. Goldenberg, and Lutz Erbring, "Type-Set Politics: Impact of Newspapers on Public Confidence," *American Political Science Review* 73 (March 1979): 67–84.

64. Joseph N. Cappella, and Kathleen Hall Jamieson, *The Spiral of Cynicism: The Press and the Public Good* (New York: Oxford University Press, 1997).

65. Murray Edelman, *Politics as Symbolic Action* (New York: Academic Press, 1976), and Murray Edelman, *Constructing the Political Spectacle* (Chicago: University of Chicago Press, 1988).

66. Susan Hearold, "A Synthesis of 1043 Effects of Television on Social Behavior," in *Public Communication and Behavior,* vol. 1, ed. George A. Comstock (New York: Academic Press, 1986), 66–133. Also see George E. Marcus, W. Russell Neuman, and Michael MacKuen, *Affective Intelligence and Political Judgment* (Chicago: University of Chicago Press, 2000), and Antonio R. Damasio, *Descartes' Error: Emotion, Reason, and the Human Brain* (New York: Grosset/Putnam, 1994).

67. The desire to be politically informed varies widely. News selection criteria are discussed in Graber, *Processing the News,* chap. 4.
68. Center for Media and Public Affairs, "Florida Trouble Triples TV Attention," www.cmpa.com/pressrel/electpr13.htm.
69. Harold W. Stanley and Richard G. Niemi, *Vital Statistics on American Politics, 1997–1998* (Washington, D.C.: CQ Press, 1998). Published every two years. Also see Pew Center for the People and the Press, "Trends, 2005."
70. For dire predictions see Jarol B. Manheim, *All of the People All the Time: Strategic Communication and American Politics* (Armonk, N.Y.: M.E. Sharpe, 1991), 204–209; Robert Entman, *Democracy without Citizens: Media and the Decay of American Politics* (New York: Oxford University Press, 1990), chap. 7. For a more positive view see Doris Graber, "Mediated Politics and Citizenship in the Twenty-First Century," *Annual Reviews of Psychology* 55 (2004): 545–571; Doris A. Graber, "Framing Politics for Mass Consumption: Can American News Media Meet the Challenge?" in *Advances in Political Psychology* vol. 1, ed. Margaret G. Hermann (Amsterdam: Elsevier, 2004), 19–39; and Page and Shapiro, *Rational Public,* 383–390.
71. None of these studies focuses on the effects of exposure to nonfictional violence in the media because the First Amendment would be a strong bar to censorship of news. Surgeon General's Scientific Advisory Committee on Television and Social Behavior, *Television and Growing Up: The Impact of Televised Violence* (Washington, D.C.: U.S. Government Printing Office, 1971). For a critical review of the follow-up report, see Thomas D. Cook, Deborah A. Kendzierski, and Stephen V. Thomas, "The Implicit Assumptions of Television Research: An Analysis of the 1982 NIMH Report on 'Television and Behavior,'" *Public Opinion Quarterly* 47 (spring 1983): 161–201.
72. "Violence Dominates on TV, Study Says," *Chicago Tribune,* February 7, 1996.
73. Russell G. Geen, "Television and Aggression: Recent Developments and Theory," in Zillmann, Bryant, and Huston, *Media, Children, and the Family,* 151–162; Jerome L. Singer, Dorothy G. Singer, and Wanda S. Rapaczynski, "Family Patterns and Television Viewing as Predictors of Children's Beliefs and Aggression," *Journal of Communication* 34 (summer 1984): 73–89. The politics of research on the effects of television violence are discussed by Willard D. Rowland Jr., *The Politics of TV Violence: Policy Uses of Communication Research* (Beverly Hills, Calif.: Sage, 1983).
74. James M. Carlson, *Prime Time Law Enforcement: Crime Show Viewing and Attitudes toward the Criminal Justice System* (New York: Praeger, 1985); Marjorie Heins, "Blaming the Media: Would Regulation of Expression Prevent Another Columbine?" *Media Studies Journal* 14, no. 3 (2000): 14–23; Marjorie Heins, *Not in Front of the Children: Indecency, Censorship and the Innocence of Youth* (New York: Hill and Wang, 2001).
75. James T. Hamilton, ed., *Television Violence and Public Policy* (Ann Arbor: University of Michigan Press, 1998); George Comstock and Haejung Paik, "The Effects of Television Violence on Antisocial Behavior: A Meta-Analysis," *Communication Research* 21 (1994): 516–539; David Gauntlett, *Moving Experiences: Media Effects and Beyond,* 2d ed. (London: J. Libbey, 2005).
76. Robert P. Snow, "How Children Interpret TV Violence in Play Context," *Journalism Quarterly* 51 (spring 1974): 13–21.
77. *Attorney General's Commission on Pornography: Final Report,* 1986; see also Richard A. Dienstbier, "Sex and Violence: Can Research Have It Both Ways?" *Journal of*

Communication 27 (summer 1977): 176–188; Presidential Commission on Obscenity and Pornography, *Report of the Commission on Obscenity and Pornography* (New York: Bantam Books, 1970).

78. David O. Edeani, "Critical Predictors of Orientation to Change in a Developed Society," *Journalism Quarterly* 58 (spring 1981): 56–64. The carefully measured impact of the introduction of television into a Canadian community is presented in Tannis MacBeth Williams, ed., *The Impact of Television: A Natural Experiment in Three Communities* (Orlando: Academic Press, 1985).

79. James B. Lemert, Barry N. Mitzman, Michael A. Seither, Roxana H. Cook, and Regina Hackett, "Journalists and Mobilizing Information," *Journalism Quarterly* 54 (winter 1977): 721–726.

80. Ronald E. Rice and Charles K. Atkin, eds., *Public Communication Campaigns*, 3d ed. (Thousand Oaks, Calif.: Sage, 2001).

81. Douglas S. Solomon, "Health Campaigns on Television," in *Television and Human Behavior*, ed. George Comstock, Steven Chaffee, Natan Katzman, Maxwell McCombs, and Donald Roberts (New York: Columbia University Press, 1978), 316–319.

82. John L. Crompton and Charles W. Lamb Jr., *Marketing Government and Social Services* (New York: Wiley, 1986); Marc L. Lame, "Communicating in the Innovation Process: Issues and Guidelines," in *Handbook of Administrative Communication*, ed. James L. Garnett and Alexander Kouzmin (New York: Marcel Dekker, 1997), 187–201.

Readings

Bennett, W. Lance, and Robert M. Entman. *Mediated Politics: Communication in the Future of Democracy*. Cambridge, U.K.: Cambridge University Press, 2001.

Entman, Robert M., and Andrew Rojecki. *The Black Image in the White Mind: Media and Race in America*. Chicago: University of Chicago Press, 2000.

Graber, Doris A. *Processing Politics: Learning from Television in the Internet Age*. Chicago: University of Chicago Press, 2001.

Gunther, Richard, and Anthony Mughan, eds. *Democracy and the Media: A Comparative Perspective*. Cambridge, UK: Cambridge University Press, 2000.

Jackson, David J. *Entertainment and Politics: The Influence of Pop Culture on Young Adult Political Socialization*. New York: Peter Lang, 2002.

Kubey, Robert, and Mihaly Csikszentmihalyi. *Television and the Quality of Life: How Viewing Shapes Everyday Experience*. Hillsdale, N.J.: Erlbaum, 1990.

Lupia, Arthur, and Mathew D. McCubbins. *The Democratic Dilemma: Can Citizens Learn What They Need to Know?* New York: Cambridge University Press, 1998.

Neuman, W. Russell, Marion R. Just, and Ann N. Crigler. *Common Knowledge: News and the Construction of Political Meaning*. Chicago: University of Chicago Press, 1992.

Shanahan, James, and Michael Morgan. *Television and Its Viewers: Cultivation Theory and Research*. Cambridge: Cambridge University Press, 1999.

Zillmann, Dolf, Jennings Bryant, and Aletha Huston. *Media, Children, and the Family: Social Scientific, Psychodynamic, and Clinical Perspectives*. Hillsdale, N.J.: Erlbaum, 1994.

Elections in the Internet Age

T HE PRESIDENTIAL ELECTION OF 2000 was one of the closest in U.S. history. Polls throughout the final months of the campaign showed Republican Texas governor George W. Bush and Democratic vice president Al Gore in a dead heat race that pollsters said was too close to call. The closeness of the race gave special excitement to election-night broadcasts that were recording actual votes.

On election day, about 8:00 p.m. eastern time, the Associated Press and the major networks announced that Gore had won Florida's electoral votes. Earlier reports had declared him the winner in other states essential for amassing a majority of the electoral college votes. The Florida win made it almost certain that Gore would be the next president.

The problem was that the announcements were premature. The press made them when a small number of polling stations in counties favoring Bush were still open in Florida even though news venues had agreed to delay predictions until all polls were closed in a state to avoid influencing the decisions of voters. Even worse, the Voter News Service exit poll data, on which the predictions were based, were flawed because of data processing and sampling errors.[1] When officials discovered the errors roughly two hours later, the networks negated their earlier announcements and put Florida back into the "undecided" category at a time when voting was still continuing in many western states. In the wee hours of the day following the election—almost eight hours later—the media finally called Bush the winner of the Florida contest. Still, that was not the last word. A recount battle to determine the correct winner of the state's electoral votes dragged on for five more weeks and was finally settled in favor of Bush by a highly controversial U.S. Supreme Court decision.

In the wake of the flawed election-day announcements, longstanding arguments reemerged about the impact of releasing election results before voting has ended in a particular state—or even in any state in the nation. The political consequences of premature designations of winners and losers can be major if the announcement discourages citizens from voting. Contenders in close elections may lose votes that might have spelled victory for them. Winners may show smaller margins of victory and thereby encourage future opponents. Candidates for low-level offices may lose crucial votes when voters do not show up to vote for high-level officials. The key question underlying all of these concerns is the extent of the media's influence on various aspects of elections. Although the link between the media and election outcomes has been studied more thoroughly than other media-politics links, the dynamics remain unclear. Definitive answers are lacking for many cause-and-effect questions in this area.

The State of Research

Imbalances in research hamper understanding of the role that the news media play in elections. Presidential elections have been most extensively studied, followed at some distance by congressional elections. Far less is known about the media's role in gubernatorial elections and local elections. The limited evidence suggests that the media's role varies substantially, depending on the importance of the particular office at stake and the news appeal of a campaign. The media cover exciting campaigns for high-level positions while ignoring routine ones.

Even at the presidential level little genuinely comparative research has been done on the differences in the role of the media from one election to the next. The influence of such factors as incumbency, three-way competition, or major national crises has not been thoroughly investigated either. It stands to reason that the effects of the media will vary depending on the changing political scene, the type of coverage chosen by newspeople, and the fluctuating interests of voters. Before the 2000 presidential campaign, high costs discouraged most researchers from studying media influences throughout entire campaigns from the preprimary period, when candidate selection takes place, to the general election. Generous funding by several foundations alleviated that problem and created a massive data pool for the presidential contest in 2000, and the trend continued during the 2004 presidential contest.[2]

Another serious obstacle to understanding media influence on elections is the dearth of media content analyses. Only rarely have researchers examined election news content, including commercials, and the context of general news in which it is embedded, making it impossible to test what impact, if any, diverse messages have on viewers' perceptions. Another problem is researchers' failure to ascertain media exposure accurately. Investigators frequently assume that people have been exposed to all election stories in a particular news source without checking precisely which stories have come to the attention of which individuals and what these individuals learned.

A shortage of good data also prevented researchers prior to the Reagan era from ascertaining the effects of political advertising on political campaigns. Candidates and their supporters spend a large share of their campaign budgets on political advertising that is displayed on bumper stickers and billboards, printed in newspapers, disseminated through videotapes, or broadcast with clockwork regularity on radio and television. Researchers who study television commercials now know that these messages are major factors in campaigns. But the role commercials play when they are carried by venues other than television remains largely unexplored. In addition, Internet messages of all types are a new and constantly changing territory where much analysis remains to be done.

The Consequences of Television-Dominated Politics

The ready availability of television in nearly every home, the pervasiveness of public opinion polling, the easy access to the Worldwide Web where election-related sites abound, guarantee that the news media will play a major role. What are the major facets of that role? We will consider three: the power of journalists to influence the selection of candidates, the requirement for candidates to "televise well," and the emergence of made-for-media campaigns.

Media as King Makers

More than ever before, journalists can influence the selection of candidates and the key issues of the campaign. Television brings candidates, especially presidential contenders, directly into the nation's living rooms, giving voters a basis for making their own choices rather than depending almost entirely on party labels, as was the case before the advent of television. Party affiliation remains more important at the state and local levels where media information about candidates is scant, particularly on television. Of course, this is not true in many local elections when candidates run without party designation and endorsement or when candidates of the same party compete against each other in primary elections. Candidates, like actors, depend for their success as much on the roles into which they are cast as on their acting ability. In the television age, media people usually do the casting for presidential hopefuls, whose performance is then judged according to the assigned role. Strenuous efforts by campaign directors and public relations experts to dominate this aspect of the campaign have been only moderately fruitful.

Casting occurs early in the primaries when newspeople, on the basis of as yet slender evidence, predict winners and losers to narrow the field of eligibles who must be covered. Concentrating on the front-runners in public opinion polls makes newspeople's tasks more manageable, but it often forces trailing candidates out of the race prematurely. Early highly speculative calculations become self-fulfilling prophecies because designated "winners" attract supporters whereas "losers" are abandoned.

For example, in 2003—the "preseason" year for the 2004 presidential race—only Democrats who scored well in public opinion polls received more than scattered attention from television news. On the Democratic side, after the campaign had started in earnest, Vermont governor Howard Dean, followed by Gen. Wesley Clark and senators John Kerry and Joseph Lieberman received the lion's share of coverage. On the Republican side, incumbent president George W. Bush, who was running for reelection, monopolized media attention. These imbalances persisted throughout the primary season, seriously handicapping the campaigns that remained in the shadows.[3]

Candidates who exceed expectations in garnering votes are declared winners; candidates who fall short are losers.[4] When journalist Pat Buchanan finished sixteen points behind George Bush in the 1992 New Hampshire Republican presidential primary, the media declared Buchanan the winner because he had exceeded their expectations. They did the same for Bill Clinton, who had trailed former senator Paul Tsongas in the Democratic primary in New Hampshire in 1992. The candidacy of Republican senator Bob Dole during the 1996 primaries was prematurely declared dead when he finished behind his competitors in a few early and insignificant contests.

Media coverage and public opinion polls tend to move in tandem in the early months of a campaign. Candidates who receive ample media coverage usually do well in the polls. Good poll ratings then bring more media coverage. Once the caucus and primary season has started in the spring of the presidential election year, the outcomes of these contests become more important predictors of media attention. One other pattern is common, though not universal. The substance of stories tends to be favorable for trailing candidates in the race and unfavorable for front-runners. During the 2004 primaries, for example, Howard Dean's favorable ratings plunged while he was the Democratic frontrunner, only to soar again when he became the underdog.[5]

The media's role as king maker or killer of the dreams of would-be kings is often played over a long span of time. Image making for presidential elections now begins on a massive scale more than a year before the first primary. The "pre-pre-campaign," on a more limited scale, begins shortly after the previous election with newspaper and magazine stories about potential presidential candidates. Senators and governors who have received favorable publicity over many years may gradually come to be thought of as likely presidential nominees.

In the past, captains of the media industry often used their personal influence and the power of the media under their control to support nominations for their favorites and to harm opponents. That practice may be vanishing. Examples include the efforts of publisher Henry Luce to entice popular war hero Dwight Eisenhower to run for the presidency in 1952 and Col. Robert McCormick's use of his powerful *Chicago Tribune* to defeat policies favored by Presidents Franklin D. Roosevelt and Harry S. Truman.[6]

Media coverage can be shaped to destroy candidacies. This happened to two Democratic candidates for the presidency in 1988. Sen. Joseph Biden of Delaware was forced out of the campaign by widely publicized charges that his speeches contained plagiarized quotations from other political leaders. Sen. Gary Hart of Colorado withdrew after charges of philandering. Recurrent media references to the Chappaquiddick incident, which linked Sen. Edward Kennedy, D-Mass., to the drowning of a young woman on his staff, also have kept his supporters from drafting him as a presidential contender. However, adverse publicity can be overcome. In the 1992 campaign Bill Clinton was accused of adultery and draft dodging, charges that caused his poll ratings and positive media appraisals to plummet. Despite the bad publicity, Clinton managed to win major primaries and the presidency, earning the title "come-back kid."

Television images can be vastly important during general election campaigns. For instance, the Kennedy-Nixon television debates of 1960, the Reagan-Mondale debates of 1984, and the Bush-Gore debates of 2000 helped to soften the public's impressions that John F. Kennedy, Ronald Reagan, and George W. Bush were unsuited for the presidency.[7] Kennedy was able to demonstrate that he was capable of coping with the presidency despite his youth and relative inexperience, and Reagan in 1984 conveyed the impression that despite advanced age he remained mentally fit for a second term. Bush's performance in the second debate served to counteract charges that he lacked sufficient intellect and debating skills to become an effective president.

The media's choice of policy issues to air during crucial phases of the campaign sharply diminished the chances of Presidents Jimmy Carter and the senior George Bush to be elected for a second term and undercut John Kerry's effort to defeat a rival who was thoroughly unpopular with Democratic voters. In Carter's case, just before the 1980 presidential election, the media chose to commemorate the anniversary of a major foreign policy failure—Carter's inability to win the release of U.S. hostages in Iran. Disapproval of Bush in the 1992 election was directed mainly at his highly publicized failure to solve major domestic economy problems during the last year of his term. In Kerry's case, reminders about the incumbent's strong war policies in Iraq and Afghanistan, coupled with stories about Kerry's waffling on these issues, reinforced voters' belief that security needs required Bush's reelection.

Media-operated public opinion polls are yet another weapon in the arsenal for king making. The major television networks, in collaboration with such newspapers as the *New York Times,* the *Washington Post,* and *USA Today,* all conduct popularity ratings and issue polls throughout presidential elections. The results are publicized extensively and then become benchmarks for voters, telling them who the winners and losers are and what issues are crucial to the campaign. Depending on the nature and format of the questions asked by the pollsters and the political context in which the story becomes embedded, the responses spell fortune or misfortune for the candidates. Polls may determine which candidates enter the tray and which keep out. In the 1992 presidential campaign, major Democratic politicians shunned the race because they believed that President Bush's high approval ratings in national polls following the Persian Gulf War doomed their candidacies. That provided an opening for a little-known governor from Arkansas named Bill Clinton to propel himself into a two-term presidency.

Television-Age Recruits

Another important consequence of television-dominated politics is the change it has wrought in the types of candidates likely to be politically successful. Because television can bring the image of candidates for high national and state office directly into the homes of millions of voters, a candidate's ability to look impressive and to perform well before the cameras has become crucial. People who are not telegenic have been eliminated from the pool of available recruits. Abraham Lincoln's rugged face probably would not have passed muster in the television age. President

Truman's "Give 'em hell, Harry" homespun style would have backfired had it been presented nationwide rather than to small gatherings. Franklin D. Roosevelt's wheelchair appearances would have spelled damaging weakness. Roosevelt, in fact, was keenly aware of the likely harmful effects of a picture of him in a wheelchair and never allowed photographs to be taken while he was being lifted to the speaker's rostrum.

Actors and other celebrities who are adept at performing before the public now have a much better chance than ever before to be recruited for political office. Ronald Reagan and Arnold Schwarzenegger, who were seasoned actors; John Edwards, a spell-binding trial lawyer; and Jesse Jackson, a charismatic preacher, are examples of typical television-age recruits whose chances for public office would have been much slighter in an earlier era. As columnist Marquis Child has put it, candidates no longer "run" for office; they "pose" for office.[8]

In fact, good pictures can counterbalance the effects of unfavorable verbal comments. When CBS reporter Leslie Stahl verbally attacked President Reagan for falsely posturing as a man of peace and compassion during the 1984 presidential campaign, a Reagan assistant promptly thanked her for showing four-and-a-half minutes of great pictures of the president. He was not in the least concerned about Stahl's scathing remarks. The pictures had shown the president

> basking in a sea of flag-waving supporters . . . sharing concerns with farmers in a field, picnicking with Mid-Americans, pumping iron . . . getting the Olympic torch from a runner . . . greeting senior citizens at their housing project, honoring veterans who landed on Normandy, honoring youths just back from Grenada, countering a heckler . . . wooing black inner-city kids. . . .[9]

During the 2004 campaign, an emotional ad showing President Bush hugging a fifteen-year-old orphan in Lebanon, Ohio, was credited with driving home the crucial message that Bush cared about people and would protect them. The ad, reproduced on page 225, showed an obviously grieving president cradling the youngster whose mother had died in the 2001 World Trade Center attack. Young Ashley Faulkner's voice could be heard saying, "He's the most powerful man in the world, and all he wants to do is make sure I'm safe, that I'm OK." [10]

Television advisers have become year-round members of presidential and gubernatorial staffs. These experts coach candidates about proper dress and demeanor for various occasions, create commercials for the candidates, and handle general news coverage of the campaign. Presidential contenders spend roughly two-thirds of their budgets on television contests. In 2004 candidates, political parties, and independent groups spent more than $1.6 billion on close to 2 million television ads in the nation's

During a campaign stop in Ohio in 2004, President Bush hugs fifteen-year-old Ashley Faulkner after learning her mother had died in the 2001 terrorist attacks on the World Trade Center.

05/04/2004

one hundred largest media markets. These spenders forked over additional sums in 111 smaller markets that often feature very active campaigns. Another $64.5 million covered commercials on cable venues. Compared to prior elections, the costs were enormous despite the fact that the presidential contenders narrowed their ad blitz to just fourteen key states in the fall, including Florida, Iowa, New Mexico, Ohio, Pennsylvania, West Virginia, and Wisconsin.[11]

Given the high cost of television commercials and of gaining news exposure, a candidate's personal wealth or ability to raise money remains an important consideration, even when federal funding is available. Candidates shun activities, statements, and policy proposals that are likely to alienate donors. Although evidence shows that the best-financed candidates do not always win, folklore says they do. Hence, falling behind in the race for money to finance media exposure is a sharp brake on political aspirations. The political consequences in recruitment and post-election commitments that spring from such financial considerations are huge.

Media Campaigning Strategies

In the age of television-dominated campaigns, receiving coverage has become a pivotal concern. Campaigns are structured to garner the best media exposure before the largest suitable audience and, if possible, with the greatest degree of candidate control over the message. To attract media coverage, candidates concentrate on photo opportunities, talk show appearances, or trips to interesting events and locations. Even when candidates meet voters personally in rallies, parades, or visits to shopping centers, they generally time and orchestrate these events to attract favorable media coverage.

The New Venues.   Appearances on entertainment shows, once considered "unpresidential," have become routine. Maverick candidate Ross Perot started the pattern during the 1992 presidential race by announcing his presidential aspirations on CNN's *Larry King Live* call-in television show. The other candidates followed the talk show trek, preferring the lighter banter and the respectful questions of callers to the pointed inquisition in interviews by the national press. Adorned with shades, Governor Clinton played the saxophone on the hip *Arsenio Hall Show*; he even bought television time to stage his own call-in show. By 2000 it seemed almost obligatory for presidential contenders to appear on talk shows hosted by television personalities Larry King, Oprah Winfrey, Jay Leno, and David Letterman. In fact, nearly half of voters younger than thirty mentioned late night television comedians as major sources of campaign information.[12]

Candidates' escape from the highly critical national press to friendlier environments also takes the form of satellite interviews in which contenders chat directly with local correspondents, most of whom are unlikely to ask hostile questions or limit the candidate's speech to brief sound bites. Even network morning news shows now devote entire hours to conversations with the candidates and accept telephoned questions from viewers during the show. All in all, the trend seems to be toward more direct contact by candidates with voters and increased candidate control over campaign messages, all at the expense of message control by the major media.

Candidate-sponsored Web sites, are another addition to the venues that campaigners have used since 1996 to offer voters a carefully selected information diet. Most Web sites show videos about the candidates' issue positions and other topics, allowing candidates to present their case at length in their own words and with carefully chosen pictures. Many Web sites allow visitors to register to vote, to donate money to the campaign or volunteer to work for it, and to check campaign sites in their states. There may be special interest pages for groups like senior citizens or veterans or

President George W. Bush shakes supporters' hands during an election rally in Minneapolis, Minnesota, October 30, 2004. Bush campaigned in the battleground states of Michigan, Wisconsin, Minnesota and Florida in the final days before the November 2 presidential election.

college students or young children. Many Web sites provide e-mail connections which then enable candidates to stay in regular contact with Web site visitors. E-mail lists have been exceedingly useful as a get-out-the-vote device during the final days of the campaign.

For the average voter, the consequences of the availability of these more candidate-centered approaches to campaigning are not entirely clear. Compared with the 2000 presidential election, use of the Internet as a mainstay of election information has almost doubled (Table 8-1). Still, television remains the chief source of election news, with cable increasing its hold on the audience. Among cable channels, Fox news, deemed on the conservative side, enjoyed a meteoric rise in audience visits, reaching twice as many viewers as its more liberal rival CNN.[13] To what extent such choices affect election outcomes is unclear because people tend to choose news venues in tune with their existing political orientations.

Cable television's growing importance as a source of campaign information is partly due to network policies that deemphasize election events. The political party conventions are good examples in 2000 and 2004. The major television networks largely ignored the conventions, estimating cor-

TABLE 8-1   Voters' Main Sources of Campaign News, 1996, 2000, and 2004
(in percentages)

News source	1996	2000	2004
Television	72	70	76
Cable	21	36	42
Network	36	22	33
Local	23	21	12
Newspapers	60	39	46
Radio	19	15	22
Internet	3	11	21
Magazines	11	4	6

SOURCE: Pew Research Center for the People and the Press, "Voters Liked Campaign 2004, but too Much 'Mud Slinging,'" http://people-press.org. Based on a survey of 1,209 voters conducted November 5–8, 2004.

NOTE: Respondents were asked, "How did you get most of your news about the presidential election campaign? From television, from newspapers, from radio, from magazines, or from the Internet?" Television users were then asked, "Did you get most of your news about the presidential election campaign from local TV news, ABC, CBS, NBC network news, or from CNN, MSNBC, or Fox News Channel cable news networks?" Respondents could name multiple sources.

rectly that most of their audiences would prefer regular programming instead. Cable television stations offered full coverage.

If the Web remains a secondary source of campaign information for the general public, is it worth major time and resource commitments by candidates? For the 2004 election, the answer was a resounding "yes." The candidates did budget most money for over-the-air television, spending little on Web advertising. But the Web was tremendously helpful on other fronts. First of all, it became a major source of collecting money from millions of citizens who responded to Web site appeals. Howard Dean, the initial front-runner on the Democratic side, raised more than $6 million in record time to jumpstart his campaign. By the end of the 2004 campaign, roughly one-third of the money raised by John Kerry, the ultimate standard bearer, came from Web contributions. In fact, John Kerry highlighted the importance of e-mail contacts with his supporters by announcing his vice-presidential choice first on e-mail.

The Web became a virtual pied piper, luring thousands of supporters to the campaign. Web appeals enlisted them in e-mail recruiting efforts and mobilized them to go to the polls and bring their friends and neighbors along. By election day, literally billions of e-mails had been sent soliciting support for the candidates. Every major political figure got into the act. That feat would have been impossible to achieve through direct mail or phone calls.

The Web also served as a rallying tool for political activists who would have found it difficult to be heard without it. MoveOn.org used its Web site and e-mail blitzes to raise millions of dollars and rally more than 2 million passionate liberals to the cause of unseating President Bush and driving Republicans from office. Such conservative groups as "Swift Boat Veterans for Truth," which brought an avalanche of negative attention to John Kerry's war record, countered the liberals' efforts. The traditional media picked up the messages circulated by activists on the Web and in e-mails, giving these often extreme views a huge national audience. In addition, hundreds of Web sites, including blogs, devoted to election information provided a rich diet of information to voters who wanted to explore election issues in depth. The audience for political blogs grew in 2004 to equal in size as the audience reached by the major news weeklies.[14]

Much of the contents of Internet campaign information and the manner in which it is framed follows familiar journalistic patterns, even for stories produced by amateurs. Quality typically ranges from excellent to vile. Lacking shared ethics or other controls, campaigning on the Internet is a free-for-all, used wisely as well as irresponsibly.

Attracting Coverage.   Candidates maximize their chances of attracting coverage by planning their schedules around events that are known to attract reporters. Contenders spend disproportionate amounts of time during the primary season campaigning in Iowa and New Hampshire, where media coverage of the earliest contests is usually heavy. In 1996, for example, primary coverage for each of these states dwarfed television news coverage of later primaries by more than a four-to-one ratio.[15] To keep a favorable image of candidates in front of the public, campaign managers arrange newsworthy events to familiarize potential voters with their candidates' best aspects. Managers show candidates dressed informally, mixing with enthusiastic crowds of average people and looking relaxed and happy and confident. If vigor has to be demonstrated, the candidate performs expertly in some popular sport. John Kerry, for example, was shown duck hunting, but an aid carried the dead ducks lest animal lovers take offense.

Incumbents have a distinct advantage over challengers. Although they may attract about the same number of campaign stories, incumbents receive additional attention through coverage of their official duties. Incumbents may also be able to dictate time and place for media encounters. When a president schedules a meeting for reporters in the White House Rose Garden, he ensures ample coverage. There even is a quasi-incumbency status for promising challengers. Once they have attained wide recognition as front-runners, newspeople compete for their attention. These candidates' power to grant or withhold attention can be translated into influence over the quality and quantity of coverage.

Media judge the newsworthiness of campaign stories by general news criteria. Therefore, they pay little attention to minor candidates and newcomers whose chances for success are questionable. Lack of coverage, in turn, makes it extremely difficult for unknowns to become well known and increase their chances of winning elections. This is one of many examples of unintentional media bias that redounds to the benefit of established politicians.

Media Content

What kinds of newspaper and television coverage have recent elections received? Did the media sufficiently cover the issues likely to require attention from the new president, and did they supply adequate criteria to enable voters to decide which of several policy options would best suit their priorities and which candidate would be most likely to govern successfully? Following some general comments about the media mix, we will address these questions and assess the adequacy of the information supply for making sound voting choices.

Unscrambling the Message Omelet

When Humpty-Dumpty, the egg, fell off the wall in the nursery rhyme, all the king's horses and all the king's men couldn't put him together again. The many components of the media message omelet have had a similar fate. Campaign commercials, for instance, have become a major ingredient of contemporary campaigns and often bestow a distinctive flavor to them. But it is well-nigh impossible to isolate their contribution because all of the ingredients—print and electronic news stories, editorials, talk-show banter and punditry, Internet messages, advertisements, even political jokes and skits on entertainment shows—mix inextricably with each other and become transformed in the process. Ads generate and influence news stories and news stories induce and influence ads that, in turn, lead to other ads and news stories and editorials. And so it goes, on and on.

This is why I discuss campaign information as a whole without, in most instances, making distinctions among the unique contributions of different media. Distinctions exist, of course—studies show, for example, that television and news magazine formats are superior to newspapers for conveying particular messages, and that the content of advertising messages is often discounted because they are regarded as self-serving propaganda even though they provide more information about policy issues than most campaign news stories.

However, television commercials often provide the only chance to gain attention for the many candidates the media ignore.[16] That includes the vast majority of also-rans for national office who seem unelectable to the major media as well as most candidates competing for local and even state offices. Locally, the impact of commercials can be decisive. Indeed, wisely spent advertising funds can buy elections, even for congressional candidates who receive news story coverage.[17] To quote political scientist Michael Robinson, commercials for congressional candidates "can work relative wonders," especially when they are not challenged by the other side. "A well-crafted, heavily financed, and uncontested ad campaign does influence congressional elections."[18] This fact raises the chilling specter that wealthy candidates may be able to buy major public offices by investing their fortunes in expensive advertising campaigns. That fear has escalated with the entry of such multimillionaires as Ross Perot and Steve Forbes into the presidential sweepstakes. Perot bought large blocks of television time for infomercials—data-packed commercials—in the 1992 presidential campaign. Forbes used personal funds to finance an expensive advertising blitz in the 1996 Republican primaries. Since neither of the candidates became president, it is obvious that superior funding is not a sure trump card in the presidential election poker game.

Patterns of Coverage

Any evaluation of how the media perform their tasks must also take into consideration the commercial pressures that journalists face. It is extremely difficult to mesh the public's preference for simple, dramatic stories with the need to present ample information for issue-based election choices. Information that may be crucial for voting decisions often is too complex and technical to appeal to much of the audience. Hence newspeople feel compelled to write breezy infotainment stories that stress the horserace and skim over policy details.

Prominence of Election Stories. In a typical presidential election year, election stories constitute roughly 13 percent of all newspaper political coverage and 15 percent of television political news. That puts these stories on a par with foreign affairs news or coverage of crime. Election news receives average attention in terms of headline size, front-page or first-story placement, and inclusion of pictures, but stories are slightly longer than average. Although election stories are quite prominent when primaries, conventions, and significant debates are held, they do not dominate the news. Normally, it is quite possible to read the daily paper without noticing election news and to come away from a telecast with the impression that election stories are just a minor part of the day's political developments.

Election news competes for audience attention with many other types of stories; this accounts, in part, for its limited impact on news audiences.

Uniformity of Coverage Patterns.   Patterns of presidential election coverage are remarkably uniform, regardless of a newspaper's partisan orientation. The major difference generally is that small newspapers carry fewer election stories and that news stories vary in their evaluation of candidates, issues, and campaign events.[19] Television news patterns, as well as blogs, are also uniform. Compared to newspaper coverage, the usual one- or two-minute television story gives little chance for in-depth reporting and analysis. To conserve limited time, television newscasters create stereotypes of the candidates early in the campaign and then build their stories around these stereotypes by merely adding new details to the established image. Once established, stereotypes stubbornly resist change. There is a feeling that leopards never change their spots.

Content analysis studies during congressional, state, and local campaigns show similar patterns. The political portraits that various media paint of each candidate match well in basic outlines and in most details. But the time and space allotted to various aspects and the tone of evaluations can vary significantly. Campaign news on public television, for example, covered the 2000 election in far greater depth and in a far more positive tone, stressing strengths as well as weaknesses, than ABC, CBS, and NBC, collectively.

Election news patterns are quite stable in successive elections and are uniform for all media covering a particular election. Thus Americans receive similar types of information on which to base their political decisions. Similarity in coverage of election campaigns has benefits as well as drawbacks. The large degree of homogeneity introduced into the electoral process is an advantage in a heterogeneous country such as the United States, where it can be difficult to develop political consensus. But it also means uniform neglect of many topics and criteria for judging candidates. Shared ignorance mars shared knowledge. A uniform information base obviously has not produced totally uniform political views throughout the country. Differences in political evaluations, even among audiences that share the same news, must be attributed to news commentators' varying interpretations of the same facts and to the different outlooks that audiences bring to the news. As the previous chapter pointed out, the impact of news frequently is perceiver determined rather than stimulus determined.

Of the factors that encourage uniform coverage, journalists' professional socialization appears to be the most important. Newspeople share a sense of what is newsworthy and how it should be presented. Reporters cover identical beats in fashions that have become routine for election coverage. That means keeping score about who is winning and losing and reporting dramatic incidents and juicy personal gossip. It means avoiding dull facts as much as possible without totally ignoring essential, albeit unglamorous, information.

Coverage does not follow the campaign model of reporting.[20] In this model—the utopia of campaign managers—the rhythm of the campaign as produced by the candidates and their staffs determines what media cover. Reporters dutifully take their cues from the candidates. Press coverage conforms instead to an incentive model. Whenever exciting stories provide an incentive for coverage, the media publish them in a rhythm dictated by their needs and the tastes of their audiences. The needs and tastes of the candidates may be ignored unless they manage to generate the kinds of stories and pictures that journalists find irresistible. This is why most candidates now employ professionals who know how to get good media coverage for their clients.

Substance of Coverage: Candidate Qualifications.   The candidate qualifications that media highlight fall into two broad groups: those that are generally important in judging a person's character and those specifically related to the tasks of the office. Included in the first group are personality traits (integrity, reliability, compassion), style characteristics (forthrightness, folksiness), and image characteristics (confidence, levelheadedness). Professional qualifications at the presidential level include the capacity to develop and execute effective foreign and domestic policies, the ability to mobilize public support, and a flair for administration. The candidate's political philosophy is also a professional criterion. Presidential candidates over the years have been most frequently assessed in terms of their trustworthiness, strength of character, leadership capabilities, and compassion. Media have covered professional capacities—the very qualities that deserve the fullest discussion and analysis—only scantily and often vaguely even when an incumbent is running.[21]

The handful of professional qualifications that news stories mention from time to time include general appraisals of the capacity to handle foreign affairs, which has been deemed crucial in a global society, and the capacity to sustain an acceptable quality of life for all citizens by maintaining the economy on an even keel and by controlling crime and internal disorder. The same types of qualities reappear from election to election, but not necessarily in every candidate's profile. Disparate coverage then makes it very difficult for the electorate to compare and evaluate the candidates on important dimensions. Effective comparisons are also hindered by contradictions in remarks reported about the candidates. Bound by current codes of objective reporting and neutrality in electoral contests, the media rarely give guidance to the audience for judging conflicting claims.

Verbal news commentary about the political candidates tends to be so negative that voters' choices have seemed dismal in recent elections, though 2004 commentary spared Kerry the usual negative onslaught. The typical downbeat mood of election coverage is epitomized by the lead paragraph in a *Time* magazine story at the end of the 1980 race between Reagan and Carter: "For more than a year, two flawed candidates have been floundering toward the final showdown, each unable to give any but his most unquestioning supporters much reason to vote for him except dislike of his opponent." [22] Such negative characterizations, which have marred all recent presidential elections, are hardly fair to capable candidates who often possess great personal strengths and skills that should be praised rather than debased.

Substance of Coverage: Issues and Events.   Journalists' overriding consideration in reporting about particular issues, as in other political coverage, is newsworthiness rather than intrinsic importance. This is why the changing record of happenings on the campaign trail, however trivial, receives extended coverage. Rather than exploring policy issues in depth, news stories emphasize brief, rapidly paced, freshly breaking events. In fact, the amount of coverage for particular issues often seems to be in inverse proportion to their significance. For instance, during the 1992 primaries, one of every six campaign stories on the television networks referred to Governor Clinton's personal life. Sexual foibles, reputed drug use during college days, slips of the tongue, and bad jokes all made headlines and were repeated endlessly on various entertainment programs. The pattern persisted during the 1996 campaign. In the 2000 campaign, a story about George W. Bush's arrest on drunken driving charges twenty-four years earlier received more coverage during the last three days of the campaign than all foreign policy issues had received since Labor Day.[23]

Three major features stand out in coverage of issues and events. First and most significantly, the media devote a large amount of attention to "horse race" aspects of campaigns. Three categories in Table 8-2—campaigns, candidate momentum, and debates—were framed largely in terms of who was ahead or behind in the race. By comparison to the "game frame" that dwells on each candidate's odds for winning or losing, the media slight political, social, and economic problems facing the country and say little about the merits of the policies proposed by the contenders, unless these issues can be made exciting and visually dramatic. Second, information about issues is patchy because the candidates and their surrogates try to concentrate on issues that help their campaigns and try to avoid issues likely to alienate any portion of the huge and disparate electorate from which all are seeking support. Third, there is more issue coverage, albeit unsystematic, than scholars have acknowledged in the past. In fact, it

TABLE 8-2   Major Story Themes, October 1–14, 2004 (in percentages)

Story theme	National paper	Regional paper	Network a.m.	Network p.m.
Iraq/terrorism	9	9	7	10
Other foreign policies	3	4	0	1
Domestic issues	11	13	8	18
Campaign issues in battleground states	10	16	6	16
Candidate momentum, stump speeches	8	9	12	18
Debates	36	29	59	33
Role of news and entertainment media	7	10	6	3
Advertising	4	1	0	1
Vice presidents, first ladies	3	3	1	0
General musings	5	2	0	0
Other	5	2	2	0

SOURCE: Adapted from Project for Excellence in Journalism, "The Debate Effect," *Reports and Surveys—Campaign 2004*, 2005, www.journalism.org/.

NOTE: Data for the 311 stories from national newspapers come from the *New York Times* and *Washington Post*; data for the 143 stories from regional newspapers come from the *Columbus Dispatch* and the *Miami Herald*; data for the 222 network news stories come from ABC, CBS, and NBC. Roughly one-third come from morning shows and two-thirds from evening shows.

slightly surpassed horse race coverage in the 2004 election.[94] Audiences often overlook commentary about issues because it is embedded in many horse race stories and discussions of candidates' qualifications. For example, the claim that a candidate is compassionate may be linked to his or her concern about health care laws. When content analysis designs focus narrowly on recording only one issue per news story, multifaceted stories are forced into a single category and important facets become obscured.

In recent elections, some twenty-five issues, like taxes or social security or education, have usually surfaced intermittently in the press; for television the number hovers around twenty. Typically only half of these receive extensive and intensive attention. Many important policy questions likely to arise during a forthcoming presidential term are totally ignored. Although candidates like to talk about broad policy issues, such as war and peace or the health of the economy, newspeople prefer to concentrate on narrower, specific policy positions on which the candidates disagree sharply.

As is the case for coverage of presidential qualifications, issues discussed in connection with individual candidates vary. Voters thus receive little aid from the media in appraising and comparing the candidates on the issues. Compared with print media, television news usually displays more uniform patterns of issue coverage for all the candidates and involves a more limited range of issues. Television stories are briefer, touch on fewer aspects of each issue, and contribute to the stereotypic images developed for particular candidates. Events are often fragmented and barren of context, but what is left is dramatized to appeal to the audience. No wonder that most people turn to television for news about the candidates and their campaigns.

We should assess media coverage not only in terms of the numbers of stories devoted to various topics but also in terms of political impact. There are times when election politics is particularly volatile and a few stories may carry extraordinary weight. Rapid diffusion of these stories throughout the major media enhances their impact. Michael Robinson calls such featured events *medialities*—"events, developments, or situations to which the media have given importance by emphasizing, expanding, or featuring them in such a way that their real significance has been modified, distorted, or obscured." [25] Medialities usually involve policy scandals, economic disasters, and personal foibles. Such key stories can have a far more profound impact on the campaign than thousands of routine stories and should be appraised accordingly.

Political and Structural Bias. Does election coverage give a fair and equal chance for all viewpoints to be expressed so that media audiences can make informed decisions? Are the perennial charges of bias that disappointed candidates level evidence that newspeople always show favoritism? Or are they merely reactions to coverage that did not advance the candidates' causes? In general, journalists try to produce balanced coverage for all major candidates for the same office. They aim for rough parity in the number of stories about each candidate and rough parity in the balance of overtly favorable and unfavorable stories.

Nonetheless, imbalanced coverage occurs frequently. In the 2004 election, for example, coverage of the president was predominantly negative while the reverse was true for Senator Kerry. For network television, the ratio of negative coverage was 63–41 percent.[26] That then raises the question whether political or structural bias is involved. Political bias reflects ideological judgments, whereas structural bias reflects the circumstances of news production. Balanced reporting may be impossible when candidates' newsworthiness and willingness to talk to reporters vary or when their campaign is linked to different issues. Incumbent president Reagan, dubbed "the Great Communicator," was far more newsworthy than his challenger, Sen. Walter Mondale, throughout 1984 because Reagan was the president. In 2004 it was appropriate to discuss the president in terms of his role as commander-in-chief in an ongoing unpopular war while focusing on Senator Kerry's far more popular domestic policy proposals. Structural bias, even though it lacks partisan motivations, nonetheless may profoundly affect people's perceptions about campaigns.[27]

Major studies of bias in presidential campaigns from 1948 to 1996 concluded that there was no evidence of significant political bias in newspapers, news magazines, or television.[28] The studies encompassed bias in gatekeeping that might affect story selection, bias in coverage that might give some candidates short shrift, and bias in the amounts of positive and negative coverage.

Editorials, of course, are intrinsically biased because their primary purpose is to express opinions. As part of the editorial function, many news media endorse candidates. That has little impact at the presidential level but does seem to matter for lower-level offices, particularly in elections in which voters have little information to make their own decisions.[29] Influential papers, such as the *Los Angeles Times,* the *Washington Post,* and the small but influential Manchester, New Hampshire, *Union Leader,* can be extraordinarily successful in promoting the election of candidates they have endorsed and in defeating unacceptable contenders. At the presidential level news coverage tends to be essentially evenhanded, regardless of the candidate endorsed. Below the presidential level, the media tend to give more coverage to their endorsed candidates than to those they have not endorsed.

The effort to keep coverage balanced does not extend to third-party candidates. Anyone who runs for the presidency who is not a Republican or Democrat is out of the mainstream of newsworthiness and is slighted or even ignored by the news profession. Especially newsworthy third-party candidates, such as Robert La Follette of the Progressive Party in 1924, George Wallace of the American Independent Party in 1968, John Anderson of the National Unity Campaign in 1980, independent Ross Perot in 1992, and the Green Party's Ralph Nader in 2000, were notable exceptions. Newsworthiness considerations also account for the sparse coverage of vice presidential candidates despite the importance of the office, including the possibility that the vice president may have to replace a deceased incumbent. A total of 95 percent of the coverage in a typical presidential election goes to the presidential contenders and only 5 percent to their running mates.

Adequacy of Coverage

How adequate is current election coverage? Do the media help voters to make decisions according to commonly accepted democratic criteria? As discussed, the media do not make comparative appraisals of candidates and issues easy for voters. In presidential contests information is ample about the major, mainstream candidates and about day-to-day campaign events. It is sketchy and often confusing about the candidates' professional qualifications and about many important policy issues. Most primary contenders, candidates of minor parties, and vice presidential candidates are largely ignored. This is not surprising because the field of candidates is usually much larger than most Americans realize. Usually several hundred individuals register as formal candidates for the presidency. The prevalence of negative information makes it seem that all of the candidates are mediocre or even poor choices. This negative cast appears to be a major factor in many voters' decisions to stay home on election day. It also undermines the ability of newly elected officials to command essential support after the election, especially from members of the opposing party.

Nonetheless, voters are generally satisfied with the amount of election information they receive (Table 8-3). In the 1996, 2000, and 2004 presidential campaigns, at least three out of four voters felt adequately informed. Many scholars and pundits would disagree with that assessment because it does not match the high standards of civic knowledge that democratic theory prescribes for citizens. The most serious deficiencies in the news supply are inadequate analyses of policy issues so that voters do not learn about the key points at stake, the scope and nature of various tradeoffs, and the impact of their vote on the resolution of major political problems. The patterns of coverage force voters to make choices based more on the candidates' campaigning skills than on their governing skills and policy preferences. These are valid criticisms if one accepts the premise that policy issues, rather than leadership characteristics, should drive voting choices.

If the public's chief role is to choose a good leader, along with a general sense of the directions this leader will take, then judgments about the adequacy of the information supply become far more positive, in line with the public's own appraisal. The proliferation of news venues that has occurred in the Internet age allows average people easy access to a vast variety of information offered at diverse levels of depth and sophistication. Links on Internet election sites are an especially rich source for facts and interpretations that facilitate in-depth analyses, whenever voters feel the need—which they rarely do.[30]

The mainstream media do fall short when it comes to supplying the needs of political elites in ready fashion. Opinion leaders would benefit from more complete coverage of the candidates' stands on major and minor issues, more point-by-point comparisons of candidates and policies, and more ample evaluations of the political significance of differences in candidates and their programs. Stories covering important topics that candidates neglect would be useful, as would more coverage of third-party

TABLE 8-3   Adequacy of Campaign Coverage, 1996, 2000, 2004
             (in percentages)

Adequacy of coverage	Campaign 1996	Campaign 2000	Campaign 2004
Learned enough	75	77	86
Did not learn enough	23	20	13
Don't know	2	3	1

SOURCE: Pew Research Center for the People and the Press, "Voters Liked Campaign 2004, but Too Much 'Mud Slinging,'" http://people-press.org. Based on a survey of 1,209 voters conducted November 5–8, 2004.

NOTE: Respondents were asked, "During this campaign, did you feel you learned enough about the candidates and the issues to make an informed choice between [respective candidates for years] OR did you find it difficult to choose because you felt you did not learn enough from the campaign?"

candidates and vice presidential contenders. In the end, though, no news consumer need hunger for information in the Internet age. With a little effort, a global cornucopia of facts and opinions is readily available to anyone with access to a computer and the Internet.

In presidential contests the deficiencies of media coverage are most noticeable during the primaries, when large slates of same-party candidates are competing in each primary. The media meet this challenge by giving uniformly skimpy treatment to all candidates except those designated as front-runners. It is not uncommon for two or three front-runners to attract 75 percent or more of the coverage, leaving a pack of trailing contenders with hardly any attention at all. As political scientist Thomas Patterson has noted, "Issue material is but a rivulet in the news flow during the primaries, and what is there is almost completely diluted by information about the race." [31] Whereas the quality of coverage during the primaries may be thin, the quantity is substantial, although it is unequally distributed so that the races in well-covered states become disproportionately influential. By the middle of the primary season, interest in these contests dwindles. Coverage shrivels. It perks up slightly during the conventions and when the final campaign starts following the Labor Day holiday in September.

What People Learn from Campaign Coverage

What do people learn from campaign coverage? The answer varies, of course, depending on their interest in the campaign, prior political knowledge, desire for certain information, and political sophistication. But several general trends emerge from national surveys, such as those conducted biannually by the Survey Research Center at the University of Michigan and from intensive interviews of smaller panels of voters.

Learning about Candidates and Issues

The foremost impression from interviews with voters is that they can recall very little specific campaign information. That does not necessarily mean that they have not learned anything. As discussed in Chapter 7, when people are confronted with factual information, such as news about a particular presidential candidate, they assess how it fits into their established view of that candidate. If it is consonant, the information strengthens that view and the person's feelings about the candidate. If it is dissonant, the person is likely to reject it outright or note it as a reasonable exception to their established schema. The least likely result is a major revision of their established beliefs about the candidate. Once people have processed the news they forget most of the details and store only their summary impression in memory. That approach is called "on-line processing." When people are later quizzed about details, they are likely to recall only what was frequently repeated in recent news stories. Online processing thus creates the false impression that the average person has formed opinions about the candidate without having learned the appropriate facts.[32]

In the past, comparisons of election information supplied by respondents' newspapers with information mentioned by respondents during interviews revealed roughly similar patterns. That was not true in 2000, possibly because newspaper use for campaign information had plunged dramatically along with confidence in the media (Table 8-4). Researchers asked a nationwide sample of people to mention good and bad points about the 2000 presidential nominees, Al Gore and George W. Bush, that might affect their voting choices. Overall news stories emphasized personal suitability more in judging the candidates' fitness for office, while the respondents gave more weight to each candidate's professional competence.

The issues people typically mention as important in the campaign represent a much abbreviated and imprecise version of media issue coverage. As Table 8-5 indicates, people express much more concern about economic and social issues than do the media. This is not surprising; these issues affect them personally. People do not need media coverage to know that inflation, unemployment, poverty, crime, race relations, and environmental pollution are serious problems requiring the president's attention. Nor is it surprising that people put much less emphasis on campaign hoopla, covered so plentifully by the media. Although audiences find these fleeting events entertaining, people make little effort to remember them.

TABLE 8-4   Presidential Qualities Mentioned by Individuals and
by Their Newspapers, 2000 (in percentages)

	Likes		Dislikes		
Qualities	Gore	Bush	Gore	Bush	Newspapers
Personal suitability					
Personality traits	21	33	29	24	40
Presidential traits	5	6	10	7	20
Style	6	3	5	6	6
Total	32	42	44	37	66
Professional competence					
Capacities	20	11	20	20	16
Philosophy	14	18	13	14	18
Policies	33	28	21	28	n.a.
Don't know/other	1	1	2	1	n.a.
Total	68	58	56	63	34

SOURCE: Survey data from the 2000 Election Survey, obtained from the Inter-University Consortium for Political and Social Research, University of Michigan; newspaper data from author's matching research in the *Boston Globe, Chicago Sun-Times, New York Daily News, Minneapolis Star Tribune, Christian Science Monitor, Los Angeles Times, New York Times,* and *Washington Post,* September 1–October 15, 2000.

NOTE: The percentages are based on responses to the question, "Is there anything in particular about Mr. Gore/Mr. Bush that might make you want to vote for/against him?" $N = 912$ for Gore likes, 822 for Bush likes, 860 for Gore dislikes, 885 for Bush dislikes. $N = 2,434$ mentions of qualities by newspapers.

Voting Behavior

Do media-intensive campaigns change votes? The answer to this perennial question so dear to the hearts of campaign managers, public relations experts, and social scientists hinges on the interaction between audiences and messages. Crucial variables include the voters' receptivity to a message urging change, the potency of the message, the appropriateness of its form, and the setting in which it occurs. For most voters, the crucial attitudes that determine voting choices are already firmly in place at the start of the campaign so that their final vote is a foregone conclusion. Vote changes are most likely when voters pay fairly close attention to the media and are ambivalent in their attitudes toward the candidates. Campaign messages are most potent if they concern a major and unpredicted event, such as a successful or disastrous foreign policy venture or corruption in high places, and when individuals find themselves in social settings where a change of attitude will not constitute deviant behavior. This combination of circumstances is fairly rare, which explains why changes of voting intentions are comparatively uncommon. Fears that televised campaigns can easily sway voters and amount to "electronic ballot box stuffing" are therefore unrealistic.

TABLE 8-5   Comparison of Mention of Issues and Events by Newspapers, Television, and Survey Responses (in percentages)

Issues and events	Newspapers	Television	Survey responses[a]
Campaign events	47	61	0
Domestic politics	21	15	27
Foreign affairs	16	7	10
Economic policy	10	11	16
Social problems	6	6	44

SOURCE: Survey data come from the 2000 Election Survey, Center for Political Studies, Survey Research Center, University of Michigan; media data come from author's research.

NOTE: Survey respondents specified the most important national problem. The question asked of survey respondents was, "What do you think are the most important problems facing this country?" $N = 4,726$ for newspapers, 985 for television, and 905 for survey responses. Media survey periods (newspapers and television) = September 1–October 15, 2000. The newspaper survey material was gathered from a Lexis-Nexis search of the *Boston Globe, Chicago Sun-Times, Daily News, Star Tribune, Los Angeles Times, New York Times, Christian Science Monitor,* and *Washington Post.* The television survey material was gathered from ABC, CBS, and NBC.

[a]Three percent of survey respondents answered "don't know" to the most important issue; this makes up the remainder of the total.

However, even small numbers of media-induced vote changes might be important. Tiny percentages of votes, often less than 1 percent, decide many elections at all levels. That was demonstrated dramatically in the 2000 election, which was ultimately decided by fewer than a thousand votes. The media may also skew election outcomes whenever they can stimulate or depress voter turnout, which is more likely to occur than changes in voting choices. Do broadcasts that predict election results before voting has ended affect turnout? The answer remains moot despite several investigations of the problem. Current evidence indicates that the effects, if they do occur, have rarely changed election outcomes.[33]

Attempts to stop projections of winners and losers while voting is still in progress have run afoul of First Amendment free speech guarantees. This may explain why the laws passed in more than half of the states to restrain exit polling are seldom enforced.[34] Congress has tried since 1986 to pass a Uniform Poll Closing Act. Although the measure has thus far failed to pass, prospects for ultimate success are good, especially after the presidential election of 2000, in which the issue of broadcasting election results while polling places remained open in parts of the United States became a huge political controversy. A smaller dispute arose in 2004 when media published exit polls that wrongly suggested a Kerry victory before the polls had closed. The concern about the impact of exit polls and early forecasts may be overdrawn. Voters are bombarded throughout the election year with information likely to determine their vote and turnout. Why should the media be squeamish on the campaign pay-off day?

The most important influence of the media on the voter does not lie in changing votes once predispositions have been formed, but in shaping and reinforcing predispositions and influencing the initial selection of candidates. When newspeople sketched out the Clinton image and held him up as a potential winner during the 1992 primaries, ignoring most of his rivals, they made the obscure governor of a small southern state into a viable candidate. Millions of voters would never have cast their ballot for the unknown Arkansas politician had not the media thrust him into the limelight as a likely winner.

By focusing the voters' attention on selected individuals, their characteristics, and issue stands, the media also determine to a large extent the crucial issues by which the public will gauge the competence of the candidates. Very early in the campaign, often long before formal campaigning starts, media interpretations of the significance of issues can shape the political and emotional context of the election. As Leon Sigal noted many years ago, the media

> play less of an independent part in creating issues, sketching imagery, and coloring perceptions of the candidates than in getting attention for their candidacies. Newsmen do not write the score or play an instrument; they amplify the sounds of the music makers.[35]

A final, potentially crucial impact on election outcomes is the role that the media play in turnout, especially in close elections. The negative tone of news coverage obviously plays a part. So do personalized appeals to voters. E-mails by the millions sent by personal friends and celebrities, often stimulated by Web site appeals, may well be the most potent electioneering weapon of the twenty-first century.

Summary

The media's role, especially that of television, in recent campaigns has been powerful and pervasive. Campaigns have become battles for favorable coverage by traditional and by new media venues. The main quest is for a place in the limelight and a "winner" image. Candidates expect that public recognition and support—or opposition—are likely to follow, particularly at the presidential level.

In this chapter we have scrutinized newspaper, television, and Internet election coverage, considering general coverage patterns, the substance and slant of coverage, and the manner of presentation. The evidence shows that the media have placed heavy emphasis on the candidates' personal qualifications for the office and on the ups and downs of the race. The media frequently mention policy issues but rarely explore them in depth. Stories are chosen primarily for their newsworthiness, not their educational value. Structural biases abound and have important political consequences, but outright political bias is uncommon.

Although the public claims, off and on, to be very interested in learning about the election, it absorbs only a small portion of the considerable amount of available information. Nonetheless, the bits of information that people absorb create sufficient political understanding to permit sound voting choices based primarily on whether the chosen candidate seems trustworthy and capable to lead the country. Although news stories rarely change people's minds, they can influence undecided voters. Along with media impact on turnout, shaping the views of even small numbers of voters can determine the outcome in close elections and change the course of political life.

Before television, conventional wisdom as well as research suggested that news media impact on elections was minimal because election stories persuaded few people to change their votes. Television and Internet-age research has cast the net much wider to include the media's effects on all phases of the election campaign, from the recruitment and nomination stages to the strategies that produce the final outcome. In addition to studying the media's impact on the final voting choice, social scientists now look at political learning during campaigns and at the information base that supports voting decisions. Television news stories and massive numbers of highly sophisticated commercials have changed the election game, especially at the presidential level. The Internet has rekindled the possibility of retail politicking through personalized appeals to individual voters. The difference now is that personalization is taking place on a mass scale that was unimaginable before the Internet. One thing is certain: candidates and media have become inextricably intertwined. Those who aspire to elective office must play the media game by rules that continue to evolve.

Notes

1. Pippa Norris, "Too Close to Call: Opinion Polls in Campaign 2000," *Press/Politics* 6, no. 1 (2001): 3–10.
2. In 2000 the most extensive data archives were created at the Annenberg School for Communication in Philadelphia and the Shorenstein Center at Harvard University's Kennedy School. Other major studies in 2000 and 2004

involved these institutions as well as Brookings, the Pew Internet and American Life Projects, and scholars at UC Los Angeles, University of Wisconsin, Brigham Young University, University of Minnesota, and Princeton University. For one of the first major attempts to study the full campaign cycle, covering multiple phases of the 1992 presidential campaign, see Marion R. Just, Ann N. Crigler, Dean E. Alger, Timothy E. Cook, Montague Kern, and Darrell M. West, *Crosstalk: Citizens, Candidates, and the Media in a Presidential Campaign* (Chicago: University of Chicago Press, 1996).

3. Media Tenor, "U.S. Presidential Elections, 2004," www.mediatenor.com/ specialr.htm.

4. Larry M. Bartels, "Expectations and Preferences in Presidential Nominating Campaigns," *American Political Science Review* 79 (September 1985): 804–815. The importance of the winner image is discussed in Henry E. Brady and Richard Johnston, "What's the Primary Message: Horse Race or Issue Journalism?" in *Media and Momentum: The New Hampshire Primary and Nomination Politics,* ed. Gary R. Orren and Nelson W. Polsby (Chatham, N.J.: Chatham House, 1987), 127–186.

5. "Campaign 2004—The Primaries," *Media Monitor,* March/April 2004, 3.

6. Richard Rubin, *Press, Party, and Presidency* (New York: Norton, 1981), 129, 138.

7. For analysis of the impact of debates, see David J. Lanoue and Peter Schrott, *The Joint Press Conference: The History, Impact, and Prospects of American Presidential Debates* (Westport, Conn.: Greenwood, 1991). Also see Judith S. Trent and Robert V. Friedenberg, *Political Campaign Communication: Principles and Practices,* 4th ed. (Westport, Conn.: Praeger, 2000), chap. 8; and Sidney Kraus, *Televised Presidential Debates and Public Policy,* 2d ed. (Mahwah, N.J.: Erlbaum, 2000). Full texts of presidential debates can be found on the web site of the Commission on Presidential Debates, www.debates.org.

8. Quoted in Edwin Diamond, *Sign-off: The Last Days of Television* (Cambridge: MIT Press, 1982), 175.

9. Martin Schram, *The Great American Video Game: Presidential Politics in the Television Age* (New York: Morrow, 1987), 26.

10. Clarence Page, "How 'The Hug' Helped," *Chicago Tribune,* December 8, 2004.

11. Alliance for Better Campaigns, "Political Standard—Local Stations," www.bettercampaigns.org.

12. "Campaign 2004 Final," *Media Monitor,* November/December 2004, 9.

13. Jacques Steinberg, "Fox News, Media Elite," *Chicago Tribune,* December 8, 2004.

14. Drew Neisser, "2004: The Internet Election," *iMedia Connection,* www.imediaconnection.com.

15. "Campaign 1996—The Primaries," *Media Monitor,* March–April 1996, 2.

16. W. Russell Neuman, Marion Just, and Ann Crigler, *Common Knowledge: News and the Construction of Political Meaning* (Chicago: University of Chicago Press, 1992), 39–59; Just and others, *Crosstalk,* 62–66; Darrell M. West, *Air Wars: Television Advertising in Election Campaigns, 1952–2000,* 3d ed. (Washington, D.C.: CQ Press, 2001), 13–19.

17. Bruce E. Gronbeck, "Mythic Portraiture in the 1988 Iowa Presidential Caucus Bio-Ads," *American Behavioral Scientist* 33 (1989): 351–364; J. Gregory Payne, John Marlier, and Robert A. Baucus, "Polispots in the 1988 Presidential Primaries," *American Behavioral Scientist* 33 (1989): 365–381.

18. Michael J. Robinson, "The Media in 1980: Was the Message the Message?" in *The American Elections of 1980*, ed. Austin Ranney (Washington, D.C.: American Enterprise Institute, 1981), 186.

19. For comparisons of coverage in Boston, Los Angeles, Fargo–Moorhead, N.D., and Winston-Salem, N.C., see Just and others, *Crosstalk*, 92–96. Also see Project for Excellence in Journalism, "Reports and Surveys—Campaign 2004," 2005, www.journalism.org.

20. C. Richard Hofstetter, *Bias in the News: Network Television Coverage of the 1972 Election Campaign* (Columbus: Ohio State University Press, 1976), 39–41; Paul S. Herrnson, "The Congressional Elections," in *The Election of 2000*, ed. Gerald M. Pomper, Anthony Corrado, E.J. Dionne Jr., Kathleen A. Frankovic, Paul S. Herrnson, Marjorie Randon Hershey, William G. Mayer, Monika L. McDermott, and Wilson McWilliams (New York: Chatham House, 2001). For a comparison of campaigns in Senate and House elections, see Paul Gronke, *The Electorate, the Campaign, and the Office: A Unified Approach to Senate and House Elections* (Ann Arbor: University of Michigan Press, 2000), chaps. 4 and 5.

21. Doris A. Graber and David Weaver, "Presidential Performance Criteria: The Missing Element in Election Coverage," *Harvard International Journal of Press/Politics* 1 (winter 1996): 7–32. A companion analysis of the 2000 election yielded similar findings.

22. Quoted in Anthony King, "How Not to Select Presidential Candidates: A View from Europe," in Ranney, *American Elections*, 305.

23. S. Robert Lichter, "A Plague on Both Parties: Substance and Fairness in TV Election News," *Press/Politics* 6, no. 3 (2001): 12.

24. "Campaign 2004 Final," 5.

25. Robinson, "The Media in 1980," 191.

26. "Campaign 2004 Final," 5.

27. Hofstetter, *Bias in the News*, 32–36. For an interesting discussion of the special concerns involved in covering African American candidates, see Jannette Lake Dates and Oscar H. Gandy Jr., "How Ideological Constraints Affected Coverage of the Jesse Jackson Campaign," *Journalism Quarterly* 62 (autumn 1985): 595–600.

28. Dave D'Alessio and Mike Allen, "Media Bias in Presidential Elections: A Meta-Analysis," *Journal of Communication* 50, no. 4 (2000): 133–156. The reasons behind unwarranted bias claims are discussed in David Domke, Mark D. Watts, Dhavan V. Shah, and David P. Fan, "The Politics of Conservative Elites and the 'Liberal Media' Argument," *Journal of Communication* 49, no. 4 (1999): 35–58.

29. Byron St. Dizier, "The Effect of Newspaper Endorsements and Party Identification on Voting Choice," *Journalism Quarterly* 62 (autumn 1985): 589–594.

30. For a more detailed discussion of the quality of the information supply and its adequacy for informing voters, see Doris Graber, "The Media and Democracy: Beyond Myths and Stereotypes," *Annual Review of Political Science* 6 (2003): 139–160; and Doris Graber, "Mediated Politics and Citizenship in the Twenty-First Century," *Annual Review of Psychology* 55 (2004): 545–571.

31. Thomas Patterson, *The Mass Media Election: How Americans Choose Their President*, 3d ed. (New York: Praeger, 1988), 250. Also see Eric R.A.N. Smith, *The Unchanging American Voter* (Berkeley: University of California Press, 1989).

32. Doris A. Graber, *Processing the News: How People Tame the Information Tide*, 2d ed. (New York: Longman, 1988). Milton Lodge and Patrick Stroh, "Inside the Mental Voting Booth: An Impression-Driven Process Model of Candidate Eval-

uation," in *Explorations in Political Psychology,* ed. Shanto Iyengar and William J. McGuire (Durham: Duke University Press, 1993).

33. Paul Wilson, "Election Night 1980 and the Controversy over Early Projections," in *Television Coverage of the 1980 Presidential Campaign,* ed. William C. Adams (Norwood, N.J.: Ablex, 1983), 152–153; Percy H. Tannenbaum and Leslie J. Kostrich, *Turned-On TV/Turned-Off Voters: Policy Options for Election Projections* (Beverly Hills, Calif.: Sage, 1983); and Paul J. Lavrakas and Jack K. Holley, eds., *Polls and Presidential Election Campaign News Coverage: 1988* (Evanston: Northwestern University Press, 1988).

34. For a discussion of how state laws have fared in the courts, see Stephen Bates, "Lawful Exits: The Court Considers Election Day Polls," *Public Opinion* 8 (summer 1986): 53–54.

35. Leon V. Sigal, "Newsmen and Campaigners: Organization Men Make the News," *Political Science Quarterly* 93 (fall 1978): 465–470.

Readings

Bimber, Bruce, and Richard Davis. *Campaigning on Line: The Internet in U.S. Elections.* New York: Oxford University Press, 2005.

Ceaser, James W. *Red over Blue: The 2004 Elections and American Politics.* Lanham, Md.: Rowman and Littlefield, 2005.

Farnsworth, Stephen J., and S. Robert Lichter. *The Nightly News Nightmare: Network Television's Coverage of U.S. Presidential Elections, 1988–2000.* Lanham, Md.: Rowman and Littlefield, 2003.

Hart, Roderick P. *Campaign Talk: Why Elections Are Good for Us.* Princeton: Princeton University Press, 2000.

Hart, Roderick P., and Daron R. Shaw. *Communication in U.S. Elections: New Agendas.* Lanham, Md.: Rowman and Littlefield, 2001.

Hollihan, Thomas A. *Uncivil Wars: Political Campaigns in a Media Age.* Boston: Bedford/St. Martin's, 2001.

Just, Marion R., Ann N. Crigler, Dean E. Alger, Timothy E. Cook, Montague Kern, and Darrell M. West. *Crosstalk: Citizens, Candidates, and the Media in a Presidential Campaign.* Chicago: University of Chicago Press, 1996.

Kaid, Lynda Lee, and Anne Johnston. *Videostyle in Presidential Campaigns: Style and Content of Televised Political Advertising.* Westport, Conn.: Praeger, 2001.

Patterson, Thomas. *The Vanishing Voter: Public Involvement in an Age of Uncertainty.* New York: Knopf, 2002.

West, Darrell M. *Air Wars: Television Advertising in Election Campaigns, 1952–2004.* 4th ed. Washington, D.C.: CQ Press, 2005.

The Struggle for Control: News from the Presidency and Congress

H AD PRESIDENT GEORGE W. BUSH REVIEWED how television news stories rated his performance late in 2003, he would have found mostly failing scores. Seventy-seven percent of the comments about his Iraq policy were negative, as were 80 percent of the comments on his handling of international terrorism and 79 percent of the comments on his defense policies. Comments on his handling of the economy were 84 percent negative. His best rating was a 44 percent positive score for health care policy thanks to some plaudits for a prescription drug plan for senior citizens.

The ratings sound pretty dismal, but press commentary has been harsher in the past. The late Katherine Graham, publisher of the *Washington Post,* reminded her listeners during a speech that personal invective once was a common feature of press criticism. For example, the press smeared Andrew Jackson's reputation by calling his mother a prostitute. The *Post* routinely referred to President Rutherford B. Hayes as "his fraudulency" following a disputed election.

Graham praised the press for its strong tradition of independence, skepticism, and irreverent journalism. She deemed periods of truce between the press and presidents as contrary to the spirit of the First Amendment, which ordains the press as the watchdog that alerts the public to government sins. The depression years, World War II, the Korean War, and the cold war were exceptions to the hallowed tradition. Much of the Washington, D.C., press then viewed itself as responsible adjuncts to the government's efforts to cope with these problems. There was criticism, of course, but it did not impugn the government's veracity and motivations, nor did it attack the substance of policies.

The tone of media evaluations of the president changed sharply with Vietnam and Watergate, which journalists saw as ventures based on false premises and involving government propaganda, lies, and cover-ups. From then on the press again became suspicious and adversarial, assuming flawed policies, bad motivations, and deceptive spinning of news most of the time, unless proven otherwise. Graham thought that there had been some softening over time as journalists became more sophisticated and realized the complexity of the contemporary political scene. But President Clinton and his immediate predecessor and successor would likely disagree when thinking about media coverage of their presidencies.[1]

Why do political leaders in democratic nations worldwide put so much energy into their media strategies when, in the end, the media may be their undoing? Why do they expose themselves to frequently hostile interrogations by journalists who routinely write stories attacking them and their policies? The answer is that politicians desperately need the media to achieve their goals. Politicians think that they exercise some control over journalists because the media need politicians to get information for important stories. Because the two institutions have conflicting goals and missions and operate under different constraints, they cannot live comfortably with each other. Yet they dare not part company. Interdependence tempers their love-hate relationship.[2]

The Adversarial Relationship

To gain and retain public support and maintain power, executives and legislators want to influence the information that media pass on to the public and to other officials. They want to define situations and project images in their own way to further their objectives. Newspeople, however, have different goals. They want to monitor and appraise government performance, and they feel bound by the economics of the news business to present exciting stories that will attract large audiences. This often means prying into conflict, controversy, or ordinary wheeling and dealing — matters that government officials would like to keep quiet. Government wants its portrait taken from the most flattering angle; at the least it wants to avoid an unflattering picture. The media, eager to find chinks in government's armor and to maximize audience size, prefer candid shots that show government at its worst.

In this chapter we will take a closer look at the interrelationship of the media and the executive and legislative branches of government at the national level, leaving the interface of the media and the court system and subnational levels of government for chapter 10. Casual as well as systematic observations readily establish that the media devote much attention to the affairs of national government, particularly the presidency. From July 2003 to June 2004 the early evening news broadcasts of ABC, CBS, and NBC ran an average of forty-five network television stories per month about some aspect of the presidency (Table 9-1). It was the most common story topic by far. The numbers for Congress and the Supreme Court were considerably lower, with a monthly average of thirty-five congressional stories and just twelve stories about the Court. However, the number of congressional stories would increase sharply if stories devoted to individual members were added. Compared to 1999–2000 coverage data, the 2003–2004 scores represent a significant increase in attention to the three branches of government in length of stories, even when story numbers have increased only moderately. Sparse coverage of the Supreme Court has remained constant.

Changes in patterns of news coverage are not uncommon (Table 9-2). Emphasis on traditional political news wanes in times of relative political calm, only to rise again during crises like the Persian Gulf and Iraq wars, the 2001 terrorist attack on U.S. soil, and the disputed 2000 presidential election. Overall, however, there appears to be a slight permanent shift on television and in news magazines—though not in newspapers—away from political news toward economic and social policies. Differences among the three networks in news allotments within each network's broadcasts are small (Table 9-3). NBC spent the most time on stories about the three branches of government. It used twenty-five hours and fifty minutes compared to seventeen hours and thirty-five minutes for ABC and twelve hours and thirty-nine minutes for CBS. The president received slightly more than half of network television time, compared to 37 percent for Congress and 10 percent for the Supreme Court.

The similarities between print and broadcast media in covering particular topics do not mean that stories project identical images. For example, when a local newspaper, an elite newspaper, and network television covered two items—a proposal by President Ronald Reagan to cut taxes and the president's 1984 trip to Europe—three different sets of images emerged from the stories.[3] The *Durham Morning Herald,* a local paper from North Carolina with limited resources for independent news analysis, presented accounts drawn largely from the wire services. These stories featured the themes, ideas, and perspectives provided by the White House and, as is typical for local media, cast the president and the events into a favorable light. The elite *New York Times* also reported the White House version of events, but subjected the White House reports to critical analysis. This created a much less rosy impression of the state of affairs. The *CBS Evening News* presented a more mixed picture. Verbal images were predominantly negative,

TABLE 9-1   Evening Network News Coverage of the Three Branches of Government, July 2003–June 2004

	President		Congress		Supreme Court	
	Number of stories	Time	Number of stories	Time	Number of stories	Time
2003						
July	50	2:24	41	1:49	9	0:18
August	28	0:56	26	0:59	10	0:27
September	30	1:41	41	2:11	6	0:12
October	35	1:34	35	1:25	6	0:13
November	41	2:13	40	1:46	9	0:20
December	20	0:34	35	1:00	11	0:20
2004						
January	57	2:31	43	2:05	10	0:12
February	64	3:32	43	1:43	15	0:33
March	56	3:00	47	2:02	19	0:40
April	48	2:50	25	1:05	20	0:25
May	40	2:05	20	1:13	11	0:24
June	69	2:42	28	0:52	22	0:46
Total	538	26:09	424	18:25	148	4:57
Monthly average	45	2:10	35	1:32	12	0:24
Comparison data for July 1999– June 2000	41	1:21	23	0:44	8	0:11

SOURCE: Compiled by the author from the Vanderbilt Television News Archive.

NOTE: Three major networks (ABC, CBS, and NBC) have been combined; time is listed in hours and minutes.

but visual images, based as usual on controlled photo opportunities, were highly favorable. Audiences for these three news sources thus learned about the same events, but the tint of the interpretive lenses varied.

The Media and the Executive Branch

The media perform four major functions for government executives.[4] First, they inform them about current events, including developments in other parts of the government. This information sets the scene for policy making. When the media highlight such problems as environmental hazards or growing homelessness, major or minor executive action often follows. Not infrequently, the media furnish daily news more quickly than

TABLE 9-2   Changing News Story Emphasis (in percentages)

Media source	Traditional political			Economic and social			Entertainment and weather		
	1977	1997	2003	1977	1997	2003	1977	1997	2003
Network news	67	41	60	18	26	20	15	32	20
Newspapers	70	65	73	18	20	14	13	14	13
News magazines[a]	48	19	54	31	44	37	33	27	9

SOURCE: Condensed from "State of the News Media," 2004, www.stateofthenewsmedia.org; and Committee of Concerned Journalists, "Changing Definitions of News: Subject of News Stories by Medium," 1998, www.journalism.org.

NOTE: The "traditional political" category combines the 1997 categories of government, military, domestic affairs, foreign affairs, and in the case of the news magazines, the "other" category. The "economic and social" category combines the 1997 categories of business/commerce, science, technology, arts, religion, personal health, and crime. The "entertainment/weather" category combines entertainment/celebrities, lifestyle, celebrity crime, sports, and weather/disaster. Front pages of newspapers and network news were coded for March 1997; the 2003 front page newspaper and network news data are a constructed-week analysis conducted between January 1 and October 7.

[a] The 1977 and 1997 data reflect only *Time* magazine cover stories; the 2003 data reflect the pages dedicated to each topic in *Time, Newsweek,* and *U.S. News* during the first half of the year.

bureaucratic channels. Stories about foreign affairs often reach presidents faster through the *New York Times* on the Web or CNN than through State Department bulletins that first must be coded and then decoded.

Second, the media keep executive branch officials attuned to the public's major concerns. They do this directly by reporting on public opinion and indirectly by featuring the stories likely to shape public opinion. Public officials assume that newspeople keep in touch with popular concerns, which are then reflected in their stories. Readers and viewers, in turn, take their cues about what is important from the media.

Third, the media enable executives to convey their messages to the general public as well as to political elites within and outside of government. These channels of communication, to which presidents have fairly ready access, provide unparalleled opportunities to explain the administrations' policies. Political elites need them as much as the public does because there is no effective communication system that directly links government officials who are dispersed throughout the country. As one pundit noted cynically:

> Nearly all of our political comment originates in Washington. Washington politicians, after talking things over with each other, relay misinformation to

TABLE 9-3   Evening Network News Coverage of the Three Branches of
Government, July 2003–June 2004 (percentage of network time)

Network	President	Congress	Supreme Court
ABC	52.9	35.5	11.4
CBS	52.1	36.4	11.4
NBC	52.4	38.7	8.8
Average	52.5	37.0	10.4

SOURCE: Compiled by the author from Vanderbilt Television News Archives.

NOTE: Total annual coverage time for the three branches of the national government:
ABC = 17 hours, 35 minutes; CBS = 12 hours, 39 minutes; NBC = 25 hours, 50 minutes.

Washington journalists who, after further intramural discussion, print it where it is thoughtfully read by the same politicians. It is the only completely successful system for the recycling of garbage that has yet been devised.[5]

Political elites also use media channels to publicly attack opponents' positions.

Fourth, the media allow chief executives to remain in full public view on the political stage, keeping their human qualities and professional skills on almost constant display. Newspapers, television, and radio supply a steady stream of commentary about a president's daily routines. Coverage of personal life may be extensive, even for the vice president. For instance, when Vice President Dick Cheney underwent minor heart surgery in 2001, extensive daily medical news briefings kept the public apprised of his progress. The media reported intimate details of the vice president's condition, including his energy level, his tolerance of medical procedures, and his daily diet. Beyond providing human-interest tidbits, such coverage reassures the public that it is fully informed about the disability and the patient's fitness to serve. Human-interest stories help to forge close personal ties between people and their leaders. They make it easier for them to trust leaders and therefore support their policies. But they may also diminish the stature of presidents by revealing their human flaws, which can seem even more pronounced when contrasted with the majesty of the office.

Media Impact

The political significance of the relationship between the media and the executive branch is much greater than the few functions just described. Media coverage is the very lifeblood of politics because it shapes the perceptions that form the reality on which political action is based.

Media do more than depict the political environment; they *are* the political environment. Because direct contact with political actors and situations is limited, media images define people and situations for nearly all participants in the political process. The quantity and richness of such images is rising thanks to new technologies.

As we saw in previous chapters, the age of television politics that began in the 1950s has vastly enhanced the impact and, hence, the power of the media. In the past a story might have caused ripples on the political seas when thousands of people in one corner of the country read it in the paper or heard it on the radio. Today that same story can cause political tidal waves when millions worldwide see and hear it simultaneously on television and computer screens. Politicians feel compelled to react. They now can visit with millions of potential followers in their living rooms, creating the kinds of emotional ties that hitherto came only from personal contact. Electronic contacts may affect the political future of a member of Congress more than service on an important congressional committee.

Television has tipped the political scales of power among the three branches of government in favor of the presidency, although increasing coverage of Congress is lessening the imbalance. We have already described how strongly the news media influence who becomes eligible for the presidency and how profoundly they affect the conduct and outcome of elections. After elections, the length, vigor, and effectiveness of a president's political life and the general level of support for the political system depend heavily on images that the media convey. Making sure that these images are favorable therefore becomes a prime concern. Staffs of various presidents concur that "the national media play a very significant role in the White House decision-making process . . . in White House meetings, on the whole, more time is spent discussing the media than any other institution, including Congress . . . all policies are developed and presented with media reaction in mind." [6]

The media frequently raise issues that presidents and other public officials would prefer to keep out of the limelight. Budget deficits, crumbling highways and bridges, and inefficient veterans' hospitals are just a few examples. The Whitewater real estate scandal that harmed the Clintons throughout their White House years demonstrates how constant media prodding can keep a damaging issue at the top of the public agenda. The list of major and minor scandals that the media have highlighted to the government's dismay is seemingly endless.

Media coverage can also increase public support for a president's policies and raise approval ratings. This is particularly important in national emergencies when backing by Congress and the public is vital. Following the 2001 terrorist attacks on the United States, President Bush's positive evaluations in the news jumped from 36 percent to 63 percent. Such steep gains may be short lived, because memories fade quickly. By 2002 Bush's positive media scores had slumped again to 38 percent. They rose to 56 percent during the Iraq War and sank to 32 percent afterward.[7]

Sensational adverse publicity can kill the president's programs and abort new policies. For instance, welfare programs, such as financial aid for minority businesses or Head Start's prekindergarten training for underprivileged children, were sharply cut in the wake of news about inefficient management and corrupt handling of money in these programs. Media publicity can also be crucial in determining whether a presidential appointee will be confirmed by the Senate. During the Clinton administration, negative media publicity was instrumental in killing the nominations of Zoë Baird and Kimba Wood for attorney general. Media stories about womanizing, heavy drinking, and other personal excesses by former senator John Tower were blamed in his failure to gain Senate approval in 1989 as secretary of defense during the senior George Bush's administration. As television critic Tom Shales said about the failed Supreme Court nomination of Judge Robert Bork in 1987, "Television may not have cooked 'his goose' but it certainly did some gourmet basting." [8]

Direct and Mediated Transmission

News about the government reaches the public either directly or indirectly. Direct transmission allows government officials to convey their messages with a minimum of media shaping. President Harry S. Truman was the first to use the direct mode by broadcasting his entire State of the Union message in 1947 to a nationwide audience. In January 1961 President John F. Kennedy further expanded direct coverage by allowing news conferences to be broadcast live. Among public officials, presidents enjoy the greatest opportunities for uncontrolled access to the American people, although C-SPAN's gavel-to-gavel coverage of Congress has leveled the playing field. Other political leaders competing with the president for power and public support have tried for matching privileges with only moderate success.

Of course, even live television and radio broadcasts by the president are not totally devoid of media influence, because camera angles and other photographic techniques used by journalists slant all presentations somewhat. For example, in 1985, when President Reagan visited a military cemetery in Bitburg, Germany, to honor the war dead, CBS filmed the president against the backdrop of Nazi storm troopers' graves to suggest that the ceremony could be interpreted as support for the Hitler movement. The White House, disclaiming any intent to honor fallen Nazi soldiers, tried but failed to persuade the network to film the scene from a different angle.[9]

Instant commentary following presidential speeches has often blunted their impact. This happens, for example, when the media invite the opposing party to present an instant rebuttal to the speech. Likewise, print news stories describing a presidential news conference, even when such stories are followed by the full transcript, involve shaping by media personnel. However, compared with the great leeway that newspeople usually have in choosing and interpreting information about the presidency, post-speech rebuttals constitute a very minor type of control.

Indirect or mediated transmission—the shaping of news presentations by media personnel—lies at the heart of the tensions between media and government because it bestows more power on the media than governments like. Mediated transmission permits journalists to pick and choose among the facts given to them. They routinely chop lengthy official statements into brief one- or two-sentence quotations and then weave them into an account often supplemented with information from hostile sources. Television sound bites featuring a speaking president averaged forty-five seconds in earlier decades; now they average less than nine seconds and rarely exceed twenty seconds. Thus media present the story in a framework of their choosing.

By judiciously selecting spokespeople for specific points of view, and by structuring questions to elicit answers that fit neatly into desired scripts, newspeople can counteract politicians' progovernment spin and control the evaluations of public officials and policies. These appraisals are predominantly negative, especially when the popularity of an administration is low or falling. Newspeople are often accused of using mediated coverage deliberately, or at the least carelessly, to hurt public officials and their policies. During the six months following the formal end of the Iraq War, three out of four comments on the major networks about Bush's policies came from Democratic sources (Table 9-4). Predictably, Democratic sources were highly negative (97 percent) compared to Republican sources (18 percent). CBS was the leader in negative news (77 percent), ABC was in the middle (67 percent), and NBC trailed (62 percent).[10]

Media personnel deny that they go out of their way to show incumbent administrations in a bad light. They contend that they see themselves as guardians of the public interest who help to make government more honest and efficient. The politicians who produced the problematic situation, not the newspeople who reported it, should be blamed, they argue. They point out that news focuses on nonroutine aspects of political life and therefore deals with isolated instances of socially undesirable behavior that, unfortunately, reflect badly on government. Journalists periodically

TABLE 9-4   How Network Sources Rated President Bush's Policies,
May 1–October 31, 2003

	Positive	Negative	Number of evaluations
Foreign policies			
International terrorism	20%	80%	134
Defense (general)	21	79	511
Iraq	23	77	969
9/11 attacks	28	72	120
Homeland security	36	64	97
Average score	26	74	
Domestic policies[a]			
Select economic issues	16	84	80
Taxes	25	75	60
Environment	28	72	21
Health policy	44	56	21
Average score	28	72	

SOURCE: "George Bush's Postwar Blues,"Media Monitor 17, no. 4 (November/December 2003): 4.

NOTE: Figures combine ABC, CBS, and NBC nightly news broadcasts. There were a total of 1,876 stories—659 from ABC, 632 from CBS, and 585 from NBC. There were 2,013 evaluations.

[a]Media evaluations focused on foreign policy issues. Evaluations of domestic policies were scant.

generate major political upheavals by blowing up minor sins as if they were major transgressions, particularly if politically influential opponents voice attacks. For example, during the 2004 presidential primaries, Howard Dean's campaign was badly hurt by reports that he uttered an unseemly scream when told about his disappointing third place finish in the Iowa caucus.

Managing a Rocky Marriage

All presidents profess to believe in a free press and to run an open government, but they rapidly develop a distaste for many of the reports about their administration. As President Kennedy told a news conference midway into his term in 1962, "[I am] reading more and enjoying it less." [11]

Presidents' displeasure with media coverage is readily understandable. Media coverage not only embarrasses them regularly and deprives them, to varying degrees, of control over the definition of political situations, it also forces them to talk in sound bites that reporters find attractive and, in the process, to put themselves on record in ways that may narrow their options for future action. Media disclosures of secret activities, such as an impending military intervention or a planned tax hike, may actually force the president's hand. Bargaining advantages may be lost through premature publication of news; trivia, conflict, and public wrongdoing may receive undue emphasis.

In the rocky marriage between the press and the president, open battles are comparatively rare. Despite traded accusations that the government manipulates and lies and that the press distorts and entraps, each side is fully aware that it depends on the other. If presidents refuse to talk to reporters, as happened periodically during the Nixon and Reagan years, or if they instruct their staffs, major departments, and agencies to refuse interviews, important stories cannot be covered firsthand. Alienating the prime news maker and source of government news is a major catastrophe for any news organization. Reporters' eagerness to get the news firsthand gives the president a tremendous advantage in influencing the substance and spin of news stories.

The media, for their part, can withhold publicity that the president needs or damage his administration through unwanted publicity. Journalists can stress the positive or accent the negative. They can give instantaneous live coverage or delay broadcasts until a time of their choosing. In 1993, for example, NBC broadcast only thirty minutes of President Clinton's first evening news conference. ABC and CBS, despite presidential pleading, refused to carry the event. All of the networks refused to broadcast the senior President Bush's last primetime news conference in June 1992.[12] In 2000 and 2004 network news slighted the presidential election debates as well as the nominating conventions.

The upshot of interdependence between the press and the government is a good deal of fraternizing and cronyism between these two "enemies," often to the dismay of those who favor an adversarial relationship. Each side works hard to cultivate the other's friendship. They often collaborate in examining political issues and problems. Such coziness may sap journalists' zeal to investigate government's misdeeds. Indeed, charges of collusion arise particularly when media suppress news at the request of government departments or the White House. Many of these instances have concerned national security. In 1980, for example, the press delayed publicizing plans for a U.S. invasion of Iran to rescue U.S. hostages. In 1987 it suppressed technical data about eavesdropping devices designed to intercept information from Soviet marine cables. Similarly, television executives agreed in 2001 not to broadcast messages from Al Qaeda leader Osama bin Laden.[13]

The relationship between the media and the chief executive generally goes through three distinct phases.[14] There is an initial honeymoon period, a time of cooperation when the media convey the president's messages about organization of the new administration, appointments of new officials, and plans and proposals for new policies. At this early stage few policies and proposals have been implemented, minimizing opportunities for adverse criticism. Presidents and their advisers, eager to get their stories across, make themselves readily available to the media and supply them with ample information.

Once the administration embarks on controversial programs, it becomes vulnerable to criticism of its record and the honeymoon ends. That is happening earlier and more abruptly now than in the past.[15] For example, President George W. Bush received far less favorable attention from newspapers, news magazines, and network television news during his early days in office than either Clinton or the elder Bush had garnered.[16] The White House may retaliate by withholding news, by restricting presidential contacts with the press, and by increasing public relations activities. If the rifts between media and the executive branch become exceptionally wide, there may be a third phase in which both sides retreat from their mutually hostile behavior to take a more moderate stance. This phase frequently coincides with a reelection campaign, when newspeople try harder to provide impartial coverage, and presidents are more eager to keep newspeople happy. The president may also arrange numerous trips abroad so that the focus of coverage switches to diplomatic ventures. That ordinarily is the area least likely to generate hostile coverage. There is political magic in scenes of U.S. presidents meeting with world leaders in foreign capitals. While presidents are abroad, domestic criticism abates because the president's foes do not want to be accused of undermining U.S. foreign policy.

The ability of administrations to get along with the media differs considerably. The president's interpersonal skills as well as the nature of the political problems faced by an administration account for much of the variation. In recent history the Kennedy and Reagan administrations were particularly good at press relations, whereas the Nixon administration was especially bad. Nixon's Watergate problems might never have developed into a major scandal had he been able to charm the press. The Clinton years featured a mercurial relationship, fluctuating between passionate love and passionate hate on both sides.

The relationship between the chief executive and the media varies not only from one administration to the next but also from one part of the country to another. Frictions are greatest between the White House and the Washington, D.C., press corps because they are most interdependent. Familiarity breeds a certain amount of contempt and dependence breeds resentment. The northeastern seaboard press has a reputation of being more caustic than the press in the rest of the country. This is why recent presidents

British prime minister Tony Blair and President Bush hold a press conference in the White House, June 7, 2005. Mrs. Bush and Secretary of State Condoleeza Rice are seated in the front row.

have often scheduled news conferences in other parts of the country and made major policy announcements away from the East Coast. They have also made concerted efforts to schedule media interviews for cabinet members and other high-level officials away from the Washington, D.C., area.

Presidents Ronald Reagan, George Bush, Bill Clinton, and George W. Bush all arranged to visit small communities throughout the country to bask in the adulation of local audiences and local media for the benefit of nationwide television viewers. Taking advantage of new satellite technology, presidents can now be interviewed from the White House television studio by local television and radio stations throughout the country. Presidents can tailor unedited, unfiltered messages for specific demographic groups and transmit them to local anchors in selected locations pleading for their support. All recent presidents have broadcast weekly radio addresses, hoping to bring their unfiltered messages to the public.

Presidential Communication Strategies

Besides circumventing the eastern press, presidents use an array of strategies to control the substance and tenor of news. Four approaches are particularly common. First and most important, presidents try to win reporters' favor. This is not difficult because presidents are constantly surrounded by people who must have fresh news to earn their pay. Second, presidents try to shape the flow of news to make good publicity more likely and bad publicity less likely. Third, they pace and arrange their work schedules to produce opportunities for favorable media coverage. Fourth—and this is a recent trend—they try to evade news media gatekeeping hurdles by publishing their news on government Web sites or through video news releases. We will discuss each of these strategies in turn.

Winning Favor. To woo reporters, presidents offer good story material as well as occasional scoops that may bring distinction to individual reporters. They cultivate reporters' friendships by being accessible, treating them with respect, and arranging for their creature comforts. To keep reporters in line, presidents may threaten them directly or obliquely with a withdrawal of privileges. Privileges include accommodations on the presidential plane, special interviews, or answers to their questions during news conferences. Presidents may also publicly condemn individual reporters or their organizations for undesirable reporting.

Shaping the News Flow. Presidents try to guide the flow of news by the thrust of their commentary and by controlling contacts with the press. For example, when publicity about illegal transfers of arms to Nicaragua had damaged President Reagan's administration, he managed to divert media attention from the affair by sponsoring a popular Economic Bill of Rights, which included a balanced budget and line-item veto. Simultaneously, his office distributed a monthly economic bulletin nationwide. It contained camera-ready copy praising the economic successes of the Reagan administration, including his records on job growth and lowered inflation. When President Clinton retaliated with extraordinary speed to a terrorist bombing of U.S. embassies in Kenya and Tanzania in 1998, observers wondered about the link to Clinton's domestic troubles caused by his affair with a young White House intern. Was the retaliatory strike a diversionary move to shift attention away from the scandal?

To avoid questions about embarrassing failures, presidents periodically restrict their contacts with the media to picture sessions. Presidents also may space out news releases to create a steady, manageable flow of news. If they want emphasis on a particular story, they may withhold competing news that breaks simultaneously. Sometimes administrations release a barrage of news or even create news to distract attention from sensitive developments. Administrations have averted criticism by the eastern press by withholding advance copies of speeches or by timing them late enough in the evening to preclude adequate coverage in the morning papers.

To control news flow and assure that the administration speaks with a single voice, presidents may prohibit their staffs, on pain of dismissal, from publicly disagreeing with their policies. In addition, they may require administrative departments to clear interviews through the White House to avoid conflicting pronouncements on public policies. Some recent administrations have insisted that officials who are privy to sensitive information receive approval of their superiors prior to granting interviews to the press.

Orchestrating Coverage. The many available tactics for generating favorable publicity include creating newsworthy events, heightening suspense through news blackouts before major pronouncements, and staging public ceremonies as media spectacles at times when there are few competing events. Political successes may be coupled with political failures in hopes that publicity for the success will draw attention away from the failure. The Carter administration reportedly timed its announcement of the opening of formal relations with the People's Republic of China late in 1978 to buffer negative publicity in case its attempts to clinch a peace settlement between Israel and Egypt failed. In the same way, the Reagan administration hoped that pictures of the U.S. Marines' successful military takeover of the tiny island of Grenada would counteract the images of the 1983 bombing of U.S. marines in Lebanon.

Occasionally administrations may even intentionally deceive the press in hopes that false messages will accomplish important political goals. For instance, in 1961 the Kennedy administration told Miami reporters that 5,000 U.S. troops had invaded Cuba's Bay of Pigs. This news was intended to encourage Cubans to rise up in support of a large invasion force. In truth, only one thousand troops had been sent. When reporters discovered that the administration had used them to spread false stories, they were furious. The credibility of the executive branch plummeted. In 2003 the Bush administration was accused of duping Congress, the press, and the public by falsely claiming that war against Iraq was necessary because that country was poised to unleash weapons of mass destruction. At the time, the press reported these claims as reliable news. No such weapons were ever discovered despite extensive searches. However, congressional investigations failed to find solid proof that the Bush administration had deliberately distorted the facts.

Presidential Web Sites. The White House maintains its own Web site at www.whitehouse.gov. It is an electronic portal to the president, his family, the official mansion, and to messages prepared for public display by the incumbent and the presidential staff. It is also the gateway to www.firstgov.gov, which contains electronic links to the entire national government. From there visitors have access to the Web sites of all three branches of the national government as well as state government, local government, and international sites. Visitors can search for specific agencies or for such policy areas as consumer services, education, or veterans' benefits. Many sites are interactive so that people can ask questions as well as request forms that can then be submitted electronically. The main sites, their links, and links to the links form a fantastic treasure trove of information.

What sorts of information do these links contain? They contain only what the site owners—the government and its agencies—wish to include in the manner in which they wish to frame it. Site owners can add or delete information at will, depending on their appraisals of the political scene. Aside from that important shared characteristic, sites vary tremendously in the completeness and timeliness of their offerings. Some are little more than public relations portals, while others genuinely try to meet citizens' needs and to be transparent about their activities.

A great deal of research is still needed to assess how useful these sites are for the president's communication within the executive branch, with Congress, with interest groups, and with the citizenry at large. By and large we do not know who visits and for what purposes. We do know that these sites are widely used, and this suggests that they may be quite influential. We also know that service-oriented sites have more visits than policy-oriented sites.[17] Finally, we know that the executive branch considers these sites important enough to allocate ample resources to them. This translates into attractive, user-friendly sites that present the government's story in words and pictures that reflect official, rather than journalistic, preferences.

Institutional Settings

Relations between the president and the media are so important and so complex that they require involvement by established as well as specially created institutions.

On the President's Side. A president can shape the news indirectly through appointments to the Federal Communications Commission (FCC) and other public agencies concerned with media regulations and through informal contacts with personnel in these agencies. Presidents can control financial lifelines through the Office of Management and Budget (OMB), which screens the budgetary requests of all federal agencies, including those dealing with the mass media. An administration can also wield control through the Justice Department. For instance, the Antitrust Division can challenge the FCC's approval of mergers and can carry appeals through the courts and ultimately to the Supreme Court.

Presidents involve themselves directly in media policy making through White House organizations, study commissions, and task forces. In 1970

President Nixon created the Office of Telecommunications Policy—the first permanent agency within the White House to plan communications policy. Since then every president has tinkered with institutional arrangements. Changes have generally revolved around four standing offices: the Press Office, the Office of Communication, the Office of Media Affairs, and Speechwriting—to use the post-Clinton nomenclature.[18] Staffs for these offices usually total fewer than fifty people, but communications experts in other offices in the executive branch perform much additional work.

The Press Office supplies Washington, D.C.–based reporters with news about the White House. By custom, the press secretary meets almost daily with the White House press corps to make announcements and take questions. These briefings supply reporters with the president's interpretation of events, which reporters then cast into perspectives of their own choice.

The Office of Communications is concerned with long-range public relations management of the presidency. In consultation with the president, it determines the images that the administration needs to convey to gain and retain the approval of important constituencies in the public and private sectors and to win support for desired policies. The office also coordinates the public relations activities of executive branch departments and agencies to make sure that the chorus of public voices is harmonious. If the president's approval ratings plunge, the communications director is likely to get the ax. As George Stephanopoulos, a victim of the communications wars during the Clinton administration, explained, "By definition, if the President isn't doing well, it's a communication problem. That's always going to be a natural place to make a change."[19]

The Office of Media Affairs serves the regional and local press and various ethnic news organizations in Washington, D.C. It also handles publicity during the president's travels. The office lets the president know how well his messages are faring with audiences. It also handles the president's Web site.

Officials in the Speechwriting Office keep busy by composing remarks for some 650 annual public events featuring the president.[20] Following the 2001 terrorist strike on the United States, President Bush added a unit to counter hostile messages emanating from the Middle East. The unit, called Coalition Information Centers, was based in London so that its operations matched Middle Eastern news cycles more readily. The president established a more broadly oriented Office of Global Communication in January 2003. Unlike the other offices, it is incorporated directly into the White House Office, indicating that its operations are high priorities for the president.

Modern public relations activities involve many different techniques. "Focus groups and polling data are used to fashion presidential messages;

sound-bites are written into the public pronouncements of the president and his underlings to articulate those messages; public appearances are choreographed so that the messages are reinforced by visual images." [21] To spread messages throughout the country, the administration sends cabinet officers and others on speaking tours and arranges satellite interviews in local markets.

It is, of course, essential for presidents to "sell" their policies by soliciting wide support for them and by presenting a united front within their administration. However, in the process democracy may be imperiled because "Style is substituted for substance. Complicated issues are transformed into simple slogans and slick sound-bites . . . timid, self-interested policy makers . . . shy away from responsibility for their actions and delude themselves and their constituents with their own symbolic spectacle." [22] Ethical issues arise when the president or executive agencies commission propaganda messages from public relations firms and then distribute them as official news releases. In 2005, for example, Congress's Government Accountability Office (GAO) criticized the Office of National Drug Control Policy for distributing what it called "covert propaganda." [23] The GAO had admonished the Department of Education earlier for paying $240,000 to a syndicated columnist for promoting the president's education reforms.[24]

On the Media's Side.   Close to 8,000 print and broadcast reporters are accredited to attend White House press operations, though only a small fraction—generally fewer than fifty—actually attend press conferences. Given the small quarters in which presidential news conferences are held, attendees are usually selected to represent a balanced pool of news venues, including wire services. Many reporters who serve routinely in the White House press corps have considerable experience and notable reputations. As a group, they are older and better educated and trained than the average U.S. journalist.[25] The *New York Times, Washington Post, Los Angeles Times, Chicago Tribune, Philadelphia Inquirer,* and other major newspapers have full-time reporters assigned exclusively to the president. So do a number of newspaper chains, such as the Scripps-Howard papers, the Hearst press, and the Newhouse papers. Smaller papers may send their Washington, D.C., bureau chiefs to the White House whenever there is news of special interest to their region.

Each of the major broadcast networks, as well as CNN, has several reporters at the White House on a regular basis; smaller networks have one. C-SPAN provides twenty-four-hour White House cable coverage as well as gavel-to-gavel coverage of the House of Representatives. The White House is also covered by several all-news cable services, Internet news operations, weekly news magazines, and periodicals, as well as photographers and their supporting staffs. Hard economic times in the early 1990s forced cut-backs in personnel and increased pooling of resources among media organizations. Even major events, such as presidential trips abroad or the national party conventions, are now covered by a smaller corps of journalists, and many reporters now work for several major news organizations simultaneously.

Most of the country's dailies and television and radio stations do not have a regular Washington, D.C., correspondent or part-time "stringer" to cover the White House. Inexpensive satellite time, however, has lowered news transmission costs and boosted the number of stations that can afford direct coverage of the Washington scene, often through the prism of local interests.

Forms of Contact

Press Releases and News Briefings.   The release of news by chief executives or their aides takes several routinized forms. Most of these represent a concerted effort to control the news output. The most common is the press release, a story prepared by government officials and handed to members of the press, usually without an opportunity for questions. In a news briefing, reporters have an opportunity to ask the press secretary about the news releases. But because executive officials furnish the news for the briefing, they control the substance and tone of the discussion.

News Conferences.   Although a news conference may appear to be a wide-open question period, the official being questioned usually tries to control it tightly. Seemingly spontaneous answers usually have been carefully prepared by experts on the executive's staff and rehearsed during extensive briefings. Theodore Roosevelt was the first president to summon reporters to the White House regularly. Before Kennedy's presidency, press conferences were not covered live, permitting the White House to make corrections before conference records were published. Kennedy, who was a gifted extemporaneous speaker, stripped away this cloak of protection by allowing live filming of the conference. At the time, press critics called it "goofy" and likened it to "making love in Carnegie Hall." [26]

The live format remains controversial because it leads to posturing by the president as well as by members of the press. It also causes embarrassment for presidents who misspeak or suffer memory lapses. Starting with the senior George Bush, presidents have lowered the risk by mostly holding informal news conferences on short notice, which makes it difficult to broadcast the live event without costly interruptions of scheduled programs. The multiplication of media channels has sharply reduced the potential audience for news conferences because the president must compete with popular entertainment shows. Presidents have therefore held fewer regular news conferences except for brief sessions when they face the press along with a visiting dignitary.

News conferences, as well as press briefings by press secretaries, often begin with a lengthy statement that is designed to set the tone as well as shrink the question period, which can be risky for the president. Presidents can often control the subject and tone of a news conference by recognizing friendly reporters for questions and avoiding follow-up questions. But no president has been able to squelch embarrassing questions entirely or to deny reporters the chance to use their questions as opportunities to express their own views about controversial issues.[27] Reporters revel in acting like prosecutors trying to extract a confession of major crimes from a hapless subject. By posing leading questions, they try to force the president or press secretary to comment on matters that these officials may not wish to discuss. The questions listed in Box 9-1 give a taste of the sorts of interrogations that presidents face.

Backgrounders. Some news conferences are off-the-record "backgrounders." High officials call such events to give newspeople important background information that they are honor bound to keep entirely secret or to publish only without revealing the source. Forms of vague attribution are usually permitted, such as "government sources say," "it has been reported by reliable sources," or even more specifically, "the White House discloses" or the "Defense Department indicates."

Government officials like backgrounders because they are a relatively safe way to "test the waters." They permit officials to bring a variety of policy ideas before their colleagues and the public without openly identifying with them. Unlike government officials, reporters are ambivalent about backgrounders. They like having access to news that might otherwise be unavailable, but they dislike being prevented from publishing all aspects of the story or from identifying the source of the information so that the story can be placed in its proper perspective.

In addition to formal encounters, reporters and the president or White House staff meet informally in work or social settings. The most probing stories about White House activities often come from reporters who are not ordinarily assigned to cover the president. The regulars would be too vulnerable to retaliation by the White House if they disclosed highly embarrassing information. Top government officials, and occasionally the president, may also agree to be interviewed on programs such as *Nightline, Good Morning America*, the *Today Show, Meet the Press*, or *Face the Nation*. Questioning on these shows can resemble a no-holds-barred cross-examination. Executive branch officials participate in this ordeal because these programs provide excellent opportunities to present the administration's

BOX 9-1
Quizzing the President

On March 16, 2005, President George W. Bush held a routine press conference at the White House. As is common, the press largely ignored his brief opening statement about Social Security that was intended to guide reporters' to an issue that the president wanted to highlight. Here, without follow-ups, are the reporters' often distressing questions from first to last.

1. Mr. President, the U.S.–led coalition in Iraq once had thirty-eight countries contributing troops. And now that number has fallen to twenty-four. And yesterday, Italy said that it was going to start pulling out some forces in September. How can you keep the coalition from crumbling? And is it time to think about a timetable for pulling out some U.S. troops, given that the Iraqi parliament was seated today, and you're making progress in training some forces?

2. . . . . The Iranians have dismissed the European incentive as insignificant. Should more incentives be offered? How long do they have until you take their case to the Security Council?

3. Mr. President, you say you're making progress in the Social Security debate. Yet private accounts, as the centerpiece of that plan, something you first campaigned on five years ago and laid before the American people, remains, according to every measure we have, poll after poll, unpopular with a majority of Americans. So the question is, do you feel that this is a point in the debate where it's incumbent upon you, and nobody else, to lay out a plan to the American people for how you actually keep Social Security solvent for the long-term?

4. Mr. President, the price of oil is at record levels, well above the $28 price point that you would prefer. The price of gasoline is projected to go above $2.50 this spring. How concerned are you that this could start to affect the American economy? Is there more you could do to talk with oil-producing nations to get the price at the wellhead down? And is there more you could do, since part of the problem is refining capacity, to encourage oil companies who haven't built a new refinery in twenty years to start increasing their capacity domestically?

5. Mr. President, can you explain why you've approved of and expanded the practice of what's called rendition, of transferring individuals out of U.S. custody to countries where human rights groups and your own State Department say torture is common for people under custody?

6. Paul Wolfowitz, who was the—a chief architect of one of the most unpopular wars in our history is your choice to be the president of the World Bank. What kind of signal does that send to the rest of the world?

7. Tom DeLay, the House majority leader, has been admonished three times by the House Ethics Committee, is currently embroiled in several con-

troversies involving a lobbyist who happened to be a pretty big fund raiser for your two campaigns. Do you have the full confidence in Tom DeLay, his tactics, and his leadership role in the Republican Party?

8. Mr. President, you have spoken out about the need for owners, coaches, and players in all sports to stop steroid use. And you've also voiced reservations about government getting too involved in that. And as you know, Congress is issuing subpoenas to Major League Baseball players during spring training. Do you think that that's an abuse of power, or is it appropriate, in your view?

9. Mr. President, your judicial nominees continue to run into problems on Capitol Hill. Republicans are discussing the possibility of ending the current Democratic filibuster practice against it. And Democrats yesterday, led by Minority Leader Harry Reid, went to the steps of the Capitol to say that if that goes forward, they will halt your agenda straight out. What does that say about your judicial nominees, the tone on Capitol Hill? And which is more important, judges or your agenda?

10. Sir, on Social Security, what is the time line that you want to see for action by Congress on a bill? When do you start to get worried about not getting something done this year? And also, if I can add, would you be willing to drop personal accounts in order to get a bill?

11. Mr. President, your administration recently called on the Texas courts to review some death—some death penalty cases down there. And during your State of the Union you talked about the importance of DNA evidence, and you talked about the possibility that maybe there were inequities in the system and the lawyers that represent death row inmates. I'm wondering if this represents a change in your feelings about the death penalty since you were governor of Texas. And if there are the possibilities—the possibilities exist of problems, why not call on—for a moratorium?

12. Mr. President, are you trying to send a message to the IRA by not inviting Gerry Adams and the other Northern Ireland politicians tomorrow?

13. Mr. President, yesterday you said that Hezbollah could prove it is not a terrorist organization by laying down arms and supporting peace. How willing and flexible, and under what conditions are you able to, as you promote democracy in the Middle East, encourage parties like Hezbollah to discontinue the use of terrorism as a tactic?

14. President Bush, a court ruling in California this week has revived debate over same-sex marriage. You support a constitutional amendment to ban such marriages. But it's not something you talk about nearly as often as Social Security and many other issues. Will you put some muscle behind that effort this year? Or is it something you'd prefer not to deal with?

15. Mr. President, you faced a lot of skepticism in the run-up to the Iraq war, and a lot of criticism for miscalculating some of the challenges of postwar

(Box continues, next page)

Iraq. Now that the Iraq elections seem to be triggering signs of democratization throughout the broader Middle East, do you feel any sense of vindication?

16. Mr. President, do you also think it will lead to America's reputation being restored? Earlier this week you brought Karen Hughes back at ambassador rank to address the question of antipathy to America around the world—particularly the Muslim world. What does that entail?

17. Mr. President, earlier this year, you told us you wanted your administration to cease and desist on payments to journalists to promote your agenda. You cited the need for ethical concerns and the need for a bright line between the press and the government. Your administration continues to make the use of video news releases, which is prepackaged news stories sent to television stations, fully aware that some—or many of these stations will air them without any disclaimer that they are produced by the government. The comptroller general of the United States, this week, said that raises ethical questions. Does it raise ethical questions about the use of government money to produce stories about the government that wind up being aired with no disclosure that they were produced by the government?

18. Mr. President, do you think there should be regime change in Iran? And if so, what are you prepared to do to see that happen?

19. . . . Do you believe that nativity scenes and the Ten Commandments should continue to be displayed on federal property or in schools?

20. Mr. President, back to Social Security, if I may. You said right at the top today that you urged members of Congress to go out and talk about the problem with their constituents. . . . Aren't you asking them to do something that you really haven't been willing to do yet?

21. Mr. President, you talked earlier about going to the Security Council if Iran turns down this EU 3 deal. Iran says they're not making nuclear weapons. Are we looking at a potential military confrontation with Iran?

SOURCE: President Bush's news conference, March 16, 2005, www.whitehouse.gov/news/releases/2005/03/20050316-3htm.

position to an interested nationwide audience. Besides, if questioning becomes excessively harsh, the audience often feels sorry for the targets and sides with them.

Leaks. An even less formal release of news occurs through "leaks," the surreptitious release of information by high- and low-level government sources who wish to remain anonymous or who do not want to release the information formally. Many leaks are sanctioned at the highest levels. But some officials may also leak information that they are not authorized to release. Sometimes low-level officials leak information to gain attention from top officials.

Leaks are mixed blessings. They can destroy the timing of negotiations, alienate the parties whose secrets have been betrayed, and cause great harm by disclosing politically sensitive matters. They also may bring important suppressed issues to needed public attention, serve as trial balloons, and permit government officials to release information anonymously. Although presidents frequently leak confidential stories, they passionately hate news leaked by others. As long as the source remains hidden, personal confrontation and punishment are impossible. All recent presidents have therefore used federal investigative agencies, such as the Federal Bureau of Investigation and the Central Intelligence Agency, to find the sources of news leaks.

A typical leak occurred in 1991 during the Senate confirmation battle over the nomination of Judge Clarence Thomas to the U.S. Supreme Court. Confidential allegations about sexual harassment by the nominee that had been presented to the Senate Judiciary Committee were leaked to the press. The leaks led to a second round of lengthy, acrimonious hearings before Thomas was confirmed. The episode did serious harm to Judge Thomas's reputation and undermined faith in the integrity of the confirmation process.

We must weigh the harm that leaks cause against their benefits. In a system in which the executive maintains tight control over the formal channels of news, leaks provide a valuable counterbalance. Take President Reagan's controversial budget proposals in 1983. Administration insiders, eager to bring their concerns to the public and to Congress, resorted to almost daily leaks of economic appraisals that contradicted the president's pronouncements. An irate Reagan proclaimed, "I've had it up to my keister with these leaks," but he modified his budget plans nonetheless.[28]

The Media and Congress

According to political folklore, the television age has permanently altered the balance of political power. The presidency basks in the limelight of publicity at all times while Congress waits in the shadows, making the president dominant and the legislature inferior. As Sen. J. William Fulbright, D-Ark., told Congress in 1970, "Television has done as much to expand the powers of the president as would a constitutional amendment formally abolishing the co-equality of the three branches of government."[29]

Image versus Reality

If one probes beyond the impression that Congress is a media step-child, the situation appears less clear. When coverage of areas of legislative concerns is added to coverage that mentions Congress explicitly, Congress and the presidency receive roughly the same amount of national news attention. Moreover, the bulk of coverage of Congress comes through stories about individual members that are published in their home states. Although local coverage does not generally attract national attention, it is politically crucial for each member.

Table 9-5 presents a comparison of ten issues that emerged in television coverage of the president and Congress from July 2003 to June 2004. The scores represent a combination of offerings by ABC, CBS, and NBC. Besides showing the number of stories in each category and the length of broadcast time devoted to them, the table also records whether the story appeared in the first, second, or last ten-minute segment of the broadcast. Four issues were covered prominently for both institutions and six issues were unique to each. The three networks chose almost identical types of issues for stories about the presidency and Congress and placed them in similar order within broadcast segments. However, the networks differed in the total amounts of time allotted to particular stories. Stories about Congress generally were fewer, shorter, and less prominently placed than news linked to the presidency, confirming that "435 members of the House and 100 members of the Senate compete for the crumbs of network time left after the president has got his share." [30]

Why does Congress fare worse than the presidency? There are several reasons. Most important, the presidency makes a better media target because it is a single-headed institution readily personified and filmed in the visible person of the chief executive. This gives media audiences a familiar, casily dramatized focus of attention. A president is like a superstar surrounded by a cast of supporting actors. Even stories originating from congressional sources frequently feature the president as the main actor. As the personification of the nation, the president can usually command national television or radio time, often at primetime and simultaneously on all major networks. In the past the press was more likely to refuse than grant Congress members' requests for coverage. That has changed dramatically, starting with the Clinton presidency, most likely because respect for the president as a person has declined in the wake of numerous well-publicized scandals. Still, the president retains the lead in coverage, but the gap is narrowing. [31]

There are many reasons why Congress is unable to attract as much media coverage as the president. Unlike the chief executive, Congress is a many-headed Hydra with no single widely familiar personal focus. It conducts its activities simultaneously in more than one hundred locations on Capitol Hill. No individual member can command nationwide media coverage at will because no one is regarded as a spokesperson for Congress as

TABLE 9-5　Top Ten Issues on Network Evening News about the President and Congress, July 2003–June 2004

Issue	Story rank (in percentages)[a]			Time	Number of stories	Percentage of total stories
	1	2	3			
President						
U.S. elections	69	20	10	6:07	124	23.1
Iraq War	90	7	3	7:40	87	16.2
Economy	81	19	0	1:11	31	5.7
Middle East policy	71	21	7	0:22	14	2.6
CIA leak	64	14	21	0:33	14	2.6
September 11 Commission hearing	92	8	0	0:40	13	2.4
Environment	60	20	20	0:12	10	1.8
President's military record	78	22	0	0:27	9	1.6
Judicial appointments	50	50	0	0:09	8	1.4
Abortion	71	29	0	0:09	7	1.3
Average (Totals)	73	22	6	(17:30)	(317)	(58.7)
Congress						
Iraq War	97	3	0	4:37	72	16.9
Health care	33	49	17	2:43	63	14.7
September 11 Commission hearing	86	11	3	1:30	28	6.6
Economy	68	28	4	1:00	25	5.8
U.S. elections	36	36	28	0:39	14	3.3
Energy legislation	45	36	18	0:24	11	2.6
Gas prices	54	45	0	0:32	11	2.6
Airline security	70	0	30	0:26	10	2.3
Abortion	56	44	0	0:19	9	2.1
Gun legislation	33	56	11	0:17	9	2.1
Average (Totals)	58	31	11	(12:27)	(252)	(59.0)

SOURCE: Compiled by the author from the Vanderbilt Television News Archives

NOTE: *N* for president = 317 for top ten and 537 for all stories; *N* for Congress = 252 for top ten and 426 for all stories. The numbers are combined scores for ABC, CBS, and NBC early evening newscasts. Stories are rank ordered by time, in hours and minutes. Some percentages have been rounded.

[a] Position of story in first, second, or third ten-minute segment of broadcast.

an institution. Consequently, most stories about Congress deal with individual members or legislative activity on specific issues rather than with the body as a whole.

Another reason why stories about Congress escape wide attention lies in the nature of its work. The legislative branch drafts laws, makes compromises among conflicting interests, forges shifting coalitions, and works out legal details. Stories about the executive branch that describe *what* is actually done are far more memorable than reports about *how* the laborious process of hammering out legislation works. Besides, the most interesting aspect of the legislative process, the shaping of broad guidelines for policy, is usually reported by the media as part of the work of the executive branch.

Congressional coverage is frequently useless for the public because it tends to be sparse in the early stages of the legislative process, when there is still time for citizens to influence a bill. Coverage usually focuses on final action after the shape of the legislation is already firm.[32] Citizens then learn what the new policies are without being exposed to the pros and cons and the political interplay that led to the ultimate compromise.[33] Live television coverage of congressional sessions is changing this tradition; it is making Congress more vulnerable to pressures from constituents and interest groups.

Fearing that legislative floor sessions would present an unedifying, boring spectacle, Congress resisted live radio and television coverage of most sessions until the late 1970s. Before 1979 only selected committee hearings were televised, primarily those involving spicy topics such as labor racketeering, communists in government, or high-level corruption. In 1979 the House of Representatives lifted the prohibition on televising its floor sessions. The action was prompted in part by the desire to counterbalance the political advantages the executive branch was reaping from heavy media attention. The rules for coverage by the House-run closed circuit system are strict: only the member speaking may be filmed, not the listeners, unless the speaker of the House decrees otherwise. This stipulation bars the public from seeing the typically near-empty House chamber and inattentive members during routine sessions. Commercial, cable, and public television systems have access to House broadcasts but rarely cover them, except for live gavel-to-gavel coverage by C-SPAN. In 1986 the Senate finally followed suit and permitted live coverage of its proceedings. It was prodded by Sen. Robert Byrd, D-W.Va., who was concerned that the Senate was "fast becoming the invisible half of Congress," compared to the White House and the House of Representatives.[34]

Unlike the presidency, Congress has rarely become a first-rate "show" for the U.S. public, although its media coverage is vital for inside-the-Beltway Washington politics. Representatives themselves are among the most avid watchers of House coverage because the television cameras permit them to keep up with floor action and issues reported by committees other than their own. Members of Congress try to use their appearances to create favorable images for themselves and their pet political projects among congressional and executive branch constituencies and the elite media. Some members claim that recent sharp increases in the time spent to pass legislation are largely due to television coverage. More members want to be heard, and they are likely to take more extreme positions because the media tend to focus on such confrontations.[35] Broadcasting may make it more difficult for congressional leaders to muffle dissident members to reach legislative compromises once representatives have publicly committed themselves to definite positions. However, there is little solid proof thus far that television coverage has harmed consensus-building in the chamber, or that the added publicity is making incumbents even more unbeatable at the polls than they are now.

Congress on the Web

Congress entered the Internet scene in earnest in 1995 with a formal House Web site that features all texts of bills, resolutions, and amendments introduced on the House floor along with brief, nontechnical descriptions of the contents of these documents.[36] The Web site also provides a minute-by-minute summary of floor action. The actual contents of debates can be monitored on an online version of the *Congressional Record*. The Senate now has a similar Web site. In addition, members of Congress have long had their own Web sites. Besides featuring the member's vital statistics and major accomplishments—but not failures—most sites also link to the Web sites of committees on which the member serves and describe committee actions and the current status of specific bills. This type of ongoing coverage is extremely useful for lobby groups and other Congress-watchers. It has enhanced their ability to air their views at key junctures in the legislative process. The Web site and its links are also a gold mine of information for reporters who want to incorporate detailed current information into their stories. In fact, three out of four Web sites provide "online newsrooms" to cater to the special needs of the press.[37] There also are a few sites, such as the Legislative Information System, which offers research material on legislation, and sites operated by each party and its subdivisions, that are purely for internal use by members of Congress.

E-mail has become the most prolific Internet message system linking Congress with its various publics. But like the multiplying buckets in Paul Dukat's *Sorcerer's Apprentice*, the floodtide of e-mails threatens to overwhelm congressional navigation resources. Given their limited staffs, members of Congress find it impossible to cope promptly and adequately with e-mail from constituents, not to mention e-mailings from outsiders, including spammers, and from computer hackers who generate mail to clog communication arteries. Efficient electronic sorting and automatic response protocols ameliorate the problem but are far from resolving it.

Writing Stories about Congress

Journalists assigned to the congressional beat use normal criteria of newsworthiness and gatekeeping to decide who and what to cover and who and what to ignore. They prefer exciting, novel, or controversial topics that can be made personally relevant to the public and be simply presented over recurrent complex and mundane problems, such as congressional reorganizations or the annual farm bill. Orderly, dispassionate debate usually is passed over in favor of pompous rhetoric and wild accusations that can produce catchy headlines. Heated confrontations are more likely to occur in the more intimate committee hearings than in full sessions. Accordingly, committee hearings attract most extensive coverage, particularly on television.

Because congressional coverage is a regular beat, daily press briefings are conducted by the leaders of each chamber. Major media organizations, such as the *Washington Post* and the *New York Times,* major newspaper chains, such as Gannett, Hearst, and Knight, and the television networks and wire services have full-time reporters covering Congress. Some of these reporters are specialists in various areas of policy or concentrate on news of interest to specific regions, such as the West or South. There are also Washington, D.C., "stringer" bureaus whose reporters serve assorted subscriber news services throughout the country. Specialized news services such as *Congressional Quarterly* and two highly competitive newspapers—*Roll Call* and the *Hill*—cover the congressional beat in detail for particular audiences. Faxed newsletters and several online publications also cover the beat. Among these, Thomas, the Web site of the Library of Congress (named for Thomas Jefferson), is most comprehensive; most congressional Web sites link to it. Thomas (http://thomas.loc.gov/) provides much information that is sparse on the Web sites of individual representatives. For example, it contains information about bill sponsorship and the texts of otherwise unrecorded speeches. In all, more than 7,000 correspondents are accredited to the press galleries in the House and Senate. The ratio of journalists to senators thus is seventy-one to one; for representatives it is sixteen to one.[38]

Congressional press releases and written reports provide news to media sources that lack regular reporters on Capitol Hill. These documents are prepared and distributed via Web sites and by congressional press secretaries because reporters accredited to Congress are unable to attend the many hearings occurring simultaneously. Press releases enable members of Congress to tell their stories in their own words. They often use this opportunity to highlight problem areas, hoping that news media publicity will shame Congress into action.[39] On certain topics, such as tax policy or investigation of executive activities, journalists routinely seek out congressional spokespersons rather than the president. Although all representatives now assign staff to serve the needs of the press, fewer than 10 percent of House members receive weekly coverage on national television. The rest appear rarely or not at all.[40]

Senators generally receive considerably more press coverage than do representatives, even though an equal number of reporters cover both houses. On network television, stories about senators outnumber those about representatives almost seven to one, probably because senators have greater prominence, prestige, and publicity resources; their larger constituencies also make them of interest to a wider audience. In general, high media visibility for senators as well as representatives hinges on serving in important leadership positions and being a congressional veteran. By contrast, sponsoring legislation or service on important committees matters little. Who one is obviously counts more than what one does. In practice, this means that more than half of the congressional membership receives no national television exposure at all. A mere twenty members of the Senate garner the lion's share of attention.[41]

In addition to national coverage, many members of Congress receive regular local coverage through their own news columns or radio or television programs.[42] They usually find their relations with the local media far more congenial than relations with a national press corps, which cares little about the problems of particular congressional districts. Local media depend on senators and representatives for local angles to national stories because local slants make these stories more attractive to the target audiences. Because Washington, D.C.–based senators and representatives are ideal sources, local newspeople are loath to criticize them. The Washington press corps lacks such qualms. During the first year and a half of the 103rd Congress, during the Clinton presidency, 64 percent of all congressional stories broadcast on national news were negative. Senate scores were a bit worse than House scores, whereas the president's press was a shade better than both Houses during this time.[43]

Functions of Media

The functions performed by the national media for Congress and by Congress for the national media parallel press-presidency relations. However, there are major qualitative differences. Neither Congress nor the media need the services of the other as much as the presidency needs the press. The national media can afford to alienate some legislators without losing direct access to congressional news. Similarly, except when the passage of major controversial laws is involved, legislators can ignore national publicity and rely instead on publicity in their own districts. News items about national events and national public opinion are also somewhat less important to most members of Congress than to the president. The home media, rather than national news providers, are particularly important to legislators as sources of news relevant for their own constituents and as channels for transmitting messages to the home district while they are in Washington, D.C.

Publicity is especially important for minority party leaders, who may need the media to pressure an unresponsive majority to consider their concerns. However, most members cannot use "outsider strategies," as publicity efforts by the out-of-power party are called, because Congress members rarely receive enough coverage. Once members achieve visibility, their fame often grows by its own momentum. They become regulars on interview shows, and their opinions are solicited on national issues. For most members, however, media attention carries few benefits and has several drawbacks; for example, elected officials become more visible targets for lobby groups, and their exposure provides ammunition for rival candidates during the next election campaign. For members of Congress who do not need nationwide attention to achieve their legislative goals, favorable media coverage by traditional media in their districts is the key objective. Local newspaper, radio, and television coverage lets their constituents know what they are doing and paves their way for reelection. Many members also communicate through newsletters and individual correspondence sent to selected constituents. Some prepare cable television programs for their district or transmit carefully chosen video excerpts from committee meetings to the media in their home districts. Still others, eager to push their legislative agendas, write op-ed pieces for the local and national media.

A Cautious Relationship

Just as the functions that media perform are similar for the executive and legislative branches, so is the love-hate relationship. But it, too, is less ardent for Congress, even though mutual recriminations are plentiful. Senators and representatives compete with peers for media attention and bemoan the lack of coverage for their pet projects and pronouncements. They complain that reporters treat them like scoundrels conspiring to defraud the public and resent the cross-examinations that reporters love to conduct with an air of infallibility. Legislators charge and can prove that the media emphasize trivia, scandals, internal dissent, and official misconduct, but often ignore congressional consensus and the passage of significant legislation. They blame the media for the declining prestige of Congress. Still, despite ample negative coverage, the media generally treat congressional leaders and Congress with a fair amount of deference and respect. Individual presidents have been more bloodied by adverse publicity than have individual members of the House. As Michael Robinson concluded from a detailed analysis of the impact of media coverage on Congress, the media have fostered a stronger presidency but weaker presidents, and a weaker Congress but more durable representatives.[44]

Journalists, in turn, complain with justification about legislators' efforts to manage the news through their professional publicity staffs. They point to members' lack of candor and grumble about being excluded from many congressional meetings and executive sessions. Broadcasters also resent the strict controls placed on their coverage of congressional sessions. They are barred from taping their own stories and are limited in the subjects they can photograph.

The realization of interdependence smoothes the ruffled feathers. Senators and representatives realize that they need the media for information and for the publicity that is crucial to passing or defeating legislation. They know that the media will discreetly ignore their personal foibles so long as no official wrongdoing is involved. Newspeople, in turn, understand that they need individual legislators for information about congressional activities and as a counterfoil and source of leaks to check the executive branch. Members are valuable for inside comments that can personalize otherwise dull stories. Congress often creates story topics for the media by investigating dramatic ongoing problems like auto or aircraft safety. A congressional inquiry may be the catalyst that turns an everyday event into a newsworthy item. The story then may ride the crest of publicity for quite some time, creating its own fresh and reportable events until it recedes into limbo once more. Newspeople do not want to dry up these sources; nor do media enterprises want to forgo the financial rewards generated by paid campaign commercials.

Congress and Communications Policy

Journalists, particularly those who work in radio and television, appreciate the power Congress has over regulatory legislation. In the past Congress used its power to legislate communications policy sparingly, viewing it as a hornet's nest of political conflict best left alone. The major exception was passage of the Communications Act of 1934 and its 1996 sequel and of supplementary laws dealing with technical innovations and other changes in the mass communication scene. Whenever strong, unified pressures from industry or consumer groups develop and overcome the strong resistance to change in this controversial policy field with multiple major stakeholders, Congress's powers to legislate communications policy become extremely important. As the sixty-two-year time gap between major communications laws demonstrates, there usually is a vacuum in both policy formulation and oversight that neither the president nor the FCC has been eager to fill.[45] Communications industry representatives occasionally jump into the breach. They are in a strong position to push their ideas because they enjoy close relationships with government officials whose interests they are able to serve.

The communications subcommittees of the Commerce, Science, and Transportation Committee in the Senate and of the Energy and Commerce Committee in the House also influence communications policy primarily through the power of investigation. They have investigated the FCC more frequently than most regulatory bodies. In fact since 1970 more than fifty different congressional committees and subcommittees have reviewed FCC activities, with few dramatic results. Investigations have included reviews of specific FCC actions, studies of corruption in television game shows, and examinations of such broad policy issues as the impact of television's portrayal of the aged or of alcohol and drug abuse. The appropriations committees have occasionally denied funds for FCC operations or explicitly directed which particular programs should be funded.[46] However, monetary control became stricter when Congress changed the FCC in 1982 from the status of a permanently authorized agency to one requiring biennial renewal.

Although the Senate has seldom used confirmation hearings to impress its views on new FCC commissioners, this does not mean that agency staff have ignored the views of powerful senators. Prospective commissioners are likely to study past confirmation hearings carefully and take their cues from them. Most presidential nominees have been confirmed. Appointments are usually made to reward the politically faithful. Although congressional control over the FCC has generally been light, there is always the possibility of stricter control. All the parties interested in communications policy, including the White House and the courts, pay deference to that possibility.

Congressional control over the media also includes such matters as postal rates and subsidies, legislation on permissible mergers and chain control of papers, and laws designed to keep failing newspapers alive. Copyright laws, which affect print and electronic media productions, are involved, too. So are policies and regulations about telecommunication satellites, broadcast spectrum allocations, and cable television. The vast, congressionally guided changes in the telephone industry are yet another area of major concern to media interests.

Laws regulating media procedures occasionally have a strong impact on media content and policies. For instance, FCC encouragement of the diversification of radio programs was largely responsible for the development of a sizable number of FM rock music stations that provide alternatives to more conventional programs. Congressional scrutiny of documentaries may chill investigative reporting, as may have happened when Congress probed the circumstances surrounding a documentary on drug use at a major university to assess whether the events had been staged. Congress has also investigated the accuracy of charges of illicit public relations activity by the Pentagon. Congressional failure to act may also have far-reaching consequences for news media. Congress has barely regulated cable television since 1996, leaving this medium mostly under control of the courts and state and local governments.

Summary

In this chapter we have examined the relationship between the media and the presidency and Congress, which is rocky because the goals of the media differ from those of government officials. Officials want favorable stories that mirror their sense of what is important and unimportant. Newspeople want stories that please their publics. Newspeople believe that their audiences are more interested in exciting events and human-interest tales than in academic discussions of public policies, their historical antecedents, and their projected impact expressed in statistics. Newspeople also feel a special mission, like Shakespeare's Mark Antony, "to bury Caesar, not to praise him." And, like Brutus, they claim that their criticism is not disloyalty. They do not love the government less; they only love the nation and its people more.

Each side in this tug of war uses wiles and ruses as well as clout to have its own way. The outcome is a seesaw contest in which both sides score victories and suffer defeats, but each is most attuned to its own failures rather than to its victories. The public interest is served in equally uneven fashion. If we equate the public interest with a maximum of intelligible information about important issues and events, media presentations fall short. But coverage also is good because it is continuous, often well informed, with sufficient attention to audience appeal to make dry information palatable. Investigative reporting has brought to light many shortcomings and scandals that otherwise might have remained hidden.

The fear of exposure by the media has undoubtedly kept government officials from straying into many questionable ventures, although this effect is hard to document. On the negative side, fear of media coverage and publicity has probably inhibited many desirable actions.

Because the contacts between officials of the national government and the media are so constant, a formal institutional structure has been established to handle their interactions. In this chapter we have described the fairly elaborate setup at the presidential level and the simpler arrangements for Congress. We also have indicated some of the problems that newspeople face in covering a flood tide of complex news expeditiously, accurately, and with a modicum of critical detachment and analysis.

Problems in communications policy making remain. All three branches of government shape communications policy, but there is little coordination among them. Even within the executive and legislative branches, so many different committees and agencies share control that the outcome tends to be a compromise that pleases nobody. Few major policy decisions have been made except during crises. Even then the weaknesses of government structures have made it easy for industry spokespersons to dominate decision making.

The government's weakness in this area may be a blessing in disguise and in the spirit of the First Amendment. Because the Constitution commands that Congress shall make no law abridging the freedom of the press, it may be well to keep all communications policy making to the barest minimum. As Chief Justice John Marshall warned early in the nation's history, the power to regulate is the power to destroy.[47] Policy making and regulation overlap. A uniform, well-articulated communications policy, however beneficial it may seem to many people, still puts the government imprint indelibly on the flow of information.

Notes

1. "George Bush's Postwar Blues," *Media Monitor,* 17, no. 4 (November/December 2003): 4–5; Katherine Graham, "The Presidency and the Press," *Miller Center Report,* 16, no. 1 (2000): 4–8.
2. Joe S. Foote, *Television Access and Political Power: The Networks, the Presidency, and the "Loyal Opposition"* (New York: Praeger, 1990), 135, reports that just before President Carter publicly announced that he would recognize the People's Republic of China, he invited the anchors of the three major networks to Washington, D.C., to break the news to them first. "This incident was tacit recognition that network anchors had assumed a status comparable to congressional leaders for whom this special type of briefing was usually reserved. The media stars had become a powerful force who deserved special handling."
3. David L. Paletz and K. Kendall Guthrie, "The Three Faces of Ronald Reagan," *Journal of Communication* 37 (fall 1987): 7–23.
4. Presidential communication in general is discussed by John Tebbel and Sarah Miles Watts, *The Press and the Presidency* (New York: Oxford University Press, 1985); and Barbara Hinckley, *The Symbolic Presidency: How Presidents Portray*

Themselves (New York: Routledge, 1990). Also see Samuel Kernell, *Going Public: New Strategies of Presidential Leadership,* 3d ed. (Washington, D.C.: CQ Press, 1997). Martha Joynt Kumar, "The White House 2001 Project," reports 31–34, http://whitehouse2001.org provides an excellent observation-based account of White House press operations. Books about the relations of individual presidents with the press include Frederic T. Smoller, *The Six O'Clock Presidency: A Theory of Presidential Press Relations in the Age of Television* (New York: Praeger, 1990); and Carolyn Smith, *Presidential Press Conferences: A Critical Approach* (New York: Praeger, 1990). Also see Mark J. Rozell, *The Press and the Ford Presidency* (Ann Arbor: University of Michigan Press, 1992).

5. John Kenneth Galbraith, quoted in William L. Rivers, *The Other Government: Power and the Washington Media* (New York: University Books, 1982), 19.

6. Quoted in Timothy E. Cook, *Governing with the News: The News Media as a Political Institution* (Chicago: University of Chicago Press, 1998), 131.

7. "George Bush's Postwar Blues," 5.

8. Quoted in S. Robert Lichter and Linda S. Lichter, eds., "Bork: Decline and Fall," *Media Monitor* 1 (October 1987): 5.

9. Martin Linsky, *Impact: How the Press Affects Federal Policymaking* (New York: Norton, 1986), 37–38.

10. "George Bush's Postwar Blues," 4–5; also Cook, *Governing with the News,* chap. 6; and Lori Cox Han and Diane J. Heith, eds. *In the Public Domain: Presidents and the Challenge of Public Leadership* (Albany: State University of New York Press, 2005), chaps. 4, 11.

11. *Kennedy and the Press: The News Conferences* (New York: Crowell, 1965), 239.

12. Refusal problems are discussed in Matthew A. Baum and Samuel Kernell, "Has Cable Ended the Golden Age of Presidential Television?" *American Political Science Review* 93 (1) (1999): 99–114.

13. Doris A. Graber, "Terrorism, Censorship and the 1st Amendment: In Search of Policy Guidelines," in *Framing Terrorism: The News Media, the Government, and the Public,* ed. Pippa Norris, Montague Kern, and Marion Just (New York: Routledge, 2003), 27–42.

14. Michael Baruch Grossman and Martha Joynt Kumar, *Portraying the President: The White House and the News Media* (Baltimore: Johns Hopkins University Press, 1980); Martha Joynt Kumar and Alex Jones, "Government and the Press: Issues and Trends," in *The Institutions of American Democracy: The Press,* ed. Geneva Overholser and Kathleen Hall Jamieson (New York: Oxford University Press, forthcoming); Martha Joynt Kumar, "The Importance and Evolution of Presidential Press Conferences," *Presidential Studies Quarterly,* 35, no. 1 (2005): 166–192.

15. Smoller, *The Six O'Clock Presidency,* 61–77.

16. "The Disappearing Honeymoon: TV News Coverage of President George W. Bush's First 100 Days," *Media Monitor* 15, no. 3 (May/June 2001): 1–5; Committee of Concerned Journalists, "The First 100 Days: How Bush Versus Clinton Fared in the Press," www.journalism.org/publ_research/100days1.html, May 2001.

17. Michael Margolis and David Resnick, *Politics as Usual: The Cyberspace "Revolution"* (Thousand Oaks, Calif.: Sage, 2000), 79–93.

18. John Anthony Maltese, *Spin Control: The White House Office of Communications and the Management of Presidential News,* 2d ed. (Chapel Hill: University of North Carolina Press, 1994), chap. 8; also see Martha Joynt Kumar, "The Office of the

Press Secretary," report 31, and "The Office of Communications," report 33, in "White House 2001 Project," http://whitehouse2001.org.

19. Kumar, "The Office of Communications," 5.

20. Martha Joynt Kumar, "Communications Operation in the White House of President George W. Bush: Making News on His Terms," *Presidential Studies Quarterly* 33, no. 2 (2003): 366–393; Martha Joynt Kumar, "The White House and the Press: News Organizations as a Presidential Resource and as a Source of Pressure," *Presidential Studies Quarterly* 33, no. 3 (2003): 669–683; Kumar and Jones, "Government and the Press."

21. Maltese, *Spin Control*, 253.

32. Ibid., 6.

23. Mark Silva, "Is It Public Relations or Propaganda?" *Chicago Tribune*, March 14, 2005.

24. David Barstow and Robin Stein, "Under Bush, a New Age of Prepackaged TV News," *New York Times*, March 13, 2005.

25. Kumar and Jones, "Government and the Press"; Kumar, "The Importance and Evolution of Presidential Press Conferences." Also see Stephen Hess, "A New Survey of the White House Press Corps," *Presidential Studies Quarterly* 22, no. 2 (spring 1992): 311–321.

26. Smith, *Presidential Press Conferences*, 41.

27. For a thorough analysis of presidential press conferences, see Smith, *Presidential Press Conferences;* Blaire Atherton French, *The Presidential Press Conference: Its History and Role in the American Political System* (Washington, D.C.: University Press of America, 1982); and Frank Cormier, James Deakin, and Helen Thomas, *The White House Press on the Presidency: News Management and Co-Option* (Lanham, Md.: University Press of America, 1983); and Kumar, "The Importance and Evolution of Presidential Press Conferences."

28. Steven R. Weisman, "Reagan, Annoyed by News Leaks, Tells Staff to Limit Press Relations," *New York Times*, January 11, 1983. For a list of measures taken by the Reagan administration to stop leaks, see Ronald Berkman and Laura W. Kitch, *Politics in the Media Age* (New York: McGraw-Hill, 1986), 195–197. The Bush administration tried equally unsuccessfully to stop further leaks following the Thomas affair.

29. Robert O. Blanchard, ed., *Congress and the News Media* (New York: Hastings House, 1974), 105.

30. Kathleen Hall Jamieson, *Eloquence in an Electronic Age: The Transformation of Political Speechmaking* (New York: Oxford University Press, 1988), 14.

31. Stephen Hess, *The Washington Reporters* (Washington, D.C.: Brookings Institution, 1981), 99. The figures are based on 921 newspaper and 87 television stories.

32. Ronald D. Elving, "Making News, Making Law," *Media Studies Journal* 10 (winter 1996): 50.

33. Hess, *The Washington Reporters*, 104–105; and Karen M. Kedrowski, *Media Entrepreneurs and the Media Enterprise in the U.S. Congress* (Cresskill, N.J.: Hampton Press, 1996), chap. 5.

34. Quoted in Steven V. Roberts, "Senators Squint into a Future under TV's Gaze," *New York Times*, February 4, 1986.

35. Timothy E. Cook, *Making Laws and Making News: Media Strategies in the U.S. House of Representatives* (Washington, D.C.: Brookings Institution, 1989), and Kedrowski, *Media Entrepreneurs,* provide detailed analyses of congressional

news making. Also see R. Douglas Arnold, *Congress, the Press, and Political Accountability* (Princeton: Princeton University Press, 2004).

36. Diana Owen, Richard Davis, and Vincent James Strickler, "Congress and the Internet," *Press/Politics* 4, no. 2 (1999): 10–29.

37. Daniel Lipinski and Gregory Neddenriep, "Using 'New' Media to Get 'Old' Media Coverage: How Members of Congress Use Their Web Sites," *Press/Politics*, 9, no. 1 (2004): 7–21.

38. "Media and Congress," *Media Studies Journal* 10, no. 1 (winter 1996); and Stephen Hess, *Live from Capitol Hill: Studies of Congress and the Media* (Washington, D.C.: Brookings Institution, 1991), 117. Also see Kedrowski, *Media Entrepreneurs*; and Arnold, *Congress, the Press and Political Accountability*. For an excellent discussion of congressional press galleries, see Melissa Merson, "Big Picture and Local Angle," *Media Studies Journal* 10, no. 1 (winter 1996): 55–66.

39. Patrick J. Sellers, "Congress and the News Media: Manipulating the Message in the U.S. Congress," *Press/Politics* 5, no. 1 (2000): 22–31.

40. "How TV News Has Covered the 103rd Congress," *Media Monitor* 8, no. 5 (September/October 1994): 2.

41. Ibid.; Timothy E. Cook, "House Members as National Newsmakers: The Effects of Televising Congress," *Legislative Studies Quarterly* 11 (summer 1986): 203–226; and Stephen Hess, *The Ultimate Insiders: U.S. Senators and the National Media* (Washington, D.C.: Brookings Institution, 1986). Also see Hess, *Live from Capitol Hill*, 55–58, and Kedrowski, *Media Entrepreneurs*, chaps. 5, 8.

42. Girish J. Gulati, "Members of Congress and Presentation of Self on the World Wide Web," *Press/Politics* 9, no. 1 (2004): 22–40.

43. "How TV News Has Covered the 103rd Congress," 2.

44. Michael J. Robinson, "Three Faces of Congressional Media," in *The New Congress*, ed. Thomas E. Mann and Norman J. Ornstein (Washington, D.C.: American Enterprise Institute, 1981).

45. For a history on the politics of communications policy formulation, see Erwin G. Krasnow, Lawrence D. Longley, and Herbert A. Terry, *The Politics of Broadcast Regulation*, 3d ed. (New York: St. Martin's, 1982), 87–132; and Robert Britt, *The Irony of Regulatory Reform: The Deregulation of American Telecommunications* (New York: Oxford University Press, 1989), chap. 6; also Patricia Aufderheide, *Communications Policy and the Public Interest* (New York: Guilford Press, 1999), chaps. 1, 5.

46. Krasnow, Longley, and Terry, *The Politics of Broadcast Regulation*, 99.

47. *McCulloch v. Maryland*, 17 U.S. (4 Wheat.) 316 (1819).

Readings

Arnold, R. Douglas. *Congress, the Press, and Political Accountability*. Princeton: Princeton University Press, 2004.

Cook, Timothy E. *Governing with the News: The News Media as a Political Institution*. Chicago: University of Chicago Press, 1998.

Fleischer, Ari. *Taking Heat: the President, the Press, and My Years in the White House*. New York: William Morrow, 2005.

Fritz, Ben, Bryan Keefer, and Brendan Nyhan. *All the President's Spin: George W. Bush, the Media, and the Truth*. New York: Simon and Schuster, 2004.

Hess, Stephen. *Live from Capitol Hill: Studies of Congress and the Media.* Washington, D.C.: Brookings Institution, 1991.

Kedrowski, Karen M. *Media Entrepreneurs and the Media Enterprise in the U.S. Congress.* Cresskill, N.J.: Hampton Press, 1996.

Kernell, Samuel. *Going Public: New Strategies of Presidential Leadership,* 3d ed. Washington, D.C.: CQ Press, 1997.

Kumar, Martha Joynt. "The White House 2001 Project." Reports 31–34. http://whitehouse2001.org.

Maltese, John Anthony. *Spin Control: The White House Office of Communications and the Management of Presidential News,* 2d ed. Chapel Hill: University of North Carolina Press, 1994.

Spragens, William C. *News Media for the New Millennium: Federal and State Executive Press Aides and Ambition Theory.* Lanham, Md.: University Press of America, 2003.

Covering the Justice System and State and Local News

In a classic study of media and public opinion, the renowned U.S. journalist Walter Lippmann likened the performance of the media to "the beam of a searchlight that moves restlessly about, bringing one episode and then another out of darkness into vision." The media were not a "mirror on the world," as others had claimed. Lippmann concluded, "Men cannot do the work of the world by this light alone. They cannot govern society by episodes, incidents, and eruptions." [1]

What Lippmann observed in 1922 is still true today. The media provide spotty coverage, leaving much of the political landscape obscured. The political life of the institutions that will be covered in this chapter—the courts, state governments, and local governments—have been in the shadows of media coverage. We know too little about them, and so it is difficult for us to become informed citizens. Just like journalists, social scientists have largely ignored these less glamorous areas of politics. Fortunately, that is beginning to change.

The Media and the Courts

Of the three branches of the national government, only the judiciary has been sparsely covered. This is the case even for the highest court in the nation (see Table 9-1). The pattern of sparse coverage is evident at the major television networks as well as major newspapers. For example, between July 2003 and June 2004 the three networks allotted 53 percent of their coverage of the three branches of government to presidential stories,

37 percent to congressional stories, and 10 percent to stories about the Supreme Court (see Table 9-3).

Federal-level judges are rarely in the limelight. They infrequently grant interviews, almost never hold news conferences, and generally do not seek or welcome media attention, lest their impartiality and mystique be compromised. Remoteness enhances the impression that judges are a breed apart, doling out justice to lesser mortals. At the state and local levels, where many judges are elected rather than appointed to office, media coverage is somewhat more common, especially during judicial elections. The aura of judicial majesty recedes accordingly. On the rare occasions when the Supreme Court has been widely accused of unduly meddling in politics, its luster also dulls for many court watchers. That happened in 2000 when its decision on the legality of vote counts in Florida decided the outcome of the presidential election.[2]

The immunity from personal media scrutiny that U.S. Supreme Court justices generally enjoy does not extend to the hearings conducted before their appointment to the Court is confirmed. These hearings, and the public debate they engender, can be highly acrimonious. Examples include the 1987 political battle that scuttled the nomination of conservative judge Robert Bork and the soap operatic hearings about alleged sexual improprieties committed by judge Clarence Thomas, whose appointment was ultimately approved in 1991. Because dramatic hearings have great audience appeal, they are now often broadcast live by Court TV, a cable channel that specializes in reporting sensational judicial proceedings, along with commentary by selected pundits.

Hearings also demonstrate how pressure groups use the media to influence judicial politics. For instance, during the confirmation hearings for Bork and Thomas, liberal as well as conservative groups mounted a massive media campaign to publicize their perceptions of the merits of these appointments. Spokespersons for such groups as the American Civil Liberties Union, the National Association for the Advancement of Colored People, the National Organization for Women, and the American Federation of Labor and Congress of Industrial Organizations spoke for the liberal camp, and conservatives lobbied through Pat Robertson's Christian Coalition and the Conservative Victory Committee. Tactics included television and radio advertisements, talk-show appearances, essays in the editorial opinion sections of newspapers, wining and dining of media personnel, and careful research and coordination work.

The institutional aspects of the federal courts also receive comparatively little coverage. There are exceptions, of course. The courts' difficulties in coping with the flood of legal actions, the problems of disparate sentencing policies, and the flaws in the correction system have all been the subject of sporadic media investigations. The speeches by Supreme Court justices to such public bodies as the American Bar Association have been telecast and reported nationwide. Chief Justice Warren E. Burger even consented to regular questioning about his annual State of the Judiciary speech. The news conference before the speech remained off the record, however, and the media could not quote the chief justice directly.

Although federal judges and court systems are not very newsworthy because they generally do not become embroiled in open battles about policies, their work—judicial decisions—does make the news. This is particularly true of U.S. Supreme Court decisions, which frequently have major consequences for the political system. For example, *Brown v. Board of Education* (1954) was widely publicized because it declared the separate schooling of children of different races unconstitutional. *Roe v. Wade* (1973) and *Planned Parenthood v. Casey* (1992) received ample media attention because they involved the emotional issue of a woman's right to have an abortion.[3] In general the news media give disproportionately heavy attention to civil rights and First Amendment cases; they slight cases involving economic and business matters. Overall, the media cover only a fraction of the Court's decisions. In 1998, for example, newspapers reported about 11 percent of the Court's decisions, and the television networks covered 7.6 percent.[4] The focus of news stories is limited to the formal decision; the Court's decision-making process remains largely shrouded in secrecy.[5]

Impact of Coverage

Publicity about Supreme Court decisions is very important because it informs public officials at all government levels, as well as the general public, about the law of the land in matters of heated controversy. A small corps of reporters is responsible for choosing the decisions to be covered. Some fifty reporters cover the Supreme Court, and of those only a dozen correspondents for major wire services and for major newspapers are full-time.[6] In 1998, for example, six reporters filed 88 percent of the 211 news stories about Court decisions. They represented just five news organizations: the Associated Press, *Los Angeles Times, New York Times, Washington Post,* and *USA Today.*[7]

Supreme Court coverage is difficult for reporters. The justices usually announce multiple decisions on a single day, forcing reporters to digest voluminous and often contradictory opinions rapidly. This must be done without help from the justices who authored the opinions. Reporters' deadlines may be only minutes away and the news may be stale after more than twenty-four hours have elapsed. Advice from outside commentators, including legal experts, is usually unavailable initially because such experts are not allowed to preview the opinions and advance leaks are rare. The Supreme Court does have a press office, which provides some reference materials and bare-bones records of the Court's activities. But it refuses to interpret the justices' decisions in laypersons' terms, fearing entanglement in legal controversies. However, publications sponsored by the legal profession make brief analyses of important pending cases available to the media. In addition, universities and major newspapers have Web sites featuring archived decisions and even audiotapes of arguments the Court has heard.[8]

Because of the shortage of skilled legal reporters, much reporting on the courts—even the Supreme Court—is imprecise and sometimes outright wrong. Justice Felix Frankfurter once complained that editors who would never consider covering a baseball game through a reporter unfamiliar with the sport regularly assigned reporters unfamiliar with the law to cover the Supreme Court. This situation has improved considerably in recent years, but it is far from cured. Many editors do not want to assign reporters whose knowledge of fine points of the law might make their stories too technical and dull.

Two landmark decisions—*Engel v. Vitale,* which outlawed school prayer, and *Baker v. Carr,* which invalidated many electoral district boundaries— provide examples of faulty reporting.[9] Stories about these two decisions in sixty-three metropolitan daily papers featured misleading headlines and serious errors.[10] Ill-informed statements by well-known people opposing the Court's decisions made up the major part of the stories. For instance, the wrong clause of the Constitution was cited as the basis for the decision outlawing classroom prayer in public schools. Arguments made in lower courts were erroneously attributed to Supreme Court justices. Moreover, the media covered the prayer decision more heavily because it was relatively easy to grasp and presented an emotionally stirring story, although the duller reapportionment decision was far more significant. When the media pay careful attention to a case, coverage can be excellent, including commentary on legal issues and the long-range implications of the case.[11] For example, a study of network coverage of the 1978 *Bakke* racial discrimination case and the 1989 *Webster* abortion rights case revealed that three out of four news stories about these prominent cases featured interpretations along with the factual account.[12]

The thrust of complaints about sketchy, inaccurate, and out-of-context judicial reporting is the same as for coverage of the presidency and Congress. But complaints appear to be more justified. Reporting of Court activities seems to be more superficial and flawed than its presidential and congressional counterparts.[13] The reasons are not difficult to understand. The volume of decisions clusters near the end of the annual term. The subject matter is often highly technical and is hard for reporters to understand and make understandable. With notable exceptions, stories about judicial decisions lack the potential to become exciting, front-page news. They are hard to boil down into catchy phrases and clichés. They rarely lend themselves to exciting visual coverage. The Supreme Court beat tends to be understaffed. All of these factors make it difficult for the assigned reporters to prepare interesting, well-researched accounts.

The information supplied to the public, though inadequate for providing important insights into the law and the judicial process, usually sustains respect for the judiciary and compliance with its rulings. Most people hold its work in high esteem.[14] This is crucial because the Court lacks the power and institutional structure to enforce its decisions. Occasionally Court publicity has the opposite effect, however. For instance, Justice Tom Clark, one of the participants in the 1962 prayer decision, complained that misunderstanding of *Engel v. Vitale* made this ruling unpopular. He blamed inadequate reporting for failures to comply with the decision, and an abortive movement to nullify it through a constitutional amendment.

Public reactions to Supreme Court decisions may affect future decisions of the Court because justices are influenced in their work by what they read and hear from the media. Media reports of crime waves, or price gouging by business, or public opposition to aid for parochial schools are likely to set boundaries to judicial policy making.[15] This makes it tragic that much of the reporting leaves the public unprepared to make sound assessments of the Court's rulings. Recent research provides evidence that news stories can influence court personnel. For example, the amount of publicity given to a crime influences prosecutors. When there is little publicity, prosecutors are less likely to press for a trial of the case and more likely to agree to a plea-bargain settlement. In federal murder trials, longer sentences tend to follow more pretrial publicity for defendants.[16] The effects of media coverage tend to persist for subsequent similar cases.

News about Crime and the Justice System

Publications of decisions by the Supreme Court and lower courts are by no means the only significant news about the judiciary. General news about crime and the work of the justice system is also important in creating images of the quality of public justice. Here a plentiful media diet is available, especially on local television news where nearly 16 percent of the coverage is devoted to the topic. Business and consumer news issues receive less than one-third as much attention.[17] Like stories about other government activities, crime and justice system stories tend to focus on sensational events, often at the expense of significant trends and problems in the legal system that might benefit from greater public attention.[18]

Reporters and photographers on February 13, 2004, surround Michael Jackson's attorney, Mark Geragos, and Jackson supporters after a hearing in a child molestation case at the courthouse in Santa Maria, California.

The nature of crime news coverage and its prevalence in the media, particularly television, has long been a matter of concern to public officials and the public. It is widely believed that current coverage practices deflect attention from the social causes of crime and the policies needed to curb it. Sensational stories lead to exaggerated fear of crime because the focus is on the most violent incidents, which in real life constitute only a tiny portion of crime. Nearly 66 percent of the crime stories in the *Chicago Tribune* in 2002 dealt with murder or sexual assaults in a year when these crimes constituted slightly under 2 percent of the actual crimes in the city (see Table 4-3). By contrast, white-collar crime, which is widely prevalent and often threatens public health and safety, received little coverage, which concealed its seriousness as a social problem.[19] These figures are typical for crime coverage by local news media.[20] Many experts on criminal behavior contend that extensive graphic coverage of crime can glamorize it and thereby encourage imitation. News stories that focus selectively on sensational aspects of the case can also mislead the public— and possibly jurors—about who is guilty and who is innocent. When that happens, guilty defendants may escape justice and innocent ones may be convicted.[21]

Probably the most graphic aspect of the "tabloidization" of crime news is overemphasis on crimes involving celebrities or crimes that seem particularly heinous (Box 10-1). The total amount of coverage is disproportionate, especially since much of it is little more than a repeated spinning out of insignificant, often irrelevant details. Coverage is also disproportionate compared to other important stories that need attention. For example, there were 22,610 stories in sixty-five major newspapers about the murder case involving football legend O.J. Simpson between 1994 and 1997, including 1,471 front-page stories.[22] During the same period, the three national networks aired 1,225 Simpson stories, roughly four times the number of stories given to Medicare and welfare policies combined. The Simpson celebrity crime story was topped only by reports about the investigation of President Clinton's relations with intern Monica Lewinsky that totaled 25,975 stories in the sixty-five papers in just one year (1998), including 1,959 front page stories. There is no record to show how many more significant stories news sources omitted to make room for these celebrity crime accounts.

Such stories are bonanzas for media enterprises because they sharply increase audience size and with it rates that can be charged for advertising. CNN, for example, more than tripled its average ratings at the height of the Simpson trial and more than quadrupled them during the peak phases of the Lewinsky affair.[23] A Web browser search in November 1998 found 498,932 Web pages on Netscape mentioning the Simpson trial and 622,079 mentioning either Monica Lewinsky or Paula Jones, two principals in the Clinton saga. No wonder, then, that 97 percent of the public were familiar with these cases, compared with 12 percent who could identify William Rehnquist as the Chief Justice of the U.S. Supreme Court.

If there is widespread agreement that current patterns of crime news coverage are excessive and undesirable, why do they continue in daily newspapers and on national and local television throughout the country? There are several reasons. Most important, despite their complaints, audiences flock to crime news, partly because it involves personal security but mostly to satisfy a hunger for excitement. This has been the case since the birth of tabloid newspapers more than 150 years ago. When crime news makes huge front-page headlines, paper sales rise sharply and audience ratings for television news channels skyrocket. The local television news, with its heavy crime component, has eclipsed national news, which carries more serious political stories and less crime, in the battle for high audience ratings. In the entertainment world, crime shows are highly popular. Besides audience appeal, crime news has the advantage of ease of coverage. The police beat can supply a steady diet of new crimes for hungry reporters who prefer to mine a news-rich source rather than working leaner beats.

BOX 10-1
When News Is Sparse, Fiction Trumps Reality

When actor Robert Blake was tried in 2005 on charges that he murdered his wife, television news had made millions of Americans familiar with the crime. In fact, there had been so much exposure that prosecutors feared that the "guilty" verdict they sought would be overturned as another case of "conviction by television."

That did not happen. Most Americans who had watched the ample dramatic stories about a celebrity accused of a heinous crime were familiar with the details of the charges in the Blake case, but not with the painstaking detailed forensic work that goes into constructing a viable court case. The news media don't dwell on such tedious matters. But crime shows like *CSI: Crime Scene Investigations* and *Forensic Files* do so dramatically—and viewers learn from them and form opinions about the work that forensic laboratories should and can do.

Prosecutors call it the "*CSI* effect" and complain that it makes it difficult to get convictions because jurors apply the hyped forensic science observed in these fictional shows to the real trials that they are asked to judge. In Blake's case, jurors refused to render a "guilty" verdict because the evidence lacked the absolute certainty that crime shows produce to solve capital crimes in the brief span of time allotted to each case. The Blake jurors concluded that there was not enough conclusive proof that Blake had shot his wife, and they dismissed circumstantial evidence that should have been sufficient to yield a conviction. One juror even admitted outright that crime shows had created high expectations and that she wanted more of the kind of evidence that she had seen in *CSI* cases.[1] Like 70 percent of the jurors in a recent survey, she was among the 60 million Americans who tune in weekly to *CSI* shows.[2]

The *CSI* effect—drawing on fictional events for forming opinions about unfamiliar scenarios in real life—has other manifestations as well. Most people lack experience in courtroom behavior. What they know about it comes from watching *Judge Judy* (more than 7 million people did in 2001) or the *People's Court* and the dozens of shows like them.[3] Surveys show that jurors who watch such shows frequently believe—contrary to the facts—that judges should let the trial participants know their own opinions about the case and should ask leading questions. The judge's facial expressions and often sarcastic remarks should guide the jury's deliberations about guilt or innocence of the defendant. Cases should be settled quickly with verdicts instantly executed without further motions and appeals delaying the final outcome.

Applying false standards to reality is obviously harmful. What can be done about it when millions of Americans absorb a mixture of truth and fiction from their daily television exposure? One solution would be for journalists to provide more detailed coverage of the procedures involved in resolving criminal cases. They also could explode *CSI*-generated myths like DNA tests done in minutes, rather than a week, or automatic instant matching of fingerprints to a national crime database. Given media norms, such a focus on public education is unlikely to happen. The more likely solution is to demand higher standards for fictional shows when it is clear that people believe what they see there and accept it as accurate. Television producers take great pains to produce accurate historical dramas and political shows, such as the *West Wing*. They should strive for the same standards of accuracy in fictional crime stories that are cast as quasi-reality and, in the process, become reality for millions of citizens.

1. Andrew Blankstein and Jean Guccione, "The Blake Verdict and the '*CSI* Effect,'" *Chicago Tribune,* March 22, 2005.
2. Richard Willing, "'*CSI* Effect' has Juries Wanting More Evidence," *USA Today,* August 5, 2004.
3. Kimberlianne Podlas, "Should We Blame Judge Judy? The Messages TV Courtrooms Send Viewers," *Judicature* 86, no. 1 (2002): 38–43.

Judicial Censorship

There are several significant systematic omissions in media coverage of the U.S. crime and justice system. The Supreme Court bars reporters from all of its deliberations before the announcement of decisions. On the few occasions when a source has leaked information about a forthcoming decision ahead of time, justices have reacted with great anger and have curtailed contacts between newspeople and Court personnel. Television cameras are barred most of the time from federal courts, and their proceedings may not be broadcast live. Federal district and appellate courts allowed cameras in the courtroom as a three-year experiment in 1991. They ended coverage in 1994 on the grounds that the cameras were distracting to the jurors and witnesses even though appraisals of the experiment had found little or no impact on the administration of justice.

For years many state courts prohibited radio and television reporters from covering trials and other proceedings. This restriction was grounded in fears, spawned by the sensational 1935 Lindbergh baby kidnapping trial, that recording devices might produce a carnival atmosphere that would intimidate participants, endanger witnesses, and harm the fairness of the proceedings. To allow citizens to watch how their courts operate, all states now allow cameras to record court proceedings subject to rules that protect the parties in the judicial drama from undue invasion of their privacy.[24] The debate about the wisdom of televising court proceedings surged in the wake of the massive media attention to the O.J. Simpson murder trial, which drowned out much other news for nearly a year. Critics of televised sessions claimed that the judges' and lawyers' showboating distorted and delayed the verdict and diminished the public's regard for the legal system. Televised trials tend to focus on court room drama at the expense of explaining legal issues. Others argued that the public is entitled to monitor the courts' performance via television in a public trial.[25]

Restraints on live audio- and videotape coverage are not the only limitations on judicial publicity. In the interest of ensuring fair trials, courts also limit the information that may be printed while court proceedings are in progress. These types of restrictions were discussed in Chapter 3.

Covering State and Local Affairs

It is an axiom of U.S. politics that "all politics is local." Decentralized politics is essential and invigorating in a nation that spans a continent and embodies diverse political cultures and contexts. Because national politics is glamorous and important, it is easy to ignore the grassroots that nourish and shape it. It is therefore not surprising that most research has focused on the national level, despite the significant impact that coverage of local politics and local perspectives has on national politics.[26]

The Changing Media Grid

Mirroring the nation's political geography and culture, U.S. newspapers and radio and television stations have been primarily structured to serve a multitude of local markets. At the start of the twentieth century, every large and medium-size city and even many small towns had at least one newspaper, and often more, geared to local political needs. The numbers of newspapers have shrunk so that most cities are now served by a single newspaper, and some no longer have their own paper. Electronic media, too, at first were situated in nearly every city to serve local audiences. Technological changes and large-scale migration of former inner-city dwellers to the suburbs have eroded this local focus so that electronic media now are serving ever larger regions. It is not uncommon for television stations and metropolitan dailies to reach people in fifty counties, making comprehensive local coverage impossible. Reporting, of necessity, becomes highly selective and superficial. Typically coverage areas include some 1,300 government units, whose policies should be reported because they involve important public issues, including the power to tax. Numerous state legislators, as well as several national legislators, are elected within these counties. Media critic Ben Bagdikian describes the consequences:

> News distribution is no longer designed for individual towns and cities. American politics is organized on the basis of the 20,000 urban and rural places in the country, which is the way citizens vote. But the media have organized on the basis of 210 television "markets," which is the way merchandisers and media corporations sell ads. As a result, the fit between the country's information needs and its information media has become disastrously disjointed.[27]

The Vanishing Metropolitan Focus. Because market areas and political communities no longer coincide, reporting has turned away from strictly local problems to more generalized topics of interest to the entire market area. That has meant more focus on soft news and less information about important local problems that face citizens.[28] This is happening despite the fact that nationwide polls show that interest in local news is growing. In 2004, 59 percent of respondents to a nationwide poll said that they watched local news regularly. Only 34 percent expressed similar interest in nightly national newscasts.[29]

Ironically, Internet news, despite its unique global reach, may ease the problem of insufficient local news. A comparison of print and Internet versions of six Colorado newspapers that varied in circulation from less than 50,000 to more than 250,000 subscribers found more local content in the Internet versions.[30] Local stories constituted 22–38 percent of the coverage in 3,403 print stories and 24–68 percent of the coverage in 1,383 online stories. Another boost for access to local news comes from community access cable channels that allow citizens to watch local government in action. City council meetings, committee hearings, and court procedures have become directly accessible to the public without the intervention of journalists. The suburbs, where such channels have been scarce in the past, are joining the parade, thereby providing more competition for suburban newspapers. However, audiences for broadcasts of local government activities are generally quite small.

Umbrella Competition Patterns.   In response to major population shifts from inner cities to sprawling suburbs, print media have developed a structure of "umbrella competition" in which smaller units operate within the area covered simultaneously by the larger units.[31] Suburban newspapers have been thriving, and metropolitan newspapers have developed special sections targeted to different communities in the metropolitan area and suburbs.[32] Despite these efforts to better serve their audiences, newspapers have shrunk in circulation, often drastically. In 1970 roughly 78 percent of U.S. adults read the daily papers; by 2004 that number had shrunk to 42 percent.[33]

The umbrella pattern consists of four layers. In the first layer, large metropolitan dailies provide substantial amounts of international, national, and regional coverage. In the second layer, smaller satellite dailies resemble their larger cousins but carry more local news. The third layer contains suburban dailies. They emphasize local news, much of it nonpolitical, and are a rapidly growing sector. Though still below the metropolitan circulation figures, suburban papers are profitable because they offer an attractive advertising opportunity to the many businesses whose customers now cluster in suburban areas. The fourth layer consists of weekly newspapers and "shoppers" that are distributed free of charge because they contain mostly advertising and only a sprinkling of news and feature stories.

The emphasis on local news increases as one moves through these layers. This has happened because newspapers with a narrower reach try to distinguish themselves from the metropolitan papers and thereby make themselves more attractive to their clientele. But because of the lack of fit between media markets and political units, most of the local news avoids detailed discussion and in-depth analysis of localized public issues, leaving these issues bereft of essential coverage. The fact that metropolitan papers now must share the advertising pie with suburban papers, as well as with shoppers has been a major factor in the death of dailies in multipaper cities. That leaves most of them without the kind of competition that invigorates political dialogue.

Television stations in smaller markets also tend to feature more local and less national and international news than their larger cousins.[34] Citizens rely heavily on these broadcasts, especially when print sources fail to cover the local scene.[35] Most radio news stations likewise devote more than half of their airtime to local news. However, stations in smaller radio markets tend to present fewer stories simply because there is less local news available.[36]

The Alternative Press.   In addition to the four layers discussed, there is also an alternative national and local press. It tends to focus narrowly on issues of interest to people representing minority political cultures or people with distinctive lifestyles and cultural and political tastes. For example, many specialized media are targeted to ethnic, racial, linguistic, and religious groups, as well as to groups with unorthodox lifestyles, such as gays and lesbians. Examples of popular alternative papers include Boston's weekly *Dig*, San Francisco's *Bay Guardian,* and the *Isthmus* in Madison, Wisconsin. Some specialized media are published in foreign languages to meet the needs of immigrants. Although these media provide in-depth coverage of local, national, and international news of interest to their clientele, they omit news covering broader concerns. Their readers may therefore live in a narrow communications ghetto that keeps them from fully understanding their surroundings.

Specialized media also often try to generate support for issues favored by their audiences and may play a role in influencing local elections. Media serving African American and Hispanic communities are good examples. Besides having their own print media, large subcultural groups in the United States are also served by electronic news media tailored to their special concerns. Over-the-air and cable television and radio stations geared to the needs of subcultures, especially Spanish speakers, are multiplying and flourishing throughout the country. They serve a relatively youthful population that is hungrier for televised news than the general population. They are a growing media force bound to carry increasing weight in U.S. politics, especially in urban areas. In New York City, for example, a dozen ethnic press ventures, out of fifty, claim circulations of more than 100,000. The five largest among them serve Jewish, Chinese, Hispanic, black, and Korean populations.[37]

Government-Press Relations at Subnational Levels

Subnational news is important for state and local politics for the same reasons that make the media important on the national scene. Subnational news sets the agenda for public policies. It helps or hinders politicians in achieving their goals. It influences the election and appointment of public officials. It informs the public and officialdom about political affairs and politicians' wrongdoings. However, there are differences in emphasis between national and subnational political coverage, largely because subnational politics operates on a much smaller scale and often performs different functions. Scholars have largely neglected the subnational media, despite unmistakable signs of their importance.[38]

How Officials Use the Press.   At the subnational level, public officials find it much easier to stay in touch with each other without relying on news stories. They also remain in closer direct contact with a comparatively tiny corps of reporters so that formal press conferences are less necessary. Moreover, their news is rarely so exciting that they can count on decent attendance if they do schedule a news conference.

Fewer subnational officials are experts in media relations. The public information and public relations materials they present to the media are often so poorly done that they do more harm than good. Many tasks performed by mayors and city managers are highly technical and difficult to condense into brief news stories suitable for lay publics. When officials do make the effort to tell their stories, reporters generally lack technical expertise to judge the accuracy of the account. Consequently, when the story relates to a policy decision involving major technical issues—for example, whether to start, continue, or stop a sewer project; how to finance it; and similar matters—the official views are likely to define the situation with little media scrutiny.

Media scholar Phyllis Kaniss identified six media styles that are especially common among public figures at the subnational level.[39] The *paranoid media-avoider* fears the press and tries to avoid it as much as possible. Information-hungry journalists are likely to retaliate with unfavorable publicity at every opportunity. The *naive professional* supplies the media with information and talks freely with journalists without realizing that uncontrolled release of information empowers reporters to determine what will be published and how it will be framed. The *ribbon cutter* is a media junkie heavily concerned with arranging events, however trivial, that are likely to attract journalists. The ensuing publicity may have few political payoffs. *Dancing marionettes* take their cues from media editorials and report and take action in areas suggested by newspeople, rather than initiating policies independently. The reward is likely to be favorable coverage, although the policy agenda favored by newspeople may be undesirable from the official's perspective. *Colorful quotables* excel in creating attractive sound bites and making sure that these come to the attention of reporters. Like ribbon cutters, their political rewards are apt to be small. Finally, *liars* conceal or slant information or distort it outright to put themselves in a favorable light.

The era of informal, inexpert handling of the press by subnational officials seems to be ending. Currently, all governors and most big-city mayors have press secretaries or public information offices. Like their counterparts at the national level, public figures try to use these offices to push their programs through recalcitrant legislatures and to disseminate news about their activities to various political elites and interested citizens. However, as on the national level, such efforts often fail. Fearing to be hoodwinked by clever professionals, the media have become suspicious, cynical commentators rather than trusting friends.

Elected officials are not alone in craving good media coverage. Appointed officials, too, need favorable images to help them win funding and support for the policies their agencies pursue. A poll of high-level federal officials showed that 79 percent thought that positive coverage increased their chances of achieving major policy goals.[40] Legislatures rarely deny support to popular agencies. By the same token, bad publicity hurts. When media frame stories in ways that subvert official goals, public officials may have to recast their own focus of attention. For example, city sanitation departments have been forced to concentrate on cleaning up lesser problems and neglecting more serious ones when publicity has highlighted a particular situation.

As on the national level, local strategies designed to win media attention include press conferences, press releases, staging events that media are likely to cover, writing op-ed pieces, and writing letters to the editor. Contacting media personnel directly seems to be the best approach, and apparently it is quite successful. Press releases are least productive. Estimates are that more than half of the content of the print and electronic media originates with publicity seekers rather than journalists.[41] Government officials at all levels provide a large share of these so-called news subsidies.[42]

In the past, most efforts to gain media coverage at the subnational level were directed at the print media, which governors, lieutenant governors, attorneys general, secretaries of state, and various legislative leaders deemed to be the most effective transmitters of state and local political news.[43] That is changing. More local officials realize that television and the Web are most important for mobilizing public opinion. Therefore, they try harder to get television and Web site coverage for themselves and their agencies.[44]

How Reporters Operate at Subnational Levels. Reporters are also somewhat different at the subnational level. Taken as a group, they have less formal education and considerably less job experience. In fact, the officials' level of education may rank considerably above that of reporters. Turnover rates are high among reporters. They are often forced to move to a different market when they switch jobs because clauses in their contracts forbid them to work for a competitor in the same area. Unfamiliarity with local politics in their new surroundings may strain relations between reporters and officials when they disagree in their analyses of political events. However, most of the time, personal relations between reporters and officials tend to be more cordial at the subnational level because these people interact more. In fact, ties of friendship have been blamed for the dearth of press criticism of local officials and local businesses.[45]

Aside from metropolitan newspapers, news organizations at the subnational level are usually considerably smaller than their national counterparts. Consequently, reporters have to cover many beats rather than becoming specialists. Roving reporters must depend more heavily on routine sources, such as daily inquiries at the police and fire departments, local newspapers, assorted press releases, tips from viewers, wire service stories, and the wire service "day books" that list major local events.[46] Because most government business stops in the early evening hours, late evening local news broadcasts depend heavily on the staples supplied by police and fire department records.[47] Serious political news featured on early evening national newscasts is deemed "stale" by nine or ten at night.[48] Stories with the best pictures and best sound bites tend to become leads, even when they are not necessarily the most important stories. Because many state and local stories are technical and undramatic, journalists strive mightily to make them entertaining. That means bypassing opportunities for detailed exposition of problems because that might bore the audience. In the process of tabloidizing news, the importance of events and their broader and long-term consequences may be lost.

Journalists who work in large metropolitan areas tend to pay more attention to inner-city affairs than to the politics of outlying areas. For Philadelphia, Kaniss reported the ratio as roughly two to one for newspapers. On local television, nearly all of the political stories covered inner-city politics, ignoring the suburbs.[49] Unfortunately, suburban reporters did not pick up the slack. A look at the contents of suburban news showed that 73 percent of the stories dealt with crime, accidents, disasters, and the like, slighting stories about other suburban concerns.

There are several reasons for "city myopia" by metropolitan media.[50] Among them is the fact that metropolitan newspaper offices usually are closer to the central city hall than to the suburbs. That makes inner-city officials and other news sources located in the inner city easier to reach. City officials are more likely to visit newspaper offices and radio and television studios that are located nearby than are their geographically distant suburban colleagues. Inner cities are also more likely to generate the kind of news that political reporters ordinarily cover, such as political wheeling and dealing, ample doses of corruption, and heavy slices of crime. Stories of spectacular fires are more common in inner-city neighborhoods, as are stories about ethnic and racial strife and protest demonstrations.[51] Most journalists find the city more exciting and relate its problems to events in the suburbs rather than the other way around. When reporters are assigned to suburban stories on a regular basis, they view it as akin to exile in Siberia. The smaller size of the press corps also accounts for the lack of coverage for many important subnational stories and for more pack journalism, generated by the close contacts that often characterize smaller groups.

The Contents of Subnational News

All of the news media—print, radio, and audiovisual—slight news about state politics. News media situated in state capitals are the only exception. Among stories about government and politics, the share of state news is less than 10 percent in all the media. It averages around 6 percent. The share allotted to local news garners one-quarter to close to half of the stories in newspapers and on local newscasts (Table 10-1).

State News: A Neglected Stepchild

Why does state news receive the least attention when states play such important roles in politics? Some media specialize in national news, like the national television networks, and other media specialize in local news, like many network affiliates. But few daily publications specialize in state news.

The Local Emphasis. Within states, the major media enterprises that have enough resources to cover news at several levels of government are usually located in the state's most populous cities where local news abounds. Very few are located in state capitals. Moreover, most state coverage has traditionally focused on the legislature rather than the governor. Because many state legislatures have relatively brief sessions, the flow of news from the capital is intermittent. Most daily papers therefore do not make the state capital a regular full-time beat. In some cases—New Hampshire is an example—the state's media markets overlap state boundaries so that news must appeal to residents of more than one state. That also puts a damper on state news.[52]

The National Emphasis. State news is a double loser on the national scene. It is extremely sparse on national television and is also extremely spotty. National television highlights a small number of states and neglects the rest. Some regions of the country receive more ample coverage than one might expect from the size of their populations, whereas others receive considerably less. Table 10-2 presents the data using electoral votes as a surrogate for population size. The concerns of people in the Midwest perennially rate the least attention relative to the size of their populations, whereas people in the Northeast and Pacific regions regularly dominate. This discrepancy has shrunk in the past five years.

Table 10-3 provides a closer look at individual states. It shows the ten most-covered and the ten least-covered states and the degree of overcoverage or undercoverage when judged by percentage of electoral vote. As usual, California and New York are in the limelight, in part because of their size and in part because of their importance in a presidential election year. In past election years Texas was also at the top. That makes it surprising that it

TABLE 10-1 Distribution of News on Government and Politics (in percentages)

Level of news	New York Times	Chicago Tribune	National ABC	National CBS	National NBC	Local ABC	Local CBS	Local NBC
National	43	38	32	41	39	24	26	29
International	38	32	56	49	50	16	8	9
State	6	5	6	6	6	9	9	9
Local	13	25	6	3	5	50	60	53
Total stories examined	232	233	188	196	217	465	160	254

SOURCE: Author's research. National television news based on data from the Vanderbilt Television News Archive. ABC local news obtained from the Museum of Broadcast Communication. CBS and NBC local news were recorded by the author.

NOTE: Newspaper and national television data and ABC local news are for forty-five days, November 1–December 15, 2004. CBS and NBC local news are for twenty-three days because they were recorded on an alternate-day schedule, November 15–December 30. During that period, CBS news was preempted repeatedly for football or movies. Presidential election news was excluded. Totals may not equal 100 percent due to rounding.

is now undercovered. However, stories about Texas still rank in fourth place overall in terms of frequency of mention. Iowa and New Hampshire rank high among overcovered states, largely because they are lead-off states in the presidential campaign. Florida joined them in 2004 thanks to its pivotal role in determining the outcome of the electoral college vote for president.

Journalistic criteria largely explain the placement of the other states. The states that offered the best story materials at a place and time that was most convenient for the media received the most ample coverage. States lacking in unusually stirring events suffered from neglect, which can harm the state's economic and political welfare. Compounding such problems, state news coverage on the national networks also is short on political substance, focusing primarily on disaster, crime, and trivia stories. State economic, political, and social conditions and policies usually are ignored even when they have major national ramifications. Print media coverage of state news tends to be more ample and considerably better.[53] That suggests that the networks could report more state news if they chose to do so.

Complaints about inadequate coverage must always be evaluated in light of the fact that media space and time are limited. What kinds of stories should the networks have omitted to make room for more news about the states? The solution is painful, given the fact that audiences love the entertainment and trivia stories that should be cut to make room for more politically meaty content. Nonetheless, the growing importance of state

TABLE 10-2   Regional Focus of Network News Coverage, September 2003–
August 2004

Region	Percentage of mentions	Percentage of electoral vote	Discrepancy
Northeast			
(D.C., Del., Md., N.J., N.Y., Pa.)	23.4	16.0	+7.4
Pacific			
(Alaska, Calif., Hawaii, Ore., Wash.)	17.4	14.7	+2.7
Middle Atlantic			
(N.C., S.C., Va., W.Va.)	8.2	7.5	+0.7
New England			
(Conn., Maine, Mass., N.H., R.I., Vt.)	6.8	6.5	+0.3
Mountain			
(Ariz., Colo., Idaho, Mont., Nev., N.M., Utah, Wyo.)	7.3	7.4	−0.1
South			
(Ala., Fla., Ga., Ky., Miss., Tenn.)	13.1	13.6	−0.5
Plains			
(Kan., Neb., N.D., S.D)	2.2	3.2	−1.0
Southwest			
(Ark., La., Okla., Texas)	7.0	10.2	−3.2
Midwest			
(Ill., Ind., Iowa, Mich., Minn., Mo., Ohio, Wis.)	14.7	20.9	−6.2

SOURCE: Author's research based on the Vanderbilt Television News Archives.

NOTE: Data come from 4,117 mentions in news stories. Figures for the three major networks (ABC, CBS, and NBC) have been combined. The distribution of 537 electoral votes is based on the Federal Election Commission's 2000 election results. Regions have been arranged from most advantaged to least advantaged by network news coverage. Figures are rounded.

politics has made it essential to provide more adequate coverage for the benefit of interested publics, as well as political leaders.

Local News Characteristics

Local television news has become the biggest game in town. When audiences are asked which news topics they follow "very closely," crime news, which is a local news staple, is number one, and news about people and events in the respondent's own community ranks in second place.[54] These preferences are typical among news consumers across the board, including print media and radio.

Primary Concerns.   What do eager news audiences get when they turn to the nightly local news broadcasts? Research by the Project for Excel-

TABLE 10-3   State Distribution of Network News Attention, Ten Leaders and Trailers, September 2003–August 2004

| State | Overcovered states | | |
	Percentage of mentions	Percentage of electoral vote	Discrepancy
California	14.5	10.0	+4.5
New York	10.2	6.1	+4.1
Iowa	3.5	1.3	+2.2
Florida	6.5	4.7	+1.8
New Hampshire	2.6	0.8	+1.8
Colorado	3.0	1.5	+1.5
Virginia	3.7	2.4	+1.3
South Carolina	2.0	1.5	+0.5
Nevada	1.1	0.8	+0.3
Massachusetts	2.6	2.3	+0.3

| State | Undercovered states | | |
	Percentage of mentions	Percentage of electoral vote	Discrepancy
Illinois	2.2	4.1	−1.9
Indiana	0.6	2.2	−1.6
Michigan	1.8	3.4	−1.6
Pennsylvania	2.9	4.3	−1.4
Missouri	0.9	2.0	−1.1
Minnesota	1.1	1.9	−0.8
Texas	5.2	6.0	−0.8
Louisiana	0.9	1.7	−0.8
Tennessee	1.4	2.1	−0.7
Oklahoma	0.8	1.5	−0.7

SOURCE: Author's research based on the Vanderbilt Television News Archives.

NOTE: Data based on 3,835 mentions in news stories. Figures for the three major networks (ABC, CBS, and NBC) have been combined. The distribution of 535 (Washington, D.C., was excluded) electoral votes is based on the Federal Election Commission's 2000 election results. Figures are rounded.

lence in Journalism tells the story. From 1998 to 2002 the project commissioned researchers to study 2,400 local newscasts presented by 154 randomly selected U.S. television stations. The stations varied in size and geographic location as well as in the kind of news they presented. Nonetheless, the investigators were able to draw some general conclusions: Local news tends to be "live, local, and late breaking," with a heavy dose of crime reports. News also tends to be formulaic, reactive, and short.[55]

To flesh these judgments out with data, researchers report that three quarters of all stories featured on local broadcasts do involve local events. Because of the heavy emphasis on crimes and accidents, roughly a third feature local law enforcement and fire-fighting personnel and crime suspects and victims. Another 14 percent feature local government officials or members of Congress representing the local community. One in five stories is a live report of a locally breaking event. Many of these involve common accidents or crimes, which are plentiful in most communities, especially when one considers that most local broadcasts cover multiple urban and suburban communities.

News is formulaic because it features similar types of stories in similar fashion night after night. The most common topic is crime. On average, 24 percent of all stories on local broadcasts—more than double any other topic—are drawn from local police department records. The reason is simple. Crime is considered exciting breaking news that is easily and cheaply available from local police stations. It can be aired night after night to audiences whose thirst for it seems unquenchable. Accidents, bizarre events, fires, and other catastrophes along with plain human interest stories account for another 22 percent of the local news pie. In general, 40 percent of all stories encompass fairly typical everyday events.

Stories tend to be brief. Roughly 70 percent are less than one minute and 42 percent are less than thirty seconds long. Such brevity does not permit in-depth analysis and turns local newscasts largely into a headline service that provides a nibble for everyone but satisfies no one's hunger. The Project for Excellence in Journalism researchers complained that the presentation of controversial stories was predominantly one-sided, depriving audiences of the chance to fully assess the merits of different positions. Sixty percent of the stories involving controversies reported it from just one perspective. The researchers also faulted local broadcasts for avoiding original investigative stories almost entirely. On most stations only 7 percent of the stories originated from reporters' efforts to cover important issues on their own initiative, rather than relying on press releases or merely recording ongoing events.

As part of its mandate to ensure that the electronic media serve the public interest, the Federal Communications Commission (FCC) has urged local television and radio stations to gear their programming to local needs, including reporting about local politics. Obviously, that mandate is honored more by lip service than by actual performance. Local stations do carry some local political news, but it constitutes only 10 percent of the average broadcast. This is hardly what the FCC has in mind when it calls for "local" programming.

Although these figures show that local news is light on politics, one must keep in mind that there are generally multiple nightly local newscasts. The proportion of serious political news available to citizens may therefore be fairly substantial. Several studies of the consequences associated with watching local newscasts indicate that most viewers feel better informed about the local scene, trust and appreciate newscasts more, and are more prone to fear crime and develop false stereotypes about the perpetrators and their victims. Readers of local print media are also more likely to participate in local politics.[56] Whether reading stimulates participation or participation stimulates reading remains an open question.

Just as one cannot lump all national media together for purposes of analysis, so one must differentiate local media along a number of dimensions. Size is one of them. Stations in the largest markets offer considerably more political news than stations in smaller markets.[57] Likewise, larger television stations devote a slightly smaller percentage of news space to local news and pay somewhat more attention to national and world events.[58] Stations in larger markets seem to be moving away from emphasizing local news as urged by the FCC's "localism doctrine."

National News on Local Media.   One reason for growing attention to national and world news by local stations is greater ease of access. New satellite and microwave technology permits local stations to tap into the pool of national news at will and report it from a local angle. In addition, local stations are increasingly entering into cooperative news-gathering systems, such as Conus and Newsfeed, that allow member stations to send their stories to other members in the system via satellite. Local stations consequently have become less dependent on network coverage for national and world events.

As we saw in Chapter 9, national newsmakers are eager to reach the hinterlands, where coverage tends to be gentler and more in tune with the newsmakers' agendas. Members of Congress rely heavily on publicity in their home states and strive to supply local media with stories and video-tapes originating in the nation's capital. Washington, D.C., also abounds with news bureaus that transmit national news, often presented from local angles, to member organizations or independent local clients. Washington news gathered by the Washington press corps but presented locally has a distinctive flavor. It often is more upbeat and less critical than its Beltway counterparts. Lacking insider knowledge, local reporters are less likely to subject national political leaders to tough questioning. They tend to pay more attention—and more favorable attention—to their senators and representatives than the national media.[59] National issues viewed from a local perspective can also be more somber. For example, stories about victims of war or terrorism that are featured in their hometown media are far more wrenching and opinion-shaping than the blander accounts in national media.[60]

Election Coverage at the Local Level

The entire U.S. electoral system is organized to reflect local and state-wide politics. All national officials—the president, senators, and representatives—are selected from state-based electoral districts, as are state officials and the half million local officials who occupy legislative, executive, judicial, and administrative positions throughout the states. Candidates for most of these offices, including scores of positions on local government boards and committees, are of prime interest to geographically limited constituencies. They rarely attract the attention of nationwide broadcasts or the few newspapers that have a nationwide circulation. Their political fate—and that of the areas they serve—therefore depends largely on coverage by local media.

News about the Candidates. The role of the local media in promoting candidates in state and local campaigns is similar to what was described in Chapter 8 for national campaigns. It is a growing role because state officials are spending more money on their media campaigns now. A large share of campaign spending goes toward efforts to obtain news story coverage rather than relying primarily on advertisements. In the past subnational officials relied heavily on radio advertisements because of the high costs of television. Cable channels have changed that situation because their advertising rates are much cheaper.

Although data remain scarce, some evidence suggests that, compared to national television news, local stations generally provide citizens with less information about the comparative merits of the candidates. A study of thirty-one stations in fourteen television markets during the last month of the 2000 presidential election campaign found that local election news broadcasts were much briefer, taking up only a small slice of the newscast, averaging around 10 percent.[61] Studies of gubernatorial races in Ohio and Michigan yielded similar conclusions. These studies also show the characteristic local patterns of one-sided coverage with incumbents usually receiving the lion's share of favorable attention.[62]

Newspaper endorsements are more important below the national level because most candidates for state and local offices are less familiar to the voters, who therefore turn more to the news media for guidance.[63] When viewers were asked to compare debates among presidential contenders at the national level with debates among candidates for state and local offices, they reported that they found the presidential debates more important and interesting, but learned more and were influenced more by the state and local debates.[64] Before watching the debates, 70 percent of the viewers in the local debate were undecided about their voting choices, compared with 40 percent of viewers in the presidential debate. If lack of information is a disease that plagues national elections, it apparently occurs in a far more virulent strain at state and local levels.

The fact that news media are now organized to serve larger markets often makes it difficult for candidates whose districts overlap several markets, or just a small slice of a large media market, to gain coverage. The media will not report about them as part of regular news coverage because limited time for news is reserved for stories of wider interest. Paid advertising coverage may be too expensive because rates are based on the numbers of people within the market, not on the much smaller numbers that are constituents of the candidate. A state representative who serves a district of 50,000 voters rarely can afford to pay for access to many times that number just because the advertising "area of dominant influence" in which her or his district is located covers a multitude of urban, suburban, and rural counties.

News about Referenda.   Elections involving local politics often are completely issue centered. Referenda on prospective policies are examples. Although these political contests have low visibility, their impact on the average citizen can dwarf that of the more publicized contests. After studying seventy-two referenda in California, Massachusetts, Michigan, and Oregon between 1976 and 1982, political scientist Betty Zisk concluded that they were impartially covered. Despite the liberal stance of the papers under investigation (the *Boston Globe,* the *Detroit Free Press,* the *Portland Oregonian,* the *Los Angeles Times,* and the *San Francisco Chronicle*), issues were amply discussed from a variety of perspectives.[65] However, Zisk faulted newspeople for merely reporting charges and countercharges rather than analyzing the merits of proposals and unmasking misleading rhetoric and advertisements.[66] When ballots were tallied, voters had agreed with newspaper recommendations about 68 percent of the time.[67] It is impossible to know with certainty whether this indicates media influence or merely an independently occurring concurrence of views. The side spending the most money, much of it to gain media coverage, won in three out of four cases (fifty-six of the seventy-two campaigns—78 percent). Zisk argues that money purchased victory, rather than good causes attracted the most money.

Radio and television, the main sources of political information for average voters, carried little news and few editorials about the referenda. Thirty- and sixty-second television spot advertisements were totally inadequate to cover the important points of most of these complex issues. However, some radio talk shows gave extensive coverage to referenda, albeit often generating more heat than light.[68] Unlike television, major regional newspapers provided comprehensive coverage of referendum issues. They carried extensive background features, pro and con articles and editorials, and news about campaign activities in the major urban centers, though not elsewhere in the jurisdiction covered by the referenda.[69]

The Quality of Local News

Maintaining high-quality coverage is often more difficult for local than for national media. As mentioned, compared to most national television networks, local television has a far greater need for a steady stream of news because it usually has three or more daily newscasts. That puts a premium on broadcasting the latest news, rather than repeating more important stories that were featured earlier in the day. To maintain profitability through a wide audience reach, local television usually pitches its programs to a moderately educated middle-income audience that, presumably, is uninterested in sophisticated political analysis.

It is also more difficult for local newscasters to get high-quality news commentary for local political stories. Many local officials lack the skills and experience required to be good media information sources. Because their jobs are often technical—fire chiefs or health commissioners, for example—they are chosen for their technical abilities and managerial skills, with no regard for public relations expertise. The end result is a dearth of political commentary on local stations. One content analysis of fourteen television stations of assorted sizes from five different markets found that only 43 (1.4 percent) of 3,037 stories that were examined included commentary.[70]

Lack of economic resources is also a problem for local stations and for local newspapers. It may explain why they use the most readily available stories, including press releases from government and the business community and why they rarely feature original, in-depth investigations. In a study of three network affiliates in the western United States, 75 percent of the news at small, economically weak stations came from handouts, 20 percent started with tips that were investigated, and 5 percent originated with reporters. For the largest, economically soundest station the figures were 50 percent from handouts, 36 percent from tips, and 13 percent originated by staff.[71] As Ben Bagdikian has put it in his inimitable style, journalism is "a daily battle between God and Mammon. Too much of the time, it's Mammon 100 and God 5." [72] Larger local stations and newspapers with greater financial resources do somewhat better in seeking out important news, providing context for their stories, and resisting pressures from advertisers.[73] Smaller news outlets cannot afford to antagonize the advertising hand that feeds them.

The difficulties in maintaining high-quality news have serious consequences at the local level because there are few competing information sources for local politics. Reporting by the local media may be the sole source of information available to interested citizens as well as government officials. It therefore matters if reporters, too, are soft on local politicians whom they know personally or spare local projects and policies from criticism out of a sense of local boosterism. Reporters rarely question estimates of costs and benefits of local development projects. They tend to be upbeat in reporting about local business leaders and economic trends. As Kaniss has noted, "While there is much in the news and editorial columns that is critical of local officials, this criticism is limited when compared with the amount of information that is taken directly, and almost unquestioningly, from official bureaucratic sources."[74] There are, of course, major exceptions to these appraisals, particularly in large cities with well-staffed news media. But even there, whenever budgets get tight, probing investigative reporting is among the first casualties.

Summary

The media spotlight falls unevenly on the body politic. In this chapter, we examined institutions that do not receive sufficient light for the U.S. public to adequately assess these institutions and the roles they play in the nation's political life. At the national level, the judicial branch suffers from inadequate news coverage. We have explained the reasons for neglect and some of the political consequences given the federal courts' importance in shaping U.S. politics. We have also noted problems that arise in reporting about the crime and justice system especially when the media focus on sensational matters rather than political substance.

At the subnational level, state news is neglected nearly everywhere in the United States. Hence, most citizens remain uninformed about state politics in their own as well as sister states. However, coverage seems to be adequate for the needs of state-level politicians, who find it easy to work with the local press. We also noted that local government publicity efforts are becoming more professional.

There is far more ample coverage of local than state news. Many regions within metropolitan areas, as well as suburbs and outlying communities, have local newspapers. But the quality of coverage of politics has deteriorated since the beginning of the twentieth century. Markets reflect technological and merchandising requirements rather than political needs. News media design their offerings accordingly. Fewer cities now have their own daily newspapers, and intracity competition among major dailies has almost vanished. The political dialogue has suffered. However, it seems too early to mourn the death of solid local politics coverage. The new technologies that make it feasible to tailor broadcasts to the needs of small audiences may restore the vigorous publicity that is essential at all political levels in a democracy.

Notes

1. Walter Lippmann, *Public Opinion* (1922; repr. New York: Free Press, 1965), 229.
2. Herbert M. Kritzer, "The Impact of *Bush v. Gore* on Public Perceptions and Knowledge of the Supreme Court," in *Judicial Politics: Readings from Judicature*, 3d. ed., ed. Elliot E. Slotnick (Washington, D.C.: CQ Press, 2005), 500–506.
3. *Brown v. Board of Education*, 347 U.S. 483 (1954); *Roe v. Wade*, 410 U.S. 113 (1973); *Planned Parenthood v. Casey*, 112 S. Ct. 2791 (1992).
4. Rorie L. Spill and Zoe M. Oxley, "Philosopher Kings or Political Actors? How the Media Portray the Supreme Court," in Slotnick, *Judicial Politics*, 462–470.
5. Richard Davis, "Lifting the Shroud: News Media Portrayal of the U.S. Supreme Court," *Communications and the Law* 9 (October 1987): 46; and Bob Woodward and Scott Armstrong, *The Brethren* (New York: Simon and Schuster, 1979), claim to present an insider's view of Court proceedings.
6. Richard Davis, *Decisions and Images: The Supreme Court and the Press* (Englewood Cliffs, N.J.: Prentice Hall, 1994), chap. 4.
7. Spill and Oxley, "Philosopher Kings."
8. Ibid., chap. 3.
9. *Engel v. Vitale*, 370 U.S. 421 (1962); *Baker v. Carr*, 369 U.S. 186 (1962).
10. Chester A. Newland, "Press Coverage of the United States Supreme Court," *Western Political Quarterly* 17 (1964): 15–36. Also see Kenneth S. Devol, *Mass Media and the Supreme Court*, 2d ed. (New York: Hastings House, 1976).
11. Stephanie Greco Larson, "How the *New York Times* Covered Discrimination Cases," *Journalism Quarterly* 62 (winter 1985): 894–896; also see Stephanie Greco Larson, "Supreme Court Coverage and Consequences" (paper presented at the annual meeting of the Midwest Political Science Association, Chicago, April 1989).
12. *Regents of the University of California v. Bakke*, 438 U.S. 265 (1978); *Webster v. Reproductive Health Services*, 109 S. Ct. 3040 (1989); Elliot E. Slotnick and Jennifer A. Segal, *Television News and the Supreme Court* (New York: Cambridge University Press, 1998).
13. Davis, *Decisions and Images*, chaps. 4–6; also see Frank J. Sorauf, "Campaign Money and the Press: Three Soundings," *Political Science Quarterly* 102 (spring 1987): 25–42.
14. Gregory Caldeira, "Neither the Purse Nor the Sword: Dynamics of Public Confidence in the Supreme Court," *American Political Science Review* 80 (December 1986): 1209–1228; John M. Scheb II and William Lyons, "Public Perception of the Supreme Court in the 1990s," in Slotnick, *Judicial Politics*, 496–499.
15. Robert E. Drechsel, *News Making in the Trial Courts* (New York: Longman, 1983), 19–22; Thomas R. Marshall and Joseph Ignagni, "Supreme Court and Public Support for Rights Claims," in Slotnick, *Judicial Politics*, 487–495.

16. David Pritchard, "Homicide and Bargained Justice: The Agenda-Setting Effect of Crime News on Prosecutors," *Public Opinion Quarterly* 50 (spring 1986): 143–159; Jon Bruschke and William E. Loges, "Relationship Between Pretrial Publicity and Trial Outcomes," *Journal of Communication* 49, no. 4 (fall 1999): 104–120; Dorothy Imrich, Charles Mullin, and Daniel Linz, "Measuring the Extent of Prejudicial Pretrial Publicity in American Newspapers: A Content Analysis," *Journal of Communication* 45, no. 3 (summer 1995): 94–117.

17. Doris A. Graber, *Processing Politics: Learning from Television in the Internet Age* (Chicago: University of Chicago Press, 2001), 137–139; C. Danielle Vinson and John S. Ertter, "Entertainment or Education: How the Media Cover the Courts," *Press/Politics* 7, no. 4 (2002): 80–89.

18. A detailed account of coverage of crime and justice system news is presented in Doris A. Graber, *Crime News and the Public* (New York: Praeger, 1980); also see Roy E. Lotz, *Crime and the American Press* (New York: Praeger, 1991); and Gregg Barak, ed., *Media, Process, and the Social Construction of Crime: Studies in Newsmaking Criminology* (New York: Garland, 1994).

19. George Comstock, "Paths from Television Violence to Aggression: Reinterpreting the Evidence," in *The Psychology of Entertainment Media: Blurring the Lines Between Entertainment and Persuasion*, ed. L.J. Shrum (Mahwah, N.J.: Erlbaum, 2004), 193–211.

20. Vinson and Ertter, "Entertainment or Education." Also see Daniel Romer, Kathleen Hall Jamieson, and Sean Aday, "Television News and the Cultivation of Fear of Crime," *Journal of Communication* 53, no. 1 (2003): 88–104.

21. Mira Sotirovic, "How Individuals Explain Social Problems: The Influence of Media Use," *Journal of Communication,* 53, no. 1 (2003): 122–137.

22. Richard L. Fox and Robert van Sickel, *Tabloid Justice: Criminal Justice in an Age of Media Frenzy* (Boulder, Colo.: Lynne Rienner, 2001), chap. 2.

23. Ibid., chap. 3.

24. Susanna Barber, *News Cameras in the Courtroom: A Free Press–Fair Trial Debate* (Norwood, N.J.: Ablex, 1987), especially 18–19. Also see Vinson and Ertter, "Entertainment or Education."

25. Fox and Sickel, *Tabloid Justice,* chap. 4; Fred Graham, "Doing Justice with Cameras in the Courts," *Media Studies Journal* 12, no. 1 (winter 1998): 32–37.

26. John J. Pauly and Melissa Eckert, "The Myth of 'The Local' in American Journalism," *Journalism and Mass Communication Quarterly* 79, no. 2 (2002): 310–326 explains why Americans venerate local news.

27. Ben H. Bagdikian, *The Media Monopoly,* 3d ed. (Boston: Beacon Press, 1990), 174. Also see Richard Campbell, Christopher R. Martin, and Bettina Fabos, *Media and Culture: An Introduction to Mass Communication,* 4th ed. (Boston: Bedford/St. Martin's, 2005).

28. Frederick Fico and Stan Soffin, "Fairness and Balance of Selected Newspaper Coverage of Controversial National, State, and Local Issues," *Journalism and Mass Communication Quarterly* 72, no. 3 (fall 1995): 621–633; Janet A. Bridges and Lamar W. Bridges, "Changes in News Use on the Front Pages of the American Daily Newspaper, 1986–1993," *Journalism and Mass Communication Quarterly* 73, no. 4 (winter 1997): 826–838. Also see Project for Excellence in Journalism, *State of the News Media 2004,* www.stateofthenewsmedia.org.

29. Pew Research Center for the People and the Press, "News Audiences Increasingly Politicized," 2004, http://people-press.org.

30. Jane B. Singer, "The Metro Wide Web: Changes in Newspapers' Gatekeeping Role Online," *Journalism and Mass Communication Quarterly* 78, no. 1 (spring 2001): 65–80.

31. James N. Rosse coined the term. See James M. Bernstein, Stephen Lacy, Catherine Cassara, and Tuen-yu Lau, "Geographic Coverage by Local Television News," *Journalism Quarterly* 57 (winter 1990): 664, note 4.

32. Phyllis Kaniss, *Making Local News* (Chicago: University of Chicago Press, 1991), 5.

33. Newspaper Association of America, "U.S. Daily and Sunday/Weekend Newspaper Reading Audience," in *Facts about Newspapers,* 2000, www.naa.org/info/facts00/02.html.

34. See Bernstein and others, "Geographic Coverage," 671; Project for Excellence in Journalism, *State of the News Media.*

35. William R. Davie and Jung-Sook Lee, "Sex, Violence, and Consonance/Differentiation: An Analysis of Local TV News Values," *Journalism and Mass Communication Quarterly* 72, no. 1 (spring 1995): 128–138; also see David C. Coulson, Daniel Riffe, Stephen Lacy, and Charles R. St. Cyr, "Erosion of Television Coverage of City Hall? Perceptions of TV Reporters on the Beat," *Journalism and Mass Communication Quarterly* 78, no. 1 (spring 2001): 81–92; and Guido H. Stempel III, "Where People Really Get Most of Their News," *Newspaper Research Journal* 12 (fall 1991): 2–9.

36. Daniel Riffe and Eugene F. Shaw, "Ownership, Operating, Staffing, and Content Characteristics of 'News Radio' Stations," *Journalism Quarterly* 67 (winter 1990): 684–691; Project for Excellence in Journalism, *State of the News Media.*

37. Project for Excellence in Journalism, *State of the News Media.*

38. Daniel M. Shea, "All Scandal Politics Is Local: Ethical Lapses, the Media, and Congressional Elections," *Press/Politics* 4, no. 2 (spring 1999): 45–62.

39. Kaniss, *Making Local News,* 175–179.

40. Martin Linsky, *How the Press Affects Federal Policymaking* (New York: Norton, 1986), 236.

41. Dan Berkowitz and Douglas B. Adams, "Information Subsidy and Agenda-Building in Local Television News," *Journalism Quarterly* 67 (winter 1990): 725.

42. Judy Van Slyke Turk and Bob Franklin, "Information Subsidies: Agenda-Setting Traditions," *Public Relations Review* 13 (1987): 29–41; Dan Berkowitz, "TV News Sources and News Channels: A Study in Agenda-Building," *Journalism Quarterly* 64 (autumn 1987): 508–513.

43. Thad Beyle and G. Patrick Lynch, "The Media and State Politics" (paper presented at the annual meeting of the Midwest Political Science Association, Chicago, April 1991), 5.

44. Roza Tsagarousianou, Damian Tambini, and Cathy Brian, eds., *Cyberdemocracy: Technology, Cities, and Civic Networks* (London: Routledge, 1998).

45. Claire E. Taylor, Jung-Sook Lee, and William R. Davie, "Local Press Coverage of Environmental Conflict," *Journalism and Mass Communication Quarterly* 77, no. 1 (spring 2000): 175–192.

46. Kaniss, *Making Local News,* 107.

47. News selection criteria are discussed in Camilla Gant and John Dimmick, "Making Local News: A Holistic Analysis of Sources, Selection Criteria, and Topics," *Journalism and Mass Communication Quarterly* 77, no. 3 (fall 2000): 628–638.

48. Kaniss, *Making Local News,* 118–120.

49. Ibid., 126–127.

50. The term is used in Kaniss, *Making Local News,* 126.
51. Ibid., 76.
52. This discussion is based on Stephen Hess, "Levels of the Game: Federalism and the American News System" (paper presented at the Hofstra University Conference, Hempstead, N.Y., April 1992).
53. For a discussion of state news in the *New York Times,* see Doris Graber, "Flashlight Coverage: State News on National Broadcasts," *American Politics Quarterly* 17 (July 1989): 277–290.
54. Pew Research Center for the People and the Press, "News Audiences Increasingly Politicized."
55. Project for Excellence in Journalism, *State of the News Media.*
56. Patricia Moy, Michael R. McCluskey, Kelley McCoy, and Margaret A. Spratt, "Political Correlates of Local News Media Use," *Journal of Communication* 54, no. 3 (2004): 532–546; Romer, Jamieson, and Aday, "Television News and the Cultivation of Fear of Crime"; Franklin D. Gilliam Jr. and Shanto Iyengar, "Prime Suspects: The Influence of Local Television News on the Viewing Public," *American Journal of Political Science* 44, no. 3 (2000): 560–573; Dietram A. Scheufele, James Shanahan, and Sei-Hill Kim, "Who Cares about Local Politics? Media Influences on Local Political Involvement, Issue Awareness, and Attitude Strength," *Journalism and Mass Communication Quarterly* 79, no. 2 (2002): 427–444.
57. Stephen Hess, *Live from Capitol Hill! Studies of Congress and the Media* (Washington, D.C.: Brookings Institution Press, 1991), 49. Also see Taylor, Lee, and Davie, "Local Press Coverage of Environmental Conflict," 175–192.
58. Bernstein and others, "Geographic Coverage by Local Television News," 668, 670; for similar results, also see Stephen Lacy and James M. Bernstein, "Daily Newspaper Content's Relationship to Publication Cycle and Circulation Size," *Newspaper Research Journal* (spring 1988): 49–57.
59. Hess, *Live from Capitol Hill!,* 53.
60. Scott Sigmund Gartner, "Making the International Local: The Terrorist Attack on the USS Cole, Local Casualties, and Media Coverage," *Political Communication* 21, no. 2 (2004): 139–159; also see the author's earlier study, "All Politics Are Local: An Analysis of the Effects of Proximate War Losses on Individual Opinions in the Vietnam War," *Journal of Conflict Resolution,* 41 (1997): 669–694.
61. Stephen J. Farnsworth and S. Robert Lichter, "Increasing Candidate-Centered Television Discourse: Evaluating Local News Coverage of Campaign 2000," *Press/Politics* 9, no. 2 (2004): 76–93.
62. Frederick Fico, Geri Alumit Zeldes, and Arvind Diddi, "Partisan and Structural Balance of Local Television Election Coverage of Incumbent and Open Gubernatorial Elections," *Journalism and Mass Communication Quarterly* 81, no. 4 (2004): 897–910.
63. Byron St. Dizer, "The Effects of Newspaper Endorsements and Party Identification on Voting Choice," *Journalism Quarterly* 62 (autumn 1985): 589–594.
64. A. Lichtenstein, "Differences in Impact between Local and National Televised Political Candidates' Debates," *Western Journal of Speech Communication* 46 (1982): 291–298; also see Dianne Bystrom, Cindy Roper, Robert Gobetz, Tom Massey, and Carol Beall, "The Effects of a Televised Gubernatorial Debate," *Political Communication Review* 16 (1991): 57–80.
65. Betty H. Zisk, *Money, Media, and the Grassroots: State Ballot Issues and the Electoral Process* (Newbury Park, Calif.: Sage, 1987), 28.

66. Ibid., 246.
67. Ibid., 109.
68. Ibid., 247–248.
69. For an excellent overview of the referendum process, see Claes H. de Vreese and Holli Semetko, *Political Campaigning in Referendums* (London: Routledge, 2004).
70. James M. Bernstein and Stephen Lacy, "Contextual Coverage of Government by Local Television News," *Journalism Quarterly* 69 (summer 1992): 338.
71. John McManus, "How Local Television Learns What Is News," *Journalism Quarterly* 67 (winter 1990): 678.
72. Quoted in Ibid, 672.
73. Bernstein and Lacy, "Contextual Coverage," 339.
74. Kaniss, *Making Local News,* 90–91.

Readings

Chiasson, Lloyd Jr. *Illusive Shadows: Justice, Media, and Socially Significant American Trials.* Westport, Conn.: Praeger, 2003.

Fox, Richard L., and Robert van Sickel. *Tabloid Justice: Criminal Justice in an Age of Media Frenzy.* Boulder: Lynne Rienner, 2001.

Halton, William. *Reporting on the Courts: How the Mass Media Cover Judicial Actions.* Chicago: Nelson Hall, 1998.

Heider, Don. *White News: Why Local News Programs Don't Cover People of Color.* Mahwah, N.J.: Erlbaum, 2000.

Kaniss, Phyllis. *Making Local News.* Chicago: University of Chicago Press, 1991.

―――. *The Media and the Mayor's Race: The Failure of Urban Political Reporting.* Indianapolis: Indiana University Press, 1995.

Lipschultz, Jeremy H., and Michael L. Hilt. *Crime and Local Television News: Dramatic, Breaking, and Live from the Scene.* Mahwah, N.J.: Erlbaum, 2002.

Slotnick, Elliot E., and Jennifer A. Segal. *Television News and the Supreme Court.* New York: Cambridge University Press, 1998.

Surette, Ray. *Media, Crime, and Criminal Justice: Images and Realities.* 2d ed. Belmont, Calif.: Wadsworth, 1998.

Vermeer, Jan P. *The View from the States: National Politics in Local Newspaper Editorials.* Lanham, Md.: Rowman and Littlefield, 2002.

Foreign Affairs Coverage

WHEN ISRAEL AND JORDAN PREPARED TO SIGN a peace agreement in the fall of 1994, they scheduled the ceremony for midday at a barren desert patch two miles north of the Gulf of Aqaba. The place was subject to sudden desert sandstorms and the appointed hour was the hottest time of the day. Why the location and the time? The answer is simple: It provided an excellent photo opportunity. As Israeli officials explained, midday at the Arava (near the Jordan border) is time for morning news in the United States—just the right time to show Americans that their president, depicted in a dramatic setting, was the godfather of the Jordanian–Israeli peace settlement.[1]

Is television coverage really important enough to make major sacrifices to schedule an important diplomatic event to meet broadcasting schedules? What, if any, are the links between the mass media and the process of creating foreign policy and producing policy outputs? How do governments use the media to further their policy objectives around the world? Do the media perform their watchdog role appropriately in times of war? In this chapter we will try to answer such provocative questions about how the mass media influence U.S. foreign policy.

We will first focus on the overall significance that U.S. media and U.S. citizens assign to news about foreign countries. Then we will point out the main differences between the production of foreign and domestic news. We will consider the unique problems newspeople face in collecting news and shaping it to meet newsworthiness criteria while heeding the canons of journalistic ethics and independence. Securing high-quality foreign news in times of peace and times of war is an extraordinarily difficult task.

We shall note how well it is currently carried out and point to accomplishments and failures.

The Foreign News Niche

Newspeople commonly assume that the U.S. public is interested primarily in what goes on in the United States. Reports about the public's ignorance about foreign countries and foreign affairs lend credence to these assumptions. Americans profess modest interest in foreign news, but when given a choice, they do not seek it out. When survey researchers asked a randomly selected national sample of people in 2004 about the types of news that they watched routinely, or only when the story seemed especially important or interesting, only half (52 percent) of the respondents claimed to watch international news routinely, whereas 47 percent said they watched only selectively. Three years earlier, only 37 percent had claimed to be regular watchers. The 15 percentage point jump illustrates how interest in foreign affairs waxes and wanes depending on the visibility of U.S. foreign involvements.[2]

Even when interest rises, it is rarely profound. Among regular readers, viewers, and listeners to news during the years of U.S. military engagement in Iraq, only 24 percent claimed to follow stories about international events very closely. That figure was surpassed by news about people in their own communities and news about crime, health, and sports. It was on a par with news about prominent politicians and events in Washington, D.C.[3]

Although most Americans do not make foreign news a prime focus of attention, print and electronic media give it considerable coverage. Foreign news receives 21 percent of the newshole in morning and early evening national network news programs and in the elite print press (see Table 4-4). That share drops to 8 percent in the nonelite print media, which constitute the main print news sources for most Americans.[4] Compared with attention to domestic affairs, foreign news is a neglected stepchild in terms of space, time, and prominence of display. News selection criteria are also more rigorous. To be published, foreign news must have a more profound impact on the political, economic, or cultural concerns of the United States than domestic news. It must involve people of more exalted status and entail more violence or disaster.[5] During crises, particularly prolonged ones that endanger U.S. lives, foreign coverage often doubles or even triples; it may even drown out most other news. Conversely, the number of stories and their length shrinks when times seem unusually calm, as happened right after the cold war ended with the collapse of the Soviet Union.[6] The number of active foreign news correspondents fluctuates in similar fashion.

The country's foreign policy elites, including government officials, depend heavily on foreign news covered by prestigious media. As a State Department official attests, "The first thing we do is read the newspaper— *the newspaper*—the *New York Times.* You can't work in the State Department without the *New York Times.*" [7] Members of the U.S. Congress, particularly those concerned with foreign affairs, and foreign officials in the United States have made similar comments. All feel that elite newspaper reports keep them informed better and often faster than their own official sources.

Making Foreign News

Although news making for domestic stories and for foreign stories differs substantially, there are many similarities. To make comparisons easier, we will follow the organization of domestic news making and reporting described in Chapter 4. First we will consider the gatekeepers—the corps of foreign correspondents who are the front-line echelon among gatherers of foreign affairs news. Then we will discuss the setting for news selection, the criteria for choosing stories and the means of gathering them, the constraints on news production, and finally the effects of gatekeeping on foreign affairs coverage.

Gatekeepers: The Vanishing News Bureaus

A combination of advancing technology, globalization of news, and efforts to cut costs is changing gatekeeping for foreign news. Most news about events happening throughout the world used to be collected by four major wire services: the U.S.–owned Associated Press (AP), Britain's Reuters, France's Agence France-Presse, and ITAR, which replaced the Soviet news agency Tass in 1992. [8] Among these world-class wire services, AP has always been by far the largest. It has now become the dominant international news wire. [9] Other wire services have been shrinking or disappearing. Britain's Reuters has financial difficulties that may force it to outsource much of its work to India; France's Agence France-Presse is surviving only because the French government subsidizes it.

In 2005 the Associated Press maintained 242 bureaus worldwide with a staff of 3,700 employees. [10] It provided print and broadcast news in multiple languages to clients in 121 countries. AP reporters are initial gatekeepers who ferret out the stories that make up the pool from which other gatekeepers select reports or find leads to pursue stories more fully. Because wire service reporters work for a variety of clients throughout the world, their news reports must be bland so that they do not offend people whose views span a wide political spectrum. Wire service news therefore emphasizes fast and ample factual reports of ongoing events. It does not provide interpretations but leaves that to the users of its reports.[11]

Besides the news reports provided by the wire service bureaus, much foreign news once came from news bureaus maintained by various news organizations. That has changed. Permanent international bureaus are no longer the model for handling most international coverage. There are a few notable exceptions, like the *New York Times,* which has actually expanded its foreign correspondents corps abroad. The *Times* can afford to operate its bureaus because their cost is defrayed largely by income from selling syndicated stories to other media enterprises. On the broadcast side of the ledger of gathering international news, CNN, the twenty-four-hour Cable News Network, has been a major player in the international news game since the 1980s. It has nearly 4,000 reporters scattered in regional offices throughout the world who collect and report news in multiple languages for worldwide audiences. As is typical of live broadcast coverage, CNN reports are a mixed bag of events and interviews ranging from the trivial to the significant, but with less time given to analysis and expert commentary than is typical for network television news. The emphasis is on taping whatever is readily and inexpensively available so that viewers are the first to see a breaking news event at close range. Table 11-1 shows the types of news that CNN offers to its global audiences on a typical day. It represents an impressive romp through the scenes of newsworthy events happening in diverse locations north and south of the equator.

Gatekeepers: The New Types of Foreign Correspondents

In the past foreign correspondents reported much of the foreign news available in the U.S. press. These elite journalists are becoming an extinct breed. Some are still around, but new types of foreign correspondents are joining and replacing them. Who are these new types of reporters? Journalism scholars John Maxwell Hamilton and Eric Jenner identify several.[12] In addition to the traditional U.S. correspondents stationed abroad, there are now a large number of foreigners who supply U.S. news media with news about their home countries and adjacent regions. Their stories may lack the traditional U.S. perspective, but they are gathered at a fraction of the roughly $250,000 that it costs to station a U.S. newspaper correspondent abroad. The price doubles for broadcast correspondents. Given these cost differentials, it should come as no surprise that by 2005 only 31 percent of the correspondents reporting news from abroad to the United States were Americans.[13] The belief that only

TABLE 11-1   One Day of CNN World News Headlines, May 2, 2005

EUROPE	ASIA PACIFIC
Italy: Italy hits back over agent's death.	*South Korea:* S. Korea–Japan play down
France: "Yes" vote in France gains	test.
ground.	*Afghanistan:* Twenty-eight die in Afghan
Britain: Blair keeps healthy lead in polls.	blast.
	Taiwan: Chen urges Taiwan-China "par-
AFRICA	ity."
Togo: More than 1,600 flee Togo.	
Mauritania: Protests precede visit of	MIDDLE EAST
Israeli envoy.	*Egypt:* Three dead in Cairo attacks.
Uganda: Ugandan president rips western	*Israel:* Pilgrims participate in holy fire
"meddling."	rite.
	Iran: Iran "may restart nuke activities."
AMERICAS	
Mexico: Poll: Support for Mexico City	UNITED STATES
mayor grows.	*Georgia:* Bridge charges possible.
Honduras: Plane carrying president goes	*Texas:* Abu Ghraib: England pleads
down.	guilty.
United States: Chilean chosen to head	*North Carolina:* Teens rescued after six
OAS	days at sea.

native Americans are capable of reporting news with an appropriate U.S. flavor has given way to the idea that foreign news reported by foreigners may have a different flavor, but that may actually be beneficial. It may tell Americans how people in other countries interpret the political scene.

Encouraged by easy international travel and cheap airline fares, more and more U.S.–based print and broadcast media are sending correspondents abroad for short jaunts to report about a particular event. These newer types of foreign correspondents have been dubbed "parachute" journalists. Most of them travel from the United States; a few are stationed at overseas jumping-off points. For example, *USA Today* uses its seven overseas bureaus as regional jumping-off points for parachuters. Parachute journalism has become almost routine for large news organizations and fairly common for smaller ones. The horde of U.S. parachute journalists dispatched to report about the death of Pope John Paul II in 2005 and the selection of his successor is a good example. The majority of the news organizations that sent more than 6,000 journalists to Rome were newcomers to gathering foreign news.[14]

So-called premium service foreign correspondents are another innovation. Hamilton and Jenner cite the example of the Bloomberg subscription news service.[15] Besides its contingent of U.S.–based print and broadcast reporters who cover economic stories in the United States, Bloomberg has 1,000 print reporters and 200 broadcast reporters stationed all over the globe. A single subscription to Bloomberg news cost $1,650 monthly in 2004 and paid for access to global financial news gathered by this large, international corps of correspondents.

News from all over the world may not be a high priority for most Americans. But in the age of globalization, foreign news is essential for large corporations with customers or branches all over the world. Nearly all of these corporations have their own reporters who often are professional journalists located abroad to dispatch salient news via computer to their U.S. bases. Much of this news is not confidential and spreads beyond the confines of the company to the networks to which company employees are linked.

Another stream of special interest news comes from public relations agencies hired by foreign countries to promote their images. More and more countries are contracting for professional image management. Citizens for a Free Kuwait, a front organization for the government of Kuwait, for example, spent nearly $11 million with just one public relations firm to burnish Kuwait's image in the months after it had been invaded by Iraq.[16] By either stimulating or suppressing media coverage, public relations agencies try to improve their clients' media image. Presumably this then changes the news images that Americans receive about the international scene and influences the conduct of politics in ways that benefit particular countries.[17]

The largest group of foreign correspondents—if they indeed deserve that name—are nonprofessionals who use Web sites to report their observations from abroad or from U.S. locations. The more serious and successful ones of this breed may become bloggers whose Web sites may be visited by hundreds of amateurs. The visitors then distribute this news—and the blogging responses it has provoked—to people far and wide. In fact, Web sites have become an important information source for journalists throughout the globe who either relay blog stories through established news organizations or use them as the basis of creating their own news organization.

Finally, large numbers of Americans now draw their information about events beyond the U.S. borders from Internet visits to foreign newspapers and foreign broadcasts. They can learn about events abroad like the turmoil in Iraq in 2005 from an Arab perspective by turning to Al Jazeera, or from a French perspective by reading *Le Monde*. Or they can listen to news from Britain's BBC or turn to English-language news from China transmitted by CNN. Scanning international news can be done very easily and inexpensively by anyone who has a computer linked to the Internet. How many people use foreign news sources and what the consequences are remain uncertain for now.

U.S. soldiers deployed in Iraq engaged in a major offensive to recapture Falluja. Embedded cameramen accompanying U.S. troops shot the picture, November 9, 2004.

Given that news reporting through diverse cultural lenses varies in perspective, the same story raw materials yield different end-products. At times the versions vary so widely that they seem to cover totally different situations. For instance, faced with the same information about global warming before, during, and after a 1997 international conference in Kyoto, Japan, U.S. reporters focused on U.S. stances on the issue, with little mention of international views; German reporters favored international views but slighted European opinions. The U.S. media split attention about evenly between the substance of the debates at Kyoto and the strategies used by negotiators; the German media focused more heavily on policy substance and barely touched on strategy.[18] Once established, story stereotypes become fixed. The initial impressions gate-keepers have conveyed about countries, leaders, and specific policies remain stable even when the reality changes in major ways.

It has become impossible to profile the "typical" foreign correspondent because there are so many new types, including the horde of nonprofessionals whose reports appear on the Internet. Foreign correspondents used to be elites among journalists: better educated, more experienced, more worldly wise, and better paid. They were U.S. citizens and, like most journalists working for elite media, they were politically liberal, taking positions to the left of mainstream views. Nonetheless, they rarely challenged the U.S. government's stance on foreign policy issues, unless prominent leaders questioned the policy. That demographic profile is unlikely to fit most of the women and men who report from abroad in the twenty-first century.

Although much has changed, one unfortunate persistent characteristic of U.S.–born foreign correspondents is their inability to communicate in most of the world's languages other than English. Deficient foreign language skills continue to hamper U.S. reporters abroad in local interviews and investigations. They must depend on translated newspaper reports and on handouts prepared by other governments for the foreign press.[19] This sharply curbs their effectiveness as reporters, especially because most of them have few direct contacts with average local people and lack the personal ties that may supply good insights. Some countries supply official translators for foreign journalists. That is a mixed blessing because the presence of government officials during interviews dampens the free exchange of ideas that might otherwise take place.

Attempts to profile foreign journalists dispatched to the United States by foreign media institutions face the same difficulties. A fair amount of information is available about the roughly 1,500 formally accredited correspondents who are stationed in Washington, D.C., or in New York, but little is known beyond these elites. Media scholars Lars Wilnat and David Weaver conducted a mail survey in 2000 that confirmed that accredited foreign reporters are an extremely well-educated group.[20] Forty-five percent are college graduates, 38 percent hold masters degrees, and 9 percent have earned Ph.D.s. Most are fluent English speakers, and a majority are fluent in a third language as well. Nevertheless, their contacts with Americans are limited. In an earlier survey, only 7 percent said that their best and closest contacts were Americans. In political orientation, foreign newspeople covering the United States tend to be further to the left than most U.S. reporters and quite critical about U.S. policies and lifestyles.[21]

Most news about the United States goes to the press in friendly countries.[22] The poorer regions of the world find it too costly to send correspondents to Washington, D.C.[23] In the 2000 survey, half of the correspondents (51 percent) represented western European countries. The next largest contingent (12 percent) came from East Asian nations and 11 percent from Latin America. Only 7 percent came from poor countries in Africa and the Middle East.

It is difficult for foreign reporters to cover the whole United States adequately. Most correspondents are kept busy in Washington, D.C., and New York. They rarely travel to other parts of the United States except to cover special events, such as spacecraft launchings or major sports competitions.

Thus the impressions that foreigners receive about U.S. politics largely reflect official Washington perspectives. Many foreign reporters complain that top-level U.S. officials rarely grant them interviews, making it difficult for them to file original reports. The frustrations such slights produce, coupled with the leftward orientation of most overseas reporters, produces a substantial amount of criticism of the United States's economic, military, and foreign aid policies. The damage done to the conduct of U.S. foreign relations by hostile news coverage abroad is only slightly balanced by U.S. government broadcasts designed to polish the country's image.

The Setting for News Selection

News cannot be gathered and produced in a vacuum. It always reflects the spirit of a particular historical period and the reporters' backgrounds and experiences.

Cultural Pressures. The journalists who gather news for mainstream U.S. media, like journalists who report domestic stories, must operate within the context of U.S. politics and political culture. Besides reflecting the U.S. value structure, stories also must conform to established U.S. stereotypes. Leaders widely characterized as either villainous or virtuous must be depicted true to their image in news stories. The ready availability of contrary images on the Internet may make it more difficult eventually to maintain stereotypes.

Because the wire services perform the initial gatekeeping tasks for most newspapers and electronic media, topic selection is quite uniform. In the United States elite papers then take the lead in framing the stories, and editors and reporters throughout the country follow suit. The upshot is a foreign news menu that is far more limited in scope than the menu of domestic news.

Political Pressures. Overt and covert political pressures to publish or suppress news stories play a greater role in foreign news production than on the domestic scene. Correspondents reporting from various regions of the world often must do their host country's bidding. Many host governments are politically unstable and fear for their survival if they receive unfavorable publicity. Hence they censor all news stories. If foreign correspondents want to remain in the country, they must write dispatches acceptable to the authorities or face severe penalties. These include refusal of contact by public officials, confiscation of their notes and pictures, closure of transmission facilities, and expulsion or criminal prosecution. These circumstances have produced a strange phenomenon: The most undemocratic countries often receive the least criticism, whereas more open societies are freely reproached.

When countries previously closed to foreign journalists suddenly open their borders, journalists may be totally unprepared for insightful coverage. The opening of the People's Republic of China in 1972 is an example. Reporters arrived with President Richard Nixon and Secretary of State Henry Kissinger. During the journalists' short stay in China, they dutifully reported those stories that the Chinese arranged for them to report. Not surprisingly, their U.S. audiences were treated to a romanticized travelogue rather than solid political analysis.

Scores of countries have barred foreign reporters entirely from entering or have expelled them after entry. Albania, Cambodia, El Salvador, Iran, Nicaragua, North Korea, South Africa, the Soviet Union, and Vietnam provide vivid examples from recent decades. Britain kept foreign reporters away from the embattled Falkland Islands in 1983, and Israel has repeatedly imposed tight censorship on coverage of its activities in the occupied West Bank and Gaza Strip. Large areas of Central America and of the former Soviet Union have been closed to reporters, making it almost impossible to cover hostilities adequately there. The United States has also used a variety of tactics to limit reporters' access to sites where U.S. military operations were in progress.[24] Bureaucratic hurdles imposed on journalists range from difficult visa requirements to failure to provide transportation to outlying areas to hurdles in transmitting the news to a reporter's home base.

In some countries reporters face physical danger. Not infrequently, they have been jailed, assaulted, and sometimes murdered. In a ten-year span between 1993 and 2002, 366 journalists were killed while performing their duties. Among them, 76 percent were murdered in revenge for their reporting; most of the remainder were killed in crossfire incidents or violent street demonstrations.[25] The Helsinki Accords of 1975, in which signatory countries promised free and safe access to each other's newspeople, have done little to improve the situation.

Media Diplomacy.   The extreme measures that many political leaders take to silence individual reporters or entire media organizations are sad testimony to the pervasive belief that media can subvert public policies and topple governments.[26] That belief also fuels the many efforts by image-conscious governments around the world to plant favorable stories in the news, often through paid public relations agents, or to suppress unfavorable ones. At times, political leaders use interviews with foreign journalists to circumvent normal diplomatic channels and instead send messages to other leaders via the published interviews. Alternatively, leaders may send their messages directly to a news channel. For example, Al Qaeda leader Osama bin Laden has repeatedly communicated with the United States and other countries by sending taped messages to Al Jazeera.

That channel has obliged him by broadcasting his words directly rather than merely reporting about them.

Journalists may even take the initiative in serving as go-betweens for hostile governments. The turbulent politics of the Middle East present the most dramatic examples of journalists turning into quasi-diplomats. A celebrated incident involves CBS anchor Walter Cronkite, who became a peacemaker in 1977 when he used a television interview to draw a promise from Egypt's president Anwar al-Sadat to visit Jerusalem if this action would further peace. In a separate interview, Cronkite secured a pledge from Israeli prime minister Menachem Begin that he would personally welcome Sadat at Ben Gurion airport. With such mutual commitments, the scene was set for the historic meeting.[27]

When Sadat arrived in Israel, flanked by anchors from the three U.S. networks, 2,000 journalists from all over the globe were part of the welcoming crowds. This was media diplomacy in the broadest sense. The event was covered live on U.S. television and radio, giving the principals a chance to woo U.S. audiences. In the weeks that followed, more than 30 million people in the United States and millions more worldwide watched and judged the peacemaking process. Television alone devoted twenty-four hours of broadcasts to the spectacle, supplemented by radio and print news.

The lesson that media diplomacy can succeed where more ordinary government-to-government contacts fail has not been lost on other world leaders. For instance, in 1979 Iran's revolutionary leader, Ayatollah Ruhollah Khomeini, rebuffed official emissaries from the United States who were sent to negotiate the release of the U.S. embassy personnel held hostage by Iranian students. Instead, he arranged a series of interviews with U.S. television correspondents, requiring prior approval of questions so that he could control the discussion. To ensure maximum exposure for the Ayatollah's views, Iranian leaders granted an especially lengthy interview for the popular CBS program *60 Minutes*. The Iranian embassy also bought full-page advertisements in the *New York Times* and other U.S. newspapers to offer Iran's version of the hostage story to the U.S. public. Even when diplomatic relations are carried out through normal channels, reporters often become part of the political process by choosing the issues to be aired during interviews with political leaders and by covering selected activities during negotiating sessions and when leaders travel abroad. Reporters cover these events as they see them.[28] In the longstanding conflict in Northern Ireland, reporters have given voice to formally excluded parties, like Sinn Fein, the political wing of the Irish Republican Army, by publicizing their views about ongoing negotiations.[29]

Although media diplomacy is often helpful, it also is fraught with disadvantages and dangers. Government officials, who have far more foreign policy expertise than journalists, may be maneuvered into untenable positions. They may have to react to unforeseen developments with undue haste, especially when twenty-four-hour newscasts may also arouse interest groups who see peaceful or disruptive protests in front of television cameras as a way to promote their causes worldwide. That has been a common occurrence at the annual economic summit meetings of world leaders.[30] Also, journalists may inadvertently provide a propaganda forum for foreign leaders. This is why many Americans harshly condemned CNN's Peter Arnett when he engaged Iraqi president Saddam Hussein in a long television interview during the Gulf War. The interview permitted the Iraqi leader to broadcast accusations against his antagonists to a worldwide audience.

Economic Pressures. Economic considerations, like cultural and political factors, also impact foreign news selection. Given the fact that most major media enterprises are owned by large public corporations, profits have become a huge concern. Accordingly, there is the usual pressure to present appealing stories that attract big audiences and keep the advertisers happy. This constraint is even more burdensome for foreign correspondents than for their domestic counterparts, because their stories must be exceptionally good to attract large audiences. There is also pressure to avoid or minimize huge production costs. Some stories may be shut out when they cannot be transmitted cheaply; others may be included merely because they are comparatively inexpensive and convenient to produce.

Gathering the News: The Beat

The international beat system is quite similar to local beats. Foreign news bureaus usually are located in the world's major capital cities. From there, correspondents cover entire countries rather than particular types of stories. In the past London, Paris, Bonn, and Rome were the main newsgathering spots. In the wake of the Vietnam War and perennial troubles in the Middle East, capitals in these regions became important news centers. China moved into focus with the opening of diplomatic relations with the United States in 1972.

Despite the greater ease of travel to all parts of the world, the bulk of foreign affairs news for U.S. media still originates in Washington, D.C., from various beats in the executive branch, especially the White House, the State Department, and the Pentagon. When journalists try to cover foreign policy–relevant news, they often face officials who are reluctant to talk because delicate negotiations or the prestige of the United States may be at stake. That makes it difficult for the media to construct cohesive stories about some of the most important political issues facing the nation.

Foreign news bestows unequal attention on regions and countries of the world just as domestic news covers regions of the United States unequally. There is no correlation between size of population and amount of coverage. In general, stories cover the countries with which the United States has its most significant diplomatic contacts. In recent years that has usually meant England, France, Germany, Italy, and Russia in Europe; Egypt, Iran, Iraq, and Israel in the Middle East; and, more recently, the People's Republic of China and Japan in the Far East. Aside from Canada and Mexico, the western hemisphere is covered lightly, except when Americans become concerned about production and export of illicit drugs, civil strife, or international business issues. Asian coverage was light until the Vietnam War, when it replaced stories from other parts of the world for several years. Overall, coverage has dropped off sharply in all types of media since the end of the Cold War. Similar to domestic news, traditional political content is fading and social and economic news is becoming more plentiful.[31] The softer focus is particularly apparent on news Web sites.[32] There is a preference for covering predictable events like elections or international conferences because coverage can be planned in advance.

Table 11-2 provides data on network television coverage of major regions of the world from October 1 to November 5, 2004. It illustrates how a heavy focus on one region can eclipse news from the rest of the world almost totally. The table therefore reports comparison data for 2000, which was a more normal year for foreign news. Clearly, coverage is unevenly distributed. Heaviest coverage goes to areas involved in bloody conflicts, including massive injuries to civilians. If it bleeds, it definitely leads. Stories about the Middle East conflict are most abundant, followed by tales of woe from Eastern Europe and Asia. Attention to North America was a bit above average for that region in 2000, largely because of increased U.S.–Mexican dealings. By contrast, news about Western Europe was exceptionally light.

In general, stories with visuals are more attractive to viewers than stories that are purely verbal. Pictures are especially important for foreign news because they bring unfamiliar sights, which might be hard to imagine, directly into viewers' homes. Starvation in India or Somalia, the lifestyles of tribes in New Guinea or Australia, or street riots in Spain or China become much more comprehensible if audiences can experience them visually. Still, not even words and pictures combined can tell a whole story if the audience is unfamiliar with the setting in which the reported events are happening. Ugly street scenes of protesters attacking police, torching buildings, and looting stores may be misinterpreted if the audience does not know the even uglier events that might have provoked the protest.[33] For more than 30 percent of the stories the chances are slim that they will

TABLE 11-2   Network Coverage of World Regions, October 1–November 5, 2004
(comparisons to same period in 2000 in parentheses)

Region	Total number of stories		Stories with visual	Stories with link to United States
Middle East	180	(180)	122	110
Western Europe	14	(18)	12	0
Asia	8	(49)	7	0
North America	5	(21)	4	2
Eastern Europe	4	(51)	1	2
Latin America	4	(11)	3	1
Africa	2	(12)	2	0
Caribbean	0	(1)	0	0
Australia	0	(2)	0	0

SOURCE: Author's research compiled from Vanderbilt Television News Archives data.

NOTE: Data tapped 217 stories in 2004 and 345 in 2000.

be noticed and remembered because they lack pictures. Audiences are
also more likely to pay attention to stories that are linked explicitly to U.S.
interests. This is especially important for regions with which average Americans are least familiar, such as Africa and Asia, and even Latin America
and the Caribbean. In 2004 only 53 percent of foreign news stories made a
link to U.S. interests.

Criteria for Choosing Stories

Foreign news, like domestic news, is selected primarily for audience
appeal rather than for political significance. This means that stories must
have an angle that interests Americans. Sociologist Herbert Gans examined foreign affairs news in television newscasts and in news magazines
and identified seven subjects that media cover frequently.[34] First in order
of frequency of coverage are U.S. activities in foreign countries, particularly when presidents and secretaries of state visit. Second are events that
affect Americans directly in a major way, such as oil embargoes and international economic problems. Third are relations of the United States with
communist and formerly communist states, particularly when stories
emphasize internal political and military problems. Fourth, the media
cover events abroad if they involve a change in the head of state or activities of European royalty. Fifth are stories about dramatic political conflicts.
Most wars, coups d'état, and revolutions are reported; protests, as a rule,
are covered only when they are violent. Sixth are disasters, if they involve

massive loss of lives and destruction of property. There is a rough calculus by which media measure severity: "10,000 deaths in Nepal equals 100 deaths in Wales equals 10 deaths in West Virginia equals one death next door." [35] In general, the more distant a nation, the more frequently a newsworthy event must happen to be reported. Seventh are the excesses of foreign dictators, particularly when they involve brutality against political dissidents. Genocide in Rwanda and Bosnia are examples. Noticeably absent from U.S. broadcasts and newspapers are stories about ordinary people and ordinary events abroad. These would be news to Americans, but, except for occasional special features, they are not news in the professional dictionary of journalists.

Foreign news stories also must be exciting and engaging. Emphasis on violence, conflict and disaster, timeliness or novelty, and familiarity of persons or situations are the major selection criteria. Stories from areas that are familiar because of ample prior coverage or because they are common travel destinations are more likely to be published than stories from more remote parts of the world. When news from countries with unfamiliar cultures is published, the rule of "uncertainty absorption" comes into play. Only plausible stories are acceptable, and they must be cast into a familiar framework, such as the battle against poverty and racism or the moral bankruptcy of military dictators.[36] Such biases make it exceedingly difficult to change images of culturally distant countries.

The media's preference for news about current happenings has led to concentration on rapidly breaking stories in accessible places. More significant long-range developments, such as programs to improve public health or reduce illiteracy or efforts to create new political parties, do not fit the bill if they lack a recent climax. When major events are reported without analysis of the context that spawned them, they acquire an unwarranted air of suddenness and unpredictability. They have no past, and without appropriate follow-ups, they also have no future. They are merely a brief presence in the parade of current events.

Space and time limitations are particularly troubling for reporting foreign events, which are often unintelligible without adequate background information or interpretation. Complexity therefore becomes a major enemy and avoidance or oversimplification the defensive strategy. Reporters must write stories simply and logically even if the situation defies logic. Usually a single theme must be selected to epitomize the entire complex story. The dominant theme of the story about China's detention of a downed U.S. plane and crew in 2001, for example, was that innocent Americans were held hostage by a dictatorial, anti-American regime—a gross oversimplification of a multifaceted situation. The complexities of China's internal politics, particularly the influence of its military institutions, received little attention because they could not be easily incorporated into a dramatic, visually appealing story.

At times coverage errs in the opposite direction. The story of Americans held hostage in Iran from November 4, 1979, to January 20, 1981, was vastly overcovered. During the first six months of the crisis, nearly one-third of each nightly network newscast was devoted to the story.[37] A similar situation developed during the 1991 Gulf War, when 57 percent of the foreign news focused on the Middle East. Much of that coverage was repetitious and uninformative. With media attention riveted on one international trouble spot, most other foreign news is slighted. Table 11-2 records a similar situation for 2004. In the five weeks from October 1 to November 5, 83 percent of the news from abroad concerned the Middle East. Four years earlier, Middle East coverage constituted just 52 percent, leaving time for sizable coverage of eastern and western Europe and Asia.

Wars in the Television Age

In the wake of the Vietnam War, many politicians and other political observers believed that fighting lengthy wars had become nearly impossible for democratic societies in the age of full-color, battlefront television. When battle scenes are broadcast nightly in bloody colors, public support for wars is likely to weaken or even vanish. To avoid images that could interfere with the conduct of the war, the United States, like other countries, often restricts war coverage. Accordingly, no reporters were permitted to witness the first phases of the U.S. invasion of Grenada in 1983. The military is especially disinclined to take time out to deal with reporters during these initial stages because it is preoccupied with fighting and wants to keep its action plans secret. Journalists, on the other hand, want to be at the scene of action from the start with full access to the troops.

The press complained loudly that its exclusion from initial coverage amounted to undue muzzling of the media at a time when its watchdog functions were particularly crucial. In response to these complaints the military allowed access to a small rotating group of reporters to record operations in Grenada. A similar pool system failed miserably in Panama in December 1989 during a mission designed to depose Panamanian president Manuel Noriega. The fourteen reporters in the pool reached Panama four hours after the fighting began, but they were not allowed to file stories until six hours later. Then their movements were restricted to tours under military escort.[38]

The situation was not much better during the 1991 Gulf War, even though the military had revised the rules again to permit journalists more freedom of movement. The pool system allowed only 100 of the more than 1,600 U.S. reporters in the area access to some 500,000 troops. Reporters who went to the front without authorization were arrested and detained. The upshot was military-controlled, sanitized coverage of the war. Flawlessly executed precision maneuvers were shown but not failures or pictures of the dead and wounded, friend or foe. Although military censorship was to blame for glamorizing the battlefield, journalists must share the blame for inadequate coverage. Most of them were unfamiliar with the history and politics of the peoples of the region and with the policies of various outside powers interested in the area, including the United States. Had they done their homework, their coverage could have been far more insightful.[39]

After the war executives from the major U.S. media formally complained to Defense Secretary Dick Cheney about the pool system and efforts to sanitize and delay the news.[40] The complaints led to yet another revision of the rules, which was endorsed by the journalism community.[41] When hostilities against Afghanistan began in the winter of 2001, the familiar problems surfaced because it is well-nigh impossible to reconcile journalists' demands for press freedom with the military's security concerns. Whenever such conflicts make it into the courts, judges usually side with the military and public opinion supports their decisions.[42] However, the balance of forces shifted moderately in the media's favor when U.S. civilian and military officials realized that the impending war in Iraq would receive detailed coverage from Al Jazeera and other potentially hostile Middle Eastern sources. U.S. media were likely to pick up this coverage in the absence of frontline news from U.S. sources.

A new approach announced in February 2003 therefore provided for a pool of approximately 600 print and broadcast war correspondents from the U.S. and other countries to accompany troops from all branches of the military. These "embedded" journalists would be screened and trained by the Pentagon so that they would fit smoothly into the units to which they were assigned. The "embeds" had to sign an agreement on ground rules of coverage and pledge that they would submit potentially sensitive stories to pre-publication scrutiny by military censors. The Defense Department promised only light censorship. Journalists who remained outside the embedded group, the so-called "unilaterals," were not subject to restrictive rules. But, in line with history, their access to front-line operations was severely restricted. Roughly 40 percent of journalists ultimately chose to be unilaterals.

When the plan was announced, critics immediately questioned whether embedded journalists would be able to retain their objectivity when they shared their lives with the troops and were likely to become close friends with many of them. Being embedded might simply be another form of government news management that amounted to "being in bed" with the military. Judging from the reports of journalists and observers, that apparently did not happen, and the embedding process received a good deal of praise. As one observer noted: ". . . embedding allowed far greater access to the battlefield than the press has enjoyed in more than two decades and has dampened the long hostility between the Pentagon and the press." [43] Yet another report warned that collaboration with the military comes at a price. "The weakness is that the embeds' accounts necessarily become the story of the war as seen through the eyes of American soldiers. No reporter is going to be 'objective' about those who are protecting his or her life." [44]

It is unlikely that the time will ever arrive when the military and the press will be fully satisfied with each other's conduct. Their respective goals are much too antagonistic. War is a dirty business that will never be photogenic when pictured in all its brutality. As long as "just" wars for "good causes" (whatever they may be) are condoned and even celebrated by the world community, full coverage of the horrors of war remains a sensitive issue. Cries for formal or informal censorship under the banner of patriotism will drown cries for press freedom.

Flaws in Gatekeeping

Foreign affairs coverage is dramatic and up to date, but it lacks depth and breadth. It stereotypes and oversimplifies, and it often distorts facts by failing to embed them in a realistic context. Analysis of forty-six years of news coverage of the Soviet Union between 1945 and 1991 revealed that the lion's share went to military aspects of the cold war while economic and science issues were neglected. Table 11-3 records the topics covered by the *New York Times,* the prime source of international news in the United States, when the spotlight focused on the Soviet Union during press conferences and in the paper's editorials. It was no wonder, then, that most Americans, including political leaders, were taken by surprise when economic deficiencies led to the disintegration and ultimate collapse of the Soviet Union in the 1990s.[45] These topics had failed to capture media attention. Similarly, a twelve-year study of international terrorism stories led to the conclusion that "network coverage bore little relationship to actual patterns of occurrence. On the whole, the limitations of production and presentation, concerns over audience share, and the narrow focus of journalistic notions of professionalism result in coverage more notable for its erratic nature than for its systematic biases." [46]

Good Frames for Friends, Bad Frames for Foes. The fact that foreign news reported in the U.S. press is based heavily on U.S. sources who tend to support government policies explains why the media tend to cast U.S.

TABLE 11-3   Soviet News Story Topics in the U.S. Press, January 1945–January 1991 (in percentages)

Topic	Press conference themes	Editorial themes
Soviet foreign relations	23	14
U.S. attitude about Soviets	21	33
Soviet military policy	18	9
U.S.–Soviet meetings	14	5
U.S. military policy	5	6
U.S.–Soviet comparisons	5	4
Soviet attitudes about United States	4	7
Human rights	3	11
Soviet leaders' quality	2	4
Communism as ideology	2	3
U.S. policy about Soviet Union	1	2
Soviet technology	1	1

SOURCE: Author's research.

NOTE: Data encompass 2,636 press conference themes and 5,310 editorial themes.

policies into a favorable light. Coverage of the downing of two planes, one by Soviet fire and the other by U.S. fire, illustrates the practice.

In 1983 a Soviet fighter plane shot down Korean Airlines Flight 007 with a loss of 269 lives. Five years later, in 1988, the *Vincennes,* a U.S. Navy ship, shot down Iran Air Flight 655 with a loss of 290 lives. The Soviets justified the shooting by saying the Korean plane was a hostile target; the Americans made the same claim for their action. Though the cases differed in detail and in the context in which they occurred, they were sufficiently alike to expect rough similarity in coverage. That did not happen, judging from coverage of the events in *Time, Newsweek,* the *New York Times,* the *Washington Post,* and the *CBS Evening News.* As the saying goes, outcomes are judged by whose ox is gored. The manner in which the news was framed, including the language and pictures used in the stories and the overall context into which the stories were placed, cast the Soviet action as a moral outrage and the U.S. action as a regrettable technological failure.[47]

For example, the media gave almost twice as much coverage to the tragedy caused by the Soviets than to its U.S. counterpart, even though the loss of life was greater in the Iran Air case. Following the Korean Airlines crash, *Newsweek* proclaimed on its cover "Murder in the Air"; *Time*'s cover read "Shooting to Kill: The Soviets Destroy an Airliner." *Newsweek*'s cover on the 1988 crash was headlined, "The Gulf Tragedy: Why It Happened," omitting any reference to a suspected villain. In the same way, *Time,* in a small insert on its cover, said innocuously, "What Went Wrong in the Gulf." The stories inside the magazines repeatedly accused the Soviets of knowingly destroying a civilian plane, whereas U.S. actions were excused as pardonable ignorance. The press characterized the Soviets' action as typical behavior for that country and attributed guilt to its leaders. Not so for the Americans.

The stories about the Korean airliner dwelled on the human tragedy; the Iranian airliner story slighted that aspect. Such words as *atrocity, crime, massacre,* and *murder* abounded in media descriptions of Soviet actions. For the Americans, the media emphasized the accidental nature of the event. During the investigation of the action of the *Vincennes,* doubts about the innocence of the U.S. crew were mentioned inconspicuously. So was commentary that suggested the Soviet action might have been accidental.

There is no evidence that the distortions that spring from such chauvinistic framing are deliberate. Rather, the framing reflects the actual perspectives of the journalists, based on their choice of sources and the predispositions with which they approach stories involving countries identified as friend or foe. Nonetheless, many scholars believe that this type of coverage has undesirable political consequences. In 1983 heightened anti-Soviet feelings among members of Congress and the public were attributed to media coverage, as was a sharply reduced momentum of the nuclear freeze movement that had been gaining ground.[48] In the Iran Air case in 1988, coverage defused potential pressure for withdrawal of U.S. forces from the Persian Gulf region. Instead of seeing the tragedy as an example of harm caused by the United States's presence in the area, warranting reconsideration of the policy, the incident presumably consolidated U.S. support behind the Reagan administration's foreign policies in the Gulf.

Uncritical Flashlight Coverage. Reporting of foreign news usually lacks a sense of history and a sense of the meaning of successive events so that it often confuses the public. The news does not provide sufficient information to permit most Americans to understand the rationale for major foreign policies such as support of the North American Free Trade Agreement (NAFTA) or the limitations of humanitarian interventions. Some stories, even those directly involving U.S. security, are ignored until events reach crisis proportions or until there is a precipitating incident. *New York Times* correspondent James Reston put the problem this way:

> We are fascinated by events but not by the things that cause the events. We will send 500 correspondents to Vietnam after the war breaks out . . . meanwhile ignoring the rest of the world, but we will not send five reporters there when the danger of war is developing.[49]

When news about the aftermath of the Iraq War turned sour in 2004, the news media were chided for neglecting their watchdog role. The *New*

York Times and *Washington Post* apologized for supporting the president's policies too wholeheartedly, true to their usual stance in covering news about U.S. military ventures abroad.[50] They had featured a limited amount of dissent about war strategies, without questioning the overall goals and the need for war. Failure to present a mix of stories that might raise questions about the rationale and justification for war amounted to abandoning the media's important duties to alert the public to possible mistakes by their government. Robert Entman's research, which covers the first Gulf war, does not support the claim that critical comments about the war were comparatively scarce. Neither does it support the claim that most of the criticism concerned procedural rather than substantive matters. Follow-up research covering the second Gulf war confirms that judgment (Table 11-4).[51] Nonetheless the criticism and self-criticism regarding the adequacy of prewar debates is important because it reflects the fact that the media did not live up to the expectations of political elites about the watchdog role in the foreign policy realm. Unfortunately, there are no satisfactory solutions to the dilemmas faced by journalists during international crises when their feelings of patriotism demand support for the government while their journalistic duty calls for raising red flags of caution.[52]

News Distortions. Just like domestic news, foreign news neglects major social problems, particularly political and economic development. The reasons are readily apparent. Such problems are difficult to describe in brief stories, pictures are scarce, and changes come at a glacial pace. Some social problems are extremely complex; most reporters are ill equipped to understand let alone report about them. When news stories address development issues, the focus is on dramatic negative aspects like famines, health crises, and conflicts. As Rafael Caldera, former president of Venezuela, told a press conference at the National Press Club in Washington, D.C., "The phrase 'no news is good news' has become 'good news is no news.' . . . Little or nothing is mentioned in American media about literary or scientific achievements" or "about social achievements and the defense against the dangers which threaten our peace and development." Instead, "only the most deplorable incidents, be they caused by nature or by man, receive prominent attention."[53] It is small consolation for such ruffled feelings that news selection criteria for events in developing nations are typical for news from everywhere.[54] The situation is aggravated by the fact that many developing countries depend for their international news on western news media, especially the Associated Press and CNN. These countries complain about "media imperialism."[55] Critics in developing nations also decry the corrupting effects of western news and entertainment programs that feature violence and sexually explicit episodes. Western pro-

TABLE 11-4   Objections to the Impending Gulf War (percentage of Iraq coverage
that was negative)

Coverage period	New York Times (number of negative assertions)	Washington Post	ABC
November 8–16, 1990	63.2 (175)	53.6 (156)	36.7 (40)
November 27– December 5, 1990	54.3 (109)	54.3 (109)	43.9 (36)
Both periods	59.9 (284)	53.9 (265)	39.8 (76)
Total stories (positive and negative)	755	687	191

SOURCE: Adapted from Robert Entman, *Projections of Power: Framing News, Public Opinion, and U.S. Foreign Policy* (Chicago: University of Chicago Press, 2004).

NOTE: The table is based on assertions in leading stories that questioned the appropriateness of the Bush administration's Iraq War policies during periods when ample criticism could be anticipated. November 8–16, 1990, follows the administration's announcement of massive increases in U.S. troops in the region; from November 27 to December 5, 1990, Congress held hearings on Iraq policy.

grams allegedly damage the cultural identity of people in developing nations, drawing them away from their own heritage.[56]

Over-Emphasis on Conflict. Negative and conflictual news is more prevalent in the U.S. media than in the media of many other societies. Comparisons of news coverage in the United States and in Canada, societies that are culturally close, are revealing. The rate of violence on Canadian television news is half the U.S. rate.[57] When the people of Quebec voted in 1980 on the question of separatism from Canada, the *Washington Post* warned that civil war might erupt. U.S. papers featured stories about serious rioting by separatists in English sectors of Montreal. By contrast, the *Toronto Globe and Mail* buried a small story about minor unrest in Quebec in the back pages. The prospect of civil war was never mentioned and was characterized as "ludicrous" by knowledgeable observers.[58] During the Iranian hostage crisis, *New York Times* coverage featured stereotypical portrayals of Muslims and tales of violence. Far more peaceful images emerged from reading the French paper *Le Monde*.[59]

By and large, news media in democracies feature more conflict than do media in authoritarian and totalitarian societies. In part this happens because government-controlled and supported news organizations can afford to forgo dramatic negative news, since their financial health is unrelated to audience size. The approach used by U.S. news media draws attention to conflict rather than to peaceful settlement and makes much of the world beyond U.S. borders seem chaotic. Routine foreign news languishes in the back pages or is condensed into the briefest broadcast accounts. Usually the issues are oversimplified and instead of interpreting what the conflict means to the country and its people, the dominant focus is on what, if anything, the conflict portends for U.S. politics.

Distortions in domestic news are not likely to mislead most U.S. audiences, because past experiences and socialization provide corrective lenses.[60] The foreign scene, by contrast, must be viewed without correction for myopia and astigmatism. Americans may be skeptical about the accuracy of the images, but they lack the means to judge the nature and degree of distortion.

The Impact of Foreign Affairs Coverage

Support of the Status Quo.   Finally, the thrust of most foreign news stories supports government policies. The media usually accept official designations of who are friends and enemies of the United States and interpret these friends' and enemies' motives accordingly. Whenever relationships change, media coverage mirrors the change. Coverage of the Soviet Union's attack on Korean Airlines Flight 007 is a good example of the approach used for disfavored countries. In the same way, a comparison of *New York Times* coverage of strife in Cambodia and East Timor and of elections in Nicaragua and El Salvador showed that the paper judged "communist-tainted" Cambodia and Nicaragua unfavorably. By contrast, comparable events in East Timor and El Salvador, countries deemed friendly to the United States, were cast in a favorable light.[61] Because the president and executive branch are the prime sources of foreign affairs news, they can, most of the time, set the agenda of coverage with stories that are framed to reflect official perspectives.[62]

On the whole, despite some coverage that challenges the official version of international politics and U.S. foreign policies, the tenor of news stories in mainstream media and on the Internet supports prevailing stereotypes about the world. Preoccupation with the developed world reinforces many Americans' beliefs about the importance of these nations. In the same way, portrayal of less developed countries as incapable of managing their own affairs makes it easy to believe that they do not deserve higher status and the media attention that accompanies it.

Newspeople usually are willing to withhold news and commentary when publicity would severely complicate the government's management of foreign policy. For example, the media suppressed information about the United States' breaking of Japanese military message codes during World War II and refrained from sharply criticizing Iranian leaders during the 1979 hostage crisis to avoid angering them. Both are examples in which major political interests were at stake. Likewise, news of delicate negotiations among foreign countries may be temporarily withheld to avoid rocking the boat before agreements are reached. When an invasion of Haiti by U.S. troops was in the offing in 1994, CNN and the three major television networks pledged to refrain from showing any pictures that might put the troops at risk.[63]

The Indexing Hypothesis. If the media are generally supportive of government policies, how can their adverse comments about the Vietnam War or the Gulf War be explained? The answer is that the media generally emphasize the government's positions until many respected sources voice strong dissent (Box 11-1). To use a term popularized by political scientist Lance Bennett, the media index their coverage to the degree of disagreement by powerful political leaders with the government's position.[64] The media do not care to lead dissent in this minefield of uncertainties about facts and they fear that irate audiences will accuse them of a lack of patriotism. Only when respected opposition forces publicly express their concerns do the media couple their government accounts with coverage of the dissenting voices. When protests are featured, they show primarily "respectable" dissenters, not political and social outcasts.[65]

Tests of the indexing hypothesis in the post–cold war era suggest that it may apply only in situations when major national security interests are at stake.[66] It may also be true that the end of the cold war marked a break with the past that led to the cascade model of foreign affairs coverage identified by Robert Entman. Entman contends that foreign policy consensus among elites has become the exception rather than the norm. That leaves the media free to choose among competing interpretations of events happening abroad. The president's framing still has the best chance to be reflected in the news. But other frames may trump it, depending on how they "cascade" through communications networks that reach the media. As always, journalistic news selection criteria are also a major selection factor.

The CNN Effect. The belief that graphic media coverage of events abroad on occasion forces the U.S. government to engage in unplanned and undesired interventions has been dubbed the "CNN effect." The name was coined by scholars who studied the U.S. intervention in Somalia that began in 1992, shortly after CNN had published gruesome pictures of atrocities against civilians in that country. Subsequent analyses suggest that CNN was given undue credit in that case. Officials had formulated plans for the humanitarian intervention well ahead of the airing of the CNN stories.[67]

Further investigations suggest that there is, indeed, evidence for a CNN effect in situations in which television pictures of human suffering inflicted by nature or by fellow humans have aroused sympathies for the victims among the U.S. public as well as U.S. officials. But the effect is less automatic than initially postulated and it seems to be limited to situations

BOX 11-1
What Motivates Foreign News Choices?

A plentiful supply of diverse models makes it tough to fathom why U.S. journalists create the images of foreign affairs that appear on television or in newspapers. There are hegemony models, classical watchdog models, indexing models, and cascade models. What theories and assumptions underlie these models?

The hegemony model, expounded in the work of Michael Parenti, Edward Herman, and Noam Chomsky, is based on theories about the desires of governments in capitalist societies to control the information supply so that news media have no basis for performing their watchdog functions, and citizens cannot form independent opinions about government policies.[1] As evidence, hegemony theorists point to the fact that most foreign affairs news in the U.S. press does, indeed, support the incumbent government's policies. Public opinion polls provide further evidence that the public shares the government's views and lacks insights into dissenting perspectives.

Classical watchdog models do not distinguish between domestic and foreign news when it comes to the media's watchdog function. They assume that the same rules apply for both. If there is little critical news about foreign policies, it simply means that these policies are sound and have wide approval. Under these circumstances, journalists see no need to question the wisdom of the government's decisions, especially in a policy arena that requires specialist knowledge that most journalists lack.

Contrary to the hegemony model and the classical model, proponents of the indexing model point out that the media do criticize foreign policies but not as often as one might expect from the classical model. Analysis of numerous cases showed that vocal objections by prominent public figures seem to be a precondition for airing policy conflicts in the media. If elites are silent about a controversial policy, the press remains silent as well. Journalists index their reports to elite behavior and do not act without this legitimating umbrella.

W. Lance Bennett, one of the most persuasive proponents of the indexing model, provides numerous examples to support it.[2] But other examples do not fit the model, either because the predicted media focus on dissenting views did not happen or occurred without the benefit of vocal elite criticism. Such instances prompted further research that led to the cascade model. That model, identified first by political scientist Robert Entman, postulates that post–cold war era politics generates multiple appraisals of the merits of foreign policies because there is no longer a single dominant frame for policy making.[3]

Which of these appraisals will surface as a dissenting view in the news media depends on a variety of circumstances. In general, the official version of the government will prevail because it is easier to access and more authoritative than unofficial dissenting voices. However, when newsworthy stories involving dissent come to journalists' attention, they have a good chance to be published absent earlier concerns about the ethics of challenging the country's foreign policies, especially in times of war. In other words, journalistic considerations have become the controlling factor, rather than the government's success in manipulating information or journalists' subservience to sparring elites.

Which of these models best describes the process is controversial. As is true of most happenings in political life, there probably are nuggets of truth in all the underlying assumptions and the models they support. But, as always, it is nearly impossible to unscramble the mixture of motivations when cases are put under the microscope. My own vote goes to the cascade model because it accommodates the widest array of motivations. Although neither simple nor elegant, it comes closest to the messiness of real policy formulation.

1. Michael Parenti, *Land of Idols* (New York: San Martin's Press, 1993); Edward S. Herman and Noam Chomsky, *Manufacturing Consent: The Political Economy of the Mass Media* (New York: Pantheon, 1993).
2. Lance Bennett, *News: The Politics of Illusion*, 5th ed. (New York: Longman, 2003).
3. Robert Entman, *Projections of Power* (Chicago: University of Chicago Press, 2004).

involving humanitarian crises. For example, political scientist Piers Robinson studied U.S. intervention in the conflict in Bosnia that began in 1992 and ended in 1995. He concluded that media coverage did play a role in the initial humanitarian intervention but that it was not a factor in subsequent military activities designed to end the war.[68] Similarly, intervention in northern Iraq in 1991 to protect Kurdish civilians from atrocities committed by Saddam Hussein, refugee rescue missions sent to Rwanda in

1994, and the efforts to protect civilians in Somalia are examples of media-encouraged humanitarian missions. But they never progressed to efforts to use military force to stop the conflict.

However, media coverage can influence foreign affairs even when it does not lead to military intervention. Effects include shortening the time for policy making, which in turn shrinks the pool of people regularly consulted prior to decisions and increases the chances for ill-considered policies.[69] Televised crisis coverage may pressure the president to react hastily to avoid appearing weak and vacillating. As Lloyd Cutler, White House counsel to presidents Carter and Clinton, put it, "If an ominous foreign event is featured on TV news, the President and his advisers feel bound to make a response in time for the next evening news program."[70] This may leave no time to investigate the news report or for officials of the foreign country to explain it. President Kennedy waited eight days in 1961 before commenting on the erection of the Berlin Wall; President George Bush had to respond overnight to its destruction.[71]

Madeleine Albright, President Clinton's secretary of state, commented in 2001 that the twenty-four-hour news cycle had changed things, but she saw advantages along with the disadvantages. "Some of it is very good, because you know what's going on and there is a real-time sense about things. . . . But, in other ways, it makes you have to respond to events much faster than it might be prudent. . . . So it's a double-edged sword. . . ."[72]

Summary

The quality of U.S. foreign policy and the effectiveness of U.S. relations with other countries are crucial to the welfare of people throughout the world. Sound policy and relations require a solid information base. As this chapter has shown, the foreign affairs information base on which Americans depend leaves much to be desired. The causes of this deficit are complex and cannot be altered readily. They involve the economics of reporting news from all parts of the globe, the sociopolitical setting in which news gathering takes place, and the audiences to whose world views and tastes the news must cater. Internal political considerations play a major part as well in determining which issues will come to the fore and how they will be framed.

Foreign affairs news often must be produced under trying conditions. Strange locations and inadequate technological facilities can make nightmares of the physical aspects of getting to the scene of the action, collecting information, and transmitting it. These technical difficulties are compounded by political difficulties. They include the reluctance of officials in the United States and abroad to commit themselves publicly on foreign affairs matters and the harassment of correspondents venturing into places where they are unwanted. Expulsion, imprisonment, and physical harm are common. With so much territory to cover and such limited personnel to cover it, newspeople frequently avoid areas where news is hard to get and devote their efforts instead to areas where public attitudes are supportive. This effectively removes many regions from media scrutiny and contributes to unevenness of news flow from various parts of the world.

How good is the foreign affairs news presented by U.S. news media? The picture is mixed and must be judged in light of the problems of foreign news production. News from around the globe must be at once timely, exciting, personalized, and brief, yet understandable for a U.S. audience that is not intensely interested in most events abroad. To satisfy these criteria using minimal resources of time and money, journalists focus on sensational, mostly negative news. They write stories primarily from a U.S. perspective and usually follow the current administration's foreign policy assumptions and the public's stereotyped views of the world. They open the journalistic gates primarily with the national interests and policy objectives of the United States in mind. Despite these shortcomings, Americans can obtain a reasonably accurate view of salient political events abroad, particularly if they turn to the Web and to elite newspapers that generally give more thorough exposure to U.S. foreign policies. However, U.S. newspapers rarely challenge the objectives of foreign policies, though they may question the effectiveness of executing them.

In recent years political leaders have paid increasing attention to their media images and have tried to influence them by designing story materials that journalists find difficult to refuse. Occasionally, television commentators have even become active diplomats through interviews that set the stage for subsequent political developments. Graphic accounts of human suffering abroad have from time to time spawned humanitarian interventions, but scholars have not yet fully delineated under what circumstances this "CNN effect" occurs. Many questions remain as well about the circumstances that propel the news media to cover dissenting views about foreign policy that may force a change in the goals and strategies favored by incumbent presidents. One thing is clear: It is no longer heresy in times of foreign crises to criticize the administration's foreign policy rather than rallying around the flag. In fact, criticism at such times may ultimately be deemed a hallowed duty.

Notes

1. Clyde Haberman, "Ceremony Will Be Hot, Windy, and Made for TV," *New York Times,* October 26, 1994.
2. Pew Research Center for the People and the Press, "1998 Media Consumption Questionnaire," 1998, http://people-press.org; Pew Research Center for the

People and the Press. "News Audiences Increasingly Politicized," 2004, http://people-press.org.

3. Pew Research Center for the People and the Press. "News Audiences."

4. Project for Excellence in Journalism, *The State of the News Media 2004,* www.stateofthenewsmedia.org.

5. Pamela J. Shoemaker, Lucig H. Danielian, and Nancy Brendlinger, "Deviant Acts, Risky Business, and U.S. Interests: The Newsworthiness of World Events," *Journalism Quarterly* 68 (winter 1991): 781–795.

6. Pippa Norris, "The Restless Searchlight: Network News Framing of the Post Cold-War World," *Political Communication* 12, no. 4 (1995): 357–370.

7. Bernard C. Cohen, *The Press and Foreign Policy* (Princeton: Princeton University Press, 1963), 164–165.

8. William A. Hachten, with the collaboration of Harva Hachten, *The World News Prism: Changing Media of International Communication,* 3d ed. (Ames: Iowa State University Press, 1992), 41–53. Other important international news suppliers are Germany's Deutsche Press Agentur (DPA) and Japan's Kyodo News Service, as well as China's Xinhua News Agency. United Press International, once second only to the Associated Press, has been teetering on the brink of bankruptcy for many years.

9. Fons Tuinstra, "Caught between the Cold War and the Internet," *Nieman Reports* 58, no. 3 (2004): 100–103.

10. Associated Press, www.ap.org.

11. For a brief description of how the Associated Press is adjusting to the Internet age, see Brent Cunningham, "The AP Now," *Columbia Journalism Review* (November/December 2000), www.cjr.org/year/00/4/ap.asp.

12. John Maxwell Hamilton and Eric Jenner, "Foreign Correspondence: Evolution, Not Extinction," *Nieman Reports* 58, no. 3 (2004): 98–100; John Maxwell Hamilton and Eric Jenner, "Redefining Foreign Correspondence," *Journalism* 5, no. 3 (2004): 301–321.

13. Hamilton and Jenner, "Foreign Correspondence."

14. Catholic World News, www.cwnews.com. The figure covers all reporters, not only Americans.

15. Hamilton and Jenner, "Foreign Correspondence"; Hamilton and Jenner, "Redefining Foreign Correspondence."

16. Jarol B. Manheim, "Strategic Public Diplomacy: Managing Kuwait's Image During the Gulf Conflict," in *Taken by Storm: The Media, Public Opinion, and U.S. Foreign Policy in the Gulf War,* ed. W. Lance Bennett and David L. Paletz (Chicago: University of Chicago Press, 1994), 131–148.

17. Jarol B. Manheim and Robert B. Albritton, "Changing National Images: International Public Relations and Media Agenda-Setting," *American Political Science Review* 78 (September 1984): 641–657; Robert B. Albritton and Jarol B. Manheim, "Public Relations Efforts for the Third World: Images in the News," *Journal of Communication* 35 (spring 1985): 43–59; Jarol B. Manheim, *Strategic Public Diplomacy and American Foreign Policy: The Evolution of Influence* (New York: Oxford University Press, 1994).

18. Brigitte L. Nacos, Robert Y. Shapiro, and Pierangelo Isernia, "New Issues and the Media: American and German News Coverage of the Global-Warming Debate," in *Decisionmaking in a Glass House: Mass Media, Public Opinion, and American and European Foreign Policy in the 21st Century,* ed. Nacos, Shapiro, and Isernia (Lanham, Md.: Rowman and Littlefield, 2000), 41–59.

19. Leo Bogart, "The Overseas Newsman: A 1967 Profile Study," *Journalism Quarterly* 45 (summer 1968): 293–306. Judging from more recent profile studies of American journalists in general, these early profiles are still reasonably accurate; see Chapter 4. In the United States the needs of foreign correspondents are served by the United States Information Agency (USIA). It maintains foreign press centers in major U.S. cities and arranges high-level briefings by government officials and news-gathering tours on major economic, political, and cultural themes. It also provides extensive information services and even helps with arranging appointments and filing facilities at international summits. United States Information Agency, Washington, D.C., "Foreign Press Centers," January 1996; also, Lori Montgomery presents a brief first-person account of the life of a foreign correspondent in "Foreign Correspondent's Notebook," www.freep.com/jobspage/academy/foreign.htm.

20. Lars Wilnat and David Weaver, "Through Their Eyes: The Work of Foreign Correspondents in the United States," *Journalism* 4, no. 4 (2003): 403–422.

21. Shailendra Ghorpade, "Foreign Correspondents Cover Washington for World," *Journalism Quarterly* 61 (fall 1984): 667.

22. Ghorpade, "Foreign Correspondents," 667–671; and *Editor and Publisher International Yearbook, 1991* (New York: Editor and Publisher, 1991).

23. *Editor and Publisher International Yearbook, 1991* and 2000 editions.

24. Doris A. Graber, "Terrorism, Censorship and the 1st Amendment," in *Framing Terrorism: The News Media, the Government, and the Public,* ed. Pippa Norris, Montague Kern, and Marion Just (New York: Routledge, 2003), 27–42.

25. Committee to Protect Journalists, "When Journalists Report in Dangerous Places," *Nieman Reports,* 57, no. 4 (2003): 89–90.

26. Eytan Gilboa, "Media Diplomacy: Conceptual Divergence and Applications," *Harvard International Journal of Press/Politics* 3, no. 3 (1998): 56–75.

27. Ibid.

28. For a full discussion of reporting on the Middle East peace negotiations between Israel and the Palestinians, see Gadi Wolfsfeld, *Media and Political Conflict: News from the Middle East* (Cambridge: Cambridge University Press, 1997).

29. Kirsten Sparre, "Megaphone Diplomacy in the Northern Irish Peace Process: Squaring the Circle by Talking to Terrorists through Journalists," *Harvard International Journal of Press/Politics* 6, no. 1 (2001): 88–104.

30. Patrick O'Heffernan, "Mass Media and U.S. Foreign Policy: A Mutual Exploitation Model of Media Influence in U.S. Foreign Policy," in *Media and Public Policy,* ed. Robert J. Spitzer (Westport, Conn.: Praeger, 1993), 187–211.

31. Garrick Utley, "The Shrinking of Foreign News: From Broadcast to Narrowcast," *Foreign Affairs* 76, no. 1 (1997): 2–10. Also see Brent Cunningham, "The AP Now," *Columbia Journalism Review* (November/December 2000), www.cjr.org/year/00/4/ap.asp.

32. Daniela V. Dimitrova, Lynda Lee Kaid, Andrew Paul Williams, and Kaye D. Trammell, "War on the Web: The Immediate News Framing of Gulf War II," *Press/Politics,* 10, no. 1 (2005): 22–44.

33. Wolfsfeld, *Media and Political Conflict,* chap. 4.

34. Herbert J. Gans, *Deciding What's News: A Study of CBS Evening News, NBC Nightly News, Newsweek, and Time* (New York: Pantheon Books, 1979), 30–36. See also H. Denis Wu, "Systemic Determinants of International News Coverage: A Comparison of 38 Countries," *Journal of Communication* 50, no. 2 (2000): 110–130; and Wolfsfeld, *Media and Political Conflict,* chap. 6.

35. Edwin Diamond, *The Tin Kazoo: Television, Politics, and the News* (Cambridge, Mass.: MIT Press, 1975), 94.
36. Daniel C. Hallin, "Hegemony: The American News Media from Vietnam to El Salvador: A Study of Ideological Change and Its Limits," in *Political Communication Research: Approaches, Studies, Assessments,* ed. David L. Paletz (Norwood, N.J.: Ablex, 1987), 17; Robert M. Entman, "Hegemonic Socialization, Information Processing, and Presidential News Management: Framing the KAL and Iran Air Incidents," in *The Psychology of Political Communication,* ed. Ann Crigler (Ann Arbor: University of Michigan Press, 1996).
37. William Adams and Phillip Heyl, "From Cairo to Kabul with the Networks, 1972–1980," in *Television Coverage of the Middle East,* ed. William C. Adams (Norwood, N.J.: Ablex, 1981), 26.
38. David R. Gergen, "Diplomacy in a Television Age: The Dangers of Teledemocracy," in *The Media and Foreign Policy,* ed. Simon Serfaty (New York: St. Martin's, 1991), 47–63.
39. Stephen S. Rosenfeld, "In the Gulf: The Wars of the Press," in *The Media and Foreign Policy,* 241–255. For a detailed account of news coverage before and during the war, see Bennett and Paletz, eds., *Taken by Storm.*
40. Hachten, *The World News Prism,* 165–166.
41. Robert Pear, "Military Revises Rules to Assure Reporters Access to Battle Areas," *New York Times,* May 22, 1992. Also see Philip Seib, *Headline Diplomacy: How News Coverage Affects Foreign Policy* (Westport, Conn.: Praeger, 1997).
42. Graber, "Terrorism, Censorship, and the 1st Amendment."
43. Nancy Bernhard, "Embedding Reporters on the Frontline," *Nieman Reports* 57, no. 2 (2003): 87–90.
44. Dan Kennedy, "Embedded Reporting: Is Objectivity an Acceptable Casualty of This Kind of Reporting?" *Nieman Reports* 57, no. 2 (2003): 87; Sean Aday, Steven Livingston, and Maeve Hebert, "Embedding the Truth: A Cross-Cultural Analysis of Objectivity and Television Coverage of the Iraq War," *Press/Politics* 10, no. 1 (2005): 3–21; Michael Pfau, Michel Haigh, Mitchell Gettle, Michael Donnelly, Gregory Scott, Dana Warr, and Elaine Wittenberg, "Embedding Journalists in Military Combat Units: Impact on Newspaper Story Frames and Tone," *Journalism and Mass Communication Quarterly* 81, no. 1 (2004): 74–88.
45. Author's research.
46. Michael X. Delli Carpini and Bruce A. Williams, "Television and Terrorism: Patterns of Presentation and Occurrence, 1969 to 1980," *Western Political Quarterly* 40 (March 1987): 45–64.
47. Robert M. Entman, "Framing U.S. Coverage of International News: Contrasts in Narratives of the KAL and Iran Air Incidents," *Journal of Communication* 41 (fall 1991): 6–27.
48. Ibid., 22–23.
49. James Reston, *Sketches in the Sand* (New York: Knopf, 1967), 195; for supporting evidence in the Gulf War, see Gladys Engel Lang and Kurt Lang, "The Press as Prologue: Media Coverage of Saddam's Iraq, 1979–1990," in Bennett and Paletz, *Taken By Storm,* 43–62.
50. New York Times Editors, "*New York Times* Reviews Its Own Coverage of Iraq War," *New York Times,* May 26, 2004; Howard Kurtz, "The *Post* on WMDs: An Inside Story," *Washington Post,* August 12, 2004.
51. Ingrid A. Lehmann, "Exploring the Transatlantic Media Divide over Iraq," *Press/Politics* 10, no. 1 (2005): 63–89; Robert Entman, *Projections of Power: Fram-*

ing News, Public Opinion, and U.S. Foreign Policy (Chicago: University of Chicago Press, 2004); Doris A. Graber, "News about the Gulf War Policy Debate: Comparing 1991 and 2002" (paper presented to the Midwest Political Science Association, 2003).

52. Stephen Hess and Marvin Kalb, eds., *The Media and the War on Terrorism* (Washington, D.C.: Brookings Institution Press, 2003).

53. Quoted in Fernando Reyes Matta, "The Latin American Concept of News," *Journal of Communication* 29 (spring 1979): 169.

54. Gary D. Gaddy and Enoch Tanjong, "Earthquake Coverage by the Western Press," *Journal of Communication* 36 (spring 1986): 105–112. For a conflicting analysis, see William C. Adams, "Whose Lives Count? TV Coverage of Natural Disasters," *Journal of Communication* 36 (spring 1986): 113–122.

55. For a discussion of media imperialism, see Herbert I. Schiller, *Culture, Inc.: The Corporate Takeover of Public Expression* (New York: Oxford University Press, 1989); and René Jean Ravault, "International Information: Bullet or Boomerang?" in *Political Communication Research: Approaches, Studies, Assessments,* ed. David L. Paletz (Norwood, N.J.: Ablex, 1987), 245–265.

56. The impact of foreign television is assessed in Alexis S. Tan, Sarrina Li, and Charles Simpson, "American TV and Social Stereotypes of Americans in Taiwan and Mexico," *Journalism Quarterly* 63 (winter 1986): 809–814.

57. Benjamin D. Singer, "Violence, Protest, and War in Television News: The U.S. and Canada Compared," *Public Opinion Quarterly* 34 (winter 1970–1971): 611–616; and Chris J. Scheer and Sam W. Eiler, "A Comparison of Canadian and American Network Television News," *Journal of Broadcasting* 16 (spring 1972): 156–164. For another comparative perspective on media coverage, see Richard Gunther and Anthony Mughan, *Democracy and the Media: A Comparative Perspective* (Cambridge: Cambridge University Press, 2000).

58. James P. Winter, Pirouz Shoar Ghaffari, and Vernone M. Sparkes, "How Major U.S. Dailies Covered Quebec Separatism Referendum," *Journalism Quarterly* 59 (winter 1982): 608.

59. Edward W. Said, *Covering Islam: How the Media and the Experts Determine How We See the Rest of the World* (New York: Pantheon Books, 1981), chap. 2; also see Gunther and Mughan, *Democracy and the Media.*

60. Hanna Adoni and S. Mane, "Media and the Social Construction of Reality: Toward an Integration of Theory and Research," *Communication Research* 11 (July 1984): 323–340; see also Doris Graber, *Processing Politics: Learning from Television in the Internet Age* (Chicago: University of Chicago Press, 2001), 82–91.

61. Edward S. Herman, "Diversity of News: 'Marginalizing' the Opposition," *Journal of Communication* 35 (fall 1985): 135–146. See also W. Lance Bennett, "An Introduction to Journalism Norms and Representations of Politics," *Political Communication* 13 (4) (1996): 373–384.

62. John A. Lent, "Foreign News in American Media," *Journal of Communication* 27 (winter 1977): 46–50. See also Jyotika Ramaprasad and Daniel Riffe, "Effect of U.S.–India Relations on *New York Times* Coverage," *Journalism Quarterly* 64 (summer/autumn 1987): 537–543; Hallin, "Hegemony"; and David Altheide, "Media Hegemony: A Failure of Perspective," *Public Opinion Quarterly* 48 (summer 1984): 476–490.

63. "TV Networks Say Coverage Would Not Endanger Troops," *New York Times,* September 19, 1994.

64. Bennett, "An Introduction to Journalism Norms."
65. Daniel C. Hallin, "The Media, the War in Vietnam, and Political Support: A Critique of the Thesis of an Oppositional Media," *Journal of Politics* 46 (February 1984); also see Jonathan Mermin, *Debating War and Peace* (Princeton: Princeton University Press, 1999); and John Zaller and Dennis Chiu, "Government's Little Helper: U.S. Press Coverage of Foreign Policy Crises, 1946–1999," in *Decisionmaking in a Glass House,* 61–84, for many examples.
66. Zaller and Chiu, "Government's Little Helper," 74–81.
67. Steven Livingston, *Clarifying the CNN Effect: An Examination of Media Effects According to Type of Military Intervention* (Cambridge: Harvard University, 1996).
68. Pierce Robinson, *The CNN Effect: The Myth of News, Foreign Policy, and Intervention* (New York: Routledge, 2002). Also see Nik Gowing, "Real-Time Television Coverage of Armed Conflicts and Diplomatic Crises: Does It Pressure or Distort Foreign Policy Decisions?" in *Terrorism, War, and the Press,* ed. Nancy Palmer (Cambridge: Harvard University, 2003), 139–222.
69. Eytan Gilboa, "Television News and U.S. Foreign Policy: Constraints of Real-Time Coverage," *Press/Politics* 8, no. 4 (2003): 97–113.
70. Quoted in ibid.
71. Ibid., 48. Nicholas O. Berry in *Foreign Policy and the Press: An Analysis of the* New York Times' *Coverage of U.S. Foreign Policy* (Westport, Conn.: Greenwood Press, 1990) makes the same argument.
72. Madeleine Albright, "Around-the-Clock News Cycle a Double-Edged Sword," *Harvard International Journal of Press/Politics* 6, no. 1 (2001): 105–108.

Readings

Bennett, W. Lance, and David L. Paletz. *Taken by Storm: The Media, Public Opinion, and U.S. Foreign Policy in the Gulf War.* Chicago: University of Chicago Press, 1994.

Dayan, Daniel, and Elihu Katz. *Media Events: The Live Broadcasting of History.* Cambridge: Harvard University Press, 1992.

Edwards, Lee. *Mediapolitik: How the Mass Media Have Transformed World Politics.* Baltimore: Catholic University of America Press, 2001.

Entman, Robert. *Projections of Power: Framing News, Public Opinion, and U.S. Foreign Policy.* Chicago: University of Chicago Press, 2004.

Galtung, Johan, and Richard C. Vincent. *Global Glasnost: Toward a New World Information/Communication Order?* Cresskill, N.J.: Hampton Press, 1992.

Gilboa, Eytan, ed. *Media and Conflict: Framing Issues, Making Policy, Shaping Opinions.* Ardsley, N.Y.: Transnational Publishers, 2002.

Hess, Stephen. *International News and Foreign Correspondents.* Washington, D.C.: Brookings Institution, 1996.

Manheim, Jarol B. *Strategic Public Diplomacy and American Foreign Policy: The Evolution of Influence.* New York: Oxford University Press, 1994.

Mermin, Jonathan. *Debating War and Peace.* Princeton: Princeton University Press, 1999.

Nacos, Brigitte L., Robert Y. Shapiro, and Pierangelo Isernia, eds. *Decisionmaking in a Glass House: Mass Media, Public Opinion, and American and European Foreign Policy in the 21st Century.* Lanham, Md.: Rowman and Littlefield, 2000.

Norris, Pippa, Montague Kern, and Marion Just, eds. *Framing Terrorism: The News Media, the Government, and the Public.* New York: Routledge, 2003.

O'Heffernan, Patrick. *Mass Media and American Foreign Policy: Insider Perspectives on Global Journalism and the Foreign Policy Process.* Norwood, N.J.: Ablex, 1991.

Robinson, Piers. *The CNN Effect: The Myth of News, Foreign Policy, and Intervention.* New York: Routledge, 2002.

Sylvester, Judith, and Suzanne Hoffman. *Reporting from the Front: The Media and the Military.* Lanham, Md.: Rowman and Littlefield, 2004.

Wolfsfeld, Gadi. *Media and Political Conflict: News from the Middle East.* Cambridge: Cambridge University Press, 1997.

Trends in Media Policy

"JOURNALISM IS IN THE MIDDLE OF an epochal transformation, as momentous probably as the invention of the telegraph or television." So concluded a group of distinguished researchers who analyzed news offerings in the United States in 2004.[1]

Where is this transformation leading? In 2004 journalists Robin Sloan and Matt Thompson conjectured that traditional journalism would be dead by 2014, killed by the technology that allows news consumers to select news tailored to their personal preferences and to publish their own views on the Internet. According to these soothsayers, Google will become a vastly more powerful search engine company within the next few years. It will merge with a giant Amazon.com enterprise charged with stocking media consumers' personal news caches with their preferred news items. Production of personalized news media will be fully automated so that Amazon's computers will pluck and assemble individual facts and sentences available through Google. Searches will retrieve everything published on the Web, from traditional information sources to citizens' blogs, corporate spins, and news supplied by interest groups—an eclectic mixture of gems and garbage. The venerable *New York Times,* deprived of its mission to publish "All the News That's Fit to Print," and other print media will become print-only newsletters serving elites and the dwindling numbers of senior citizens who stubbornly refuse to act as their own reporters, editors, and publishers.[2]

Not so fast! say other media observers. The announcement of traditional journalism's death, as Mark Twain once remarked, has been greatly exaggerated.

352

Journalism is changing. There are some forces, particularly the advent of computer communications, the abundance of cable television, and the global interconnectedness of communications, that clearly signal powerful change, but so did the telegraph, the transatlantic cable, and the first wire services with a global reach, all emerging in the same thirty-odd years in the mid-nineteenth century. It is not that there is nothing new under the sun. It is just that we are not in a very good position to see which of the social changes of the past five or ten or twenty-five years is likely to seem earth shattering several decades from now. And maybe these changes are not shattering the earth so much as reshaping it.[3]

So who is right, the prophets of revolution who predict an entirely new era? Or the incrementalists, who predict more gradual changes? Why are current trends so confusing that experienced journalists can see them moving in vastly different directions? What conclusions can we draw from the developments recorded in this book? Those are the questions that we will tackle in this final chapter. We will highlight the forces pushing for major changes in communications policies and practices and the obstacles that lie in the way. We will also explore some of the areas of disenchantment with mass media performance that have fueled demands for reform and the steps taken by dissatisfied communicators and audiences to improve and supplement the existing information supply. The potential impact of major new technologies on politics and policy alternatives will be examined. Finally, we will try to discern whether we are in the middle of a communications revolution or merely a period of rapid development along familiar lines.

Dissatisfaction with the Media

Dissatisfaction with U.S. mass media runs deep and wide. The public feels it, the pundits give it voice, and journalists have lately become very self-critical.

The Journalists' Perspective

According to a 2004 survey by the Pew Research Center for the People and the Press, news professionals working for print, television, radio, and Internet organizations complain about neglect of complex issues and say that the lines between commentary and reporting and between entertainment and news have become unduly blurred. Many think that news reporting is increasingly sloppy and full of errors, and that the watchdog role has gone awry. Press reports about misdeeds by public officials are geared to presenting sensational audience-grabbing exposés rather than bringing about reforms in public life. These flaws, which journalists blame largely on bottom-line pressures, have undermined the public's trust in the news media and have contributed to the shrinking of media audiences.[4]

The sample of 547 journalists tapped by the Pew Research Center survey was broadly based. It included individuals working at the top, middle, and bottom levels of national and local newspapers, magazines, wire services, news services, television, cable, radio, and Internet organizations. Table 12-1 presents their reactions to ten major criticisms leveled against the press.[5] Although the differences between local and national professionals are insignificant, it is noteworthy that each group is internally split about the validity of particular complaints. Two out of three journalists in each group do not consider the press to be too cynical, for example. Such split appraisals are common because the appropriate political role of journalism remains contested.

Regardless of which appraisal of trends is correct, journalists are dissatisfied with many aspects of their performance. Media gurus like Bill Kovach, chairperson of the Committee of Concerned Journalists, and Tom Rosenstiel and Amy Mitchell, respectively director and associate director of the Project for Excellence in Journalism, characterize the problems journalists now face as "intractable" because they are caused by unavoidable economic pressures that are eroding the quality of journalism.[6] That is a troubling judgment.

The Public's Perspective

News consumers' dissatisfaction with the news they currently receive enhances the image that journalism is in trouble. Nearly half the public (48 percent), especially media-faithful senior citizens, complain that "people who decide what to put on TV news or in the newspapers are out of touch with people like me."[7] Most crucially, consumers find news less relevant and less believable. The percentage of people who deem news venues highly credible has dropped in the past four years for every type of news (Table 12-2). Although the drop is not dramatic, it is nonetheless shocking because credibility was already low in 2000.

The sizable discrepancies in believability scores of Democrats and Republicans are also alarming. Republicans distrust news venues more than Democrats, which is in line with the widespread belief that the news bears a liberal imprint. Republicans therefore flock to the more conservatively oriented Fox News channel, while Democrats avoid it. Differential use of media then heightens partisan divisions and lessens the chances for democratic compromises. This, too, is a disturbing trend.

TABLE 12-1   News Professionals' Agreement with Press Criticism (in percentages)

Major criticism	National professionals	Local professionals
Too little attention is paid to complex issues.	78	77
The distinction between reporting and commentary has eroded.	64	59
There are too many talk shows on cable television today.	63	64
The Internet allows too much posting of links to unfiltered material.	57	58
Journalists have become out of touch with their audiences.	47	44
The press is too timid these days.	47	42
News reports are increasingly full of factual errors.	45	47
Journalists let ideological views show too frequently.	45	43
The emergence of the twenty-four-hour news cycle is weakening journalism.	42	40
The press is too cynical.	37	40

SOURCE: Adapted from the Pew Research Center for the People and the Press, "Bottom-Line Pressures Now Hurting Coverage, Say Journalists: Questionnaire," http://people-press.org.

NOTE: Based on a survey of 547 national and local, print, broadcast, and Internet journalists. Respondents were drawn from national and local media samples representing a cross-section of news organizations and their personnel. They were interviewed between March 10 and April 20, 2004. Figures add up to more than 100 percent because respondents were able to answer "yes" to more than one question.

Putting Criticism into Perspective

Most of the concerns voiced by critics of the news media have been echoed in the pages of this book. Nonetheless, the evidence does not support a blanket indictment of the media for failure to nourish democratic life adequately.[8] First and foremost, the collective noun *news media* covers a broad range of institutions. It does not refer only to newspapers and news magazines and television and radio as groupings of news media types; it also refers to individual institutions within these broad categories. In terms of supplying information essential for citizens in a democracy, there is a wide gulf between the *New York Times* on one hand and the scores of tabloids and small-town newspapers that highlight local society news on the other. There is a great deal of journalistic wheat as well as chaff in U.S. media, and the proportions of each vary widely in individual media. In fact, I contend that any citizen willing to make the effort can find essential current information more readily than ever before in U.S. media, especially in the traditional media's Internet versions.[9]

TABLE 12-2   News Consumers Who Believe "All or Most" of News Venues' Offerings (in percentages)

News venue	Survey		Democrats 2004	Republicans 2004
	2004	2000		
CNN	32	39	45	26
Fox news	25	26	24	29
Local TV news	25	33	29	21
National TV news	24	25	33	16
Your daily paper	19	25	23	16

SOURCE: Adapted from the Pew Research Center for the People and the Press, "Political Believability, May 2004," http://people-press.org.

NOTE: Based on a nationwide survey of 3,000 adults interviewed May 3–9, 2004.

Any fair indictment of the news media must also consider mitigating circumstances. This does not mean that the charges are invalid; it means that they must be put into context to assess the degree of guilt. The pressures under which journalists do their work must be considered. These have been discussed in the chapters dealing with domestic and foreign news production under normal and crisis conditions. Besides the economic constraints to produce profits for the parent organization that account for excesses of negativism and voyeur journalism, they include major journalistic conventions of news production. The zeal to rush to publication with breaking news, for example, fosters mistakes and misinterpretations; the beat system privileges newsworthy events occurring on regular beats over important happenings that occur beyond these beats; and pack journalism homogenizes criteria for news selection so that most media become rivals in conformity.

Economic developments have heightened pressures. The multiplication of news channels in the United States and elsewhere, and the ease with which they can be tapped, have forced electronic as well as print media to compete more fiercely for audiences and for advertisers. Shrinking profit margins in individual enterprises have forced cutbacks in staffs that put additional workloads on the survivors. While databases that could be used to provide context for stories have grown exponentially, the time available to individual reporters to search them has shrunk. The traditional media find their news turf eroded by the new media's ability to publish breaking stories immediately. Accordingly, print media must abandon the lure of featuring freshly breaking news for other ways to attract audiences. But when they turn to more analytical and interpretive reporting, they are accused of improperly straying into the terrain of editorial commentary. The upshot has been that the public increasingly perceives newspaper reporting as unduly biased.

Finally, complaints about the media need a historical perspective. They are occurring at a period when regard for most major institutions in the United States is at a low ebb. Nonetheless, when people were asked in 2002 how much they enjoyed keeping up with the news, only 15 percent confessed to little or no enjoyment.[10] History also shows that politicians and the general public are fickle and schizoid in their condemnations as well as their praise. The founders of our nation were the first to complain about its venal, lying press on the one hand and on the other the first to agree that, warts and all, it was the bedrock on which democratic freedoms rest.

Specialized Media

Hundreds of specialized media address information needs that are neglected or poorly served by the regular media. They are a partial antidote for the general mass media's failure to cover many important groups and issues. Ethnic media are examples. There is an abundance of foreign language newspapers and broadcasts that provide detailed news about the many regions from which U.S. immigrants hail. Their numbers are growing at a time when the English-language press is shrinking. For example, in 2000 there were thirty-four Spanish-language dailies. Four years later there were forty, a growth rate in excess of 10 percent. If one includes papers with less than daily publication schedules, there were 666 by 2004.[11]

Numerous professional and trade journals, newsletters, and Web sites are devoted to such concerns as religion, sports, fine and popular arts, automobiles, health, and animal welfare. Some specialized media, such as the *Nation, Mother Jones,* or the *Weekly Standard,* and the *Drudge Report,* on the Internet are primarily devoted to political commentary inspired by diverse ideological perspectives. Others, like New York's *Village Voice* or Chicago's *Reader* specialize in sharp-tongued, lengthy essays covering local politics and the arts. Still others, like the *Onion,* parts of the *New Yorker,* and Comedy Central's the *Daily Show* on television excel in humorous or satirical analyses. The Internet enables many special interest groups to air their views on controversial political issues, often to widely dispersed audiences. Environmental groups are an example, as are supporters of fringe candidates for political office.

Thanks to the demand for targeted information, more than 10,000 magazines are now published in the United States. In 2004 alone more than 1,000 new ones saw the light of day.[12] Cable channels are multiplying, and specialized Web sites are mushrooming. Specialized media also encompass the politically radical, iconoclastic, and counterculture media that flourish in times of social and political stress, such as the late 1960s and early 1970s. These media feature the flagrant opposition to government policy that is permitted in the United States but often forbidden in other countries. At the height of underground press popularity, during the Vietnam War era and its aftermath, readership was estimated at 10 million. The rise of the underground print and electronic press during troubled times demonstrates that mass media can be started and operated with modest means. Like most alternative media, the counterculture media of the 1960s were financed through small-scale local advertising and through classified ads. Staffs were paid meager salaries or no salaries at all.[13] At one time there were nearly 1,000 underground newspapers and 400 counterculture radio stations. Such vitality attests to the vigor and flexibility of the mass media system.[14] The abrupt decline of underground media with the end of the Vietnam War also shows that the system is able to prune its unneeded branches when demand ends.

Waning public support rather than official censorship led to the steep decline in this genre of journalism. It has been revived with the advent of the Internet, where thousands of vitriolic antigovernment sites urge opposition to established authorities and their policies and often suggest ways to implement radical ideas. Mao Tse-tung's admonition to "let a thousand flowers bloom," ignored in China, has come to fruition on the U.S. alternative media scene. However, given the explosive growth of electronic soap boxes from which citizens can broadcast their views, the competition for gaining attention has become extraordinarily fierce.

The Impact of New Technologies

Marshall McLuhan, the television guru of the 1960s, predicted that the world would become a global village where humanity would partake of a global culture via television.[15] His vision of shared audiovisual news and entertainment has largely come to pass, but the reality is quite different and, in many respects, far richer than even McLuhan imagined. The vast amounts of diverse information produced by new technologies permit people to create their own information diet. The new age of personalized mass media has arrived. Political scientist W. Russell Neuman predicted this development at the start of the 1990s when he pointed out that we now "have the opportunity to design a new electronic and optical network that will blur the distinction between mass and interpersonal communications. . . . A single high capacity digital network will combine computing, telephony, broadcasting, motion pictures and publishing."[16] The proliferation of news venues is likely to continue.

Broadening the Public's Options

The new technologies have also reduced the public's dependence on traditional media. The store of information made available through new radio, television, cable, and Internet channels, through communication satellites, and through round-the-clock news programs has grown by leaps and bounds.[17] Small as well as large communities share in this bounty, reducing the dangers of monopoly control over local information and opening up hitherto closed communication ghettos. Even newspapers can be printed and transmitted electronically, making it easier to bypass local media and rely on distant news sources. Cable television systems now can offer broadcasts from hundreds of separate channels, vastly increasing consumer choices of channels, if not content. Local television stations can tap into satellite news directly or via other carriers, as can individual consumers through backyard satellite dishes. Space for electronic transmissions, including television, can be rented by public and private parties from the satellites' owners.

DVD and videotape recorders store electronic fare, allowing people to watch broadcasts that they would have missed otherwise because of schedule conflicts. Annoying commercials can be readily suppressed. Nearly half of U.S. households have at least one video or DVD recorder. People can also subscribe to special entertainment or special interest television programs at moderate costs. They pay solely for programs they choose to watch. Public access cable channels and government Web sites keep citizens in closer touch with public institutions and political leaders. They also permit these leaders to address the public directly without having their pronouncements mutilated by hostile journalists. Cable's narrowcasting capabilities suit viewers' growing preference for news tailored to their special likes and needs and presented at times of their choosing.

The proliferation of news venues has fragmented audiences. The traditional media are faced with dwindling numbers of clients. The Internet and cable television are the only political news venues whose audiences are growing. Viewers now name cable television most often as their source of political information, ahead of network or local news. Nonetheless, cable's reach of audiences remains puny compared to the reach of the slimmed-down networks. In November 2004, when election news was at a peak, cable television attracted roughly one-eighth of the viewers that evening television news programs garnered.[18]

The Internet presents the potential, as yet largely unfulfilled, of transforming average people into broadcasters who address their messages to audiences of their choice, including journalists. Talk shows on radio and television also allow audiences to interact with others while watching the

Technology exhibited at a show in San Diego in September 2004 allows users to synchronize notes and data over the Internet and transfer them to their cell phones or mobile computers.

same programs. Two-way communication technologies using radios, telephones, and the Internet have been extraordinarily useful for connecting outlying areas with social service systems in more populated centers. In Alaska and northern Canada, for example, these technologies deliver educational and health services and give people a greater voice in government.[19]

Transforming Journalism

Thanks to the new technologies, the mass media business has made noteworthy advances on three fronts: news gathering, news processing, and news dissemination. Access to computer databases and satellites has put an enormous store of usable information within reach of average journalists wherever they may be. Even foreign countries kept off limits by hostile rulers can be explored by satellites, as can remote areas of the globe and even the private retreats of powerful elites. The ability to search databases electronically for specific bits of information and to combine these data in a variety of ways opens up countless new possibilities for creating news stories and providing valuable contextual information for fast-moving current developments.

When it comes to the distribution of news gathered at different locations, the array of channels for immediate or delayed transmission has multiplied far beyond the range deemed possible when cable television first picked up steam in 1975. When local stations import video footage from satellites, they reduce their dependence on current network programming and vastly expand their television programming options. The dependence on network programming has been reduced even further by round-the-clock news programming by cable and Internet television news venues. Broadband technology has made Internet use far more attractive because it allows nearly instant, constant access without the delays and hassles of a modem.

New broadcasting and narrowcasting technologies usually produce problems along with their benefits and require new policies. Take high-definition television (HDTV) technology, which improves picture quality and opens up space for new channels. Besides requiring many consumers to buy new television sets to receive HDTV signals, most television stations will have to spend millions of dollars for new equipment and transmitting towers. In view of these major and costly changes, the Federal Communications Commission conceived a multiyear transition plan in the early 1990s. Established broadcasters would receive a second channel free of charge to duplicate their analog programs in digital versions on this second channel. In 2007 the broadcasters would return their original channels to the government while retaining the digital channel as their sole outlet. The plan immediately became embroiled in major political battles.

Although the 1996 Telecommunications Act has embraced the principle of awarding digital channels free of charge, influential members of Congress wanted the channels auctioned off to the highest bidders. The telephone companies, which pay the government for the right to transmit information over the public airways and who fear potential competition in data transmission from the broadcast industry, joined the lobby against free channels for broadcasters. Naturally, broadcast industry leaders strongly opposed any changes in the current rules. They were eager to get high-definition television under way, as were the manufacturers of the new television sets. In fact, supporters of the plan wanted to shorten the transition period. PBS, ABC, NBC, CBS, and Fox began digital broadcasting in major television markets in 1998. They are committed to relinquish their analog broadcast spectrum and broadcast digitally exclusively by 2007.[20] By 2004 only half of the nation's commercial stations had begun digital transmissions, and consumers were dragging their feet on buying new television sets or converting older ones. Considering the complexity and costs involved in conversions, it seems unlikely that the 2007 completion date will be met.[21]

Another major problem exacerbated by the new technologies concerns the safeguarding of individual privacy. Ever smaller cameras and microphones permit reporters to spy with little chance for detection. Today reporters and other people can assemble scattered bits of information in seconds to derive a comprehensive, publishable portrait of an individual's past. Unless individual privacy becomes more fully protected, the computer age could well turn into an Orwellian nightmare—with individuals living in glass cages and exposed to instant public scrutiny by all sorts of reporters. Likewise, the new information-gathering techniques make it far more difficult to protect national security information from prying eyes. Congress and the courts have been unable to strike a sound balance between a free press and a secure society. That accounts for the heated political battles over the renewal of the 2001 Patriot Act, which the Bush administration deems essential for national security and critics condemn as a menace to their cherished privacy and to free speech.

The Internet

The technology with potentially the largest impact on the way the traditional media conduct their business is the Internet and its components, such as e-mail—its most popular feature—listservs, chatrooms, and the World Wide Web. The Internet presents the stiffest competitive threat to traditional over-the-air and cable television because it duplicates many of their news and entertainment offerings. As yet, contrary to earlier forecasts, it has not split off large chunks of their audiences or competed successfully in the battle for advertising revenues. The defining feature of Internet technology is open, nearly unrestricted access. Most people can receive Internet messages and broadcast their own at relatively low costs (Box 12-1). The political consequences have been substantial, although observers measure them with diverse scales and therefore disagree about the magnitude and significance of changes. Assessment of the precise impact of the Internet is also difficult because it is a technology in progress. Its hardware, software, types of uses, and applicable government regulations remain in flux.[22]

The Internet has diminished the traditional news media's tight control over access to mass audiences. Politicians, for example, who have felt victimized by journalists who paraphrased their comments and boiled them down to meaningless nuggets, can now reach audiences directly via e-mail and Web technology, and they often do. They can customize their messages to fit the needs of target populations. Politicians who have found it difficult to win access to a media platform—presidential contenders competing during the early primaries and candidates for local offices are examples—

now have alternative channels at their command. During the 2004 presidential contest, candidate Howard Dean raised half of his $41 million campaign chest from Internet donors. Liberal Web sites like MoveOn.org and Meetup.org helped organize campaign rallies and mobilize Democratic voters. Conservative Web sites like those sponsored by Move America Forward energized citizens on the other side of the political fence.

The Web allows average individuals, whom the traditional news media have long ignored, to make their voices heard in the public arena. Individuals and groups with modest resources can now reach widely dispersed audiences throughout the United States and most parts of the world. Their messages can be constructed to inform or deceive, to rally people for good and bad causes, or to entertain in socially approved or condemned ways. The Internet remains one of the very few venues where information transmission is largely free from censorship. It is left to message consumers to determine what is acceptable and credible and what is not.

By 2004 most Americans were using the Internet to send and receive e-mail messages, and more than half were watching Internet news broadcasts intermittently or regularly.[23] Table 12-3 shows that sites controlled by familiar enterprises are preferred by far over newcomers. Socioeconomic and demographic barriers to Internet access continue to shrink. What remains of the "digital divide" runs along higher education lines. Internet users say that it is the most up-to-date medium, the easiest to use, and the most enjoyable. Despite such high praise, television has remained their first choice, except for major rapidly breaking events. During the 2004 presidential campaign, for instance, 78 percent of the audience relied primarily on television, and 38 percent named newspapers as their primary news sources. Only 15 percent named the Internet.[24]

There is, as yet, no widely available solution to the problem of finding one's way through the Internet's lush jungles of information where search engines like Google and Yahoo provide guidance, but often from perspectives skewed to business interests.[25] Moreover, the stock of information that requires searching doubles every few months. For most news consumers, journalists remain essential, therefore—in fact they may be more essential than before—because they are trained to ferret out what seems "most important" within their cultural milieu and to present it in language that average people can understand. Journalists and major media institutions are deemed more trustworthy than unknown dispatchers of Internet information. This is why most people, for much of their political information, continue to turn to traditional media most of the time, either in their old formats or their Web site incarnations.

Newsworthy information posted on the Web is likely to trickle down to the general public through journalists' stories. In fact, journalists and

BOX 12-1
Blogs: The Newest Kids on the Block

In Horatio Alger's America, every boy could become president if he was honest, hardworking, and persevering when faced with adversity. Of course, that scenario wasn't quite true. But it is true that in twenty-first century America every boy—and girl—can become a published author with a potential audience of millions of people. And she or he need not even be honest, hardworking, persevering, or even a talented writer. Is this the age of the American dream or the American nightmare?

What are the facts?

Eight million Americans had become bloggers by the end of 2004, and 32 million had actually read blog messages. In other words, millions of people, whose identities are unknown to blog visitors, now post their views on Internet Web sites where ever-larger numbers of people read them, comment about them, and pass them on to millions more. In fact technology now allows blog fans to program their computers to automatically scan new messages on their favorite blog sites. Anyone, at little cost and with no training in news collection and verification, can become a blogger and post any message, true or false. There is practically no form of censorship, governmental or private, or requirements for ensuring transparency or accountability.

The upshot is a flourishing market place of disparate views—far more than ever before. Some blog messages have contributed to the public dialog and even spawned significant political action. Examples are the vivid, firsthand accounts through which bloggers covered the horrors of the 2004 tsunami and, thanks to news media coverage of the blogs, inspired audiences to help the victims.

Like investigative journalists, bloggers have unearthed stories that the media missed. They were the first to publicize Trent Lott's racial remarks at a birthday party for a fellow senator, which ultimately led to Lott's resignation as majority leader. Conservative bloggers engendered major upheavals at CBS news when they revealed lapses in checking the authenticity of documents alleging that President Bush had dodged National Guard service. Other blogs have become megaphones for spreading dangerous falsehoods, often without the antidotes of counter-arguments that the nation's founders anticipated. Most blog messages, of course, fall by the wayside like so many dead leaves in autumn.

So is blogging a dream or a nightmare? The answer is that it is a bit of both for the public, news media professionals, and for American democracy.

The public benefits from a richer marketplace of ideas but is harmed when messages are based on misinformation or deliberate deception, often fueled by hate. Bloggers are not bound by journalistic criteria like fairness, balance, and objectivity. News professionals benefit from blogging when the pool of ideas from which they can select their stories is enriched, particularly when the new voices cover unique slices of reality from fresh, nongovernmental sources. But journalists suffer when blogs of questionable newsworthiness dominate the news agenda and force journalists into a subordinate role of filling obvious holes in the information.

For U.S. democracy, blogging is a fulfillment of that part of the American dream that promises that every American, regardless of expertise, can have a voice in the nation's political life. Unfortunately, there is no assurance that all bloggers will use the privilege responsibly or that the falsehoods will be refuted. There is no guarantee that truth will always prevail.

other elites stand to gain most from the new riches, although everybody benefits. Information on the Web reaches journalists faster, from more diverse sources, and in modes that allow reporters to question sources quickly with the expectation of a prompt response. The potential for producing excellent news therefore has grown by leaps and bounds, which is welcome news for Americans. Regrettably, the reality has thus far failed to match the potential even for Internet newscasts. Thanks to links these broadcasts offer more background information and access to more diverse points of view than other venues. But they are still short on audiovisuals, and their interactive features are underdeveloped. A mere third of their stories are originals; the remainder come from the pool of stories available from traditional news sources.[26]

Benefits and Drawbacks of News Fragmentation

While some bemoan the fact that journalists' role as selectors and framers of news has been undercut by news consumers' ability to perform these tasks themselves thanks to Internet search engines, others hail the weakening of journalism. News consumers, they say, have been relieved of

TABLE 12-3   Typical Monthly Audiences on Top-Ten News Web Sites

Web site	Millions of viewers
CNN	23.9
MSNBC	21.0
Yahoo news	20.3
AOL news	16.4
Gannett newspapers	16.4
Knight Ridder	10.3
Systems, Inc.	10.0
New York Times	9.9
USA Today	9.6
Tribune newspapers	9.2

SOURCE: Adapted from Project for Excellence in Journalism, "The State of the News Media: Charts and Tables," http://stateofthenewsmedia.org/2005.

NOTE: Based on monthly Nielsen data for October 2004.

the tyranny of the press where unelected journalists determine what becomes news and frame it in ways that may be unappealing to audiences. They say that targeted news raises the possibility of a better fit between audience needs and public messages. Government programs may operate more successfully, given ampler opportunities for one- and two-way communication with selected audiences. The electoral chances of minority candidates and parties may also improve with increased ability to address their messages to selected audiences. The possibilities for positive changes arc staggering but are still too undefined to hazard predictions.

The multitude of broadcast channels and the even broader options created by videotape technology and the Internet have prompted fears that the national political consensus will become fragmented in the age of multimedia. When people turn to specialized fare in news and entertainment, their attention to politics may diminish. Without national media, there may be no national political consensus.[27] As discussed in Chapter 7, in the past nationwide dissemination of similar news has fostered shared political socialization. When news becomes fragmented, people are likely to be socialized in disparate ways.

If political programming becomes available only on channels dedicated to politics, will people choose to watch it? Will government leaders be able to convey their messages to the public? Will they be able to move the nation to agree with new policy directions, such as accepting equal treatment for racial minorities, the disabled, and people with divergent sexual orientations? A music fan, tuned in to an all-music station, may watch music programs only; an African American or Hispanic person may tune in only to stations concerned with African American and Hispanic affairs. Many citizens thus may become prisoners of their special interests and may miss out on happenings in the broader culture. The country may be carved up into mutually exclusive, often hostile political enclaves.[28]

Not everyone shares the fears that fragmentation of the broadcast audience will lead to political balkanization.[29] Many people point out that the national consensus was not ruptured when alternative media were used in the past. They argue that fragmented interests create the demand for fragmented media rather than the reverse. If there is political and social consensus, people will seek out information pertaining to the larger community. Others point out that commercially oriented media are unifiers because they will always try to attract large audiences by offering programs with wide appeal. That is why programming on cable television has become uniform and similar to network television. Even if the new media increase fragmentation, many people do not find this objectionable, believing that pluralism is preferable to earlier melting-pot ideals.

Media pluralism does herald more local programming. Most local governments eagerly use cable channels and Web sites to broadcast local political news. Many local school systems and police and fire departments air their concerns on their own channels. Because publicity means power, the new communications media tend to enhance the power of local institutions, frequently at the expense of national ones. The two-way capacity of the new media makes local programming more attractive for local audiences even when it lacks the polish of professional programs.[30] Although the possibilities for strengthening local communities through increased publicity are good, the new narrowcasting technologies also can deflect interest away from the local scene and produce global villages of like-minded people. As usual, major changes have their dark sides along with the bright ones.

Public Broadcast Stations

Yet another issue brought to the fore by the age of media plenty is the fate of public broadcasting. Many political leaders would like to abandon it and save the costs of public subsidies. They point out that its audiences, except for its children's programs, have been quite small. In fact, the disadvantaged groups to which the public broadcast system targets its programs largely ignore it. Instead, its audience tends to be upscale. As discussed in Chapter 2, public television was organized to provide an alternative to the typical programming available on the commercial networks. It also was intended to be an outlet for programs geared to minorities. These are the very services that cable television and other narrowcasting services now can and do perform commercially. Examples are programs offered by the History, Discovery, Learning, and National Geographic channels.

Most poor families cannot pay for access to these channels; therefore, they do not fill the niche currently occupied by the public broadcast system. Because sophisticated cultural and educational programming attracts only small audiences, it is unlikely that the free television channels will be eager in the future to feature such fare, even when HDTV technology increases the number of channels available for programming.[31]

The difficulty of keeping the public broadcasting system solvent without government subsidies may sound its death knell. PBS has been dreaming about creating a huge endowment from the money it hopes to earn when it completes conversion to HDTV and sells the spectrum space that will be released. But it is unlikely that Congress will consent to that plan. The European practice of funding public broadcasting principally through consumer fees has never been considered a realistic option in the United States.[32]

Barriers to Development

A look at technology may tell us what is possible rather than indicate what is likely to happen, particularly in the short run. A number of psychological, political, and economic barriers block the full development of new mass communication technologies. Most people are reluctant to change their media use habits, particularly when there are costs in time, attention, and effort to master new technologies. Many new developments never get off the ground because bureaucracies, often prodded by vested interests, impose too many regulations to guard against abuses. Unrealistically high standards are frequently prescribed, raising costs to unaffordable levels. For example, to stop satellite companies from effectively competing with cable companies at the local level at the turn of the century, the cable companies lobbied for imposing several costly requirements. They wanted to compel the satellite companies to carry all local channels, not just a few, at a price for rebroadcast rights that would be controlled by the satellites' competitors.[33]

State and local rules, piled on top of federal regulations, complicate the picture even further. Not only do they add more requirements, but rules issued by various jurisdictions often conflict. Every major technological revolution—and the information transmission revolution *is* major— has brought about economic and political dislocations. Such massive changes are fought by those whose knowledge and equipment will be made obsolete. Some of the new mass media offerings endanger current jobs. For instance, teachers may lose their jobs when long-distance learning programs transmit a master teacher's lessons to faraway classrooms. Medical programs that teach people better medical self-care methods may be unwelcome competition for health workers. Televised programs featuring outstanding practitioners and facilities may establish standards for professional performance that average institutions cannot match.

Communications technologies involve large investments so that their sudden obsolescence becomes a crushing financial blow. Business entrepreneurs often try to derail innovations. Early entrants in a technological field frequently develop a squatter's mentality about rights they have acquired, such as the right to use certain broadcast frequencies or particular technologies. Newcomers, on the other hand, are eager to reallocate facilities in line with their special interests. They want to mandate the use of more advanced technologies, even before they can guarantee that a market for these technologies and services will develop. This could destroy proven interests in favor of new claimants whose prospects for success are uncertain. Obstacles also arise because competing new technologies benefit groups unevenly. Power struggles, which may be prolonged, are fiercest before the status quo is determined. Meanwhile, technology continues its advance, raising problems that further delay the green light for implementing new systems.

The Cable Television Case

Cable television's rocky history in the United States illustrates the obstacles that technical innovations face. It also illustrates the many political decisions that must be made to fit a new information technology into existing legislative and administrative structures.

When cable television first became available in 1949, established broadcasters viewed it as dangerous competition that would steal their audiences and pirate their programs. When satellite technology evolved, fears mounted. The networks feared ruin if stations could pick up programs directly from satellites to broadcast nationwide via cable television.

The initial response of the Federal Communications Commission (FCC) to cable technology was typical. Prodded by established interests, the commission passed rules to protect existing stakeholders. These rules sharply limited the types of programs that cable television stations could broadcast when they competed with established network services. Consequently, the growth of the cable industry was stunted. By 1972 the FCC eased its regulations on the types of programs that cable television could broadcast. Cable advocates had argued that the technology was needed because it could reach people in locations inaccessible to regular television signals. Cable would break the near monopoly enjoyed by the networks over broadcasting. It would open up many new channels for broadcasting to groups hitherto shut out by a limited spectrum.

As usual most new communication technologies initially face very costly regulations designed to force them to serve hitherto unmet public needs. For example, the FCC asked the cable industry to offer a minimum of twenty channels, including outlets for the general public, educational institutions, and local governments. It was also required to carry signals of local broadcasters. These rules hampered rapid development of cable television; they were eased starting in 1976 after successful legal challenges.[34] In 1979 the FCC issued a lengthy research report on the economic impact of cable broadcasting. It concluded—erroneously, as it turned out—that cable was only a minor economic threat to the established television industry and that it did not endanger the industry's "ability to perform in the public interest." In the wake of these findings, the government removed its shackles from the industry, one by one.[35] With the passage of the Cable Communications Policy Act of 1984, deregulation was complete.[36] The act deregulated rates and made renewal of cable franchises nearly automatic in areas with ready access to over-the-air television—roughly 90 percent of the cabled areas.

Meanwhile, the resistance of the established industries to this new competition softened gradually. Heeding the old adage, "If you can't beat 'em, join 'em," a number of over-the-air broadcasters invested heavily in cable facilities once the FCC eased controls regarding cross-ownership and admitted the networks to the cable market. By 1993 broadcasters fully or partially controlled nearly half (47 percent) of the top fifty cable systems; newspaper and magazine publishers participated in one third (34 percent).[37] The three major cable news outlets—CNN, Fox News, and MSNBC—are all owned by media conglomerates and all have corporate siblings heavily involved in other media sectors. All have enjoyed steady growth in the number of cable news subscribers between 1995 and 2004 (Table 12-4).

FCC rules and the opposition of the established industries were not the only hurdles that the cable industry faced during its development. There were and are numerous local political hurdles as well. Laying of cables so that consumers can receive cablecasts requires permission from local authorities. To avoid undue duplication of facilities, cable enterprises must obtain franchises allowing them to serve consumers in each locality. The franchising process has been highly political in terms of both the selection of a particular cable company and the determination of the conditions of the franchise. Many small enterprises were squeezed out because they were unable to pay the costs of bidding for a contract.

TABLE 12-4   The Growth of Cable News Subscribers, 1995–2004
(millions of viewers)

Year	CNN	Fox News	MSNBC
1995	67.8	n.a.	n.a.
1996	71.3	n.a.	n.a.
1997	72.6	24.0	38.0
1998	75.6	36.4	46.0
1999	77.5	44.0	53.2
2000	80.3	57.5	61.4
2001	85.6	77.2	73.0
2002	86.6	82.0	78.5
2003	88.2	85.0	81.3
2004	90.3	86.8	84.0

SOURCE: Adapted from Project for Excellence in Journalism, "The State of the News Media: Online: Charts and Tables," http://stateofthenewsmedia.org/2004.

NOTE: Based on data from Kagan Research LLC, www.kagan.com.

In the absence of national rules, local franchising policies have been diverse.[38] Franchisers and franchisees have had to agree on the time to be allowed for constructing the system and the life of the franchise (usually fifteen years). They also need agreement on how many customers they must accept in outlying areas where costs exceed profits temporarily or permanently. Service to rural areas has posed daunting economic problems, particularly in the western plains and the Rocky Mountain states. Government agencies had to develop plans for supervising the execution of cable contracts and ensuring that programming serves the public interest. Repeatedly, major controversies have erupted over the fee and tax structure.

Despite all the obstacles, the cable television saga demonstrates that major innovations are possible in a government system built deliberately to slow change and allow minorities to block unwanted developments. There is no reason to believe that technological developments and their political fallout will continue, but most major changes will happen at a very gradual pace.

Regulatory Options

Governments have several policy options for dealing with broadcast systems. First, they can play a hands-off, laissez faire role, allowing the system to develop as its private owners please.[39] The precedent for this policy is the traditional U.S. stance toward the print media. If one believes that government should regulate information supply only when transmission channels are scarce, as happened with early radio and television, then it makes sense to leave the current rich crop of information transmission systems unregulated. When broadcast and narrowcast outlets are plentiful, market forces presumably come into play so that necessary services will be supplied in a far more flexible way than is possible when government regulations intervene. The only restraints that may be needed are safeguards to protect national security and maintain social norms and privacy. Laissez-faire is the mantra of deregulation proponents.

Second, information transmission systems can be treated as common carriers, like the telephone or rail and bus lines. Common carrier status makes transmission facilities available to everyone on a first-come, first-served basis. Under common carrier rules, the owners of cable facilities would not broadcast their own programs as they do now. Instead they would lease their channels to various broadcasters for fees regulated by government or by market forces. As common carriers they would not be allowed to selectively exclude certain programs. The FCC and many local governments like the common carrier concept. It has been adopted for dealing with communications satellites. But the U.S. Supreme Court decided in 1979 that cable could not be considered a common carrier under federal laws.[40] However, the ruling does not bar state and local authorities from designating the industry as a common carrier. Congress, too, has repeatedly imposed some common carrier features on the cable television industry. In the mid-1960s, for instance, it ordered cable systems to broadcast all local over-the-air programs. The industry brought suit and won judgments in 1985 and again in 1987 that the "must carry rule" violated the First Amendment rights of cable companies.[41] The victory for cable systems was a defeat for champions of broad public access rights to the media.

Third, the government can confer public trustee status on communication enterprises. Owners then have full responsibility for programming but are required to meet certain public service obligations. Examples are adherence to equal time provisions, limitations on materials unsuitable for children or offensive to community standards of morality, and rules about access to broadcast facilities. Access rules are designed to ensure that there are channels available to governments and various publics to broadcast information about such public issues as education, public safety, and medical and social service programs. Over-the-air television in the United States has operated under trustee rules.

The rationale for conferring trustee status on broadcasters has been twofold. In the past, the scarcity argument has been powerful but it has lost validity. The other argument for trustee status is that television is a highly influential medium. There must be assurance that valuable programs are broadcast and harmful ones avoided and that canons of fairness are observed. This is a powerful argument with strong support in much of the world. It is the argument that underlies the treatment of over-the-air television in the 1996 Telecommunications Act. However, it is not the primary argument on which the U.S. system was built.

Periodically, trustee norms clash with the First Amendment. This is why free-press purists are so alarmed about the increasingly strict enforcement of social and political correctness norms. They shudder when the majority of Americans applauds when journalists in the United States are fired for saying that some terrorist actions might be fueled by legitimate grievances or when the FCC imposes heavy fines on a network because a female entertainer's breast was accidentally bared during a broadcast. Given majority approval of such restraints on the press, especially in times of crisis, it is difficult to predict the longevity of these trends. Past experience suggests that their life is limited.[42]

Regulation Versus Deregulation

The new communications technologies require a far more complete rethinking of the scope and purpose of federal regulation of broadcast media than has happened thus far. The Telecommunications Act of 1996, although moving beyond some of the outdated assumptions of its 1934 predecessor, still falls short of matching the revolutionary technological changes with appropriate policy innovations. The difference in treatment between the unregulated print media and the regulated electronic media has become highly questionable. It was based on the assumption that there would be numerous competing newspapers while broadcast channels were scarce, encouraging monopoly. In reality, competition has been rising among broadcasters while it has been falling among daily newspapers. Besides, many newspapers are now available in broadcast formats. To bring some logic to the regulatory scheme, proponents of regulation could conceivably extend regulations to include the print media in the future. The price of progress in electronic transmission of printed news could be the loss of freedom from government regulation.

The other alternative, total deregulation of all media and reliance on traditional First Amendment values, remains a distant goal, though piecemeal skirmishes and full-scale assaults on regulatory policies continue apace. Opponents of extensive deregulation of all mass media have argued that the age of electronic plenty remains a far-off vision, because multiplying broadcast channels does not automatically mean more diversity in programming.[43] Opponents also contend that the impact of television on public life in the

United States is so profound that the public interest requires controls. Even when competition is ample, it may be necessary to mandate access to neglected viewpoints and provide programming for ignored audiences, such as children, as well as protecting children from unwholesome information.

Dissatisfaction with the services supplied by private entrepreneurs, including complaints about price gouging, have further fueled opposition to deregulation. The wave of mergers since the 1980s, which placed most major media enterprises under the control of big corporations, rekindled fears that the media might become the mouthpieces of narrow special interests, and that financial returns would be their programming lodestar. Plummeting revenues and sharp cuts in news division staffs heightened these fears. Calls for regulation to prevent misuse of power by the media, rather than deregulation, once again became the battle cry, especially among Democrats in the halls of Congress. Efforts by the Bush administration and the Republican-dominated FCC notwithstanding, congressional and public reluctance to deregulation seems to be winning out.

Paying the Piper

Whether government treats new technologies like private enterprises, common carriers, or trustees, the costs have to be paid. There are three possibilities for financing, each with different policy consequences: advertiser support, audience payments, and government subsidies. Various combinations are also possible. Print media, for example, are financed by their audiences, supplemented by advertisements and some mailing subsidies. A new idea for financing newspapers has spawned rapid growth in the numbers of newspapers distributed free of charge to all takers. The rationale is that many people will accept and read give-away, stripped-down versions of regular papers, especially when they are distributed at train and bus stations. As circulation figures mount, so will charges for advertising and so will the profits earned by the newspapers' owners.

Advertiser support requires news offerings that have mass appeal. Considering current lifestyles and the preferences of young audiences, that means infotainment with all the strengths and weaknesses of current mass media.[44] Advertiser influence may increase in the age of medium proliferation because competition for advertisers becomes keener when media multiply. Many outlets—particularly those with small audiences or audiences that lack attraction for advertisers because they represent small markets—may even find it impossible to attract enough sponsors to pay for their operations.

Most new broadcast facilities, along with cable television, rely heavily on audience payments. These have generally taken the form of a monthly service charge for the facilities, to which an installation or equipment charge has often been added. Additional programming may be available for a flat monthly rate or on a per-program basis. Service charge financing for broadcasting has been quite popular abroad. In the United States, however, it initially met with resistance because good broadcast services are available throughout the United States free of charge.

By the mid-1980s much of the initial resistance to paying for television had vanished. Half of U.S. households had been cabled, and many were paying for special programs in addition to their standard monthly fees. The worst fears of old-line broadcasting entrepreneurs had not materialized. While cable television had captured a solid slice of the networks' turf, the networks remained financially viable and even expanded into Web enterprises. News-sharing arrangements, involving major companies, became one of several ways to cut costs. One typical sharing arrangement included NBC, MSNBC, the Washington Post Company, and Newsweek.[45] As had been the case with past innovations, the new media had not mortally wounded their predecessors. When established enterprises could not throttle the newcomers in infancy, they joined them in droves by setting up Web ventures themselves.

A major social drawback of service charges for broadcasts is that poor families who most need many of the specialized programs are least able to pay to receive them. Middle-income families, who already enjoy many social advantages, benefit most from the information resources available through cable and other programs; low-income folks fall further behind.[46] This problem could be reduced through government subsidies paid to cable and Internet companies on a basis similar to financing public television, or government could pay subsidies directly to the poor. The latter system seems preferable to avoid making media enterprises financially dependent on the government, thereby endangering their freedom of action.

The Shape of the Future

The trends outlined thus far are not the only ones ahead. Many other issues will require decisions that go far beyond resolving technical issues. The direction of communications policy is at stake and with it the tone and possibly the direction of U.S. politics in general. John M. Eger, a former director of the White House Office of Telecommunications Policy, once remarked that the United States was "moving into a future rich in innovation and in social change." But this meant that the country was also moving into a storm center of new world problems. The new technologies are "a force for change throughout the world that simply will not be stopped, no matter how it is resisted." And then he asked, "Are we ready for the consequences of this change? Are we prepared to consider the profound social, legal, economic, and political effects of technology around the world?"[47]

Currently, the answer is no. In the communications field, the structure for policy making at all government levels is fragmented and ill-suited to deal with the existing problems, to say nothing of those that must be anticipated.[48] Policies are improvised when pressures become strong, yielding in a crazy quilt pattern to various industry concerns, to public interest groups, to domestic or foreign policy considerations, to the pleas of engineers and lawyers, and to the suggestions of political scientists and economists. Narrow issues are addressed, but the full scope of the situation is ignored. As political scientist W. Russell Neuman notes, "the concept of a comprehensive industrial policy or even a broadly focused reformulation of communications policy for the information age is political anathema in the centers of power."[49] The struggle over passage of the 1996 Telecommunications Act, and the compromise measure that is now the law of the land, proves that this assessment is unfortunately correct.

Summary

Many people are dissatisfied with the performance of the mass media, especially television. Critics can and do air their dissatisfaction through formal and informal channels, but criticism usually has had limited success in bringing reforms. To fill the gaps left by the major mass media, many alternative media have been created. These media either serve demographically distinct populations or cater to particular substantive concerns or political orientations. Two opposing trends are simultaneously at work. One is a trend toward concentration of media power in the hands of huge commercial conglomerates, the other is a trend towards fragmentation of news dissemination and audiences.

In this chapter we explored the social and political consequences of technological advances affecting mass media and outlined the areas in which new public policies are needed. We briefly sketched the political roles played by the medley of print media, over-the-air and cable television, and the Internet. We discussed the political and economic obstacles that media based on new technologies must overcome to compete against established competitors. We also outlined several major looming problems and hailed the arrival of the age of broadcast plenty. The impact of these changes on life and politics in the United States could be enormous unless resistance to the pace of change slows progress. Fragmentation of the broadcast audience has raised fears of political balkanization and breakdown of the national political consensus that has been deemed essential for successful democratic governance. But the extent and implications of the danger remain disputed.

Changes in regulatory policy are in progress to integrate the new broadcast and narrowcast technologies into the existing mass media regulatory structure. But a total overhaul of the current policy regime is unlikely. The forces favoring greater government control of media content continue to be strong because the public sees the media as powerful social and political forces. Whatever the outcome, the debate about media regulation and deregulation needs to focus more clearly on the merits of safeguarding First Amendment rights in the century that lies ahead. Freeing the electronic media from government supervision may lead to some misbehaviors and abuses. But that may be the lesser evil if more government regulation is the alternative. As Thomas Jefferson wrote to his colleague Edward Carrington in 1787, " . . .were it left to me to decide whether we should have a government without newspapers or newspapers without a government, I should not hesitate a moment to prefer the latter."[50]

Notes

1. Project for Excellence in Journalism, "The State of the News Media: Overview," 1, http://stateofthenewsmedia.org/2004.
2. Ibid.
3. Michael Schudson, "Orientations: The Press and Democracy in Time and Space," in *Institutions of American Democracy: The Press,* ed. Geneva Overholser and Kathleen Hall Jamieson (New York: Oxford University Press, 2005), 1–3.
4. Pew Research Center for the People and the Press, "Bottom Line Pressures Now Hurting Coverage, Say Journalists, May 2004," http://people-press.org.
5. Ibid. The survey was conducted March 10–April 20, 2004.
6. Bill Kovach, Tom Rosenstiel, and Amy Mitchell, "Commentary: A Crisis of Confidence," in "Bottom-Line Pressures Now Hurting Coverage, Say Journalists: Questionnaire," 2004, 1–6, "http://people-press.org" http://people-press.org.
7. Project for Excellence in Journalism, "The State of the News Media: Public Attitudes," http://stateofthenewsmedia.org/2005.
8. For an excellent comparative analysis of these issues, see Pippa Norris, *A Virtuous Circle: Political Communications in Postindustrial Societies* (Cambridge, U.K.: Cambridge University Press, 2000).
9. Robert M. Entman, "The Nature and Sources of News," in Overholser and Jamieson, *Institutions of American Democracy: The Press,* 48–65. Entman identifies four types of journalism: traditional, advocacy, tabloid, and entertainment, each characterized by distinctive organizational values and missions.
10. Pew Research Center for the People and the Press, "Public's News Habits Little Changed by September 11," 2002, http://people-press.org.
11. Project for Excellence in Journalism, "The State of the News Media: Ethnic/Alternative," http://stateofthenewsmedia.org/2005.
12. Ibid.

13. John W. Johnstone, Edward J. Slawski, and William W. Bowman, *The Newspeople* (Urbana: University of Illinois Press, 1976), 157–179; and Project for Excellence in Journalism, "The State of the News Media: Ethnic/Alternative," http://stateofthenewsmedia.org/2005.

14. They are described more fully in Johnstone, Slawski, and Bowman, *The Newspeople,* 157–181; Laurence Leamer, *The Paper Revolutionaries: The Rise of the Underground Press* (New York: Simon and Schuster, 1972); and Jack A. Nelson, "The Underground Press," in *Readings in Mass Communication,* ed. Michael C. Emery and Ted Curtis Smythe (Dubuque, Iowa: W.C. Brown, 1972), 212–226.

15. Marshall McLuhan, *Understanding Media: The Extensions of Man* (New York: McGraw-Hill, 1964); and Marshall McLuhan and Quentin Fiore, *The Medium Is the Message: An Inventory of Effects* (New York: Bantam Books, 1967).

16. W. Russell Neuman, *The Future of the Mass Audience* (New York: Cambridge University Press, 1991), ix–x.

17. W. Russell Neuman, Lee McKnight, and Richard Jay Solomon, *The Gordian Knot: Political Gridlock on the Information Highway* (Cambridge, Mass.: MIT Press, 1996); Helen Nissenbaum and Monroe Price, eds., *Academy and the Internet* (New York: Peter Lang, 2004); Lincoln Dahlberg, "Democracy via Cyberspace: Mapping the Rhetorics and Practices of Three Prominent Camps," *New Media and Society* 3, no. 2 (2004): 157–177.

18. Project for Excellence in Journalism, "The State of the News Media: Charts and Tables," http://stateofthenewsmedia.org/2005. The figures are based on Nielsen audience measurements in November 2004.

19. Heather E. Hudson, "Implications for Development Communications," *Journal of Communication* 29 (winter 1979): 179–186. Also see Bella Mody, Joseph D. Straubhaar, and Johannes M. Bauer, *Telecommunications Politics: Ownership and Control of the Information Highway in Developing Countries* (Hillsdale, N.J.: Erlbaum, 1995).

20. David Sharos, "HDTV Clearly Becoming the Standard to Watch," *Chicago Tribune,* July 31, 2004.

21. Hernan Galperin, *New Television, Old Politics: The Transition to Digital TV in the United States and Britain* (Cambridge, U.K.: Cambridge University Press, 2004).

22. Doris A. Graber, Bruce Bimber, W. Lance Bennett, Richard Davis, and Pippa Norris, "The Internet and Politics: Emerging Perspectives," in Nissenbaum and Price, *Academy and the Internet,* 35–70.

23. Project for Excellence in Journalism, "The State of the News Media: Charts and Tables," http://stateofthenewsmedia.org/2005.

24. Project for Excellence in Journalism, "The State of the News Media: Online: Audience," http://stateofthenewsmedia.org/2005. Respondents were allowed to name two primary sources.

25. Richard Campbell, Christopher R. Martin, and Bettina Fabos, *Media and Culture,* 5th ed. (Boston: Beford/St. Martin's, forthcoming). Google, for example, ranks its listings by their popularity, judged by how many other pages are linked to them. That puts small enterprises, featured well below the leaders, at a self-perpetuating disadvantage.

26. Project for Excellence in Journalism, "The State of the News Media: Online: Conclusions," http://stateofthenewsmedia.org/2005. University of Southern California, "The Digital Future Report: Surveying the Digital Future, Year Four," 2004, www.digitalcenter.org. Like the studies produced by the Project for Excellence in Journalism, this study has been updated annually. The Poyn-

ter Institute and Stanford University have combined forces for a long-range study of Internet audiences. Reports are posted at www.poynterextra.org.

27. James G. Webster, "Audience Behavior in the New Media Environment," *Journal of Communication* 36 (summer 1986): 77–91.

28. Lawrence K. Grossman, *The Electronic Republic: Reshaping Democracy in the Information Age* (New York: Viking, 1995).

29. W. Russell Neuman, *The Future of the Mass Audience* (New York: Cambridge University Press, 1991), 58–63.

30. Use of cable television is compared with use of other media in Gerald L. Grotta and Doug Newsom, "How Does Cable Television in the Home Relate to Other Media Use Patterns?" *Journalism Quarterly* 59 (winter 1982): 588–591, 609. Also see "Cable TV," *Consumer Reports.*

31. The reasons for this situation are explained by David Waterman, "The Failure of Cultural Programming on Cable TV: An Economic Interpretation," *Journal of Communication* 36 (summer 1986): 92–107. Also see Robert M. Entman and Steven S. Wildman, "Reconciling Economic and Non-Economic Perspectives in Media Policy: Transcending the 'Marketplace of Ideas,'" *Journal of Communication* 42 (winter 1992).

32. John Tierney and Jacques Steinberg, "Conservatives and Rivals Press a Struggling PBS," *New York Times*, February 17, 2005.

33. William Neikirk, "Satellite TV Ready to Soar," *Chicago Tribune*, November 25, 1999.

34. *Home Box Office, Inc. v. FCC*, 567 F.2d 9 (D.C. Cir.), *cert. denied*, 434 U.S. 829 (1977); and *FCC v. Midwest Video Corp.*, 440 U.S. 689 (1979).

35. Pay television had been freed from federal controls in 1977. Remaining federal controls were dropped by 1979. Benjamin M. Compaine, Christopher H. Sterling, Thomas Guback, and J. Kendrick Noble Jr., *Who Owns the Media? Concentration and Ownership in the Mass Communications Industry*, 2d ed. (White Plains, N.Y.: Knowledge Industry Publications, 1982), 381, 407.

36. "Cable TV," *Consumer Reports* 52 (September 1987): 547–554.

37. Edmund L. Andrews, "Hopes of Cable Industry Ride on Veto by Bush," *New York Times*, July 25, 1992. Also see Warren Communications News, *Television and Cable Factbook*, 2000, www.warren-news.com/factbook.htm.

38. FCC regulations prevail over conflicting state regulations. *Capital Cities Cable v. Crisp*, 104 U.S. 2694 (1984). Federal law may preempt state laws. See William E. Hanks and Stephen E. Coran, "Federal Preemption of Obscenity Law Applied to Cable Television," *Journalism Quarterly* 63 (spring 1986): 43–47.

39. Henry Geller, "Mass Communications Policy: Where We Are and Where We Should Be Going," in *Democracy and the Mass Media*, ed. Judith Lichtenberg (New York: Cambridge University Press, 1990), 290–329.

40. *FCC v. Midwest Video Corp.*, 440 U.S. 689 (1979).

41. "Cable TV," *Consumer Reports*, 555.

42. Doris A. Graber, "Terrorism, Censorship, and the 1st Amendment," in *Framing Terrorism: The News Media, the Government, and the Public*, ed. Pippa Norris, Montague Kern, and Marion Just (New York: Routledge, 2003), 27–42.

43. Jeff Chester, "Strict Scrutiny: Why Journalists Should Be Concerned about New Federal and Industry Deregulation Proposals," *Press Politics* 7, no. 2 (2002): 105–115.

44. David T.Z. Mindich, *Tuned Out: Why Americans under 40 Don't Follow the News* (New York: Oxford University Press, 2004).

45. Felicity Barringer, "Leading Media Companies Forming Joint Web Venture," *New York Times,* November 18, 1999.
46. Vincent Mosco, "Une Drôle de Guerre," *Media Studies Journal* 6 (spring 1992): 56–60.
47. John M. Eger, "A Time of Decision," *Journal of Communication* 29 (winter 1979): 204–207.
48. William A. Lucas, "Telecommunications Technologies and Services," in *Communication for Tomorrow: Policy Perspectives for the 1980s,* ed. Glen O. Robinson (New York: Praeger, 1978).
49. Neuman, "The Future of the Mass Audience," x.
50. Paul Leicester Ford, ed. *Writings of Thomas Jefferson,* vol. 5 (New York: Putnam's, 1894), 253.

Readings

Anderson, Bonnie M. *News Flash: Infotainment and the Bottom-Line Business of Broadcast News.* San Francisco: Jossey-Bass, 2004.
Becker, Ted, and Christa Dayl Slaton. *The Future of Teledemocracy.* Westport, Conn.: Praeger, 2000.
Bimber, Bruce. *Information and American Democracy.* Cambridge, U.K.: Cambridge University Press, 2002.
Downey, Leonard Jr. *The News about the News: American Journalism in Peril.* New York: Knopf, 2002.
Ferguson, Charles. *The Broadband Problem: Anatomy of a Market Failure and a Policy Dilemma.* Washington, D.C.: Brookings, 2004.
McChesney, Robert W. *The Problem of the Media: U.S. Communication Politics in the Twenty-First Century.* New York: Monthly Review Press, 2004.
Mullen, Megan. *The Rise of Cable Programming in the United States: Revolution or Evolution?* Austin: University of Texas Press, 2003.
Norris, Pippa. *Digital Divide? Civic Engagement, Information Poverty, and the Internet in Democratic Societies.* Cambridge, U.K.: Cambridge University Press, 2002.
———. *A Virtuous Circle: Political Communications in Postindustrial Societies.* Cambridge, U.K.: Cambridge University Press, 2000.
Sunstein, Cass. *Republic.com.* Princeton: Princeton University Press, 2001.

Index